LEBANON

LIBERATION, CONFLICT, AND CRISIS

Edited by Barry Rubin

LEBANON
Copyright © Barry Rubin, 2009.

All rights reserved.

First published in hardcover in 2009 by
PALGRAVE MACMILLAN®
in the United States—a division of St. Martin's Press LLC,
175 Fifth Avenue, New York, NY 10010.

Where this book is distributed in the UK, Europe and the rest of the world,
this is by Palgrave Macmillan, a division of Macmillan Publishers Limited,
registered in England, company number 785998, of Houndmills,
Basingstoke, Hampshire RG21 6XS.

Palgrave Macmillan is the global academic imprint of the above companies
and has companies and representatives throughout the world.

Palgrave® and Macmillan® are registered trademarks in the United States,
the United Kingdom, Europe and other countries.

ISBN: 978–0–230–62306–4

Library of Congress Cataloging-in-Publication Data

Lebanon : liberation, conflict, and crisis / edited by Barry Rubin.
    p. cm.—(Middle East in focus)
    ISBN-13: 978–0–230–60587–9 (alk. paper)

    1. Lebanon—Politics and government—1990–2. Lebanon—Foreign
relations. I. Rubin, Barry M.

DS87.54.L39 2009
956.9204′4—dc22   2008052683

A catalogue record of the book is available from the British Library.

Design by Newgen Imaging Systems (P) Ltd., Chennai, India.

First PALGRAVE MACMILLAN paperback edition: September 2010

10 9 8 7 6 5 4 3 2 1

Printed in the United States of America.

Transferred to Digital Printing in 2009

Contents

Preface to the
Paperback Edition

The analysis of Lebanon provided in this book has proven even more accurate with the passage of time. Within the country, the crisis has developed on the three levels laid out herein. On one hand, the high tide of independence proclaimed by the Beirut Spring has continued to recede.

First, the power of Hizballah and its allies, backed by Iran and Syria, has increased, while the March 14 coalition—especially given the lack of support from the United States, France, and the West generally—has fragmented. The defection of Walid Junblatt from the coalition in 2010 was an especially hard blow.

At the same time, though, the balance has remained very roughly the same. Hizballah may have a veto power over government decisions but March 14 is still the most important part of the government. The battle is far from over, with the issues and basic balance of forces being as presented in this book.

And, third, the two sides in the battle over Lebanon have been able to reach agreements that have avoided violence or a much larger crisis. This kind of complex framework of political arrangements—as the chapters by William Harris and Eli Fawuz show—is something that Lebanon's political culture has often built.

The reasons for this situation are very well explained in this book. As Tony Badran's chapter shows, the impossibility of one side truly winning a civil war is a great incentive for avoiding one. Similarly, as Mark Farha points out, the demographic balance also makes for a situation that can be called either an accommodation or a deadlock.

Indeed, as the other chapters explain such internal dynamics as economy, Hizballah's strategy along with the Iran-Syria factor, and the Shia community play into this pattern. Equally, the relative lack of intervention by Israel or the United States also does not challenge these arrangements.

The players and their general positions thus remain about the same, despite the tremendous stress that their very bitter conflicts place on the structure—both fragile yet surprisingly durable—that is Lebanon.

One thing remains certain. Lebanon is one of the most fascinating countries in the world. This book provides a clear and detailed picture of its dynamics.

—Barry Rubin

LEBANON

THE MIDDLE EAST IN FOCUS

The Middle East has become simultaneously the world's most controversial, crisis-ridden, and yet least-understood region. Taking new perspectives on the area that has undergone the most dramatic changes, the Middle East in Focus series, edited by Barry Rubin, seeks to bring the best, most accurate expertise to bear for understanding the area's countries, issues, and problems. The resulting books are designed to be balanced, accurate, and comprehensive compendiums of both facts and analysis presented clearly for both experts and the general reader.

Series Editor: Barry Rubin
Director, Global Research International Affairs (GLORIA)

Center Editor, *Middle East Review of International Affairs* (MERIA)
Journal Editor, *Turkish Studies*

Turkish Dynamics: Bridge across Troubled Lands
By Ersin Kalaycıoğlu

Eternal Iran: Continuity and Chaos
By Patrick Clawson and Michael Rubin

Hybrid Sovereignty in the Arab Middle East: The Cases of Kuwait, Jordan, and Iraq
By Gokhan Bacik

The Politics of Intelligence and American Wars with Iraq
By Ofira Seliktar

Hezbollah: The Story of the Party of God: From Revolution to Institutionalization
By Eitan Azani

Lebanon: Liberation, Conflict, and Crisis
Edited by Barry Rubin

The Muslim Brotherhood: The Organization and Policies of a Global Islamist Movement
Edited by Barry Rubin

CONTRIBUTORS

Tony Badran is a research fellow for the Foundation for Defense of Democracies, where he focuses on Lebanon and Syria. His articles have appeared in the *Los Angeles Times*, *Middle East Quarterly*, and *Beirut Daily Star*, among other places. He also authors the weblog, "Across the Bay" and is the editor of the Syrian Opposition Portal, a website tracking the news of the Syrian opposition movements. Mr. Badran is currently completing his doctorate at New York University.

Mark Farha is visiting assistant professor of comparative politics at Georgetown University's School of Foreign Service in Doha, Qatar. He obtained his Ph.D. in History and Middle Eastern Studies from Harvard University and is working on *Secularism under Siege in Lebanon: Global and Regional Dimensions of a Malaise*.

Elie Fawaz is a Lebanese political analyst with the Beirut offices of the Lebanon Renaissance Foundation that promotes democracy and the rule of law.

Charles Paul Freund has been a writer for *The Washington Post*, a columnist for *The New Republic*, and a senior editor at *Reason Magazine*, where he often wrote about Middle Eastern pop culture. His articles and essays have also appeared in *The Daily Star* (Beirut), *Slate*, *The New York Times*, *Los Angeles Times*, *The International Herald-Tribune*, *L'Orient-Express* (Beirut), and elsewhere. He is currently managing editor of the AEI Press in Washington, D.C.

Gary C. Gambill is the editor of *Mideast Monitor* and was editor of the *Middle East Intelligence Bulletin* from 1999 to 2004. Gambill publishes widely on Lebanese and Syrian politics, terrorism, and democratization in the Middle East.

William Harris is a professor in the department of politics at the University of Otago, New Zealand. He holds a Ph.D. from the University of Durham. Professor Harris is the author of *The Levant: A Fractured Mosaic* (Markus Wiener, Princeton, 3rd edition, 2008), which won a Choice Magazine Outstanding Academic Title award, and *The New Face of Lebanon* (Markus Wiener, Princeton, 2nd edition, 2005). He is currently working on a history of Lebanon since the Islamic conquest for Oxford University Press.

Dr. Omri Nir is a lecturer at Tel Aviv University, Hebrew University, and Ben-Gurion University of the Negev, Israel. His fields of expertise are

Lebanese politics, Lebanese Shi'a, and Shi'a in the Arab world. Among his publications, he has written "The Shi'ites during the 1958 Lebanese Crisis," *Middle Eastern Studies*. Forthcoming publications include a political biography of Nabih Berri.

Nimrod Raphaeli joined the Middle Media Research Institute in August 2001 after 28 years in the World Bank serving both in managerial and advisory capacity. Upon his retirement from the World Bank he was retained as a consultant at both the Bank and the International Monetary Fund. During his service at the World Bank Mr. Raphaeli has served on economic and technical assistance missions to more than 30 countries including Iran, Afghanistan, Malaysia, Indonesia, Yemen, Tunisia, Nigeria, the Philippines and most countries in eastern and southern Africa. He was born in Iraq in 1932. He immigrated to Israel in 1951 and eventually went to the United States on a Fulbright scholarship. He received his Ph.D. from the University of Michigan. He has published numerous articles in professional journals.

Barry Rubin is director of the Global Research in International Affairs (GLORIA) Center and editor of the *Middle East Review of International Affairs* (MERIA) *Journal*. His latest books are *The Israel-Arab Reader* (seventh edition), with Walter Laqueur (Viking-Penguin); the paperback edition of *The Truth about Syria* (Palgrave-Macmillan); *A Chronological History of Terrorism*, with Judy Colp Rubin (Sharpe); and *The Long War for Freedom: The Arab Struggle for Democracy in the Middle East* (Wiley).

David Schenker is a senior fellow and director of the Program in Arab politics at The Washington Institute for Near East Policy. In 2002–2006 he served in the Office of the Secretary of Defense as Levant country director, the Pentagon's top policy aide on the military and political affairs of Syria, Lebanon, Jordan, and the Palestinian territories. In 2005, he was awarded the Office of the Secretary of Defense Medal for Exceptional Civilian Service. David has authored two books: *Dancing with Saddam: The Strategic Tango of Jordanian-Iraqi Relations* (2003) and *Palestinian Democracy and Governance: An Appraisal of the Legislative Council* (2001). His writings have appeared in scholarly journals and newspapers, including *Middle East Quarterly*, *The Los Angeles Times*, *Chicago Tribune*, and *Boston Globe*. He has appeared as a featured commentator on NPR, CNN, Fox News, and Politically Incorrect. David holds an M.A. from the University of Michigan in Modern Middle Eastern History and a B.A. in Political Science from The University of Vermont. He has lived in the Middle East for four years, including two years in Egypt researching and studying Arabic.

Jonathan Spyer is a senior research fellow at the Global Research in International Affairs Center, IDC, Herzliya, Israel. He is the author of *The Rise of Nationalism in the Middle East* (Mason Crest, 2007) and "Lebanon 2006: Unfinished War" (*Middle East Review of International Affairs*, March 2008). Jonathan Spyer's articles and analysis of the current political situation in the Middle East are published in a number of important journals, including the *Guardian*, *Times*,

Haaretz, the Jerusalem Post, MERIA Journal, Toronto Globe and Mail, British Journal of Middle East Studies, Israel Affairs, and others.

Eyal Zisser is the director of the Moshe Dayan Center for Middle Eastern and African Studies and the head of the department of Middle Eastern and African History, both at Tel Aviv University. Zisser has written extensively on the history and the modern politics of Syria and Lebanon and the Arab-Israeli conflict. Among his books are the following: *Assad's Syria at a Crossroads* (Tel Aviv, 1999); *Asad's Legacy–Syria in Transition* (New York, 2000); *Lebanon: The Challenge of Independence* (London, 2000); *Faces of Syria* (Tel Aviv, 2003); and *Commanding Syria, Bashsar al-Asad's First Years in Power* (London, 2006).

INTRODUCTION

Barry Rubin

By any measure, Lebanon is a small country with a tiny population. It possesses no great natural resources. In ancient history, its location was more strategic as a passageway up the eastern shore of the Mediterranean. Its ports were good for seafaring trade. Yet these geographic assets were considerably diminished in the age of steamships, airplanes, and paved roads.

More recently, Lebanon's considerable asset was its people, who possessed relative education; familiarity with the outside, Western, world; and mercantile experience. The less advanced neighboring countries, especially the oil-rich Persian Gulf region, needed their services. Lebanon found a real but modest role in the modern world.

Yet all of the above does not prepare one to absorb the reality that Lebanon has become a cockpit of turmoil and a focus of controversy. It has more demographic diversity, complex internal politics, and crises proportionately than any other country in the world.

The combination of this country's apparent unimportance and centrality has created a situation in which the world alternately focuses on and neglects this small country.

Time after time, it has been wracked by upheavals, sometimes domestically generated, sometimes spillovers from neighboring countries. Once regarded as the showcase of the Arab world, with its cultural sophistication and economic success, Lebanon has been fractured by civil war and other strife in which the state has, in effect, disintegrated. Unfortunately, Lebanon remains a focal point for regional crises, terrorism, violence, Islamism, and the diverse competing influences of powers both local and Western.

While Lebanon seemed permanently mired down in civil war and Syrian occupation for decades, this long period changed virtually overnight with the Beirut Spring—the mass mobilization of long-silent Lebanese demanding the withdrawal of Syria's military. The movement succeeded, opening a new period in the country's history. However, optimism soon flagged, with a series of, apparently Syrian-inspired, attacks; the growing power of Hizballah; and a full-scale Hizballah-Israel war in the summer of 2005.

Given the dramatic changes in Lebanon and its continual role in the international spotlight a new evaluation of the country—in all its complexity of communities, politics, and crisis—is very much needed.

On the internal front, Lebanon achieved success when it was able to balance its communities. Yet this consensus, called the National Pact, was torn apart by external interventions, the Palestinian issue, changing demographic proportions, the rise of the Shi'a, and different orientations among the communities themselves. The Christians, or at least the Maronites, were from the 1950s to the 1980s traditionally Lebanese nationalist and Western-oriented; the Greek Orthodox heterodox and leftist; the Sunni Muslims pan-Arab nationalist; the Druze parochial; and the Shi'a largely silent. These are generalizations, of course, but they point to the tremendous chasms in the life of the country.

The civil war brought these rifts to the surface in bloody confrontations, including a long-term Syrian and short-term Israeli occupation. It was as if no one stood for Lebanon itself, as the country suffered a de facto partition into separate zones of control. The growing number of Shi'a and the turn of many of them toward radical Islamism added another difficult dimension. To say, as Kamal Jumblatt did in the title of his autobiography, "I Speak for Lebanon" was absurd.

However, the long, grinding Syrian presence and the country's stagnation eventually brought a reaction. Most Christians, Sunni Muslims, and Druze rediscovered the value of Lebanon as the only overriding interest that preserved them from destruction. Even while the hitherto quiescent Shi'a Muslims became clients of Iran and Syria while bidding for state power under an Islamist banner, most other Lebanese were turning back to Lebanese nationalism and paving over their differences. Rafiq Hariri, the country's wealthiest man and twice prime minister, symbolized this orientation.

Thus, when pressure began to build in Lebanon demanding a Syrian withdrawal and the end to Lebanon's satellite status, Hariri was the focal point of Syrian retaliation. On February 14, 2005, he was blown up by a very large bomb planted in a Beirut street. Twenty-two bystanders met the same fate.

This event unleashed what later became known as the Beirut Spring, with massive demonstrations by mostly Christians, Sunni Muslims, and Druze blaming and calling for Syria's withdrawal, and equally large demonstrations by Shi'a Muslim supporters of Hizballah calling on Syria to stay. The young and relatively new Syrian dictator, Bashar al-Asad, decided to avoid a crisis and bring out his forces. This was a high point of Lebanese morale. They had appeared to have won a stunning victory.

Soon, however, the Syrians showed that they had no intention of giving up Lebanon. More terrorist acts followed and as the investigation, mandated by the United Nations in cooperation with Lebanon, into Hariri's death advanced it was increasingly clear that the Syrians and their Hizballah allies were trying to destabilize the country. Hizballah pulled its members out of the cabinet in a failed attempt to block the government's support for the tribunal.

However, Hizballah also had other tactics. A year later, in 2006, it launched an attack on Israel, killing or kidnapping the members of a border patrol. This was at least the third such attack within a year and Israel retaliated, opening a war that was on one hand a full-scale conflict but on the other hand a battle between Israel and Hizballah with the Lebanese state and army as bystanders. The war ended with a UN-negotiated truce, which set up an enlarged United Nations' Interim Force in Lebanon (UNIFIL) force to keep the peace on the border.

Having had either, depending on who is giving the account, a great victory or humiliating defeat, Hizballah—backed by Syria and Iran—turned back to the domestic Lebanese scene. It demanded a blocking majority over all government actions. Lebanon once again teetered on the verge of civil war. And after a two-year struggle, through the mid-2008 Doha agreement, it achieved that goal. On one hand, Lebanon was now governed by a coalition, with the March 14 movement still nominally as its leader. On the other hand, a huge step had been taken toward establishing Hizballah's hegemony and reestablishing Syrian (and Iranian) predominant influence.

Given that this is Lebanon, however, the next roll of the dice, the complex factional-communal struggles, and the prospect of more changes, is never far away.

For the first time since the 1980s, Lebanon has been constantly in the world's attention, on governments' agendas, and the media's top story. Yet while all the basic players remained the same, there had been tremendous shifts in power balances and alignments. These factors make Lebanon a fascinating subject and outdated all the books written about the country two decades earlier, when a very different situation prevailed.

As a result of these events, a new look is needed at Lebanon, its politics, people, history, and economy, which will reveal what makes Lebanon important, fascinating, and different from the way it has been in the past.

It has been my privilege to work with a first-rate group of experts to develop a book on these issues.

William Harris explains to us, in "Reflections on Lebanon," (chapter 1) the country's history as the basis for its distinctive structure and makeup. Since the topic is Lebanon, even events of centuries ago remain controversial. Critical factors include the survival of the country's pluralism, the relationship among the communal players, and the backgrounds of their using external powers as patrons.

While religiously defined groups exist as social and political communities elsewhere in the Middle East, in Lebanon these structures were modernized and structured in a dialectical relationship with history to become almost "subnational" and "ethnic groups," overshadowing—either almost or fully—the existence of the nation-state itself.

Eli Fawaz, in "What Makes Lebanon a Distinctive Country?" (chapter 2), develops these themes. There are four basic factors that lay the basis for Lebanon as it is. First, there is the diversity of people and their identities. Most countries consist of people who at one time had different identities and loyalties. France, for example, consists of people who once considered themselves Bretons, Normans, Gascons, and so on. As recently as 1871, countries we now call Germany and Italy were not nation-states at all. However, in Lebanon, the pre-state communities not only continued to exist but became stronger.

Fawaz's second factor is geography. While itself a tiny country with a small population, Lebanon's mountains and other physical features divide it up into sections that each have their own character and distinctive population mix. Communities have been able to build and hold—even when moving to cities—their own territories.

The third aspect here is history. The way that Lebanon was usually governed maintained this decentralized situation. For example, local communities were able to keep their own laws. Religious tradition determined much of the life cycle and social framework. No single religion was imposed on the population; no one identity was forced onto it. The basis of today's political situation was laid under Ottoman and French rule.

Finally, the administrative structure and changing boundaries of the country completed the picture so that Lebanon was established as—though no one ever called it that—in effect a communal federation governed under the National Pact. All these factors plus ones cited earlier in this discussion made Lebanon distinct among the Arabic-speaking, general Muslim-majority states of the Middle East.

While there were certainly benefits to this particularity, there were also problems. Since communities continued to exist, the power and demographic relations among them changed, and foreign powers intervened (often at the request of Lebanese forces), conflict ensued. Tony Badran, in "Lebanon's Militia Wars" (chapter 3), looks both at the civil war and later events to explain how this violence has played out.

This chapter not only shows the strategy, tactics, and order of battle of the different sides but also makes an extremely important point about the nature of warfare in (and from, and into) Lebanon. No one side, either external or internal, can achieve complete victory. No community can take and hold its opponents' turf. There is a very real limit to the military achievements possible. It is always important to remember that in Lebanon there are never really just two sides but four major communities each with its own factions and individual, often competing, leaders. Consequently, the pluralist nature and unrest are long-term factors.

No one conquers Lebanon; the alignments and relative power of different forces merely changes temporarily, unleashing a new stage of either peaceful, violent, or peaceful and violent maneuvering. Of course, a given line of policy does predominate at all times, which can have either positive or devastating implications for Lebanon and the Lebanese.

The course of these ups and downs is traced by William Harris in "Lebanon's Roller Coaster Ride" (chapter 4). Between 2004 and 2008 the country experienced a cycle of turbulence unusual even given its own patterns. This era encompassed the assassination of former Prime Minister Rafiq al-Hariri, the Beirut Spring, the Syrian withdrawal, emergence of the March 14 movement, the covert Syrian campaign to subvert the regime, a

Hizballah-Israel war, and Hizballah's resurgence. Harris deftly analyzes and explains this complex sequence of events.

A combination of electoral democracy and communal competition makes the demographic composition of Lebanon one of the core controversies of the country. As a result—presumably of the relative decline of Christian and rise in Muslim, especially Shi'a, populations—no census has been conducted since the 1930s and none is likely in the foreseeable future. Mark Farha's "Demographic Dilemmas" (chapter 5) tries to provide the most accurate possible reading of the real numbers.

Farha's conclusions include two extremely important political markets for Lebanon's demography. First, contrary to many assumptions, the three largest communities—Christian, Shi'a Muslim, Sunni Muslim—are roughly equivalent. With each of these communities having one-third or less of the population, none can easily dominate.

However, Farha has an even more surprising finding: that a large group of Lebanese no longer cite communal membership as their main source of identity. In fact, he argues, communal, as opposed to national, identity in Lebanon is no higher than that in other Arabic-speaking countries. He concludes that the communally based structure is not going to change some time soon but points to its relative undermining by the modernization process.

One factor that should never be left out of discussions of Lebanon is that of culture. There are two aspects to this. First, Lebanon is an important producer of contemporary Arab culture and exports this elsewhere. Second, as a more liberal society compared to other Arab states (due to the large Christian population, a higher degree of exposure to Western culture, a free atmosphere, and other factors), Lebanon has unique aspects to its culture. Charles Freund, in "Lebanon's Culture: Popular Music as a Case Study" (chapter 6), uses music to explore these factors.

While Lebanon's economy, marked by powerful entrepreneurial skills in the population, is always one of great potential, concludes Nimrod Raphaeli in "Lebanese Economy between Violence and Political Stalemate" (chapter 7), the country's political troubles undercut stability and growth. The seemingly unending mixture of civil war, internal strife, external conflict, and unpredictability constantly sabotages the effort to advance.

Historically, Lebanon was a bright spot in the Middle East's economic situation, an oasis of efficiency, transit, and services. The civil war and the development of other countries swept away this marginal advantage, replacing it with a destitute polity. Hariri began a remarkable comeback campaign. Yet it is highly significant that this would-be architect of Lebanon's post–civil war revival himself fell victim to such violence.

Over a long period of time, in proportionate terms, there is no Arabic-speaking state that—outside of oil income—has so much potential and so little success as Lebanon. There is no question that the country pays heavily for its political unrest, yet such pragmatic considerations of course do not dissuade those who disrupt it.

One of the main factors of instability is the presence of both Shi'a (principally Hizballah) and Sunni Islamist groups in bewildering variety. Gary Gambill, in "Islamist Groups in Lebanon" (chapter 8), examines these groups in terms of their history, politics, goals, relative strength, leadership, and foreign connections.

An important feature of this situation is the many, often apparently contradictory, roles that Hizballah is called upon to play and tries to fill. These include its position as leader (but neither a unanimous nor unchallenged one) of the Shi'a community, revolutionary Islamists seeking to transform Lebanon, patriotic resistance, would-be destroyer of Israel, and ally of Syria and Iran.

Given the Sunni-Shi'a divide, the presence of large and armed Christian and Druze communities, the Hizballah-Amal competition among Shi'a, and other factors, no Islamist group seems capable of taking over Lebanon and making an Islamist (the first issue would be: Shi'a or Sunni Islamist?) state. Indeed, one of Hizballah's greatest errors is its antagonizing the overwhelming majority of the Sunni Muslim community which, even if it praises Hizballah for fighting Israel, reviles it for attacking other Lebanese and serving the interests of Damascus. The part played by Sunni Islamist groups is even more complex, with many small organizations, often local in nature or following charismatic leaders.

The developing domestic strategy of Hizballah is indeed considered by Eyal Zisser in "Hizballah in Lebanon" (chapter 9). The dilemma for the group has been among often incompatible desires to govern an Islamist Lebanese state, to head the Shi'a community, or to appear as a patriotic force concerned with Lebanon's interests. Handling this dilemma requires a delicate balance, especially hard given the fact that most Lebanese political forces see through it. Yet Hizballah has at least partly managed this transition, emerging as a powerful factor on the Lebanese national political scene as well as maintaining its Shi'a base.

There have also been considerable problems, however, in Hizballah's management of the 2004–2008 crises. By opposing Syrian withdrawal, it appeared to be unpatriotic and, indeed, protecting Syrian—not Lebanese—interests; by trying to block the state's participation in investigating the Hariri murder (the issue on which it left the government) Hizballah damaged its domestic reputation. Engaging in actions leading to full-scale war with Israel without state sanction won Hizballah more opposition than applause in non-Shi'a Lebanon.

The pressure by which it muscled its way back into government in 2008 heightened this anger. It was far more fear—both of Hizballah and of its Syrian and Iranian sponsors—than fraternity that led to concessions made in Doha that produced Hizballah's return to government. How much emphasis Hizballah will put into fighting Israel, and how much in fighting for Iranian and Syrian interests, are issues certain to shape the future of both Hizballah itself and of Lebanon.

A closer examination of the Shi'a community—in its attitude toward Lebanon, Hizballah, Amal, and socioeconomic issues—is the topic examined by Omri Nir in "The Lebanese Shi'a as a Political Community" (chapter 10). It is a fascinating story of how Lebanon's weakest and poorest group became organized and sought power, even state power.

There were many identities (Arab, Lebanese, Shi'a, communal, and Islamist) and leaderships (traditional powerful families, Arab nationalist, leftist, Amal, and Hizballah) available to the Shi'a. The development of Hizballah as the leadership of its community was by no means inevitable nor is it unanimous by any means. While demographic trends favor the Shi'a (and hence Hizballah), its future hegemony is by no means assured. Similarly, while Iranian-Syrian sponsorship gives it a real edge over its rival groups, this backing may be a handicap in future.

Among Lebanon's most controversial—and violent—relationships is that with its neighbor Israel. Jonathan Spyer in "Israel and Lebanon: Problematic Proximity" (chapter 11) looks at this situation. Lebanon has been in a formal state of war with its southern neighbor for 50 years and fought a war of its own in 2006, albeit only as an unwilling hostage of Hizballah, with it.

Still, Lebanon-Israel relations are far more complex than it appears, with different factors in the country taking drastically diverse positions. There are powerful factors in Lebanon that would prefer a de facto (or even explicit) peace with Israel and others that see this battle as a low priority for the country.

What is in Iranian, Syrian, and Hizballah's interest is to see a high degree of conflict though even here the factors involved are complex. Syria has at times a wish to use the conflict as leverage in which Israel, and the United States, accept Syrian hegemony to keep the border quiet. Iran to some extent wants this threat to be saved as leverage to prevent an Israeli attack on its nuclear arms' project. Hizballah's leaders deploy heated rhetoric but also want to choose confrontations based on its shorter-term priorities. Different considerations also, as Spyer shows, shape Israel's policy toward Lebanon.

Finally, David Schenker in "America and the Lebanon Issue" (chapter 12) shows how the United States has tremendous potential influence on Lebanon, and yet this potential has never fully been realized. Despite military interventions in the 1950s and 1980s, American policy has never had much impact on Lebanon. Indeed, it has often misjudged the balance of power there or ceded its direct goals based on other interests. Schenker looks at the successes and failures of U.S. policy with a special emphasis on current instruments and objectives.

Since Washington views Lebanon as a very secondary factor, its policy is often subsumed in other considerations: preventing conflicts, battling radical Islamists, courting Syria for making peace with Israel, or participating in other efforts (notably the 1991 coalition against Iraq's invasion of Kuwait). While the 1950s intervention was a notable success, the 1980s intervention was ill-conceived and a near-total failure.

Both the experience of the 1980s and current commitments (notably in Iraq) make the U.S. government loathe to intervene in Lebanon. While U.S. policy during the 2004 crisis succeeded in pushing out Syrian forces, it failed very badly afterward to help consolidate the March 14–led regime and to prevent the return of Syrian (and Iranian) influence. The U.S. emphasis on aiding a national army that was usually, at best, ineffective, and at worst largely sympathetic to Hizballah was a strategy that, at least ultimately, seemed to make little sense.

What is undeniable after this comprehensive review of Lebanon is that this is indeed a fascinating and complex country which will in the future again engage international attention and Western (especially U.S.) policy involvement. Civil war remains possible; a high level of conflict seems inevitable.

Is there any way that Lebanon can knit together the competing, often hostile, communities and factions within a country where multiculturalism has perhaps reached its maximum? Will violence explode on a high level or will maneuvering remain more a matter of the kind of intricate bargaining and changes of alliance that have so long characterized Lebanese politics?

In addition, there is the larger area that so often impinges on the country. The fate of Lebanon is linked with the impact it will have on questions of war and peace, democracy and dictatorship, radical Islamism and Arab nationalism in the wider region. A tiny country with a miniscule population thus becomes a focal point for the world's attention and involvement, a weather vane for the Middle East itself, for Western-Middle East relations, and for Muslim-majority societies while itself remaining unique and atypical at the same time. This is surely a topic worth studying and understanding.

1

REFLECTIONS ON LEBANON

William Harris

What distinguishes modern Lebanon? There is perhaps no other country where so much human complexity is loaded into such a small space. Four million people inhabit an area about the same size as a big national park, spread over a mountain range and its Mediterranean coastal fringe.

The primary characteristic of these 4 million inhabitants involves their belonging to 17 different Christian and Muslim sects. Belonging does not refer to attendance at places of worship; it means a sense of distinctiveness based on particular histories, myths, festivals, commemorations, localities, and—not least—different external ties. Certainly an overarching Lebanese identity has also evolved based on shared residence of the mountain and its surroundings and on give-and-take within the territorial state created by France in September 1920. However, the modern state has only functioned courtesy of power-sharing among the sectarian communities—or at least among their elites. This indicates the order of precedence among identities, in which the communal trumps the national.

As of the early twenty-first century, there has been no majority community. Indeed, there is a rough triangular balance of three great sectarian blocs: the Christians, pivoting on the Maronite Catholics; the Shi'a Muslims; and the Sunni Muslims, whose core leadership is aligned with the majority of the Druze community. The assemblage of large minorities, with no prospect of a sectarian majority, differentiates Lebanon from Iraq, where the Shi'a comprise 60 percent of the population. Lebanon is unique.

Apart from the delicate equation of identities and demography, and therefore of the jostling for political shares, Lebanon occupies a critical strategic location, and its communities have varying external connections. As regards political geography, Lebanon lies between Israel and Syria. It covers the western flank of Damascus, the capital and strategic core of Ba'thist Syria. Lebanon is therefore the target of all the ambitions and phobias of the Syrian dictatorship, which cannot function as an Arab power without commanding the Lebanese.

Lebanon also hosts a discontented Palestinian Arab refugee population, equivalent to almost 10 percent of its own people. Furthermore, the country's Shi'a community resides in the heart of the largely Sunni Arab world and on the frontline with Israel; therefore, Lebanon's Shi'a are of double interest to their coreligionists in revolutionary Shi'a Iran. Finally, Lebanon's far-flung Diaspora, its partially Westernized character, its free-wheeling pluralism, its gateway function into the Arab world, and its large Christian population all make it of political and cultural interest to Western powers.

The external connections of Lebanon's communal blocs involve antago-nists in Middle Eastern disputes. The Maronite Catholics, 60 percent of Lebanon's Christians, have relations with the West dating back to the Crusades. France has been their patron since a declaration by Louis XIV, and Maronites account for the largest Arab community in the United States. Lebanon's Shi'a provided religious scholars who assisted the conversion of Iranians to Twelver Shi'ism in the sixteenth century. As with the Maronites, the connections of the Shi'a go beyond the Arab world. In contrast, Lebanon's Sunnis relate to Sunni Arabs. Although Lebanese Sunni empathy with Damascus has decayed with non-Sunni management of Syria, Saudi Arabia has taken up the slack. The extension of Lebanon's differences reach into the divide between Sunni Arab states and Shi'a Iran and into the standoff between the United States, France, and Saudi Arabia on one hand and Syria and Iran on the other. In this sense, Lebanon really is the cockpit of the Middle East.

CONTESTING LEBANON'S PAST

Lebanon's history is the history of an assemblage of sectarian communities in and around Mount Lebanon. Therefore, the starting point is the Islamic conquest of Roman Syria in the 630s and 640s. By definition, the Islamic and Islamic-derived communities evolved out of this conquest. Lebanon's preeminent Christian community, the Maronites, took shape in the seventh-, eighth-, and ninth centuries under Arab Islamic supremacy.

Today, sectarian identity is an emotive topic. Sectarianism, meaning the assertion of cultural distinctiveness and claims to political rights or autonomy based on belonging to a religious community, has become a dirty word. Many Arabs do not want to admit to fractured identity, and they damn sec-tarian sentiment as a false consciousness stirred up by European interven-tions in the Ottoman Levant in the mid-nineteenth century. The highlighting of communal identities for earlier periods therefore can only be a Western agenda to denigrate the Arabs. Modern historical investigation of the Middle East proceeds in an atmosphere of intellectual intimidation by Arabist aca-demics.[1]

Lebanese sectarian political assertion can be seen as a nineteenth-century phenomenon, though it was rooted in historical factors even then. The mid-nineteenth century conflict between Maronites and Druze was substantially a product of local demographic and institutional evolution going back to the seventeenth- and eighteenth centuries.[2]

The medieval and early modern periods exhibit plenty of evidence of communal sensitivity and bigotry. A good example from the Arabic primary sources can be found in the travelogue of Abd al-Ghani al-Nabulusi, a famous poet and Sunni Sufi of Damascus.[3] Nabulusi toured the Biqa Valley of eastern Lebanon in 1688. He recounts a prejudicial tale of "a group of Druze" who killed a wild boar and ate it after washing the carcass in the water of a certain well. The well then dried up and no water reappeared. In fact, Druze frown on the eating of pork but the sectarianism in the story is blatant.

Even though sectarian identities did not lead to outright political claims before the nineteenth century, they did lead to collisions with political implications. For example, there were the Mamluk expeditions against recalcitrant Maronites, Shi'a, and Druze in Mount Lebanon between 1283 and 1305. The Sunni religious scholar Ibn Taymiyya went to the Kisrawan ahead of the 1305 expedition to demand that Shi'a and Alawites "return to obedience," meaning accept Sunni Islam.[4] They refused.

In general, communal identities dating back to the centuries between the Islamic conquest and the Crusades represent an essential precursor to modern political sectarianism. Fragmentary references in Syriac and Arabic primary sources provide glimpses of solid collective identities emerging in and around Mount Lebanon from the seventh century onward.

First, consider the Maronite Christians. A Syriac chronicle written in the 660s had monks of the House of Maron, a monastic foundation in the Orontes valley north of Mount Lebanon, defending the Monothelite doctrine (an attempt by the Emperor Heraclius to reconcile the Orthodox dual divine and human natures of Christ with the Monophysite single divine nature) to the Umayyad Caliph Mu'awiyya in Damascus.[5] The Arab historian al-Mas'udi, writing in the mid-tenth century, stated that this monastery and doctrine represented the origin of the Maronites.[6] In the late seventh century monks and their followers migrated to Mount Lebanon, seeking refuge from destruction caused by Arab civil warfare. The Arab historian al-Baladhuri, writing in the ninth century, referred to a tax revolt of Christians in the Biqa in 759, which provoked a vicious Abbasid punitive expedition into Mount Lebanon, condemned by the Beirut Sunni scholar al-Awza'i.[7]

Perhaps the most telling references come from the intermittent family records of the Arslans, which had the virtue of being within decades or less of events, whereas the Arab historians usually wrote one or two centuries later. The Arslans—or Tanukhs—were renowned both as Arab settlers brought in by the Abbasid caliphs to guard the Lebanese coast against Byzantine incursions and later as leaders of the Druze community. From the eighth- to the tenth centuries the family record had the Arslans repeatedly fighting off Christians—termed Marada (Mardaites)—from northern Mount Lebanon, in 845 including inhabitants of the Kisrawan district (*ahl al-aasiya*).[8] Given that the real Marada were Byzantine auxiliaries who withdrew to Anatolia in the late seventh century, it can be assumed that the Arslans were in conflict with a growing Maronite population—perhaps including Marada remnants. For his own times in the tenth century, al-Mas'udi registered the Maronites as a significant, distinctive presence.[9] The Crusader chronicler William of Tyre noted that these Mount Lebanon Christians enthusiastically aided the Franks in 1099. He estimated Maronite numbers in the twelfth century at around 40,000.[10]

Next, consider the Shi'a and the Druze. Southern Lebanese tradition, according to the prominent early twentieth-century local historian Muhammad al-Safa, holds that Arab tribes entering the southern Lebanon hills before and after the Islamic conquest gave their loyalty to the party of the Caliph Ali (the Shi'a) from the 650s on.[11] In other words, they favored the line of Muhammad's family as Islamic leaders, in opposition to the Umayyads of Damascus, who were Sunnis, accepted by most Muslims as the proper Muslim rulers. The most prominent early Lebanese partisans of Ali were the Arabian Amila tribe, mentioned by the fourteenth-century historian Abu al-Fida.[12] They gave their name to the hills south of the Litani River—Jabal Amil.

Until the tenth century, when Shi'a doctrine crystallized and differentiated between the book-oriented Shi'a Twelvers and the esoteric Isma'ilis, only proto-Shi'a in Lebanon can be referenced. In Iraq around 940, the twelfth Imam, or saintly personality in line from Ali and Muhammad, disappeared into "occultation." According to Twelver Shi'a belief, he will return to set the world right before the Final Judgment. After the 940s, Twelver Shi'a doctrine entered Lebanon from Iraq. The following century, until the Sunni Seljuk Turks seized Baghdad in 1055, saw Shi'a ascendancy in the central Islamic lands, whether the Twelver Buyids in Baghdad, the Twelver Hamdanids in Aleppo, the Fatimid Isma'ilis in Cairo, or the Carmathian Isma'ilis who raided the Levant from the desert.

Under Shi'a ascendancy, the majority of the rural Muslim population of southern Mount Lebanon, the northern Galilee, and the Biqa—whether previously Sunni or proto-Shi'a—became either Twelver or Isma'ili Shi'a. The Shi'a also penetrated the Christian Kisrawan district from the Biqa. The sectarian differentiation of Sunni and Shi'a in Mount Lebanon was obvious enough by the early twelfth century to excite Crusader interest. According to the contemporary Muslim historian Ibn al-Athir,[13] when in 1124 the Franks took Tyre the advice of a Muslim turncoat that the Shi'a of Aleppo would open the gates of their city was enough to stimulate a Frankish expedition in that direction.

The story of the Druze community begins with the Tanukh clans—mentioned earlier as early Arab Muslim settlers in Mount Lebanon, fiercely loyal to the Sunni Umayyad and Abbasid caliphs. The Abbasid decline set the Tanukhs adrift, and in the late tenth century they gave their fealty to the Isma'ili Shi'a Fatimids, who were extending their rule from Cairo into the Levant. The Fatimids presented themselves as descendants of Muhammad and Ali through Isma'il, the seventh and last Imam (saintly personality) for Isma'ili Shi'a, who are therefore also called Seveners.

In 1020 the highly eccentric Fatimid caliph, al-Hakim, died with no body discovered. Members of his immediate circle openly declared that he was an incarnation of God and sent out a "unification call" for acceptance of his divinity. The Tanukhs of central Mount Lebanon and the slopes of Mount Hermon accepted the call, and they and their peasants became the Druze, named after a disciple of al-Hakim. The sixteenth-century Lebanese historian Ibn al-Hariri claims that al-Hakim mobilized followers in Wadi al-Taym near Mount Hermon.[14] It is interesting that there is a change in the opening religious invocation of the Arslan family records to include Caliph Ali and the imams with the seventh *sijl* (entry) of 1061.[15]

Crusader rule of much of the Levant from 1099 till the mid-thirteenth century was crucial for consolidation of the Maronite, Twelver Shi'a, and Druze communities. The chiefs of the mountain sects could play off Frankish and Muslim principalities, and they were given an extra century and a half of relief from Sunni Muslim imperial authority. By the time of the Sunni Mamluk takeover in the late thirteenth century, the mountain communities all had cohesive identities and could not be expunged. The Maronites inaugurated their link with Rome, though there was dissension. They reinforced their presence in northern Mount Lebanon.

The Twelver Shi'a filled out their settlement of the southern Lebanese hills inland from Tyre under stable and relatively tolerant Frankish rule. The Druze inhabited a sensitive strategic location at the conjunction of the Kingdom of Jerusalem, the County of Tripoli, and the Muslim Emirate of Damascus. Inland from Beirut, the Crusader/Muslim frontier zone was closest to the coast, and the allegiance of the Tanukhs of the Gharb to Damascus brought a devastating Frankish response in 1110.[16] Druze, headed by the Ma'n family to the south, had generally better relations with the Franks of Sidon.[17]

The Crusader period has been particularly manipulated to suit modern agendas because of modern issues between the West and Islam. In reality, the interactions of Franks and Muslims differed from the interactions among modern states and societies. Instead of territorial boundaries there were transition zones, with the Biqa Valley an area of shared revenues between Frankish Tripoli and Muslim Damascus. Commerce proceeded as if politics did not exist, and Muslim caravans headed for the Frankish port of Acre even during military confrontations.

An interesting case of interpreting the past in the light of the present is the attempt by modern Lebanese Shi'a historians, writing in Arabic, to read today's resistance against Israel and the West back eight centuries into Frankish/Shi'a relations. In fact, the Arabic and Frankish sources are unanimous about the predominance of Frankish/Shi'a harmony, at least until the Crusader disaster at Hittin in 1187. In 1184, the Spanish Muslim traveler Ibn Jubayr went through Jabal Amil with a caravan from Damascus.

We came to one of the biggest fortresses of the Franks called Tibnin. At this place customs' dues are levied on the caravans. It belongs to the sow known as

Queen, who is the mother of the pig who is the lord of Acre—May God
destroy it....We moved from Tibnin at daybreak. Our way lay through contin-
uous farms and ordered settlements, whose inhabitants were all Muslims, living comfortably with the Franks. God protect us from such temptations....
The Muslim community bewails the injustice of a landlord of its own faith,
and applauds the conduct of its enemy and opponent, the Frankish landlord,
and is accustomed to justice from him.[18]

Further, the Damascus historian Ibn al-Qalanisi, writing in the late 1150s,
refers to "Muslims of the Jabal Amila" as military auxiliaries of the Franks.[19]
Ibn al-Athir endorses this picture,[20] and William of Tyre notes that when the
funeral procession of King Baldwin III passed southward from Beirut in
February 1163, "there came down from the mountains a multitude of infidels who followed the cortege with wailing."[21] The indicators would seem
powerful, though modern historians Muhammad Makhzum and Ja'afar
al-Muhajir have reservations.[22] Al-Muhajir appears apoplectic about even the
suggestion of collaboration. For example, he dismisses Ibn Jubayr's observations as naïve, as missing deep social antipathies that he believes must have
existed. Al-Muhajir gives his work the suggestive title "Jabal Amil under the
Crusader Occupation."

Moving on to the Mamluk and Ottoman periods, the medieval Lebanese
assemblage of communities supplied the antecedents of modern Lebanon as
a multisectarian political entity. After initially confronting the mountaineers,
the Sunni Mamluk regime generally ruled with a lighter hand through the
fourteenth- and fifteenth centuries. Kamal Salibi, the doyen of modern
Lebanese historians, disparages the idea of Mount Lebanon as a refuge for
autonomous lords of minority populations. Salibi observes that imperial
forces could march in at will.[23] However, the Mamluk historian Badr al-Din
al-Ayni, writing in the early fifteenth century, had a more nuanced view:
"The Emirs of Damascus were deterred by what they knew of the numbers
and resolution [of the mountain people], and the narrowness of the tracks to
them, which a horseman cannot negotiate."[24]

Under the Mamluks, the mountain communities acquired characteristics
relevant to later politics. The Maronite church began to evolve into a coherent
structure with a line of patriarchs, while a Maronite historian, Ibn al-Qila'i,
laid the foundation blocks for a heroic communal historical mythology. The
Twelver Shi'a of Jabal Amil also assumed more communal cohesion with the
emergence of a semifeudal order of leading rural families, beginning with
Husam al-Din Bishara in the 1190s. The fourteenth century saw the establishment of Jabal Amil as a center of Shi'a religious scholarship. This production of scholars later helped entrench the momentous sixteenth-century
conversion of Iran to Shi'a Islam.

The Mamluks soon tended to favor the leading Druze families, including
the Ma'ns and Tanukhs, as their mountain agents. The Druze chiefs knew
how to play their cards; they dominated the strategic high ground flanking the
Beirut-Damascus road, and they feigned Sunni Islam when convenient, as

their religion allows. Mamluk favor and Druze command of the center of Mount Lebanon gave the Druze lords a social and political preeminence that lasted until around 1800.

After seizing the Levant in 1516, the Ottomans initially faced resistance from some Druze clans who were not pleased with the regime change. The Ottomans, like the Mamluks, co-opted Druze leaders. In 1593 they made Fakhr al-Din al-Ma'n subgovernor for the Sidon district. Fakhr al-Din used his position to carve out a virtually independent principality, including the whole of modern Lebanon, and in the 1620s he deposed the governor of Damascus. Fakhr al-Din opened Mount Lebanon to Europe. He had intimate relations with Tuscany; he worked closely with the leading Maronite family, the Khazens; and he was permissive regarding the expanding land-holdings and influence of the Maronite church. Fakhr al-Din also gave refuge to the family of the rebel Kurdish chief Ali Janbalad, who briefly aspired to make Aleppo an independent principality. One of the Janbalads married into the Druze Tanukhs, and their descendants—the Jumblatts—are today the leading Druze political family. Although the Ottomans overthrew Fakhr al-Din in 1633, his principality persisted in reduced form. Many regard it as the origin of the modern Lebanese polity.

Some modern historians, for example Salibi and Richard van Leeuwen, have interpreted the informal principality of Mount Lebanon between the seventeenth- and nineteenth centuries as simply an Ottoman tax-gathering device.[25] The Ottoman governor of Sidon invested a leading member of the Ma'ns, and later the related Shihab family, as "emir"—chief tax farmer and judicial officer of the mountain. These historians claim the "emirate" was no different from other local autonomies in geographical Syria.

There is dissension regarding this position, however. No other local autonomy lasted more than a few decades: The emirate of Mount Lebanon lasted 250 years and developed into the Ottoman autonomous province of Mount Lebanon. No other local autonomy represented non-Sunni collaboration as did the Druze/Maronite collaboration in Mount Lebanon. No other local autonomy provided cover and encouragement for the demographic, economic, and political rise of a Christian community as the emirate of Mount Lebanon provided for the Maronite Catholics. In these respects, the informal principality was unique in the Ottoman Levant. If this uniqueness is asserted, it is automatically asserted that modern Lebanon has antecedents much deeper than those of the modern Syrian state. The current rulers of Syria perceive Lebanon as an illegitimate entity cobbled together by French imperialism in 1920. Hence, the contested meaning of the informal principality is not an arcane historical matter; it touches on the legitimacy of Lebanon as a modern country.

Similarly, contrasting perspectives on the origins of Lebanon's sectarian politics connect to different views on the legitimacy of Lebanon's modern confessional democracy. If the view is taken, as this chapter asserts, that the outburst of Maronite/Druze sectarian conflict between 1840 and 1860 was the outcome of a long, primarily indigenous evolution and related to sectarian identities going back a millennium, the idea of pluralism by communal representation is well grounded in the country's cultural landscape.

If the view of Usama Makdisi is taken, that the mid-nineteenth century sectarian conflict was a sudden development provoked by European favoring of Christians and European-sponsored division of the mountain between Maronite and Druze districts,[26] it becomes easier to scorn sectarian representation. Put simply, it becomes easier to interpret confessional democracy as an unnatural product of European imperialism. This is the Arab nationalist dismissal of Lebanon's confessional democracy as a fake pluralism. Such devaluing of the Lebanese system obviously is favored by such modern groupings as the Ba'thists, who rule Syria and formerly ruled Iraq; other autocratic regimes; and Islamists.

This chapter's perspective is that Lebanon's modern sectarian politics rose out of the seventeenth- and eighteenth-century growth of the Maronite community and the pressure that growth put on both the multisectarian landlord class and on Druze territory. Maronite population increase and the activism of the Maronite church from Fakhr al-Din onward led to Maronite migration south, displacing Shi'a Muslims in the Kisrawan and moving beyond into Druze areas, initially as invited tenants of Druze chiefs. European influence and favors sharpened the drive of the Maronite church and made Christians wealthier, but they assisted rather than created the trend toward politicization of sectarian identities.

Sectarian politicization received its initial expression in the administrative council of the Ottoman autonomous province of Mount Lebanon between 1861 and 1915. Multimember constituencies provided twelve councilors—four Maronites, three Druze, two Orthodox Christians, one Greek Catholic, one Shi'a, and one Sunni. This was roughly in line with the populations, though Maronites were a majority of almost 60 percent in the territory.

In 1920, the French mandatory regime extended the province to include the coastal cities of Beirut, Tripoli, and Sidon, as well as the Biqa Valley and the Shi'a south. This brought the substantial Sunni Muslim urban population of the coast into the political picture as the second largest community after the Maronites. The new Greater Lebanon also fully incorporated the Twelver Shi'a. Enlargement to the natural limits of the Lebanese mountains converted the Lebanese polity from a Maronite/Druze affair with a big Christian majority to a polyglot with no sectarian majority, and the Christian population soon sank below 50 percent.

INTERPRETING LEBANON'S PRESENT

In political terms, Greater Lebanon, which after 1943 was independent Lebanon, proceeded as an elaboration of the communal pluralism of the Ottoman autonomous province. According to the 1943 National Pact between sectarian leaders, the president would be a Maronite; the prime minister a Sunni; and the parliamentary speaker a Shi'a. Parliament was divided in a 6-to-5 ratio between Christians and non-Christians in line with the 1932 census (the last held) and adjusted to an even split in 1989. The Christian president could not function without a cooperative Sunni prime minister, and unstable multisectarian factions rather than ideological parties have dominated the legislature.

Lebanon's political system has many deficiencies. Between 1975 and 2005, it effectively ceased to function, with 15 years of violent breakdown followed by 15 years of manipulative Syrian hegemony—a hegemony approved by the West until about 2000. Even when operating, the system has never reconciled representation of communities with representation of individual citizens. Parliamentary deputies are elected under sectarian labels at the same time as they are constitutionally bound to act for the citizenry regardless of sect. The allocation of parliamentary seats has become out of line with the numerical weighting of the communities. Only an internationally supervised census, which no one wants, can resolve the issue. Every community has its demographic mythology, which they do not want punctured. The Shi'a community has increased from one-fifth of the population in 1932 to probably around one-third today. Even under the 1989 adjustment, it gets 27 seats out of 128 when it should have at least 40.

However, the positives of the system exceed the negatives. First, Lebanon is one of the very few Middle Eastern countries where the government arises from parliament.

Second, the Lebanese system has been the political framework for a dynamic public pluralism unheard of anywhere else in the Arab world. Even the intimidation from 1990 to 2005 by the Damascus-directed security apparatus did not destroy a freewheeling civil society and an assertive media.

Third, the reemergence of "confessional democracy" in May 2005, with Syria's enforced military withdrawal and the first free elections since 1972, produced a parliamentary balance close to the probable numerical weight of major political forces. In massive competitive demonstrations in March 2005, the "March 8" Shi'a bloc of Hizballah (the Party of God) and Amal mobilized about half the numbers brought out by the anti-Syrian "March 14" Cedar Revolution forces, mainly Sunni, Christian, and Druze. In the elections, Hizballah and Amal gained 35 seats compared to the 72 of the Cedar Revolution alignment; 21 seats went to a bloc headed by the Maronite General Michel Aoun, mainly Christians suspicious of the Sunni and Druze management of the Cedar Revolution.

It is vital to record the predominant positives because the Lebanese democratic system is at peril in Lebanon's current crisis—a crisis over the determination of a Syrian ruling clique to recover the hegemony lost when its nerve briefly failed in 2005.

The crisis commenced in September 2004 when Syria's young president, Bashar al-Asad, who succeeded his more cautious father in 2000, forced an unconstitutional extension of office for his friend, the Lebanese president Emile Lahoud. Lining up against Bashar were Lebanon's Sunni Prime Minister Rafiq al-Hariri; much of the Lebanese political class, which had previously cooperated with Bashar's father; an affronted French President Jacques Chirac; and the United States, furious about Syrian-sponsored jihadis in Iraq. On Bashar's side were Hizballah and Amal, dominant in the Shi'a community, and Iran. Syria was the central cog in the Syria-Iran-Hezbollah alignment against Israel, and many Shi'a appreciated Syrian support for themselves against Syria's other client, the Lebanese government. Throughout the 1990s, Hizballah had fought Israel and the government neglect of the Shi'a.

In reaction to Bashar's move, the United States and France sponsored UN Security Council Resolution 1559, which demanded Syrian withdrawal from Lebanon and the disbandment of militias, principally Hizballah's military wing. In February 2005, Rafiq al-Hariri, who had made it plain that he wanted to displace Syrian influence in the coming elections, was murdered in a huge truck bomb attack. The United Nations promptly established its first-ever murder inquiry, which in October 2005 named senior Syrian and Lebanese security officials as suspects, including the brother-in-law and brother of Bashar al-Asad. The fierce Lebanese and international reaction to the Hariri assassination briefly shook Syrian Ba'thist self-assurance sufficiently to obtain the Syrian military departure from Lebanon.

By early 2006, Hizballah had cause for serious concern about the threat to its Syrian missile supplier from the murder inquiry and about its own political slippage. In a national dialogue, Lebanese politicians raised the party's private weaponry and its state-within-a-state status. In July, Hizballah sought to turn the tables with its war against Israel. The war burnished Hizballah's resistance halo, but it also turned most Sunnis and Druze, more than half the Christians, and a minority of Shi'a against the movement. Hizballah received crucial cross-sectarian cover from the discontented General Michel Aoun, a Maronite whose presidential aspirations did not receive Cedar Revolution endorsement, but who tapped Christian hostility toward perceived financial colonization of Beirut by the Sunni Arab oil states of the Persian Gulf.

Hizballah's fight with Israel ended in mid-August 2006, with UN Security Council Resolution 1701 blaming the party for precipitating hostilities. The UN force in southern Lebanon tripled in size, and the Lebanese Army moved to the border, its role being defined as constraining Hizballah's military wing. Hizballah accused the Lebanese government majority of wanting the party's demise. This inflamed a dangerous Shi'a-Sunni rift.

In November 2006, when the protocol for the international court to try suspects identified by the murder inquiry came to Beirut for Lebanese government approval, all the pro-Syrian ministers, including those from Hizballah, resigned in order to derail the vote. The government still had its two-thirds' quorum and went ahead anyway. More anti-Syrian politicians died in a continuing series of political murders, and on May 30, 2007, the UN Security Council formally endorsed the international murder tribunal in Resolution 1757. The UN inquiry, loaded with the lengthening series of murders, slowed under its second chief, but the trend toward indictment of

Syrian officials was plain in the procession of reports to the Security Council.

In 2007 and 2008, the Lebanese crisis metastasized. Syria and its Lebanese allies paralyzed the Lebanese state, declaring the government illegitimate, refusing to allow parliament to meet, and blocking the election of a Lebanese president after Emile Lahoud finally left office in November 2007. Syrian military intelligence manipulated so-called al-Qa'ida elements in a Palestinian refugee camp in northern Lebanon—the Fath al-Islam group—to destabilize Lebanon, debilitate its army, and disrupt Lebanon's Sunni community.

There is a multiple triangulation of evidence from separate sources about this Syrian activity: Lebanese judicial documents, Jordanian security courts, the Gulf Arabic press, interviews with witnesses to Syrian intelligence co-opting of religious militants inside Syrian prisons, naming of Syrian security minders of Fath al-Islam by a top *al-Hayat* journalist, and so on.[27]

The Syrian regime's purpose has been transparent. It is to flaunt Syria's capability for destabilization and blockage to the international community until Bashar al-Asad gets a deal that lets him and his regime off the murder rap. Bashar personally threatened UN Secretary General Ban Ki-moon regarding the murder tribunal when they met in Damascus in April 2007. According to the secretary general's note-taker:

> Instability would intensify if the Special tribunal were established. This was particularly the case if the Tribunal were established under Chapter 7 of the Charter. This could easily ignite a conflict which would result in civil war [in Lebanon] and provoke divisions between Sunni and Shi'a from the Mediterranean to the Caspian Sea....If the Tribunal was achieved via Chapter 7, it would have grave consequences that could not be contained in Lebanon...[On diplomatic relations between Syria and Lebanon] President Assad responded by saying that establishing diplomatic relations was impossible at this point. The present government in Lebanon was not legal and the Syrian people hated the March 14 Movement. He had tried to talk to [Lebanese Prime Minister] Siniora in the past but this was now impossible.[28]

A year later, in April 2008, U.S. Senator Arlen Specter reported being told by King Abdullah II of Jordan: "The item that is most on the mind of Assad is the action of the international tribunal that could lead to his indictment."[29]

In June 2008, after a flurry of fighting, an agreement reached by the two sides in Lebanon at Doha, Qatar, provided for the election of Michel Suleiman, commander of the army, as president; gave a blocking third of cabinet seats to the Hizballah-led opposition; and provided for future elections.

The present Lebanese crisis connects to communities. The probable background to the Hariri murder was the paranoia of the Alawite rulers of Syria, members of a Shi'a-derived minority facing a Sunni majority, about the Saudi, Western, and even Syrian Sunni connections of a billionaire Sunni Lebanese prime minister whom they needed for Lebanon to be viable and lucrative under their hegemony, but whom they intensely distrusted. This is what can already be divined from the UN inquiry reports, which are clear on political motive.

There is more. Shi'a estrangement from the rest of Lebanon underlies the alliance between Hizballah leader Hasan Nasrallah and Bashar al-Asad. Druze leader Walid Jumblatt's fear of militant Shi'a ascendancy backed by Syria and Iran led him into a Sunni-Christian-Druze alliance. However, he also has looked to preserve multicommunal Lebanon by pulling moderate Shi'a away from Hizballah, using his political friendship with the Shi'a parliamentary speaker Nabih Barri. To secure the Druze community, Jumblatt is even ready to appease Hizballah, as evidenced in the aftermath of Hizballah's military and political assertion in Beirut in mid-2008.

As for the Christians, contradictory Maronite impulses have distracted Lebanon's still formidable Christian sector. There is Maronite nostalgia for the partnership with Sunnis that dominated twentieth-century Lebanese politics. There is also a Maronite commonality with the Shi'a as a fellow mountain community. There is fear of Syria, ally of the Shi'a Hizballah, but also prejudice against Saudi and Gulf money.

Walid Jumblatt believes that sectarian pluralism is the essence of Lebanon and that the arguments within each communal political compartment only reinforce the point. Muhammad Hussein Fadlallah, a leading religious scholar of the Lebanese Shi'a, concurred in 1998 remarks at a Ramadan *Iftar*: "We are several sects, but we feel that we are several states.... Is it believable that the country is occupied by an enemy [he meant Israel] and we [spend our time] debating whether the Shi'a sect or the Sunni sect or the Maronite sect has the biggest numbers."[30]

Lebanon's multicommunal history makes for problems of coherence in modern Lebanese politics. Communal suspicion—today principally on a Sunni-Shi'a fault line—produces paralysis that saps Lebanon's viability and pluralist foundations. This is fine for a Syrian Ba'thist regime that denies there is anything significant about the Lebanese and their history, despises pluralism, and regards restored command of Lebanon as vital to its own viability as the "beating heart" of Arabism.

Perception of reality is what drives policy and action, and any survey of Syrian media outlets leaves no doubt of the extraordinary sense of self-importance within the Syrian Ba'thist bubble. For inhabitants of the bubble, Syria is the hub of the Middle East, to which anyone wanting quiet in Iraq, Arab-Israeli peace, or relief from car bombs must come cap in hand. Syria is not a philanthropic society, says Bashar al-Asad, and supplicants must pay Syria's price. Lebanon has been and will again be the Syrian regime's own turf. This outlook has underpinned the Syrian regime's self-assurance that there will be benefits but no costs from political murder.

The present Syrian regime cannot tolerate or conceive a pluralist Lebanon. It cannot believe that any real Lebanese, as an Arab, can oppose Ba'thist Syria. Anyone who parts company with Ba'thist Syria must be a non-Arab and become a nonperson. Westerners find such a worldview difficult to digest. They look for the reasonable Westernized Bashar al-Asad who did eye doctor training in London in the early 1990s. Rafiq al-Hariri commented scathingly to an Irish journalist only one month before his murder: "You silly Westerners. You think your society is the best in the world, and that anyone who spends three years in London becomes just like you."[31]

A peculiarity of the Lebanese crisis is that the international community is a central player. A main focus of the crisis—the fate of a UN murder inquiry and tribunal—is unique. The U.S. administration has exhibited exemplary multilateralism. There is also the very large international military presence as a result of the Hizballah-Israeli hostilities, and the international attention to the Lebanon-Syria border. The commitment of international credibility lights the darkness just a little.

There are two possible outcomes. If there are indictments of murder masterminds, it is difficult to see the Syrian ruling clique surviving. That does not mean that Syria will be taken over by Sunni religious militants, who have no serious organizational capacity. Lebanon's pluralism will be able to consolidate, and Hizballah's absolutists will have to come to terms with their Lebanese environment. If the murder court and inquiry are gutted by shady deals, political murder will be supreme and Lebanon will slip back under the Syrian Ba'thist shadow.

It is true that it will be difficult to dispose of the Hariri affair easily since the Hariri case is a top-down investigation in which most evidence is apparently against the masterminds. Also, UN Security Council reports on fulfillment of Resolutions 1559 and 1701 are increasingly sharp toward Syria and Hizballah despite the hoary UN bureaucracy, and the establishment of the murder court grinds onward.

Nonetheless, the perspective presented here is bleak. Lebanon's only hope is international justice. When dealing with political murder the only conflict resolution is judicial resolution. In this crisis, the engagement ideas of Barack Obama, Nicolas Sarkozy, and Turkish and Israeli politicians just give oxygen to absolutists and murder suspects.

CONCLUSION

Lebanese communal identities are products of historical circumstances and accidents. In theory, they can be downscaled in favor of representative constructs that are simpler, more unifying, and less riddled with patron/client dependencies than confessional democracy.

Yet communal identities are much older and stronger than Arabist intellectuals would have it. At best, Lebanon is stuck with a long transition. Lebanon cannot be reformed as a nation-state—or even guard the existing pluralism, which is itself effortlessly superior to anything else in the Arab world—if the forces hostile to Lebanon as a nation-state win the present conflict.

Hizballah's state-beyond-the-state is incompatible with Lebanon and with Shi'a interests. For Shi'a, liberation culminated in 2000. They are now prisoners of a megalomaniac "resistance" agenda—"resistance" against anyone unenthusiastic about the private army of the Party of God. Hizballah's Shi'a base will erode if the rest of Lebanon can sustain pluralism. The problem is that the Syrian ruling clique will not leave Lebanon alone. It is determined on reassertion through its allies, and its victory will be the end of any decent Lebanon. Lebanese pluralism cannot coexist with Bashar al-Asad's regime. Those Westerners who are soft in the head about mafias such as the Syrian regime, who romanticize authoritarian machines such as Hizballah and who are comfortable with political murder—provided of course that it is always far from home—are not friends of Lebanon or of the Arabs.

NOTES

1. See, e.g., Aziz al-Azmeh, "Nationalism and the Arabs," in Derek Hopwood (ed.), *Arab Nation, Arab Nationalism* (London: MacMillan Press, 2000), p. 77. Al-Azmeh asserts as fact rather than opinion that "[c]ommunalism...belongs to the register of new identities invented under contemporary conditions of structural involution, buttressed by nearly two centuries of Balkanist policies by the Western powers.... [It is] representation of minor ethnological differences...as ethnographic incompatibilities."
2. For elaboration of the argument, see William Harris, *The New Face of Lebanon* (Princeton: Markus Wiener, 2005), pp. 95–100.
3. Abd al-Ghani al-Nabulusi, "Hullat al-Dhahab al-Ibriz fi Rihlat Ba'albak wa al-Biqa al-Aziz," in Stefan Wild (ed.), *Zwei Beschreibungen des Lebanon: Abdalgani an-Nabulusis Reise durch die Biqa und Al-Utaifis Reise Nach Tripolis* (Beirut: Orient-Institut, 1979), p. 109.
4. Salih bin Yahya, *Ta'rikh Bayrut wa Akhbar al-Umara' al-Buhturiyin min Bani al-Gharb*, edited by Louis Cheyko (Beirut, Al-Matba'at al-Kathulikiyya, 1927), p. 32. Bin Yahya was a fifteenth century local chronicler.
5. *The Maronite Chronicle*, as translated by A. Palmer, *The Seventh Century in the West-Syrian Chronicles* (Liverpool: Liverpool University Press, 1993), p. 30.
6. Al-Mas'udi, *Kitab al-Tanbih wa al-Ashraf* (Beirut: Khayyat, 1965), pp. 153–154.
7. Al-Baladhuri, *Kitab Futuh al-Buldan*, as translated by Philip Hitti, *The Origins of the Islamic State* (Beirut: Khayyat, 1966), pp. 250–251.
8. *Al-Sijl al-Arslani*, edited by Muhammad Khalil al-Basha and Riyadh Husayn Ghannam (Beirut: Nawfal, 1999), pp. 55–56.
9. Al-Mas'udi, *Kitab al-Tanbih wa al-Ashraf*, p. 153.
10. William of Tyre, *A History of Deeds Done Beyond the Sea* (trans. Emily Babcock and A. C. Krey), 2 vols. (New York: Columbia University Press, 1943), Vol. 2, p. 459.
11. Muhammad Jabir Al-Safa, *Ta'rikh Jabal Amil* (Beirut: Dar al-Nahar, 2004), p. 33.
12. Abu al-Fida, *Kitab al-Mukhtasar fi Akhbar al-Bashr* (Beirut: Dar al-Fikr, 1956–1961), Part 1, p. 131.
13. Ibn al-Athir, *Al-Kamil fi al-Ta'rikh*, 13 vols. (Beirut: Dar al-Sader, 1965–1967), Vol. 10, p. 623.
14. Ibn al-Hariri, *Muntakhab al-Zaman fi Ta'rikh al-Khulafa wa al-Ulama wa al-Ayan* (Beirut: Dar Ashtar, 1995), pp. 258–259.
15. *Al-Sijl al-Arslani*, p. 79.
16. Ibid., pp. 101–104.

17. Jean Richard, *Francs et Orientaux dans le Monde des Croisades* (Aldershot: Ashgate-Variorum, 2003), pp. 145–146; Joshua Prawer, *The Latin Kingdom of Jerusalem* (London: Weidenfeld and Nicolson, 1972), p. 52.

18. Ibn Jubayr, *Rihla*, as translated by R. J. C. Broadhurst, *The Travels of Ibn Jubayr* (London: Jonathan Cape, 1952), pp. 316–317.

19. Ibn al-Qalanisi, *Dhail Ta'rikh Dimashq*, as translated by H. A. R. Gibb, *The Damascus Chronicle of the Crusades* (London: Luzac & Co., 1932), p. 331.

20. Ibn al-Athir, *Al-Kamil fi al-Ta'rikh*, Vol. 12, p. 481.

21. William of Tyre, *A History of Deeds Done Beyond the Sea*, Vol. 2, p. 294.

22. Muhammad Makhzum, "Jabal Amil fi al-Ahdayn al-Salibi wa al-Mamluki," in *Safahat min Ta'rikh Jabal Amil*, ed. South Lebanon Cultural Council (Beirut: Dar al-Farabi, 1979), pp. 33–51; Ja'afar al-Muhajir, *Jabal Amil taht al-Ihtilal al-Salibi* (Beirut: Dar al-Haqq, 2001), pp. 31–51.

23. Kamal Salibi, *A House of Many Mansions: The History of Lebanon Reconsidered* (London: I. B. Tauris, 1988), pp. 139–140.

24. Badr al-Din al-Ayni, *Iqd al-Juman fi Tarikh Ahl al-Zaman—Asr Salatin al-Mamalik* (Cairo: Al-Hay'a al-Misriya al-Amma lil Kitab, 1987–1992), Vol. 3, p. 127.

25. Richard van Leeuwen, *Notables and Clergy in Mount Lebanon: The Khazin Sheikhs and the Maronite Church* (Leiden: E. J. Brill, 1994), p. 38: Salibi, *A House of Many Mansions*, p. 128.

26. Usama Makdisi, *The Culture of Sectarianism: Community, History, and Violence in Nineteenth Century Ottoman Lebanon* (Berkeley and Los Angeles: University of California Press, 2000).

27. Some examples follow. In *al-Hayat* (London and Beirut), May 21, 2007, the respected journalist Muhammad Shuqayr, using Palestinian informants in northern Lebanon, identified Syrian intelligence officers who were coordinating Fath al-Islam. *Al-Sharq al-Awsat* (London), June 9, 2007, reported from "Jordanian judicial sources" that Fath al-Islam leader Shakir al-Abssi ran a suicide bomber training camp in Syria. *Al-Nahar* (Beirut), August 22 and 23, 2007, interviewed former prisoners in Syrian jails on Syrian intelligence mobilization of jihadists.

28. Official UN transcript of April 24, 2007 Ban Ki-moon meeting with Bashar al-Asad, pp. 3–4.

29. *Daily Star* (Beirut), April 10, 2008.

30. *Al-Hayat*, January 1, 1999.

31. Lara Marlowe in *The Irish Times*, February 19, 2005.

2

WHAT MAKES LEBANON A DISTINCTIVE COUNTRY?

Eli Fawaz

In December 1948, at one of the earliest sessions of the United Nations, Lebanon's representative, Ambassador Charles Malik, summed up his country's self-image and unique nature:

> The history of my country for centuries is precisely that of a small country struggling against all odds for the maintenance and strengthening of real freedom of thought and conscience. Innumerable persecuted minorities have found, throughout the ages, a most understanding haven in my country, so that the very basis of our existence is complete respect of differences of opinion and belief.[1]

Throughout history Lebanon had a distinct identity and fate. Its natural environment, a symbiotic blend of the mountains and the Mediterranean sea; its social composure of diverse religious minorities; its relations with the West and that region's ideas; the consensual democratic regime it invented to suit its sectarian reality; the liberal economy it enjoyed; relative freedom that held special appeal for the intellectual dissident of the neighboring countries—all of these elements have always marked Lebanon, sometimes bringing it trouble as the center of conflicts.

Yet what makes Lebanon distinctive? What is underlying these features? How is the country distinctive in the region?

SOCIAL COMPOSITION

One of the features that distinguishes Lebanon in the region is its social composition, a spectrum of different religious minorities. It thus gained the reputation of being a safe haven for them. As early as the tenth century, a new historical era for Lebanon began as Maronite monks migrated to the northern Lebanese highlands, Druze reached and controlled the Shuf district southeast of Beirut, and Shi'a populated south Lebanon and the Biqa Valley. Despite their many differences, these populations were certainly singular in the fact that they were not all-conquering armies that would either displace all the existing people or force them to covert but were religious minorities that would remain as such.

Religion was not merely a theological distinction but an ethnic-communal one, a marker of identity. As Elie Kedourie put it: "Religion was not only a matter for the individual conscience, for personal and private devotions; it was a rule of life regulating all social activities and all relation with the suzerain power, itself suzerain by virtue of professing the dominant religion."[2]

Almost all the political, economic, and cultural events that unfolded on this land are directly related to the social composure of the inhabitants and their interactions with each other.

GEOGRAPHIC PARTICULARITY

Another important and determining factor of the distinctive Lebanese identity is the natural environment in which those minorities have evolved: The mountains of Lebanon stand defiant, overlooking the wide desert lands that spread out from their northern side and stop their march. On the other side, they are open to the infinite adventurous horizon of the Mediterranean shore. They do in places come to touch it and loom over vivacious cities and busy ports that have flourished throughout different epochs. They have witnessed numerous invasions, destruction, degradation, and rebirth.

Since the past and until the current day, these lands still attract and host many minorities seeking refuge, conquerors hunting glory, regional and international conflicts seeking a stage, and political and intellectual dissidents trying to find a ray of freedom. Phillip Hitti wrote of it thus: "The mountainous character of the land, its close proximity to the sea, its central location in the cradle of civilization and at the crossroads of the world, astride the great international highway that linked the three historic continents—these are the determining factors in its historic career."[3]

From then on it seems that the mounts of Lebanon have found their people—or is it the other way around? Was it the nature in which they came to thrive that enhanced their love for freedom, or is it their vigorous spirit of independence and their endurance of adversity that led them to inhabit those protective highlands?

Those two important features, the geographical and demographic, mark Lebanese history and have somehow distinguished this nation from its surroundings. The many events to unfold in the region have a special and different resonance in Lebanese society, precisely because of that country's special and particular features.

HISTORICAL BACKGROUND

The Lebanese state in its present form was not recognized as independent and sovereign until 1920, when France declared the formation of Grand

Liban. Nevertheless, it enjoyed a political form and had considerable special privileges throughout the Ottoman era. In the heart of those mountains, explained Kamal Salibi: "An evolving form of political authority has continued without interruption from the early seventeenth century to our time, giving Lebanon a separate and distinct identity."[4]

This nature somehow distanced the local authorities from the strong influence of the central political authorities. Later, the rulers of Mount Lebanon benefited from the Ottoman reluctance to subdue those semiautonomous regions. The Ottomans followed the policy of their predecessors in that matter and tried to deal with the inhabitants of Mount Lebanon as vassals. As long as they paid their fiscal dues and did not try to occupy the territories directly exploited by their agents, the Ottoman rulers would let them enjoy a kind of autonomy. This was exactly what the emirs of Mount Lebanon understood and successfully used. This helped the Druze Ma'n emirs to unify Mount Lebanon as early as the seventeenth century and even to extend their dominions to a good part of Syria and Palestine, with the consent of the Ottomans.

PARTICULARITY

With time "this nature will create a ray of freedom" that will permit the inhabitants of Lebanon to develop and enjoy certain customs and practices, such as religious freedom and tolerance, internal organization in matters of justice, and security and law.

The minorities in Mount Lebanon enjoyed a large degree of freedom, which was reflected in some of their practices. For instance, the Druze did not pay the poll tax and were recognized as part of the Muslim *Umma* even though they were not subscribers to Sunni Islam. As for the Christians, they were allowed to build and renovate their churches, though in other parts of the empire such activities required the Muslim sultan's permission. In Lebanon, this rule was not observed.[5]

The people of Mount Lebanon were also allowed to have their own quasi-system of law enforcement, which helped them establish security and stability. Garrisons were created in order to secure the transportation and the movement of people and goods. "Security of life and property [were guaranteed] not only for the Lebanese," wrote Hitti, "but also for foreign visitors and residents, including European travelers, missionaries' traders and political agents."[6]

"The peasant preserved his complete freedom and the possibility to be the owner of his land," noted Edmond Rabbath. "His relation to the feudal lord was based strictly on a commission system; no obstacles were put on his movement. He was free to change from one feudal lord to another without restrictions. Emirs favored local Christians, encouraging Maronites to migrate southwards into the Matn and the Shuf."

The Maronites were able to expand freely and peacefully in the Druze area and work without any constraints for a Druze feudal lord, which created a "human and tolerant aspect of coexistence, which was raised to a historical principle."[7]

The Lebanese were also successful in establishing economic, cultural, and religious ties with the West. The silk production prospered in Mount Lebanon and opened up new avenues of foreign trade, especially with Florence, Venice, and France.[8] The ties established between Lebanese—mainly the Maronites—and the papal seat in Rome had a great impact on the future of Lebanon as well. During the fourteenth- and fifteenth centuries, the Franciscan missionaries were specifically instructed to restore the effectiveness of the Maronite union with Rome.[9] To that purpose, Salibi wrote, a Maronite college was founded in Rome to educate the Maronite clergy. "Direct relations had long been established between Christian Lebanon and Europe. It was in the late twelfth century, while the Franks were in occupation of coastal Syria, that the Maronites, as their allies, became formally attached to the Roman Catholic Church."[10]

The church realized the importance of lay education for boys and many of the clergymen, who would make it back to Lebanon, would start establishing schools in different villages—some of which still stand today.[11]

The appeal of lighter taxes and military service as well as greater security resulted in more prosperity and, in turn, persuaded more people to settle in Lebanon. It also encouraged different missionaries to set a foot there. They grew numerous, especially after Fakhr al-Din first extended princely protection to them. By opening schools and universities and dispensing knowledge they contributed to the awakening of the country's social and cultural life, and eventually their presence came to affect both the Christian and non-Christian communities among whom they lived.[12]

All of this slowly transformed Lebanon, and, in Salibi's words:

> By the end of the nineteenth century, Lebanon was easily the most advanced part of the Ottoman empire in the field of popular education. Literacy was widespread in the country, particularly in Mount Lebanon and in Beirut, Sidon and Tripoli. Anyone could easily obtain primary instruction, and a good secondary education was available for those who could afford it. Two colleges in Beirut offered courses of advanced study in the arts and sciences, as well as training in medicine. The American press, the Catholic press, and thirteen other printing presses in Beirut and Mount Lebanon published books in Arabic on a wide variety of subjects, mostly literary, and issued no less than forty periodical publications, including fifteen newspapers, between 1870 and 1900.[13]

The freedom, the coexistence between sects, the diversity, the good education, and the overture to the West became, with time, integral parts of the Lebanese identity. These features constituted the foundations of the future Grand Lebanon. It is important to note that Lebanon is a nation where tradition replaces power. Every time the Lebanese experience slipped to violence, tradition was transgressed and power overcame the existing arrangements.

The Christians were prepared to benefit from the big changes the region witnessed after World War I. In their majority, they supported the independence of Lebanon. This was possible because of their close ties to circles of influence in the West and their growing number within the Lebanese community. Nevertheless, the shape of Lebanon was based on the traits that have always distinguished it throughout its history.

THE PATH TO GRAND LIBAN

For almost four centuries the populations of the Ottoman provinces were organized under a millet system, bounding people to their communities by their religious affiliations or confessional communities. Therefore, their relationship with the suzerain power was defined along those lines. The Christians and the Druze of Mount Lebanon benefitted during the Ottoman era from some privileges as religious minorities, and the different religious groups in Lebanon were settled with a system that gave them some room to control their own destiny, to preserve and elaborate some features of their culture and mores.

"The Ottoman control was hardly felt in Mount Lebanon," wrote Leila Fawuz Tarazi, "where no direct Ottoman authority existed before the nineteenth century. The Ottoman kept an eye on it but left it alone."[14] The end of the emirates in Mount Lebanon in 1842 presaged the coming of troubled times ahead. The Ottomans by then tried to rule Lebanon directly, ending "the special status of the mountain" after sectarian strife between the Maronites and the Druze started, to no avail.

The continuing sectarian strife led the Ottoman government to divide the mountains into two regions: one Maronite and the other Druze. This precarious solution was hard to implement due to the mix of lands and populations in those regions; it only complicated things more. This did not calm things down, and the Western powers found themselves obliged to intervene in order to put an end to the war. The French arrived in 1860, restoring calm to the mountains. They helped, with the weakened Ottoman Empire, to put in place a unique political system to run the daily affairs of Mount Lebanon: the *Mutasarrifiyya* system, an administrative council established in 1864 as an elected multisectarian advisory body for the provincial governor.

"In other words," William Harris explained, unique in the region,

Lebanon acquired a proto-parliament many decades before the emergence of either Israel or the Turkish republic, and far in advance of the creation of modern Arab states. When France and Britain cobbled together such entities as Syria and Iraq in the 1920s, Mount Lebanon already had more than half a century of experience of council elections and lively pluralist discourse.[15]

The decline and the fall of the Ottoman Empire created a vacuum for the many provinces it controlled in terms of political organization. Amid the uncertainty of the region's future, and in light of new ideas coming from the

West, the population was turning to the West. For that purpose, secret societies were formed in Lebanon and abroad, composed of intellectuals and a business bourgeoisie, in order to debate and foresee the best political form for the country. They tried to absorb the notions of citizenship—nationalism for instance—and to implement it in their environment. They gathered in Egypt and the United States, where they felt free to express their opinions against Ottoman persecution and to address the international community involved in deciding the future of the region.

Different ideas made their way into the public consciousness. Some called for the Greater Syria option, among them Constantine Zreik, Edmond Rabbath, and the Lebanese poet Amin al-Rihani. Others called for one united Arab nation led by the government of Faysal in Damascus. Among them was Rashid Rida, an Arab Muslim protagonist who saw the Lebanese nationalist dream as "something beyond capacity."[16]

The majority of the Christians, on the other hand, supported the idea of an independent Lebanese state. People such as Yusuf al-Sawda, Bishara al-Khuri, Emile Eddé, Alfred Naccache, and Michel Chiha formed numerous societies in Egypt, among the first and most important of which was "Alliance Libanaise," demanding the full independence of Lebanon.

By 1920, this group had become the backbone of the Lebanese state. They believed, noted Kauffman, that the separation of Lebanon from Syria was "supported by history, morés, racial affinities, geographical considerations, language, legislation, and common thinking. Syria and Lebanon were simply two different civilizations, because the coast which has turned towards the West since the days of the Phoenicians cannot consciously consent to let itself drown in an intrusive and planned pan-Arabism."[17]

All parties obviously were looking for historical justification to reinforce their cause and demands. In 1919, Patriarch Hoayek headed the Lebanese delegation at the Peace Congress in Versailles. He had no desire to see Lebanon become part of an Arab empire. The delegation demanded the conference extend Lebanon's frontiers to include the cities of Beirut, Tyre, Sidon, Tripoli, and the districts of Akkar, Biqa, and southern Lebanon. These cities and districts, they claimed, were natural parts of Lebanon but had been administratively separated by Ottoman rule.

In addition, they asked for the recognition of Lebanon's full independence, the institution of a parliament to represent the different sects, and the assistance of France in consolidating Lebanon's independence. Thus the independence party won the day; their ideas triumphed, and Grand Liban was officially recognized by the French mandatory force on September 1, 1920. A new constitution replaced the old order.

Lebanon's independence was seen as a major challenge to the pan-Arabist ideologues and the Arab public. It was also seen as cultural defiance since Lebanon itself embodied all of what pan-Arabism resented: Western involvement and influence in the Arab world both culturally and politically. Pan-Arabism was a form of a cultural nationalism, likened to a desperate yell in the face of the colonialist and superior attitude or action initiated by the

West. Pan-Arabism resented all forms of Western cultural manifestation and furthermore accused colonialism of hindering the Arabs' return to their golden age.

Lebanon's history and demographic composition, different Western and missionary interests, and the Lebanese mercantile capacities cultivated Lebanon into being a melting pot of different cultures and civilizations. Nevertheless, Lebanon acceded to its independence—with the support of the Western powers, but more importantly with the collaboration of a Sunni leader who through his wide connections with the Arab world made this statehood acknowledged and welcomed by Arab peers. It took many setbacks and a substantial amount of time before the wider Arab population accepted that any form of pan-Arabism is a matter of slow construction rather than that of a rejectionist sentiment toward the West. Unfortunately, pan-Arabism has been replaced by another angry manifestation: militant Islamism.

What Chiha and his friends fought for and tried hard to accomplish was simple: the combination of the existing society of Mount Lebanon with a fair amount of modernization. Chiha understood that the privileges the population of Mount Lebanon had were as much given by the former suzerain power as imposed by the character of the community itself. Those privileges—the equality of all Lebanese, personal liberty, freedom of conscience and beliefs, and education—were to become an inherent part of Lebanese society and thus were acknowledged in the Constitution. Chiha and his friends hoped that time and the healthy practice of the principles and traditions of the mountain would calm the respective fears of the minorities and push them to settle their differences within the democratic institutions and away from violent confrontations. They also hoped that, as Kais Ferro put it, "[e]conomic ties could be an instrument for modifying people's attitude and behavior."[18]

Chiha worked to ensure "proportional representation of Lebanon's different ethnic communities and the equality of all Lebanese before the law. The constitution was designed to create a basis for power sharing as part of the process of nation building."[19] As a result, the state was centralized by form but not by nature, and true power remained in the hands of the religious authority and the wealthy business class. If this reality created a barrier for all attempts by any of the minorities to dominate the others or the young Lebanese democracy to fall into any kind of dictatorship, it reflected the feeble ability the state possessed to counter the many crises it faced whether internal, regional, or international.

Yet despite the many crises Lebanon has encountered during the last several decades, as well as a civil war, it managed somehow to keep the institutions away from total collapse. No single party and no single leader could have overridden the institutions or ignored them in order to impose his will on the rest of the population. Even in the most chaotic of situations, like that of the summer of 1982 when Beirut was under siege by the Israeli army, Bashir Gemayel, in order to be elected president, had to go through the parliament in an orderly fashion with the blessing of his Sunni counterpart leader of that time—Sa'ib Salam.

A strange equilibrium existed between the weak state and the strong confessional system; some red lines were drawn between the two, and every time one sect felt stronger than the state itself and tried to trespass those red lines, the whole equilibrium was disrupted and a round of violence would erupt. From 1982 until 1991, Lebanon experienced a troubled era marked by sporadic wars; this last round of violence was marked by dramatic regional and international events, which led to Syrian hegemony over all of Lebanon.

With the fall of the Soviet empire, the United States was able to fill the gaps left by the Soviet absence in this region of the world. Furthermore, some of the Arabs who had allied with the Soviets were compelled to reconcile with the United States. Syria entered an era of entente with the United States, when it joined the international coalition during the Gulf War to liberate Kuwait from an Iraqi invasion and fought alongside American forces. Syria, in return, asked to have a free hand in Lebanon. For more than a decade Syrian President Hafiz al-Asad treated Lebanon as a Syrian province and succeeded in imposing his iron hold over Lebanese society.

Rage against the Syrian regime's behavior grew. The events of September 11, 2001, and the ensuing war on terror helped in changing the international community's sentiments toward Syria. This led to the Syrian Accountability Act passed by the U.S. Congress in 2003, meant to halt Syrian support for terrorism, end its occupation of Lebanon, and hold Syria accountable for its role in the Middle East. The Syrian regime did not grasp the change in the international mood and was convinced that it could revert to its old status. The Asad regime assassinated Lebanese Prime Minister Hariri, believing that in doing so it would successfully defy the international community and intimidate the Lebanese into capitulating to Syrian demands.

The sight of Lebanon's most powerful Sunni leader lying dead on a Beirut street that he had helped rebuild after the war sent the Lebanese into a raging but nonviolent revolt. Anti-Syrian slogans for the first time resonated in Beirut suburbs after news of the assassination spread, and the Cedar Revolution was launched. Most of the Lebanese demanded independence.

For the first time, a Sunni leader, the son of the slain Hariri, called for adopting a policy that took Lebanese interests into consideration first. And the world community responded unanimously by establishing a special tribunal to prosecute those responsible for the terrorist attacks that were targeting Lebanese leaders.

The Lebanese have seen the ultimate price paid by those politicians and intellectuals who dared to oppose first Syrian occupation of, and then Syrian interference in, Lebanon. They are not surprised that no one has been brought to justice for any of these murders through the years. Yet as long as this situation prevails, it discourages people from standing up for Lebanon's independence and makes that goal very difficult to achieve.

In 1949, George Naccache, in an editorial for the French-language newspaper *L'Orient*, pointed out his suspicion that the Christian rejection of pan-Arabism and the Sunni rejection of strong Western ties both meant that each side was based on a negative attitude rather than some kind of doctrine that could bring the two groups together. Today, however, both Christians and Sunnis are united in seeking Western help and promoting Lebanon's independence, while the Shi'a Muslims and some Christians take a clear anti-Western stance and seek Syrian-Iranian patronage.

It took six decades—including some 20 years of useless civil war and more than 200,000 victims and the Ta'if Accord that granted Muslims a true partnership in the ruling process, in addition to the failure of many ideologies—to make the majority of Lebanese adhere to the idea of a united, independent nation.

If Lebanon is the only example in the world of a power-sharing formula between different religious sects, and if the Lebanese political trajectory is different from that of other Arab states, this is not the work of chance but the accumulation and sum of historical experiences in a particular geographical space inhabited by a diverse group of people. Although frustrating at times, the Lebanese experience has always been attached to freedom within diversity. If there is something that is lacking in the Middle East today it is precisely that freedom in its many forms and that diversity in its many manifestations. That is why the Lebanese experience must be reinforced and kept going—it might be the only ray of light coming out of this region.

NOTES

1. Charles Malik, *The Challenge of Human Rights* (Oxford: Charles Malik Foundation, 2000), p. 16.
2. Elie Kedourie, *The Chatham House Version* (London: Weidenfeld & Nicolson, 1970), p. 287.
3. Philip Hitti, *Lebanon in History* (London: Macmillan, 1957), p. 5.
4. Kamal Salibi, *The Modern History of Lebanon* (Delmar, NY: Caravan Books, 1965), p. 15.
5. Ibid., p. 12.
6. Hitti, *Lebanon in History*, p. 6.
7. Edmond Rabath. *La formation historique du liban* (Beirut: Impr. Catholique, 1986), p. 183.
8. Hitti, *Lebanon in History*, p. 376.
9. Salibi, *The Modern History of Lebanon*, p. 121.
10. Ibid., p. 122.
11. Ibid., pp. 122–124.
12. Ibid., p. xxi.
13. Ibid.
14. Leila Fawaz Tarazi, *An Occasion for War* (London: Centre for Lebanese Studies, 1994), p. 15.
15. Will Harris, "Pluralistic Politics," unpublished paper, 2007.
16. Asher Kauffman, *Phoenicianism* (London: I. B. Tauris, 2004), p. 197.
17. Ibid.
18. Kais Ferro, *Inventing Lebanon* (London: I. B. Tauris, 2003), p. 31.
19. Ibid., p. 33.

3

LEBANON'S MILITIA WARS

Tony Badran

Lebanon's civil war has been one of the most complex, multifaceted wars of modern times due to its hybrid nature, multiple participants (both state and non-state actors), and its impact on regional, and even global balances of power.

The goal of this chapter is to identify the principal combatants during the various stages of the war, their equipment, and tactics, with an emphasis on urban warfare and military operations in built-up areas. In this context, the focus is on the Lebanese participants and not the regular, state armies involved: the Syrian Arab Army and the Israel Defense Forces (IDF). However, Syria and Israel were intimately involved in the war, and Syria in particular cannot be separated from various key battles that took place on its orders and/or through its direct intervention either with its regular armed forces or proxies. In addition, since Palestinian military capabilities and preparedness have been covered far more than their Lebanese counterparts, they will not be addressed in extensive detail here.[1]

Finally, the 2008 Hizballah military operation in Beirut and the Shuf Mountains will be examined and compared with the civil war to see what lessons can be drawn today, especially in light of this crucial development.

THE NATURE AND COURSE OF THE WAR

The causes of the war remain a matter of contention in Lebanon scholarship. Was it a war of "others" merely fought in Lebanon, using the Lebanese as tools and proxies, as Lebanese publisher and veteran diplomat Ghassan Tueni put it,[2] or was it a "Lebanese civil war" that drew in external players?

It was both. The non-Lebanese factor was central, even determinant, especially in the way the autonomous Palestinian armed presence in Lebanon strained the Lebanese system to the breaking point,[3] but also in the simple fact that the sustainability of the war effort—namely the supply of arms and ammunition—was completely dependent on foreign sources, which patronized factions that advanced their regional interests. Certain factors within the overall course of the Lebanon War were primarily regional—Israeli-Palestinian, Syrian-Palestinian, and Syrian/Iranian-Iraqi—even if they involved Lebanese proxies and/or allies.

By the same token, Lebanese parties also had the ability to torpedo unfavorable resolutions and to create situations that further involved the regional actors. The crisis was so intricately tied to regional and international dynamics that it was virtually impossible to disentangle them. Further, as the power of the militias grew and animosities deepened, the war took a life of its own—whereby even low-ranking militiamen could break a ceasefire out of sheer boredom.[4]

From a military standpoint, a defining feature of the war was that the Lebanese combatants were unable on their own to overrun each other and no single group was able to score a decisive victory over the other.[5] In order to achieve a decisive military triumph, one camp had to overtake, control, and hold the other camp's enclave. With the exception of the fights in Beirut itself, that never happened in the main sectarian enclaves throughout the war due both to domestic and regional (especially Syrian and Israeli) constraints.

Therefore, as Paul Jureidini, R. D. McLaurin, and James Price noted about the war's earliest phases, "[t]he period of April 1975 through March 1976 was in essence one of static and positional warfare."[6] This also applied to the mid-1980s, after sectarian consolidation created what became known as "cantons" not penetrable by opponents.

The increase in intensity, fighters, and weapons did not change that basic fact. Echoing this conclusion, Samir Kassir noted that during the buildup in fighters and arms, which took place during the long ceasefire in the summer of 1975, "[n]either the introduction of new arms nor the mobilization of a growing number of combatants substantially modified" the war's static nature.[7]

In many ways, this characterization serves to describe much of the war in general, not counting of course the advances and territory seizures by regular militaries—Syrian and Israeli.

Since enemy enclaves could not be overrun and taken over, artillery and rocket bombardment of enemy areas was never followed by effective infantry deployment and was thus limited to inflicting damage. It did not alter the overall military balance.[8] This was one of the major, and enduring, lessons of the Lebanese War.

The examples are numerous, but perhaps the most dramatic was the attempt by the Lebanese Forces to move into and establish a military presence in the Shuf Mountains in 1983–1984, after the Israeli invasion. Despite its significant capabilities (and its alliance with the Israel Defense Forces (IDF) at the time), the Lebanese Forces (LF) militia was not able to hold its positions in the Shuf. One year later, it was also defeated in eastern Sidon, where it had attempted to establish a presence.[9]

Fighting over and control of supply, access, and strategic routes was a prominent feature of the war, and particularly significant in terms of the sectarian/political geography of Lebanon. Strategic routes were at the heart of a number of battles: the attacks on the Dbayya and Tal al-Za'tar Palestinian camps and the Quarantina shantytown, the spring 1976 mountain offensive against the conservative Christian parties (especially the battles over Kahhala and Bologna, the gateway to Kisirwan), the Palestinian attack on the Christian coastal village of Damur, the battle of Zahla, and so on. Control of checkpoints on such roads, such as the infamous Barbara checkpoint held by the LF would play a major role in the internal coup within the LF in 1985 that saw the rise of Samir Geagea to the command of the militia. Directly related to this securing of strategic roads was the consolidation of areas of influence (mainly along sectarian lines), whereby potential or actual enemy pockets would be eliminated.

All these factors shaped the balances of power on the ground, which went through several phases; this cannot be isolated from the broader regional interventions, especially by the Syrians both in the second half of the 1970s and after 1984, and the Israelis in 1982. Still, it can be said that by the mid-1980s, the situation outside of Beirut had consolidated into sectarian "cantons" next to areas dominated by the Syrians in the east and the north, and Israel's security zone in the south. This status quo would remain until the Syrian invasion of the Christian enclave in 1989, ending the war and completing the military occupation of Lebanon—which lasted until April 26, 2005, when the Syrians withdrew their troops. The Israelis had completed their withdrawal five years earlier, in May 2000.

THE MAIN COMBATANTS

When the war broke out, the three main groupings on the scene were the conservative or status quo parties—often dubbed "rightist" or "rightist-Christian"—and the revisionist camp—often dubbed "leftist" or "leftist-Muslim"—along with the various Palestinian forces, who aligned themselves with the later camp and helped train, arm, and even man its various militias.

The exact number of fighters in each camp is difficult to ascertain given the significant divergence in available sources. This is compounded by the fact that many of the fighters were not full-time soldiers, and some left the fighting—or even the country—or even switched sides at different junctures during the war.

The Conservative Coalition

The conservative Christian parties consolidated under the banner of the "Lebanese Front," which was presided over by former President Camille Chamoun. This political coalition gave birth to a joint command for the front's respective militias. The united military body was called the "Lebanese Forces" and comprised the Phalangists, the "Tigers" of the National Liberals Party, al-Tanzim (the "organization"), and the Guardians of the Cedars.

The Phalangists made up the military backbone of the LF, and although each militia had two representatives in the joint command, the LF were clearly dominated by Bashir Gemayel, son of Phalangist leader Pierre Gemayel. By August 1980, the integration of fighting forces was complete.[10]

The largest and most organized of the Lebanese Christian parties were the Phalanges. They were also the primary and most fearsome fighting force of the conservative camp. Formed in 1936 by Pierre Gemayel, a pharmacist by profession, their sphere of influence was Gemayel's hometown of Bikfayya in the northern Matn region of Mount Lebanon.[11]

Fiercely nationalist, the Phalanges' mobilization and street-action capabilities were its hallmark. It fought alongside President Camille Chamoun in the 1958 civil war and its influence grew markedly in the 1960s, as did its national reach (though only among Christians). Around 1969–1970,[12] especially after the 1969 Cairo Accord[13] and the 1970–1971 influx of Palestinian fighters expelled from Jordan, it began training paramilitary units to confront the increased armed Palestinian presence, which the state was not able to contain and which clashed with the Lebanese Armed Forces (LAF).

This fear was sharpened especially after the clashes between the Lebanese Army and the Palestinians in 1973, which intensified the Phalanges' preparation for the inevitable showdown with the Palestinians.[14]

The estimated number of Phalangist fighters varies from source to source. A July 1975 Lebanese Army intelligence report cited by Farid el-Khazen lists 8,000 militia men, all armed with personal weapons.[15] It is unclear how many of these members actually participated in the fighting and represented the fighting core of the militia. For instance, during the Battle of the Hotels buildings could be defended by a small number of fighters, and no more than 60 fighters would participate on any given day.[16]

The party's military wing was commanded by "The War Council" (*al-majlis al-harbi*) first headed by William Hawi, who was killed during the Tal al-Za'tar offensive, which he supervised. He was succeeded by Bashir Gemayel. Hawi had been in charge of setting up and supervising training camps and oversaw the party's Regulatory Forces, which he had created.

The second major party was the National Liberals Party (NLP), formed by former President Camille Chamoun in 1959. Its immediate zone of influence was in the Shuf (Chamoun's birthplace was the Shuf town of Dayr al-Qamar) and southern Mount Lebanon (south and east of Beirut).[17]

Smaller and less organized than the Phalanges, the NLP nevertheless benefited from Chamoun's impressive charisma, wealth, and connections. It played a very important role in the early years of the war, especially in the battle of Tal al-Za'tar, and was the Phalanges' principal ally (though at times competitor) in the fighting.

Like the Phalanges, though lacking their paramilitary history, the NLP began training around 1970. In archival footage used by al-Jazeera's war documentary, Chamoun commented on the training of his followers to a Western reporter:

> The presence of the [Palestinian] Fida'iyyin is something we don't want to have here in this country. As far as we are concerned, we are training because

we don't have any military experience. And since we lack this experience, we have to handle that, because our youth has turned soft and needs training, physical as well as intellectual. That's the idea behind the military training and that's what we're doing now.[18]

The NLP's militia, the "Tigers" (al-numur), was named after Chamoun's father, Nimr (Tiger), and was led by his son Danny. Again, the exact numbers of fighters is difficult to ascertain. The same Lebanese Army intelligence report cited by El-Khazen lists 4,000 fighters, all armed with personal weapons. However, the core fighting force was most probably much smaller, as was perhaps evident from the total of fighters amassed for the Tal al-Za'tar battle.

The Tigers and Danny Chamoun took the lead in launching the Tal al-Za'tar offensive although it has been reported that the irregulars under his command were the least disciplined.[19]

On July 7, 1980, members of the Tigers militia were attacked and slaughtered by the Phalanges after Danny Chamoun resisted Bashir Gemayel's drive to unify the conservative Christian militias under his command in the LF and after attempts to find a middle ground failed to satisfy Gemayel. Danny was rushed to exile, while Camille accepted the reality of Gemayel's military leadership and integrated the Tigers into the LF under Gemayel's command. The Tigers tried to revive their militia after Gemayel's assassination, but by that time they could no longer compete with the LF.

The Tanzim, while much smaller than both the Phalanges and the NLP, was an interesting, initially secret, organization, founded in 1969 after the first major clashes between the Lebanese Army and the Palestinians. Lewis Snider had the following to say about its inception:

> It originated as a splinter group from the Katā'ib after its founders failed to persuade the Katā'ib leadership to support large-scale military training of Lebanese citizens in response to the expansion of Palestinian power in Lebanon and to Arab League pressure on the Lebanese government to neutralize Lebanese law in its application to the Palestinians. Therefore, the founding members decided to build a paramilitary organization to defend Lebanon and support the Lebanese Army....[20]

Since the Lebanese Army was against independent military preparations by private organizations, the Tanzim began secret military training programs in camps in the mountains. The rudimentary beginnings of this effort are suggested by the fact that wooden dummy rifles were used in the early stages of the program.

This military training program, which began in April 1969, was open to all Lebanese civilians who pledged to keep the source of their training a secret and to be ready to defend Lebanon in times of crisis, as the army could not do it alone. The Tanzim made its first "public appearance" in May 1973 during the prolonged clashes between the Lebanese Army and the Palestinian guerillas. The army indirectly called on the Tanzim for help when it announced over the radio for the Lebanese population to stop any "foreigners" from entering army-controlled areas. The "foreigners" in question were Palestinian guerrillas. From 1969 to 1975 the Tanzim claims to have trained 14,000 Lebanese. It did not become a truly separate and distinct organization until 1975.

With this background in mind, it is easy to see how Tanzim, Kata'ib, and NLP militia leaders could develop a close working relationship.[21]

The Tanzim was headed by the president of the Medical Association, Dr. Fu'ad Shimali, who was also a member of the executive board of the Maronite League and a founding member of the Lebanese Front (first known as the Front for Liberty and Man in Lebanon), which also included the head of the Maronite League, Shakir Abu Sulayman. There was speculation that the Maronite League financed the Tanzim.[22] Although small, the Tanzim was well organized.

There is seemingly more to the organization, perhaps further explaining its secrecy. Jureidini, McLaurin, and Price explain: "Although small in number, the Tanzim...was the secret creation of high-ranking Christian Lebanese Army officers and represents the beginning of the disintegration of the Lebanese Army."[23]

The 1975 Lebanese Army Intelligence report cited by El-Khazen does not list the Tanzim or the number of its fighters. The Tanzim's numbers are hard to determine also because they trained both local volunteers as well as affiliates of other parties. Some of its fighters, especially at the fighting in Tal al-Za'tar, were army regulars in disguise.[24] They, however, counted in the hundreds, not thousands. At the Tal al-Za'tar battle, they reportedly contributed 200 fighters.[25]

The Guardians of the Cedars were another smaller militia that was integrated into the LF in August 1976. Formed in 1974 and headed by prominent Lebanese poet and writer Sa'id Aql, its militia was under the command of a former General Security (al-amn al-am) officer, Etienne Saqr (aka "Abu Arz"), who recruited a small number of highly motivated ultranationalists.[26] An early and enduring ally of Israel, Saqr and his militia were vehemently anti-Palestinian.

The Guardians' fighters are often numbered at around 750–1,000. However, like all the militias, the actual fighting force is more difficult to assess. They contributed 100 fighters to the combined assault on Tal al-Za'tar in the summer of 1976.[27] Like the Tanzim, and unlike the Phalanges, the NLP, and other local militias, they were not tied to a particular region where they wielded political influence. Rather, as Mordechai Nisan notes, "they fought where they were needed."[28]

Notable among the small local groups was the Marada Brigade, which essentially was the private militia of the Franjiyya clan in the northern region of Zgharta, and its parochialism was evident in its original name, "Zgharta Liberation Army." The militia was commanded by President Sulayman Franjiyya's son, Tony, and it was said that President Franjiyya supplied it from the stocks of the LAF. In June 1978, after growing differences between Franjiyya and Bashir Gemayel, the latter sent a Phalangist squad that murdered Tony Franjiyya in his home along with his wife and daughter. That was also the end of Franjiyya's alliance with the Lebanese Front.

As noted earlier, the LF was first born as the joint command for the aforementioned militias (excluding the Marada) under the command of Bashir Gemayel. In 1979, as part of Bashir's ambitious rise, he formed a military force under his direct control that integrated military units independent of any of the parties and militias. The following year, all the militias were absorbed into the integrated units after Bashir attacked Chamoun's Tigers in July 1980 and incorporated their remnants.

After Bashir's assassination, the LF continued to grow and build on his legacy, becoming an impressive, sizeable, and very well-equipped fighting force (with an engineers corps, a mountain unit, an Israeli-trained special operations unit, a small navy, an artillery unit, an armored unit, counterintelligence and security, etc.). It had a complex organizational structure (though without the use of traditional military ranks), diverse sources of income, and multiple functions in the areas under its control—where it essentially took on the functions of a state authority.[29]

However, Bashir's assassination created a vacuum in leadership, which also led to an attempt by Bashir's brother, President Amin Gemayel, to seize control of the powerful militia, but to no avail. Instead, a coup resulted in a joint command under Samir Geagea and Elie Hobayka. Hobayka then decided to enter the Syrian orbit with the Syrian-sponsored Tripartite Agreement, leading to yet another coup by Geagea ousting Hobayka, torpedoing the Tripartite Agreement and consolidating his command over the LF.

The LF was attacked by Army Commander General Michel Aoun in the last two years of the war, severely weakening the Christian enclave (the last one outside Syrian control) and paving the way for the Syrian takeover in 1990.

The LF finally supported the Ta'if Accord that ended the war, and subsequently abided by its precepts concerning disarmament of all militias, handing over their arsenal to the army and the state in 1992. However, by 1994 the Syrians moved against Geagea and he was thrown in jail for crimes committed during the civil war, despite the existence of an amnesty law. The Syrians proceeded to tighten the noose on the LF, attempting several times to co-opt it, without any success.

After the Syrian withdrawal in 2005, Parliament passed an amnesty freeing Geagea, who returned to the command of the LF, which is once again an active political force in Lebanon.

The Revisionist Alliance and the Palestinians

Grouping the revisionist camp with the Palestinians is due not only to the fact that they were allied until the Palestinian Liberation Organization's (PLO) expulsion from Lebanon, but because of the intricate political-ideological (including the common roots in the Arab Nationalist Movement) and military relationship that joined them. In fact, some of the groups in the revisionist camp were essentially Palestinian creations and mere Lebanese fronts for Palestinian activity. The best example is the short-lived Army of Arab Lebanon (*jaysh lubnan al-arabi*). The effect of the Palestinian Resistance Movement on Lebanese political life, especially on the power of the traditional Muslim leaders and their ability to control their constituents, was deep.

In 1972, the revisionists (also known as "the leftist and progressive forces") formed a front, which became known as the National Movement, under the leadership of Druze leader Kamal Jumblatt, head of the Progressive Socialist Party (PSP).

Although representing the small Druze sect in Lebanon (even while managing to attract some non-Druze followers), the PSP was without doubt the backbone of the revisionists, due to the towering figure of its founder. Jumblatt's charisma was the driving force behind the revisionist alliance, and he was its unquestioned leader.

Jumblatt founded the party in 1949, and the party revolved around his powerful personality. Based in the Druze enclave in southern Mount Lebanon and the Druze quarter of Beirut, the party participated in the fighting in 1958 against President Camille Chamoun. Jumblatt was a strong supporter of the Palestinian Resistance Movement in Lebanon and called for massive reforms in the Lebanese sectarian system. In 1970, as interior minister, Jumblatt legalized three parties—which would become part of the National Movement: the Lebanese Communist Party (LCP), the Syrian Social Nationalist Party (SSNP), and the Arab Ba'th Socialist Party.

The PSP fielded a small but potent militia, which would go on to play a major role in the civil war. The exact number of its fighting force is unclear, with some placing it at 3,000 fighters,[30] while others go as high as 5,000.[31] It is likely that the core fighting force was smaller.

The National Movement received a severe blow with Kamal Jumblatt's assassination on March 16, 1977, after his conflict with Syria's President Hafiz al-Assad had crossed the point of no return, leading the latter to liquidate him. The mantle of leadership was passed on to his son Walid, who still heads the party and the Druze community.

The second major party in the National Movement was the LCP. The party traced its roots back to 1924 and had its first congress in 1943. It had a wide appeal due to its secularism and its attraction of the intelligentsia, but its popularity suffered in the heyday of Arab nationalism in the 1950s and 1960s, especially when it maintained an unsympathetic attitude toward Arab nationalism. It underwent a significant shift in ideology at its second congress in 1968, when it decided to back the Palestinian Resistance Movement.[32] Its secretary general, George Hawi (who was assassinated in Beirut in June 2005), was a dominant figure in the war and a staunch ally of the Palestinians and of Kamal Jumblatt.

The LCP were part of the "Joint Forces" (*al-quwwat al-mushtaraka*), joining Palestinian and National Movement fighters in an attempt to achieve better command and control, a problem that was even more acute among the revisionists than among the conservative Christian forces.

The LCP would maintain joint forces with the PSP. Hawi explained that at one point, "[w]e were almost a unified force, meaning each battalion would have two companies from the Communist Party and two companies from the [Progressive] Socialist Party, especially in Beirut."[33] It fought on most fronts, but the actual number of its fighters is uncertain, with some listing the total number of militiamen at 5,000,[34] while others place the number of armed fighters at 1,000.[35]

Another important Communist group was the Organization for Communist Action (OCA), led by Muhsin Ibrahim, also a close ally of Jumblatt. The OCA's roots are in the Arab Nationalist Movement (ANM) and the Socialist Lebanon Organization and had close ties with the Democratic Front for the Liberation of Palestine (DFLP), which had common roots in the ANM. The OCA drew support from intellectuals, students, and workers and together with the LCP was able to appeal widely to the Shi'a.[36] It had a small militia of about 100 fighters.[37]

The main Sunni militia in the National Movement was the Murabitun militia of the Independent Nasserites Movement led by Ibrahim Qulaylat. Qulaylat, a typical neighborhood enforcer (qabaday), began organizing the militia in his Mahallat Abu Shakir quarter in Beirut; he had allied himself with Jumblatt from the late 1960s, and like Jumblatt was against the Syrian intervention in 1976. The militia drew support from lower middle-class urban Sunnis. The militia participated in many battles during the war, especially in the Battle of the Hotels in 1975–1976.

The Murabitun were trained by the Palestinians and financed by Libya.[38] A former Sunni militiaman confirmed that the role of the Palestinians in the Murabitun could not be overstated.[39] In fact, he noted, that many a time, operations would be conducted by units led and manned by Palestinians, and supplemented by Lebanese elements for cover. This seems to be corroborated by the support the Murabitun received from Palestinian factions (Fatah, PFLP, and Sa'iqa) and Ahmad Khatib's Army of Arab Lebanon, a Palestinian-supported faction.[40]

The number of Murabitun fighters varies from source to source, but seems to have been in the low hundreds. The former Sunni militiaman expressed his conviction that, at most, the Murabitun had 100–150 fighters. This number seems to fit more or less with a Lebanese Army intelligence report quoted by El-Khazen, which lists them at 200.[41]

Though allied in the National Movement, the Murabitun clashed with the SSNP in 1981 over control of certain neighborhoods in Beirut. This was a common phenomenon in West Beirut, which highlighted the multipolarity of the National Movement.

More significantly, however, was the termination of the Murabitun alliance with the PSP in 1985, which effectively ended its role in the war and in Lebanese politics. This was the result of Syria's drive to prevent a return of Yasir Arafat's influence to Lebanon. Syria used proxies and allies—in this case the Shi'i Amal militia—to attack Palestinian camps, positions, and assets—including deciding to eliminate the Murabitun in Beirut (and the Islamist *harakat al-tawhid al-islami* militia in Tripoli), using the SSNP and Alawite proxies.

However, reflecting a typical reality of the war, Amal proved incapable of routing the Murabitun on its own. In fact, Hawi noted that the balance on the field had been shifting against Amal. Hawi was contacted by Walid Jumblatt and he expected that Jumblatt would give the order for the PSP's and LCP's "Joint Forces" to enter the fray on the side of the Murabitun. To his surprise, Jumblatt's decision was to support the retreating Amal and defeat Qulaylat's Murabitun. "It was our and the [Progressive] Socialist Party's forces that decided the battle, and not Amal's forces," Hawi said.[42]

Qulaylat left Lebanon into exile and the Murabitun faded. There was a plethora of other small Nasserist, Arab nationalist, and socialist organizations—and their ubiquitous splinter movements—whose patronage was divided among the various radical states (Syria, Libya, and Iraq). Those included factions of the Ba'th Party (pro-Iraqi, based largely in Tripoli, and pro-Syrian), the Union of the Forces of the Working People (pro-Syrian), the Arab Socialist Action Party (formed by Palestinian leader George Habash), and the Arab Socialist Union (later split in two)—which was formed in the early 1970s and recruited from the poor quarters and operated in Ras Beirut, Ayn al-Maraysa, and Basta. These militias were essentially neighborhood gangs whose control was over certain streets and quarters.

Another local group was the Sidon-based Populist Nasserist Organization led by Sidon figure Mustafa Sa'd, whose father, Ma'ruf, was a former MP and leading Nasserist activist in the Sidon region who was shot and killed at a public demonstration in Sidon in February 1975.[43]

Like the Murabitun, with which it was allied, Sa'd's militia was trained and supported by the PLO and financed by Libya. It played a somewhat significant role in the attack against the Christian coastal town of Damur (just north of Sidon on the coastal road) and was involved in the fighting in Jizzin and certain battles in Mount Lebanon. Sidon's importance was a port for supplies to the National Movement. Indeed, later in the war—during the mid-1980s—battles between Amal and the forces of the PSP and LCP, Sidon's port, and Sa'd's fishing boats were used to circumvent Amal's blockage of the Uza'i land supply route, transferring men and ammunition from Khalda to the waterfront Ayn al-Maraysa sector of Beirut.[44]

One last actor worth mentioning is the Army of Arab Lebanon (AAL, sometimes also referred to as Lebanon's Arab Army). The formation of the AAL was the result of a mutiny within the ranks of the LAF instigated by Lieutenant Ahmad Khatib in January 1976, and which drew strong support among units in the LAF. Khatib was first sought by the Syrians to join their own ill-fated splinter faction in the LAF known as "the Vanguard of the Army of Arab Lebanon," but they were not successful. Instead, Khatib was won over by the PLO (especially Ali Hasan Salama and Abu Jihad) and the Libyans.[45] The AAL participated in the spring offensive against Mount

Lebanon in 1976 and attacked President Franjiyya's residential quarters in the presidential palace in Ba'bda, forcing him to leave it for the rest of his term. The formation of the AAL was in large part an element of the Syrian-Palestinian war in Lebanon, and the Syrians eventually arrested Khatib a year later in January 1977. He was subsequently released, withdrawing from all activity, and the AAL's role was finished. At its peak, El-Khazen estimates that the AAL commanded around 3,000–4,000 fighters. Yet by the end of 1976, he adds, it had dropped to a few hundreds.[46]

Last, another important member of the National Movement was the SSNP, formed in 1932 by Antun Sa'ada, a Greek Orthodox ideologue executed in 1949 for conspiring to stage a coup. The party was to attempt another failed coup in 1961 against President Fuad Shihab. Its hostility to Arab nationalism in the 1950s led it to fight alongside President Camille Chamoun in the 1958 war. After 1967, the party's orientation shifted, giving full support to the Palestinians. It was legalized in 1970 by then Interior Minister Kamal Jumblatt and joined the National Movement he formed in 1972.

The party suffered a split, but the main faction ultimately became a Syrian proxy militia, attacking targets of the Syrian regime (especially in the war against the Palestinians and their allies in 1983–1985)—with Syrian officers involved directly in training, supplying, and supervising it.[47]

Its core area of influence was the Kura region in northern Lebanon, as well as the northern Matn, certain quarters in Beirut, and the south. The size of the fighting force is unclear, with the LAF intelligence report cited by El-Khazen placing the total number of militiamen at 4,000, and anonymous Israeli intelligence sources quoted by Ehud Ya'ari citing "a few thousand fighters, some of whom are reservists called up only in emergencies."[48] Ya'ari's observation about reservists is accurate and is reflected in Yussef Bazzi's account (the reservists were called "end of the month comrades" by the regulars).[49]

A former Sunni militiaman speculated that they counted in the hundreds but acknowledged that they could mobilize reservists from the northern Matn region (Dhur al-Shwayr). Indeed, Bazzi notes that in the fighting against the Murabitun in Beirut in 1981, the SSNP would amass about 200 fighters.[50] Bazzi also describes a "general mobilization" in 1986, which included calling on "reservists" to gather at a meeting point in order to head for Tripoli, for the battle with the Tawhid movement.[51]

As for the Palestinians, much has been written about them and so they will not be covered in detail here. Briefly, the Palestinians in Lebanon consisted mainly of Yasir Arafat's Fatah, the largest and most important faction; the pro-Syrian Sa'iqa, led by Zuhayr Muhsin; and the so-called Rejectionist Front, which included radical Marxist factions, namely George Habash's Popular Front for the Liberation of Palestine (PFLP) and a breakaway faction, Nayif Hawatma's Democratic Front for the Liberation of Palestine (DFLP). The PFLP had another splinter faction, the PFLP-General Command (GC), headed by Ahmad Jibril, and was first under Libyan patronage, but then became a full-fledged Syrian proxy and remains so to this day. The decisions and participation in the war varied between Fatah on one hand, and the Rejectionist Front on the other.

Aside from the PFLP-GC, other Palestinian organizations were also proxies for Arab regimes, like the Arab Liberation Front, which was pro-Iraqi. Arab regime interests were also reflected in the various brigades of the Palestine Liberation Army, which was supposed to be the PLO's regular military arm. However, the PLO never had an overall command over the different PLA brigades. Instead, these units were under the command of the respective Arab armies in Egypt, Syria, and Jordan. The Syrians, for example, used their units in the Lebanon War to serve their own interests.

In terms of numbers of Palestinian armed fighters, estimates vary widely. Sayigh estimates that there were probably no more than 2,000 PLO regulars in Beirut at the time of the Israeli invasion in 1982, with a part-time force of 4,000–5,000. Elsewhere in Tripoli and the Biqa, the number did not exceed 1,000 regulars and 2,000 part-timers, according to Sayigh, with another 2,000 regulars in the south.[52]

The biggest fighting force was Fatah followed by Sa'iqa and the DFLP and PFLP.

The Shi'a Militias

Shi'a militias per se were relatively late in joining the fray. Shi'i youths had joined the various leftist and Palestinian groups, and received training from the Palestinians like everyone else in the revisionist front. Hizballah commander Imad Mughniyya himself had started his career in Fatah's Force 17.

Yet the Shi'a were stuck in the middle of a dangerous triangle, between the Palestinians and the Israelis on one side, and the Palestinian-leftist front and the conservative alliance on the other. The Shi'i cleric Musa Sadr, the most towering figure in the Lebanese Shi'i community at the time, secretly began training a militia for his Movement of the Deprived. The militia's existence was discovered in 1975 due to an explosion in its Biqa training camp, and was revealed as Amal, the acronym of *afwaj al-muqawama al-lubnaniyya* (the detachments of the Lebanese resistance).[53]

The militia was weak in the early years, and in 1976, when Amal supported the Syrian intervention, the National Movement and the PLO easily routed it from areas it controlled in Beirut. Sadr's ties with the Syrians and his deteriorating relationship with the Palestinians and the leftist groups are likely the reason for his disappearance (and presumably his death) during a 1978 trip to Libya, which was allied with Sadr's Palestinian enemies, including the PLO. He was succeeded first by Husayn Husayni then by Nabih Barri, who remains the party's leader to this day.

Amal remained Syria's ally throughout the war and indeed became its main proxy. However, Amal was not particularly well organized and effective in battles against the Palestinians in the "war of the camps" and against their Arab nationalist allies as noted earlier, or against the PSP-LCP joint forces, or later against its Shi'i rival Hizballah in the final years of the war; it needed to be bailed out by the Syrians, from whom it also received weapons and training.[54]

Barri did, however, have an ally in the predominantly Shi'i 6th brigade of the LAF, together with which Amal rebelled against the authority of the U.S.-backed President Amin Gemayel in the so-called intifada of February 1984, with Syrian backing. The army collapsed once again.

This period, starting in 1983, saw attacks against the U.S. and multinational forces deployed in Beirut—resulting in their pullout. It also saw the beginning of the infamous Western hostage crisis that continued throughout the 1980s.

The factions responsible for these acts—using the suicide bomber, a tactic that Shi'i militants would proceed to hone for the next two decades—were clandestine radical Shi'i Islamist groups with ties to Iran and under Syria's protection. These groups began to emerge in the Shi'i milieu due in part to disillusionment with Amal. A breakaway faction, Islamic Amal, headed by Husayn Musawi, had already split from Amal in 1982. Aside from the religious element, there was also a regional and clannish element at play in the split,[55] and Islamic Amal was based in the Biqa. There it was soon joined by Iranian Revolutionary Guards dispatched via Syria. They set up base there after seizing an army barracks and created a zone of control in its vicinity in the Biqa. The new Islamist organization was named Hizballah, "the Party of God."

Hizballah was and remains a militant Khomeinist Islamist movement that adheres to Khomeini's doctrine of *velayet-e-faqih*, rule by a cleric in an Islamist state. Its ties to Iran are organic, multifaceted, and complex. The exact number of Hizballah's fighting force, the Islamic Resistance, is not known with certainty. In 1997 one source[56] placed it at 5,000 while another gave estimates between 500 and 600 core fighters and a reservist force of about 1,000.[57] The number during the civil war was probably in the low hundreds. It did, however, attract defectors, including military commanders from Amal who were disillusioned with that party.

During the inter-Shi'i war that began in 1987, Hizballah was able to overrun most of Amal's positions in Beirut, as Amal pleaded with the Syrians to interfere. Finally a deal was reached between the Syrians and the Iranians and the inter-Shi'i war ended with the deployment of the Syrians in West Beirut, but with Hizballah's assets safeguarded.

As a result of another Iranian-Syrian agreement after the Ta'if Accord ended the Lebanese war, Hizballah was the only militia to be excluded from handing over its weapons under the pretext that it was a "resistance movement" fighting Israeli occupation. Since the Israeli withdrawal in 2000, and more so after the Syrian withdrawal in 2005, the fate of Hizballah's armed status (which has grown massively and developed doctrinally, ironically, *after* the Israeli withdrawal) is the central issue in Lebanon today.

WEAPONS AND PROCUREMENT

Writing in 1979, Lawrence Whetten observed that both camps possessed essentially the same type of weapons, which only added to the overall stalemate of the war and its ultimately pointless destructiveness: "The war is likely to be classified as a war fought by the wrong people for the wrong reasons. No indigenous faction had an advantage in weaponry, all were equally dependent upon foreign sources."[58]

In the lead-up to the war and during its earliest weeks, many of the weapons used were mainly light but also obsolete. A former Sunni militiaman noted that early on, the main weapons in their possession were the Simonov SKS semiautomatic carbine and the Degtyarev light machinegun.

The summer truce of 1975, as Samir Kassir pointed out, was used to procure more and better weapons and ammunition, with obsolete equipment being discarded.[59] During the period between 1973 and 1975, the main light weapons that would become the hallmark of the subsequent fighting were acquired from both the Eastern bloc and from Western sources.[60] These included Soviet AK-47s, U.S. M-16s, Belgian FN FALs (acquired with the help of sympathizers in the army),[61] West German G-3s, 50mm machineguns and DU 12.7s, RPG-6 and -7s, and light 81 and 82mm mortars.[62]

Phalangist official Karim Pakraduni described his party's initial weapons procurement and distribution process as follows:

> The decision was the following: to propose that every household in our areas own a rifle, and we secured through some Eastern European countries...the purchase of weapons from Bulgaria. Each Kalashnikov rifle, arriving into Beirut with its ammunition, cost 200 Lebanese Pounds. We would distribute it for 300 Lebanese Pounds, and so, with the difference of 100 Pounds it meant that with the distribution of three rifles we would secure another rifle for the party."[63]

On November 6, 1975, a freighter was discovered delivering ammunition and weapons to the Phalanges at the Aqua Marina port in Juniya in preparation for another round of fighting even as a (twelfth) ceasefire had been declared barely five days earlier. Prime Minister Rashid Karami at the time asked Army Commander Hanna Said to confiscate the weapons and the ship, but the army did not take any action—leading Karami to threaten to resign.

Conservative Christian parties made use of the help of sympathetic army officers in receiving weapons arriving at the port and airport listed as intended for the LAF.[64] Moreover, the role of the army, especially after its disintegration, was crucial in significantly upgrading the fighters' capabilities, knowhow, personnel, and equipment—including armored vehicles (Panhards, AMXs, and Staghounds) and personnel carriers (M-113), as well as communications gear (including the army's telephone system), from which the conservative Christian camp benefited more.[65] The collapse of the army also escalated heavy weapons procurement.[66]

Ahmad Khatib's rebellion and his takeover of several LAF barracks also added heavy weaponry, including armor and artillery, to Fatah's bounty.[67]

Meanwhile, the barracks in Fayyadiya (under the command of Colonel Antoine Barakat, a supporter of the Christian militias) and Sarba supported the Lebanese Front.

As noted earlier with the Tanzim, sympathetic army officers had clandestinely helped train militia volunteers, and in the case of the final assault on the Tal al-Za'tar Palestinian camp—which was an in fact an army operation—supplied armored vehicles, communications and artillery support, and even provided disguised regulars.[68]

Once the Phalanges party established contacts with Israel, it began to receive shipments of weapons by boat at ports it controlled in East Beirut (the Aqua Marina in Juniya).[69] Phalangist official Joseph Abu Khalil describes his initial trip to Israel in 1976 as having come as a result of setbacks in the fighting in the commercial district in downtown Beirut, a shortage in ammunition, and advances by the National Movement forces—which had expanded the fighting into Mount Lebanon and the Matn (the "spring offensive"). Certain probing contacts had already been made and came back with positive results, relaying a willingness by Israel to supply weapons and ammunition. Those, according to Abu Khalil, were mainly from the stocks captured during Arab-Israeli wars.[70]

Chamoun had in fact preceded the Phalanges in reaching out to Israel, at first indirectly, for support, and became more and more dependent on it.[71] In 1976 Chamoun met secretly with then Prime Minister Yitzhak Rabin. Rabin agreed to rush supplies of antitank weaponry and communications equipment.[72] He also agreed to provide Christian militiamen with training in Israel—something that would continue into the following decade with the Lebanese Forces. "Enlarged programs" were developed for training the Christian fighters—men and women—who reportedly impressed their trainers.[73]

Bavly and Salpeter noted that the rivalry between Chamoun and the Gemayels complicated things for the Israelis who had to distribute the shipments, and the working manuals, evenly between the two.[74]

Bashir Gemayel was not pleased with this state of affairs—what he dubbed the multiple "shops" of coordination with the Israelis. He moved to monopolize all contacts with the Israelis and made his move against Chamoun on July 7, 1980, and consolidated his control over the military forces of the conservative coalition.

The various groups in the revisionist camp relied on the Soviet bloc, the Palestinians, Syrians, Libyans, and Iraqis for weapons. The LCP's George Hawi summed up the procurement process:

[Arafat] sometimes used to handle transferring arms that would come to the National Movement, sometimes bought by Kamal Jumblatt's and our supporters; they used to pay for it. We would buy it from Bulgaria and Romania and it would be transferred, and Arafat would handle transferring it from Damascus, and he would sometimes delay its delivery and sometimes the delivered weapons would be old.[75]

The Libyans financed and supported a number of the Nasserist groups, most notably the Murabitun and the short-lived AAL. The Libyan role receded by the mid-1980s, and the Syrians and their Shi'i allies moved to neutralize the Iraqi assets as well. It was in the last phase of the war, after the end of the war with Iran, that Iraq began sending weapons to the forces under General Michel Aoun's command as well as to the LF—both of whom were fighting the Syrians at the time.

The Palestinians had access to Arab money and weapons and had good ties with the Soviet bloc from which they received their weapons. Bavly and Salpeter list the inventory captured by the IDF as of October 13, 1982: 1,320 armored combat vehicles, including several hundred T-34, T-55, and T-62 tanks—some damaged; 82 field artillery pieces, 122 mm, 130 mm, 155 mm, and 25-pound guns; 62 Katyusha rocket launchers; 215 mortars, 60 mm, 81 mm, 82 mm, 120 mm, and 150 mm; 196 antiaircraft weapons, including 43 AA machine guns and 153 AA guns, 20mm, 23 mm, 30mm, 37mm, 40mm, 57mm, and 100mm; 1,352 antitank weapons, including 1,099 personal weapons, 27 antitank missile launchers, 138 recoilless rifles, and 88 antitank guns; and 33,303 small arms. "Thousands of pieces of communications and optical equipment were captured as well."[76]

During the Israeli invasion, the Palestinians opened their caches and shared them with the leftist and Muslim militias.[77] The Palestinians had received training from Jordanian regulars, although they suffered from a number of the same problems that plagued the Lebanese militias—such as lack of proper doctrine as well as other conceptual and technical problems.[78]

After their evacuation from Jordan, the Palestinians handled the training of the revisionist militias, and the Palestinian camps themselves became the main training ground for the leftist and Muslim militias. A former Sunni militiaman related to me how before the breakout of the war in 1975, Fatah officers would hold yearly summer training camps for as many as 300 youths. This militiaman's own training was in the Sabra and Shatila camp. He, along with about 150 others, was trained for 3 months in light-weapons use, as well as RPGs, explosives (including mines), mortars, and recoilless rifles.

Later, as the war intensified, time for training became sparse, and so, as the militiaman explained, training was restricted to quick familiarization with light weapons and RPGs. Quick on-the-spot training in specific weapons systems also took place sometimes.[79] Moreover, as Yussef Bazzi's account shows, training rounds for pro-Syrian proxies took place in secure areas (under direct Syrian control). These included training in field artillery.[80]

BATTLEFIELD TACTICS AND USE OF WEAPONS

Much of the war was urban warfare, involving fighting at close distance in built-up areas from one quarter to the next or even from building to building.

The basic fire-teams were small infantry units of four to six fighters. The unit leaders were often simply the most imposing and prominent persons in the group, who could command respect and maintain discipline. A former

Sunni militiaman noted how it was mainly these leaders who took charge in "storming" operations (*iqtiham*)[81] against target buildings (often depending on the availability of ammunition).[82] These leaders did not have any formal rank. Discipline and command and control were weak points among all the militias.[83]

The former Sunni militiaman explained how especially early on, before the upgrade in weapons procurement, each small unit would have only one AK-47. This then evolved when AK-47s became the standard personal weapon, which also helped unify and integrate ammunition (*tawhid al-dhakhira*). The unit then also came to include an RPG launcher.

Eventually, the small units became roughly standardized, equipped with assault rifles (mainly AK-47 but also M-16), backed by a medium machine gun (FN MAG, Kalashnikov PKM, or M-60), along with a rocket launcher (mainly RPG 7 but sometimes also shoulder-held recoilless rifles).

Mechanized support was also added, whereby a unit would sometimes be backed by a jeep or pickup truck mounted with either recoilless rifles (106mm, M40 or B-10) or medium or heavy machineguns (Gorjunov SGM, DShKM 12.7 "Dushka"). Sometimes instead of a jeep or truck, a medium tank (Super Sherman) or light armored car (Panhard, AMX, Staghound) was used, which proved quite effective in urban warfare due to its maneuverability,[84] including in antitank operations, especially against Syrian armor.

Adaptability and conversion were hallmarks of weapons use during the war, given the limited means and access. For example, all combatants relied extensively on antiaircraft guns converted for ground-support and direct ground fire roles.[85] The high rate and high caliber of the fire made the antiaircraft gun a very effective and fearsome weapon, both defensively—in stopping infantry advances—as well as offensively—especially against fixed positions, where the damage inflicted would render the position virtually indefensible.[86]

Vehicle-mounted antiaircraft guns were also very common. There were even ad hoc innovations to increase accuracy over longer ranges. The Phalangists, for example, added cameras and small monitors to their ZU antiaircraft guns, which proved most effective and was used both in urban and rural settings in Mount Lebanon.[87]

Another innovation was the conversion of the air-to-ground Sneb rockets to surface-to-surface rockets. This proved another highly effective antitank weapon especially during the 1978 battles in East Beirut between the Phalanges and the Syrian Arab Army. Fired from a pipe that had been cut in half vertically, with 28-volt batteries, it was used for direct fire at distances of about 350 meters.[88] Along with other antitank weapons (jeep-mounted 106 mm recoilless rifles, B-10, antitank 76 mm guns, and also HEAT and TOW rounds), this allowed the Phalanges to maintain control of key towns in East Beirut and to prevent the Syrians from penetrating them.

Like the antiaircraft weapons, antitank systems were also converted for direct ground fire roles, especially for breaching defensive positions.[89] They were particularly effective when mounted on jeeps/trucks and mobile platforms as they were able to deliver fire and quickly take cover. Rocket launchers were similarly effective, only not in direct fire roles but for their ability to be mounted on mobile platforms and to deliver heavy and rapid concentration of fire.

Field artillery also played a role in the war and was mainly used for suppressive effects as well as for its destructive power—especially against reinforced concrete defensive positions in buildings immune to light mortars.[90] It was also used for random shelling of enemy civilian areas for maximum destruction and psychological effect.[91]

It was a central weapon in the mountain battles (during the 1976 "spring offensive"), especially on the Farayya-Uyun al-Siman front, along with heavy mortars.[92] Together with rocket fire (Grad and Katyusha), it was also used in assault operations—providing cover and softening targets (from positions on hills overseeing the target area) for advancing and/or retreating infantry units.[93]

A tactic often seen throughout the war involved small infantry units taking cover behind corners of buildings, sometimes two parallel buildings on opposite sides of the street with the adversaries doing the same further down the street from inside or behind buildings.

The unit would take cover behind the corner of the building with the machine gunners taking turns running out to deliver rounds of suppressive fire and taking cover again. The soldiers armed with rocket launchers would take turns coming out, firing at the target (the opposing building or barricade), and then quickly return to cover. Similarly, the armed vehicle would emerge from behind the building (often on a cross street), fire, and proceed to take cover behind the parallel building. The tank or armored car would similarly emerge from behind the corner of the building, fire, and roll back for cover.

The corner of the buildings could be extended with sandbags, sand-filled barrels, and/or concrete fortification. Or sometimes the street could be blocked entirely with landfill and/or sandbags allowing the fighters to take cover behind it, standing up occasionally to fire over the barricade. Trenches could be dug behind the barricades to allow safe movement of troops and light supplies. Tunneling—including inside the Palestinian camps and inside buildings—was a standard practice during the war, especially in situations of siege and when exposed to sniper fire.[94]

This tactic was seen in particular early on in the war between the Phalangists and the National Movement forces; it was recurrent all throughout, including in the mid-1980s between rival factions of the Lebanese Forces, after Elie Hobayka had signed the Syrian-sponsored Tripartite Agreement and was overrun by Samir Geagea. This was also the case toward the end of the war in 1988—during the inter-Shi'i wars between Amal and Hizballah in Beirut and south Lebanon.

HIZBALLAH'S ASSAULT AND THE CURRENT SITUATION

Almost 40 years after the Cairo Accord and 33 years after the start of the civil war, Lebanon continues to face the basic problem of having a revolutionary militia with regional extensions operating independently as a state beyond the state, in pursuit of armed conflict with Israel, sparking similar tensions among the various Lebanese communities.

In this case, the militia in question is Hizballah, which—unlike the Palestinians—draws its rank and file from one of the main Lebanese communities but simultaneously represents a regional dimension and poses a direct threat to the state, thus causing a fundamental imbalance in the Lebanese system.

In May 2008, this contradiction, which had been building up especially since the 2005 Syrian withdrawal from Lebanon, reached its peak—or perhaps inevitable conclusion—when Hizballah and the other communities clashed militarily.

The episode carries a number of avenues for comparison with the civil war era to see what, if anything, has changed about the dynamics of war in Lebanon, and what lessons from that war remain valid today.

On May 7, Hizballah launched a military assault on West Beirut from its Shi'i neighborhoods mainly in the southern parts of the city. Hizballah—aided by its allied Shi'i militia Amal and the SSNP pro-Syrian militia—quickly took over West Beirut without organized military resistance to its encroachment. This was the result of a political decision made by Sunni leader Sa'ad Hariri and Druze leader Walid Jumblatt not to contest the advance in an area that they did not control.

Hizballah then decided to expand its operations to the Druze Shuf Mountains. What ensued allows us to draw a number of lessons in comparison with the military situation during the civil war.

During their assault on Beirut, Hizballah and its allies used standard civil war–era tactics and types of weaponry, namely assault rifles (AK-47s and M4A1s) and rocket-propelled grenades (RPG-7s).

In the months before the assault, reports about armament and Hizballah-provided training in the pro-Syrian camp abounded. Raids by the LAF and the Internal Security Forces confiscated weapons caches and shipments. One such example was the raid against the SSNP, which uncovered a large cache of civil war–era weaponry and explosives (suspected to be intended for assassinations).[95] Unverified statements by March 14 politicians constantly claimed that weapons for urban warfare (especially mortars and RPGs) were being smuggled to the pro-Syrian groups.

Similarly, intercepted shipments—intended for Hizballah—revealed the same type of urban-warfare weaponry, which only increased the suspicion of the governing March 14 movement that the pro-Syrian camp was preparing for an assault. One truck shipment intercepted in February 2007 contained forty-eight 60 mm mortars, sixty 120 mm mortars, 52 Grad rockets, and 118 cases of mortar shells.[96]

While a pro-Hizballah paper claimed that the battle plan was drawn by the slain Hizballah military commander (killed in February 2008), Imad Mughniyya,[97] the offensive tactically mirrored the preferred strategy for built-up areas detailed earlier: small units with assault rifles and RPGs tag-teaming from behind building corners. The fighters with the rifles spring out first and deliver cover fire to be followed by the RPG launcher.[98]

Communication between the fighters was carried mainly through cellular phones and short-range walkie-talkies. On one occasion during the Beirut offensive, Hizballah used supportive mortar fire in the Nuwayri neighborhood, indicating perhaps a stiffer resistance than elsewhere.

Another standard civil war feature of urban warfare was the extensive use of snipers on both sides. Sniping is an effective defensive measure, as a single sniper can cripple an offensive advance within his area of control.

On the other hand, support sniper fire was also used by the attacking Hizballah-Amal militias against defenders in residential buildings in the Sunni neighborhoods. One incident involved a sniper on the fifteenth floor of an unfinished building (owned by a business partner of Amal's leader, Nabih Barri) on the Ayn al-Tina corniche, who had a line of fire against several Sunni defensive positions in residential buildings.

Kidnappings, another grim hallmark of the civil war, also quickly resurfaced as both sides took hostages. The release of some was secured after a series of contacts between the leaderships, but others were not so lucky, either being tortured or slaughtered.

However, it was the situation in the Shuf Mountains that was of most interest for comparative analysis. Hizballah launched an assault on the Druze stronghold from multiple fronts: Shwayfat from the west on the coast, right above the Beirut airport, Baysur from the south, and the Baruk hill from the east, as well as from the two Shi'i towns Kayfun and Qmatiya, south of Alay.

As was the case in the civil war—indeed in any war—controlling strategic and access roads is crucial. Thus, in scenes very reminiscent of the civil war, rubble and sand barricades littered the streets of Beirut as Hizballah proceeded to surround Sa'ad Hariri's headquarters and the Beirut residence of Walid Jumblatt and to cut off all roads surrounding the prime minister's headquarters in the Grand Serail.

Similarly, Hizballah was trying to link the Shi'i towns of Kayfun and Qmatiya to the base of operation in the southern suburbs of Beirut (Dahiya) through the road that links the Dahiya to Shwayfat-Aramun-Dawha-Dayr Qubil-Aytat and Kayfun, and Qmatiya, so that it could establish a pocket supported by access routes and prevent the Druze from surrounding the two Shi'i towns.

The very use of these Shi'i towns to launch operations seemed to confirm suspicions and fears that Hizballah was attempting to create demographic bridges—indirectly buying land or building residential apartments—in order to link up its noncontiguous areas. This was much in the same fashion as with its fiber-optic telecommunications network, which was at the heart of the May 2008 controversy, and which penetrated non-Shi'i areas in order to link up Hizballah positions in the south, Beirut, and the Biqa.

However, the attempt in the Shuf failed. In drastic contrast to the situation in Beirut, Hizballah's infantry units were not capable of penetrating the Shuf villages. As a result, we saw the use by Hizballah of mechanized units—the civil war hallmarks: trucks mounted with heavy machine guns, recoilless rifles, and antitank guns—as well as mortar and rocket fire. Yet it was to no avail, as this support did not facilitate ground infiltration, and a number of Hizballah's vehicles were successfully destroyed, and both infantry and mechanized units were ambushed.[99] The Druze villages also used mortars in their successful defense. Of note were the extensive reports that fighters loyal to Hizballah's Druze ally, Talal Arslan, had joined the other Druze and Jumblatt's PSP in their defense against Hizballah, including in Shwayfat.

It is unclear, however, what the ammunition situation was and how long the Druze could have maintained this defense. This may have been one reason why Jumblatt moved, after the Druze made their point, to absorb and neutralize the attack by inviting the army to move into the Shuf and secure it. This would have placed Hizballah in the face of the army. Should Hizballah have decided to persist in its attempts at storming the Shuf, the army would either have had to respond or splinter. Already there were reports that 40 senior officers (many of whom were Sunnis) had threatened to resign in protest of the army command's handling of the situation.[100]

Hizballah's failure to enter Alay—specifically the Ras al-Jabal hill overlooking the airport and the Dahiya—and to take the Baruk and the strategic "three 8s" hills, meant that Hizballah, in an all-out war situation would leave its positions in the Dahiya and the Biqa as well as the south exposed to artillery, mortar, and rocket fire. Moreover, it means that the PSP, along with Sunni allies on the coast and in the middle and western Biqa, can effectively cut off access between the noncontiguous Hizballah areas—something that was seen back in January 2007, during Hizballah's riots, when PSP supporters and Sunni allies cut off the Na'ma coastal roads in an unambiguous message to Hizballah.

Hizballah's control of the airport road, as well as its de facto control of the airport, which lies in its zone of influence, is of significance. It led to a government decision to rehabilitate the Juniya port, as well as to the resurgence of calls to habilitate properly the René Mu'awwad airport in Qlay'at, in order to have options not under Hizballah's direct threat.

CONCLUSION

Several of the lessons of the civil war were confirmed once again during Hizballah's offensive.

The most significant recurring lesson was that regardless of military capabilities, militias were not really able to take over and/or hold positions in hostile territory, outside its direct area of influence. This was a feature of the civil war, and it was seen, for example, with the failure of the well-equipped Lebanese Forces in the Shuf Mountains and later in East Sidon to hold their advanced positions. Such positions are not sustainable or defensible, and "outsiders"—even well-trained and equipped ones, like Hizballah—can be repelled and made to sustain significant casualties.

The weaponry did not change much from the time of the war. The same type of weapons remain in use today, even if in newer versions (e.g., the M4A1): assault rifles, RPGs, sniper rifles, mortars, truck/jeep-mounted recoilless rifles and heavy machine guns, as well as rocket launchers and antiaircraft guns.

Battles to control strategic and access routes will continue to remain central to the fighting, especially with Hizballah's need to link up its three non-contiguous areas of influence and the ability of its opponents to block that access.

Also, access to secure ports would be crucial if war were to break out again, as evident from the calls to rehabilitate the Juniya port—which played a central role for the Christian militias in the civil war—and the Mu'awwad airport.

Finally, as with the civil war, the role of regional actors and the international community will likely be decisive. Syria and Iran would continue to support Hizballah and Amal and their smaller allies. Meanwhile, the potential exists for Saudi Arabia, Egypt, and Jordan to support the March 14 Sunni-Druze-Christian coalition. What the effect of such presumed regional roles will be cannot be stated with certainty. What role Israel might play is also unsure. Would Israel insert itself in a conflict in Lebanon? It is most likely safe to assume that the countries contributing to United Nations Interim Force in Lebanon (UNIFIL) in southern Lebanon would withdraw their troops.

The role of the Palestinians, however, will be markedly different. The Syrians still maintain the armed proxies of the PFLP-GC and Fatah Intifada, which maintain bases in the Biqa and in the southern coastal town of Na'ma. They are likely to play a supporting role alongside Hizballah, Amal, and the SSNP. What role Fatah and other smaller Islamist organizations decide to play is unclear. Sunni Islamists would also be a wildcard in such a conflict.

The biggest question, however, is whether all these elements could once again ensure that a renewed war in Lebanon would be another stalemate, or if the unitary state would survive at all this time.

NOTES

1. For more detailed studies on the Palestinians, see, e.g., Yezid Sayigh, "Palestinian Military Performance in the 1982 War," *Journal of Palestine Studies*, Vol. 12, No. 4 (Summer 1983), pp. 3–24.
2. Ghassan Tueni, *Une Guerre pour les Autres* (Paris: Editions Lattès, 1985).
3. For a good study from this vantage point, see Farid El-Khazen, *The Breakdown of the State in Lebanon 1967–1976* (London: I. B. Tauris, 2000).
4. See the various anecdotes in Yussef Bazzi's *Yasser Arafat Looked at Me and Smiled (Diary of a Fighter)* (Beirut: Dar el-Kotob, 2005).
5. Lawrence L. Whetten, "The Military Dimension," in P. Edward Haley and Lewis W. Snider (eds.), *Lebanon in Crisis: Participants and Issues* (Syracuse: Syracuse University Press, 1979), p. 88. "Military expediencies required the enlistment of foreign military forces to advance the respective belligerents' goals."

6. Paul Jureidini, R. D. McLaurin, and James Price, *Military Operations in Selected Lebanese Built-Up Areas, 1975–1978* (Aberdeen, MD: U.S. Army Human Engineering Laboratory, Aberdeen Proving Ground, Technical Memorandum 11–79, [June 1979]), p. 7.

7. Samir Kassir, *La guerre du Liban: De la dissension nationale au conflit régional, 1975–1982* (Paris: Karthala/Cermoc, 1994), p. 150.

8. Michael F. Davie, "Comment Fait-on La Guerre à Beyrouth?" *Hérodote*, 2ème & 3ème trimestre, Nos. 29–30 (Geopolitique au Proche Orient, 1983), p. 41. "Cette situation 'extrême' a un but essentiellement politique et non militaire: elle ne sert qu'à imposer une conduite politique à son adversaire en détruisant son infrastructure ou son moral, mais sans entrer dans son territoire." ["This 'extreme' situation had an essentially political, and not military, goal: It serves only to impose a political conduct on one's adversary by destroying his infrastructure or his morale, but without entering his territory."]

9. Davie echoes a similar remark in 1983: "Les combats ont duré pendant huit années: Ils n'ont 'servi' à rien, puisque le seul but était de tuer, à partir de positions bien protégées. La pensée militaire derrière ces opérations était nulle: il n'a jamais été question de prendre d'assaut les positions de l'adversaire." ["The fights lasted for eight years: They 'served' no purpose, since the only goal was to kill, from well-protected positions. The military thinking behind these operations was nil: it was never a question of storming the adversary's positions."] Ibid., p. 38.

10. Lewis W. Snider, "The Lebanese Forces: Their Origins and Role in Lebanon's Politics," *Middle East Journal*, Vol. 38, No. 1 (Winter 1984), pp. 1–33.

11. The definitive study on the Phalanges' organizational structure in the years before the 1975 war remains John P. Entelis, *Pluralism and Party Transformation in Lebanon: Al-Kata'ib, 1936–1970* (Leiden: E. J. Brill, 1974).

12. In his book on the Phalanges, Hazem Saghieh writes: "serious training and running [training] camps did not begin until 1969, the year of the April 23rd demonstration after the clash between the army and the Palestinian Resistance. However, the split of the Phalangist elements that went on to form the *Tanzim*, as we saw, suggests that this training was still limited and far from satisfying the more radical youth." See, *Ta'rib al-kata'ib al-lubnaniyya: al-hizb, al-sulta, al-khawf* (Beirut: Dar al-Jadid, 1991), p. 163. Translation by this author.

13. Veteran Phalangist official, Joseph Abu Khalil, described it thusly in his autobiography:

    On the other hand, arms had begun to spread in people's hands, rather, the Phalanges had begun to arm themselves and to encourage the people to arm themselves since 1969—specifically after the state was forced to recognize the armed Palestinian presence and its right of movement in the infamous Cairo Accord. Since then, the Phalanges had been preparing themselves for a resistance that seemed, to them, necessary after the crippling of the army and removing it from its military and security duties. (Joseph Abu Khalil, Qissat al-mawarina fil harb: Sira dhatiyya [Beirut: Sharikat al-Matbu'at, 1990, pp. 17–18], translation by this author.)

14. Saghieh, *Ta'rib al-kata'ib al-lubnaniyya*.

    In 1972, the "P. G." company was born and became "the only real regular company which could be considered as the nucleus of the Lebanese Forces." The following year, the training became more serious, and that was the year that saw the May confrontations between the army and the [Palestinian] Resistance. In 1975, with the breakout of the war, each party local section [*qism*] would handle the confrontation in its district, except for the "P. G." central company, which moved between sections. (Translation by this author.)

"P. G." stood for Pierre Gemayel, but later came to stand for Bashir Gemayel. Both letters P and B are represented by the same letter in Arabic.

15. El-Khazen, *The Breakdown of the State in Lebanon*, p. 303.
16. Jureidini, McLaurin, and Price, *Military Operations in Selected Lebanese Built-Up Areas*, p. 6.
17. See Itamar Rabinovich, *The War for Lebanon, 1970–1985*, revised edition (Ithaca and London: Cornell University Press, 1989), p. 65. See also, Marius Deeb, *The Lebanese Civil War* (New York: Praeger, 1980), pp. 25–28.
18. *Harb Lubnan* [The War of Lebanon], "*al-infijar*" ["The Explosion"], Episode 3, al-Jazeera Productions, 2001. Transcript gleaned from the audible parts of the audio in English and translated from al-Jazeera's dubbed-over Arabic translation.
19. Dan Bavly and Eliahu Salpeter, *Fire in Beirut: Israel's War in Lebanon with the PLO* (New York: Stein & Day, 1984), p. 52.
20. Snider, "The Lebanese Forces," pp. 6–7, footnote 4.
21. Ibid., pp. 6–7, footnote 4.
22. Deeb, *The Lebanese Civil War*, p. 29.
23. Jureidini, McLaurin, and Price, *Military Operations in Selected Lebanese Built-Up Areas*, p. 57, note 1.
24. Ibid., p. 15.
25. Ibid.
26. See Mordechai Nisan, *The Conscience of Lebanon: A Political Biography of Etienne Sakr (Abu-Arz)* (London: Frank Cass/Taylor & Francis, 2003). See also, Mordechai Nisan, "Dossier: Etienne Saqr (Abu Arz)," *Middle East Intelligence Bulletin*, Vol. 5, No. 1 (January 2003), http://www.meib.org/articles/0301_ld.htm.
27. Jureidini, McLaurin, and Price, *Military Operations in Selected Lebanese Built-Up Areas*, p. 15. They provide the total number of "ca. 750" in Appendix A, Table 2. Nisan, "Dossier," provides a total of "about 1,000."
28. Nisan, "Dossier." "In March 1976, they confronted Palestinian and leftist forces in West Beirut. A Guardians unit was also dispatched to Zaarour, above the mountain road to Zahle, to support Phalangist forces. In April, Guardian fighters defended a line in the area of Hadeth, Kfar Shima, and Bsaba, south of Beirut, against a coalition of Palestinian, PSP, and SSNP forces."
29. For a detailed look at the LF ca. 1982, see Snider, "The Lebanese Forces."
30. Walid Khalidi, *Conflict and Violence in Lebanon: Confrontation in the Middle East*, fourth printing (Cambridge, MA: Harvard Studies in International Affairs, 1984), p. 77.
31. El-Khazen, *The Breakdown of the State in Lebanon*, p. 302, based on the same 1975 LAF intelligence report.
32. Deeb, *The Lebanese Civil War*, p. 66.
33. *Harb lubnan*, "*al-fawda*" ["Chaos"], Episode 12. Translation by this author.
34. El-Khazen, *The Breakdown of the State in Lebanon*, p. 303, based on the 1975 LAF intelligence report.
35. Deeb, *The Lebanese Civil War*, p. 66.
36. Ibid., pp. 66–67.

37. El-Khazen, *The Breakdown of the State in Lebanon*, p. 303.
38. Ibid., pp. 332–333.
39. Private conversation, May 2008.
40. Jureidini, McLaurin, and Price, *Military Operations in Selected Lebanese Built-Up Areas*, p. 6.
41. El-Khazen, *The Breakdown of the State in Lebanon*, p. 303. Jureidini, McLaurin, and Price list their force size at 300, although they point out that during the Battle of the Hotels, "60 [fighters] were committed on any given day." Jureidini, McLaurin, and Price, *Military Operations in Selected Lebanese Built-Up Areas*, p. 6, and Appendix A, Table 2. Walid Khalidi cites a higher number of 500, which is probably too high. *Conflict and Violence in Lebanon*, p. 77.
42. *Harb lubnan*, "*al-fawda*" ["Chaos"].
43. For more on these groups, see Deeb, *The Lebanese Civil War*, pp. 68–69.
44. As related by George Hawi in *Harb Lubnan*, "*awdat dimashq*" ["Damascus Returns"], Episode 13.
45. El-Khazen, *The Breakdown of the State in Lebanon*, pp. 332–335.
46. Ibid.
47. See Bazzi, *Yasser Arafat Looked at Me and Smiled*, pp. 13–14, 45, 50, 52. Bazzi, a former SSNP militiaman himself, offers an excellent, tragically comical account of his days with the militia, providing detailed insights into the militia's involvement in the war, its armament, and its command structure. In many respects, the picture that emerges contrasts quite significantly on many of the details (e.g., when it comes to discipline) with the account offered by Ehud Ya'ari in his article "Behind the Terror," *The Atlantic Monthly*, June 1987, http://www.theatlantic.com/issues/87jun/yaari.htm.
48. El-Khazen, *The Breakdown of the State in Lebanon*, p. 302. Ya'ari, "Behind the Terror."
49. Bazzi, *Yasser Arafat Looked at Me and Smiled*, p. 52.
50. Ibid., p. 7.
51. Ibid., p. 52.
52. Sayigh, "Palestinian Military Performance in the 1982 War," pp. 17–18. For lists of numbers based on LAF intelligence reports from 1975 to 1976, see El-Khazen, *The Breakdown of the State in Lebanon*, Tables 22.1, 22.2, and 24.1.
53. See Fouad Ajami, *The Vanished Imam: Musa al Sadr and the Shia of Lebanon* (London: I. B. Tauris, 1986), pp. 168–175.
54. Both Walid Jumblatt and George Hawi were summoned to Damascus and given a stern message that Amal was a "red line" and that the PSP-LCP campaign against it should stop immediately. Jumblatt and Hawi personally related this incident in *harb lubnan*, "*awdat dimashq*" ["Damascus Returns"].
55. For more on these aspects and their role in the organizational structure of Hizballah, see Magnus Ranstorp, *Hizb'allah in Lebanon: The Politics of the Western Hostage Crisis* (New York and London: Palgrave Macmillan, 1997). See also Martin Kramer, "Hizbullah: The Calculus of Jihad," in M. Marty and R. S. Appleby (eds.), *Fundamentalisms and the State: Remaking Polities, Economies, and Militance* (The Fundamentalism Project, Vol. 3) (Chicago: University of Chicago Press, 1993), pp. 539–556, http://www.geocities.com/martinkramerorg/Calculus.htm.
56. A. Nizar Hamzeh, "Islamism in Lebanon: A Guide to the Groups," *Middle East Quarterly*, Vol. 4, No. 3 (September 1997), accessed at http://www.meforum.org/article/362.

57. Nicholas Blanford, "A Testing Time," *The Middle East*, December 1997. "Hizbollah is estimated to have between 500 and 600 hard core fighters— trained originally by Iran's Revolutionary Guards—and can draw upon a fur- ther 1,000 part time volunteers." See http://findarticles.com/p/articles/ mi_m2742/is_n273/ai_n25024599.

58. Whetten, "The Military Dimension," p. 88.

59. "Parallèlement à l'extension géographique de la guerre, l'armement aux mains des miliciens se perfectionnait. L'accalmie de l'été avait été bien mise à profit. Les fusils semi-automatiques disparurent pratiquement, de même que les fusils- mitrailleurs obsolètes comme le P.pS.H." ["Parallel with the geographic exten- sion of the war, the arms in the hands of the militiamen were being perfected. The summer truce had been put to good use. The semi-automatic rifles practi- cally disappeared, as did the obsolete submachine guns like the P.pS.H."] Kassir, *La guerre du Liban*, p. 148. The P.pS.H. is the Soviet World War II–era submachine gun, PPSh-41, aka. Shpagin.

60. Jureidini, McLaurin, and Price, *Military Operations in Selected Lebanese Built-Up Areas*, p. 1.

61. Kassir, *La guerre du Liban*, p. 149.

62. Whetten pointed out that "the problems associated with the diversification of weapons was partially compensated for by the readily available new sources and a gradually widening range of arms." Whetten, "The Military Dimension," p. 87.

63. *Harb Lubnan*, "*al-infijar*" ["The Explosion"]. Translation by this author.

64. This is according to the account of an anonymous former Christian militia com- mander (seemingly in the NLP's "Tigers" militia) interviewed for the al-Jazeera documentary. "I used to see the boats unloading weapons in the Beirut port, and even in the Beirut airport, on the basis that these weapons were for the govern- ment, and they would be distributed to some parties." *Harb Lubnan*, "*al-infijar*" ["The Explosion"] . Translation by this author.

65. Jureidini, McLaurin, and Price, *Military Operations in Selected Lebanese Built-Up Areas*, pp. 41–47, and Appendix A, Table 4.

66. Whetten, "The Military Dimension," p. 87.

67. El-Khazen, *The Breakdown of the State in Lebanon*, pp. 332–335.

68. Jureidini, McLaurin, and Price, *Military Operations in Selected Lebanese Built-Up Areas*, pp. 15, 18, 46–47.

69. Bavly and Salpeter, *Fire in Beirut*, p. 53. "Periodically, an Israeli missile boat or a smaller Dabour-class gunboat would arrive at the bay of Junieh, towing a barge full of arms. The arms would be handed over and the empty barge would be towed back to its home port."

70. Abu Khalil, *Qissat al-mawarina fil harb*, p. 61. See also Davie, "Comment Fait-on La Guerre à Beyrouth?" p. 23.

71. Bavly and Salpeter, *Fire in Beirut*, pp. 44–45.

72. For a detailed discussion of the communications equipment, see Jureidini, McLaurin, and Price, *Military Operations in Selected Lebanese Built-Up Areas*.

73. Bavly and Salpeter, *Fire in Beirut*, pp. 45–46, 54.

74. Ibid., p. 53. "Each item and each publication had to be supplied in duplicate."

75. *Harb lubnan*, "*al-infijar*" ["The Explosion"]. Translation by this author. Hawi went on to relay an anecdote of how once Jumblatt protested to Arafat that the shipment was of old weapons. Arafat told him, "Well, you know the Soviets always give us old weapons and the Bulgarians give us from their old stocks," to

which Jumblatt replied, "Yes it's true, but they don't write on their guns *abu al-mawt* [father of death] and *abu al-jamajim* [*father of skulls*], and *abu al-hawl* [*father of the sphinx*]!" Translation by this author.

76. Bavly and Salpeter, *Fire in Beirut*, p. 93. See also the 1975 LAF intelligence report cited by El-Khazen, *The Breakdown of the State in Lebanon*, p. 302. See also Yezid Sayigh's discussion of the Palestinian move toward "regularization" during the 1970s, as well as his survey of their arsenal by 1982. Sayigh, "Palestinian Military Performance in the 1982 War."

77. This is also recounted by Bazzi, *Yasser Arafat Looked at Me and Smiled*.

78. Sayigh, "Palestinian Military Performance in the 1982 War," pp. 22–24.

79. Bazzi describes how a Syrian officer headed a mortar unit—instructing SSNP fighters without any previous training how to set up the launching platform, including the trenches and ditches. Bazzi, *Yasser Arafat Looked at Me and Smiled*, pp. 13–14.

80. Ibid., p. 52.

81. Bazzi offers an example of these types of urban assault operations from the SSNP's battle with the Murabitun in Beirut in 1981. Ibid., pp. 6–7.

82. This is substantiated in Bazzi's account of the command structure in the SSNP militia. See Bazzi, *Yasser Arafat Looked at Me and Smiled*.

83. Ibid., p. 41.

84. Jureidini, McLaurin, and Price, *Military Operations in Selected Lebanese Built-Up Areas*, p. 54.

85. Jureidini, McLaurin, and Price list "the U.S. M-42, the Soviet ZU-23 and ZU-57, the Swiss Oerlikan, and the Hispano-Suiza 30." *Military Operations in Selected Lebanese Built-Up Areas*, p. 53.

86. Ibid. "These weapons were employed against outside walls with devastating effect; they denuded structures with their high volume of firepower. In addition, used in a direct-fire capacity by firing the length of streets, AAA was a strong deterrent to assaults."

87. Ibid., p. 40. "The zoom lens allowed Christian gunners to focus in on buildings and windows of buildings where the enemy was located. At distances from four to eight kilometers the ZU-57 proved very effective." For a picture of the monitor-equipped ZU in action in a rural setting in Mount Lebanon, see Joseph G. Chami, *Lebanon, Days of Tragedy 75–76* (Transaction Books: London and New Brunswick, 1984), p. 190.

88. Jureidini, McLaurin, and Price, *Military Operations in Selected Lebanese Built-Up Areas*, pp. 51–52.

89. Ibid., pp. 53–54.

90. Davie, "Comment Fait-on La Guerre à Beyrouth?" pp. 41–42.

91. Ibid., p. 41.

92. Chami, *Lebanon*, p. 195.

93. See Bazzi's description of the SSNP assault on Tripoli. Bazzi, *Yasser Arafat Looked at Me and Smiled*, p. 53. The SSNP stronghold was in the Kura hills overlooking Tripoli. Also, a former Christian militiaman had related to me how artillery fire was used to provide cover for a small special operations unit on a sabotage mission that was pulling out from enemy territory. Private conversation, summer 1994.

94. Ibid., p. 52.

95. For a report with pictures, see *al-Mustaqbal*, December 23, 2006, http://almustaqbal.com/stories.aspx?StoryID=210750.

96. "Lebanon's Army Will Keep Hizballah Seized Arms to Fight Israel," *Ya Libnan*, February 20, 2007. http://yalibnan.com/site/archives/2007/02/lebanons_army_w.php.

97. *Al-Akhbar*, May 10, 2008, http://www.al-akhbar.com/ar/node/73087.

98. *The Guardian*, May 10, 2008, http://www.guardian.co.uk/world/2008/may/10/lebanon.syria.

99. The PSP claimed on its website (link no longer available) that at least 36 Hizballah fighters were killed. Hizballah Secretary General Hassan Nasrallah admitted to 14 casualties in his speech on May 26, 2008.

100. "Lebanon: 40 Sunni Officers Threaten to Resign," *Asharq al-Awsat* (English edition), May 15, 2008, http://www.aawsat.com/english/news.asp?section=1&id=12758.

4

LEBANON'S ROLLER COASTER RIDE[1]

William Harris

Syrian President Bashar al-Asad's determination in August 2004 to force Lebanese leaders to grant an extended presidential term for his ally Emile Lahoud inaugurated a multifaceted crisis in the Levant. Bashar mistakenly assumed that he could railroad the West and the Lebanese into accepting a fait accompli on the basis of Syria having had its own way through almost 15 years of command of Lebanon, blessed by the United States in 1990 when it needed Syria's help in the crisis resulting from Iraq's seizure of Kuwait.

However, in late 2004, the United States and France surprised Damascus by refusing to continue to bend to Ba'thist Syria's demands, and a majority of Lebanese mobilized against Syrian domination. The resulting upheaval has continued down to the present, involving the need to find a new political order in Lebanon and to determine the extent of influence for foreign powers.

Two principal shocks set off this longer-term crisis. First, on February 14, 2005, Rafiq al-Hariri, several times previously Lebanon's prime minister, billionaire magnate, and the political colossus of the Lebanese Sunni Muslim community, was assassinated. Hariri opposed the extension of Lahoud's presidential term and turned against Syria's hegemony in Lebanon. His assassination outraged the international community and provoked Lebanon's Sunni, Christian, and Druze communities against the Syrian regime. It led to the first ever UN murder inquiry, which gradually assembled evidence through 2005 and 2006 and principally targeted the Syrian security apparatus and clients in its Lebanese counterpart.

In the meantime, Syria and its Lebanese allies suffered serious reverses, losing control of the Lebanese parliament and government. The United States and France mobilized the international community to compel a Syrian military withdrawal from Lebanon in April 2005, which facilitated Lebanon's first parliamentary elections free of external manipulation since 1972. Syria's allies, most prominently President Lahoud and the Shi'a religious radicals of Hizballah, retained formidable capability but were on the defensive. The Hariri murder inquiry and the prospective "tribunal of an international character" to try Hariri's assassins threatened their Syrian patron. A threat to the Syrian regime was a threat to Hizballah and its autonomy in southern

Lebanon, where that group faced Israel. How therefore could Syria and Hizballah turn the tables on Lebanon's "new majority" and its foreign backers? Provoking a destructive Israeli return to the Lebanese arena was an obvious temptation.

The second shock, the Israeli-Hizballah war, precipitated by Hizballah on July 12, 2006, could therefore be seen as an extension of the Lebanese-Syrian crisis inaugurated by Bashar al-Asad in August 2004. When Hizballah raided across the Lebanon-Israel boundary to kidnap Israeli soldiers it presumably calculated a response that would truncate Lebanese criticism of "resistance" weapons, destabilize the "new majority," and refocus world attention on Lebanon's problems with Israel, sidelining problems with Syria. It is unlikely to suppose that Hizballah did not calculate a major reaction to an unprecedented infraction in the Galilee far from the disputed Shab'a Farms on the Golan Heights, even if that response ended up being bigger than it expected.

Further, there was the prospect that sustained hostilities and their difficult aftermath would disrupt the Hariri murder inquiry. Hizballah Secretary General Hasan Nasrallah indicated in a wartime speech that the party had entered battle on behalf of the whole *Umma* [Arab and Islamic community], and that damage that occurred along the way was of small account.[2]

Hizballah gained kudos by surviving the bloody, muddled Israeli offensive of July–August 2006, but the scale of Israeli bombardment, which occurred as Hizballah was firing hundreds of rockets into Israel, brought an international intervention in southern Lebanon uncomfortable for Hizballah and Syria. The Lebanese government, dominated by the "new majority," survived, buttressed by Saudi Arabia and Egypt, while the Americans and French made sure that the Hariri inquiry suffered no body blow. After the August 14, 2006 ceasefire Hizballah moved overtly to overturn Prime Minister Fuad Siniora's cabinet of ministers, but the Lebanese stalemate persisted.

The following analysis explores these two main dimensions of Lebanon's contemporary affairs: the Hariri story as an expression of Lebanon's problematic relations with Syria, and Hizballah's confrontation with Israel. It interprets the intersection of these dimensions in the crisis inaugurated in August 2004 as well as the repercussions for Lebanon up to mid-2008.

LEBANON, SYRIA, AND THE HARIRI MURDER INQUIRY

Renaissance Italy offers an instructive comparison for the spectacular ascent of Rafiq al-Hariri, Sunni Muslim prime minister of Lebanon for 11 of the 13 years between 1992 and 2004, and for the jealousies aroused by "money power" in an overcrowded, superheated political arena. Hariri was in some respects Lebanon's Lorenzo de Medici, and his conversion of a fortune earned in Saudi Arabia into commercial and construction interests worth billions of dollars may be seen as a meteoric version of the rise of the Medici.

In a brilliant book,[3] the Renaissance historian Lauro Martines dissects the April 1478 murder plot against Lorenzo and his brother Giuliano, which involved the rival Florentine Pazzi family and implicated Pope Sixtus IV and the King of Naples. There are startling parallels between Lorenzo de Medici's assertive role in Italy and Hariri's financial freewheeling amid a jealous elite as he sought to lead Lebanon to a rebirth.

Hariri's fraught relations with Lahoud, with the Lebanese and Syrian security machines, and with the Asads of Syria resemble Lorenzo's maneuverings within and outside Florence. Unlike Hariri, Lorenzo survived the assassination attempt that took the life of his brother, but he later had to make a humiliating visit to the pope, who had earlier encouraged his would-be murderers. Would Hariri's heir, his son Sa'ad, and their Druze and Christian allies retain Western buttressing against an angry Syrian regime? Or would they have to bow to Bashar al-Asad as Lorenzo de Medici bowed to Sixtus IV?

Rafiq al-Hariri became the Lebanese prime minister in October 1992 because the Lebanese economy was collapsing. Damascus and its clients in Beirut needed a personality at the helm of the Lebanese government "capable of bringing foreign aid and loans," in the words of Syrian Vice President Abd al-Halim Khaddam.[4] Hariri, as a self-made billionaire with top-level connections in Saudi Arabia, Western Europe, and the United States, was therefore indispensable. He was amenable because he wanted to reconstruct his country and accepted that he had to adapt to Syrian supremacy in security affairs and to the venality of Syrian officials and their Lebanese cronies.

Nonetheless, his foreign connections meant that the Syrian security apparatus could never trust him, and he was never close to the Asad family. In August 1993, Syrian President Hafiz al-Asad rebuked him for "concealment" over a Lebanese arrangement with the United Nations to send the Lebanese Army south toward the Israeli-occupied "security zone."[5]

Within the Syrian leadership, Hariri developed personal and business relations with prominent Sunni Muslims such as Khaddam and Army Chief of Staff Hikmat Shihabi. The latter saw their fortunes decline in the late 1990s, when Hafiz al-Asad turned over more responsibility, for example in the case of Lebanon, to his son Bashar. Syria's military intelligence chief in Lebanon, Ghazi Kana'an, was the only senior Alawite with whom Hariri had regular interaction. Rumor held that Hariri paid Kana'an handsomely to shield him from bother, and the two established a friendship of sorts as Kana'an found himself outside the new elite around Bashar after 2000 and at odds with Lebanese President Lahoud.

Hafiz al-Asad selected Emile Lahoud as Lebanon's president in late 1998. As army commander between 1990 and 1998, Lahoud reformed Lebanon's army in line with Syrian preferences, exhibiting exemplary loyalty and Arab nationalism. By 1998, Hariri had produced significant economic improvement, and Syrian security chiefs wanted the prime minister constricted by a reinvigorated Maronite presidency. Lahoud devoted himself to shifting effective authority from the formal government organs to a secretive security machine on the Syrian model. This took its mature form after Bashar al-Asad succeeded his father as Syrian president in June 2000. Unlike Hafiz al-Asad, who cultivated aloofness, Bashar descended into Lebanese factional politics, siding with Lahoud and Hizballah and cold-shouldering Hariri and Druze leader Walid Jumblatt.[6]

In the first years of the new century, ultimate control of Lebanon was in the hands of an Asad family cartel in Damascus, headed by Bashar, his younger brother Maher, his older sister Bushra, and his sister's husband Asif Shawkat. The cartel's power flowed through Lahoud and the Syrian military intelligence commander in Lebanon to a group of Lebanese security heads, notably the Shi'a chief of the public security directorate, Jamil al-Sayyid, and the Maronite chief of Lebanese military intelligence, Raymond Azzar. In December 2002, Bashar relieved Ghazi Kana'an of his command in Lebanon, replacing him with his deputy, Rustum Ghazali.

Lahoud, a member of a prominent Maronite family from Mount Lebanon, detested Hariri and his wealth. When Hariri was in the parliamentary opposition from 1998 to 2000, Lahoud's circle ran a vindictive campaign against Hariri and his senior aides. After Hariri triumphed in the 2000 parliamentary poll despite electoral manipulation by Lahoud and Syrian military intelligence, the president worked to frustrate the returning prime minister's privatization and tax reform plans. In August 2001, Lahoud's security apparatus arrested hundreds of Christian activists after the Maronite patriarch visited Druze leader Jumblatt amid excited crowds hostile to Syrian hegemony. Bashar dispatched troop reinforcements to Lebanon to buttress Lahoud while Hariri complained that he knew nothing about the crackdown.[7]

Thereafter, Hariri's relations with the Syrian leadership deteriorated decisively. The major Kuwaiti daily *al-Ra'i al-Am* has claimed that at some time in 2003, Bashar al-Asad presided over a conclave in Damascus with the Lebanese prime minister at which "Syrian officials and officers comprehensively attacked Hariri, accusing him of secretly meeting a high-ranking American official in Lebanon and working against Syria....A close former aide of Hariri says that the prime minister felt ill and went to hospital before returning to Lebanon."[8]

Through early 2004, Hariri and Walid Jumblatt publicly opposed Bashar's wish to extend President Lahoud's period in office. According to the Lebanese Constitution, Lahoud could only have a single six-year term, due to end in November 2004. Bashar summoned Hariri to Damascus on August 27, 2004, to order him to have the Lebanese government and parliament override Lebanon's Constitution. The Syrian president reportedly threatened to "break Lebanon" if he did not get his way.[9]

Terrorization secured Lahoud his three extra years.[10] Bashar, however, reckoned without the United States and France. Syrian promoting of the insurgency in Iraq had alienated Washington, and Syrian contempt for France's aspiration for a continuing role in Lebanon provoked Paris. The Syrian action, defying appeals by the Western powers for election of a new Lebanese head of state, brought Presidents George W. Bush and Jacques Chirac together, despite divisions over the 2003 U.S. occupation of Iraq, to sponsor UN Security Council (UNSC) Resolution 1559 of September 2, 2004. Resolution 1559 required termination of Syria's 29-year-long military presence in Lebanon; disbanding of private armies, principally Syria's Lebanese Shi'a ally Hizballah; and a normal Lebanese presidential election free from foreign pressure. Syria, President Lahoud, and Hizballah scorned the resolution.

The humiliated Rafiq al-Hariri resigned as prime minister in October 2004, after a murder attempt on the Druze politician Marwan Hamada, who had left the government in protest of the Lahoud extension. Hariri became the backstage coordinator of opposition to Syrian hegemony in Lebanon's Christian, Sunni, and Druze communities. According to the respected international Arabic daily *al-Hayat*, Hariri informed the Iranian ambassador in Paris of his determination to have Syria removed from Lebanon but without targeting Hizballah.[11]

In early February 2005, Syrian President Bashar al-Asad reportedly told UN envoy Terje Roed-Larsen: "Hariri is playing dirty roles against Syria."[12] Roed-Larsen went to Beirut and warned Hariri that he feared for his physical safety.[13] Four days later Hariri was assassinated in a massive truck bomb explosion that also killed 22 others. The entire political context highlighted the Syrian regime and its clients, including security personnel and Sunni Islamists,[14] as prime suspects. A wave of fury against Syria's ruling Alawite clique swept Lebanon's Sunni Muslim community. At Hariri's funeral thousands chanted: "There is no God but God, and Asad is the enemy of God."

New domestic battle lines crystallized between February and July 2005. On March 8, Hizballah mobilized half a million followers to emphasize Shi'a Muslim alienation from the new Lebanon of the Hariri-Jumblatt camp and the traditionalist Christian politicians. On March 14, Syria's opponents replied with the largest demonstration in Lebanon's history—about 1 million Sunnis, Christians, and Druze. In May 2005, General Michel Aoun—who returned from 15 years of exile—felt sidelined by Hariri's son Sa'ad and Walid Jumblatt and separated his substantial Maronite Christian following from the "March 14" coalition. In the May–June parliamentary elections, after Syria's resentful April military evacuation of Lebanon, the rump of March 14 took 72 of the 128 seats (still allocated on a sectarian basis).

Aoun carved away 21 seats in the Maronite heartland. He accused the "new majority" of turning the Syrian-promoted 2000 electoral gerrymander—which effectively disenfranchised many Christians in northern Lebanon and the Biqa Valley—to its own advantage.[15] Hizballah, with the more secular but also Shi'a communal Amal movement of parliamentary speaker Nabih Barri as junior partner, corralled 35 seats, including 26 of the 27 Shi'a mandates.

Rafiq al-Hariri's former associate Fuad Siniora formed a government in July 2005 in which Syria's allies fell one position short of the one-third needed to block major decisions. The new majority, however, could not remove President Lahoud—whom it regarded as one of those responsible for Syrian domination, without support from Aoun, whom they were unwilling to advance to the presidency.

Aoun had emerged from the parliamentary poll as a Maronite leader equivalent to Hizballah's Hasan Nasrallah among the Shi'a. Aoun's bloc stayed outside the government, and the general criticized those, such as the Hariri group, who had turned against Damascus after profiting from Syrian hegemony through the 1990s.[16] Aoun's Free Patriotic Movement (FPM), a consistent enemy of Syria through the years of its hegemony in Lebanon, now drifted toward an alliance with Hizballah.

Meanwhile, the Hariri murder was also having international repercussions. UN Secretary General Kofi Annan sent a team headed by the Irish deputy police commissioner Peter Fitzgerald to make a preliminary report on the circumstances of the killing. Fitzgerald accused Syria of creating the atmosphere of intimidation in which the murder occurred and recommended an international investigation with broad powers. On April 7, 2005 UNSC Resolution 1595 was passed by unanimous vote, establishing the United Nation's first-ever murder inquiry. The UN International Independent Investigating Commission (UNIIIC), headed by Berlin prosecutor Detlev Mehlis, began work in Beirut in June 2005.

In late August, at the recommendation of the UN Commission, Lebanese authorities detained four commanders of the Lebanese security apparatus, all close to President Lahoud, on suspicion of involvement in the Hariri murder. In his first interim report in late October Mehlis noted "converging evidence" that the Syrian-Lebanese security machine, including top officials in the Syrian regime, had organized the assassination.[17] UNSC Resolution 1636 of October 31, 2005 rebuked Damascus for stalling the holding of interviews with prominent Syrians and invoked Chapter VII of the UN charter, meaning that noncompliance could lead to military action.

Fear in Beirut and belligerence from Damascus accompanied the UN inquiry. A series of murders and attempted murders of journalists or political figures critical of Syria emphasized that the new majority faced an existential struggle. The murder targets included Defense Minister Elias al-Murr, son-in-law of President Lahoud, who had fallen out with Syria's former military intelligence chief in Lebanon, Rustum Ghazali.[18] On October 12, 2005, one week before the Mehlis report, Syria announced the "suicide" of Syrian Interior Minister Ghazi Kana'an, Syria's superintendent in Lebanon from the 1980s until 2002 and a crucial witness for the UN inquiry. Kana'an did not have good relations with the clique around Bashar al-Asad and was rumored to have opposed Lahoud's extension.[19] Few believed the suicide story.

On November 10, 2005, Bashar accused Lebanon's new majority of moving toward Israel and being a "factory" for conspiracies against Syria. He termed Lebanese Prime Minister Siniora "the hired slave of a hired slave," the latter being Sa'ad al-Hariri.[20] Such pronouncements were viewed in Beirut as death threats. On December 12, 2005, the same day Mehlis submitted his second report to the UN secretary general, a bomb blast killed Gebran Tueni—publisher of the leading Beirut newspaper *al-Nahar*, a Hariri bloc parliamentarian, and a staunch foe of Ba'thist Syria's ambitions in Lebanon.

Armed with the reiterated focus on the Syrian-Lebanese security machine in the second Mehlis report, after interviews with Syrian officials regarded as "suspects,"[21] the UN Security Council unanimously issued Resolution 1644 on December 15, 2005. Resolution 1644 introduced the concept of a "tribunal of an international character," involving international and Lebanese judges, sitting outside Lebanon, to try murder suspects indicted as a result of the UN inquiry. It also authorized the UNIIIC to provide assistance in the investigation of other murders and bombings, from the attempted assassination of Marwan Hamada in October 2004 to the killing of Gebran Tueni.

In early 2006, Belgian prosecutor Serge Brammertz assumed the leadership of the UNIIIC after Detlev Mehlis declined a new six-month contract. Brammertz put the commission into a lower-key phase of consolidating the evidence. This was logical after Mehlis's high-impact reports had provided the commission with Security Council backing for coercing Syrian cooperation and put it on track to preparing the prosecution brief for an international court. Brammertz wanted to avoid giving Damascus excuses to persist in frustrating UNIIIC requirements for evidence, or for continued grandstanding about "politicization" of commission reports. He also needed several months to rebuild the commission into a larger apparatus to follow comprehensively each line of evidence.

Brammertz issued reports in March, June, and September 2006, according to the Security Council request for three monthly assessments of inquiry progress. In all these reports, the old Syrian-Lebanese security machine remained the central object of interest, no state or organization was named except Syria, and there was no suggestion that the four senior Lebanese security officials arrested in August 2005 should not stay in prison. Brammertz maintained the direction set by Mehlis.

Nonetheless, in the early months of 2006, Damascus may have gained the impression that the inquiry was faltering, and that by avoiding obvious provocations the regime might outlast Rafiq al-Hariri's friend President Jacques Chirac in Paris and Bashar's foes in Washington. Somewhere on the horizon, the Damascus regime hoped, there would be the kind of "deals" that Syria had pocketed in past times.[22] Anyway, the death squads took a rest after liquidating Gebran Tueni.

The June 2006 report clarified the situation. The inquiry was picking up steam on reinforced foundations. Brammertz promised that "based on the information received, further requests will be formulated and addressed to Syria," and he emphasized the centrality of "full and unconditional cooperation from Syria."[23] He indicated upcoming integration in the investigation of the 14 other bombing and murder incidents that were being pursued along with the Hariri case, a package unlikely to be comfortable for Syrian and Lebanese security operatives. He floated the idea of a "multi-layered concept" on how the murder had been planned, with multiple subcontractors that could only mean state involvement. Brammertz forecast turbulence: "The focus of the investigation increases the probability of individuals or groups attempting to execute threats against the Commission or its personnel for the purpose of disrupting its mandate."[24] UNSC Resolution 1686 of June 15, 2006 extended the UNIIIC mandate to mid-2007.

During the July–August 2006 Israel-Hizballah warfare the inquiry temporarily relocated to Cyprus. Given that the UNIIIC base in Beirut's Christian mountain suburbs was at no risk from Israeli bombardment, the primary fear was exploitation of the hostilities for an attack on the commission by Hariri's murderers. The September 2006 report demonstrated further consolidation of evidence, despite intervening upheavals. The inquiry was firming up the scenario of an elaborate murder team, with more data on individuals who had "substantive information…about the attack [on Hariri] prior to its execution."[25] Brammertz reported confirmed linkage among the murder cases and featured the discovery of Syrian "documentation" about explosives.[26] He was not satisfied with the "qualitative cooperation" of Syrian officials being interviewed[27] and again reminded Syria of the Chapter VII coercive provisions. Developments in the Hariri murder affair prefigured an international court and probable sensations in Damascus and Beirut, with far-reaching implications for Lebanese politics, especially for Hizballah and the Shi'a.

HIZBALLAH, ISRAEL, AND THE WAGES OF WAR

Through the 1990s, the radicalization of Lebanon's Shi'a Muslim community proceeded apace, driven by Israel's actions in southern Lebanon. Israel's occupation of a "security zone" in southern Lebanon anchored Syrian hegemony over the Lebanese. It invited Shi'a resistance and enabled Syria and its friends to smear Lebanese criticism of Syrian hegemony as treason. Confrontation with Israel justified Hizballah's private army and assisted the Party of God to expand its popular base and exact money from Lebanese Shi'a at home and abroad. Hafiz al-Asad cultivated Syria's ties with Shi'a parties, both Hizballah and Amal, while making sure that the Sunnis and Maronites maintained advantages that guaranteed Shi'a dependence on Syria. In turn, widening popularity, the flow of funds, and political entrenchment buttressed Hizballah's confrontation capability. This dialectic was primarily powered by Israel and entirely favorable to Hizballah.

Israeli bombardments in 1993 ("Operation Accountability") and 1996 ("Operation Grapes of Wrath") gave Hizballah windfall boosts in prestige and street support. The Lebanese government's negligence of Shi'a regions, with Hariri's reconstruction spending concentrated in downtown Beirut and the corruption and disorganization of Hizballah's Amal rival, contributed to the trend. Syrian manipulation of parliamentary elections, with Hizballah and Amal forced into an alliance, masked the effects, but the municipal polls of 1998 and 2004 demonstrated Hizballah's ascendancy among the Shi'a.

Israel's withdrawal from southern Lebanon in May 2000 also gave Hizballah a further advantage—the ability to claim victory over "the Zionist enemy"—but at the same time undercut the justifications for its continuing to field a large, well-armed militia. Israeli withdrawal also exposed Syria to protest against its domination of Lebanon. The answer was to claim to find other Lebanese territory still occupied by Israel. Hence, in mid-2000 parliamentary speaker Nabih Barri, Hizballah, and the Lebanese government asserted Lebanese sovereignty over the Shab'a Farms[28]— about 10 square miles of hillside at the northern extremity of the Golan Heights, captured by Israel from Syria in June 1967. The Lebanese government had not previously made such a claim, and the United Nations insisted that the land was Syrian territory until Syria signed documents stating otherwise. Syria backed the Lebanese demand but avoided endorsing it in writing for fear that the United Nations would then persuade Israel to pull back, thereby solving the dispute.

Hizballah's taste of regional power in compelling Israel to abandon its "security zone" inside Lebanon made it loath to confine itself to Lebanese domestic politics. The party incited the Palestinians to rise against the Israelis and provided expertise and training to the Sunni Islamists of Hamas in the West Bank and Gaza during the 2000–2004 Palestinian Intifada. In October 2000, Hizballah leader Hasan Nasrallah proclaimed: "The party has outgrown the country [Lebanon] and the [Shi'a] community."[29]

Hizballah's advance to the international boundary in southern Lebanon made it even more useful to its Iranian and Syrian patrons as a deterrent force in case of threats from Israel or the United States. Intermittent fighting in the Shab'a Farms fortified Hizballah's assertion of freedom of military maneuver in Lebanon south of the Litani River, meaning the exclusion of the Lebanese Army from the border zone. The party viewed itself rather than Lebanon's national army as the primary Lebanese spearhead against Israel.[30]

After 2000, the new Syrian president treated Hasan Nasrallah as a confidante rather than, as his father had, a hired client.[31] Bashar al-Asad's father had an instrumental attitude to Hizballah and would never have accorded its leader such status. Syria and Iran accelerated shipments of missiles to Hizballah, in coordination with Lebanese President Emile Lahoud. They also helped the party to construct hardened bunkers in the south. Most missiles came from the extensive Syrian stocks, which was confirmed by Israeli analysis of fragments in July–August 2006. Some longer-range and antiship varieties were imported directly from Iran.

By 2005, Hizballah's 12,000 or more rockets meant it could menace Israeli towns almost as far south as Tel Aviv if the United States moved to attack Syria because of its interference in Iraq or to attack Iran because of its resurgent nuclear program. The Russians later indicated that Syrian officers transferred Russian missiles to Hizballah during the April 2005 Syrian withdrawal from Lebanon.[32]

During the post-August 2004 Lebanon-Syria crisis, Hizballah found itself at the peak of its military expansionism and command of Lebanon's Shi'a at the same time as it was exposed by the pullback of its Syrian ally. Until 2005, Syrian hegemony in Lebanon allowed the party to stand aloof from Lebanese governments—with the assurance that they could never cause it any bother. However, the requirement for Hizballah disarmament in UNSC Resolution 1559, followed by Syria's withdrawal of its forces from Lebanon and the anti-Syrian triumph in Lebanese elections, compelled Hizballah to join Prime Minister Fuad Siniora's government in May 2005. For the first time, the party contributed two ministers—aside from its influence over other Shi'a appointments, because, also for the first time, it needed to restrict a potentially hostile majority. The Hariri murder inquiry reports of UN commission head Detlev Mehlis in late 2005, preceded by the arrests of the Lebanese security chiefs, intensified Hizballah's predicament. The Syrian regime was in serious danger.

Stalemate in the Lebanon-Syria crisis throughout early 2006, as the murder inquiry retooled and General Michel Aoun split from Lebanon's "new majority," gave the Hizballah-Syria-Iran alignment breathing space. Certainly, Aoun's February 2006 accord with Nasrallah, in which the Maronite general approved resistance weaponry and Hizballah signed onto the general's anticorruption crusade, supplied the Shi'a Party of God with vital Christian "street" approval. Aoun's defection made it impossible for the "new majority" to muster the two-thirds in parliament to depose President Lahoud, who gave Hizballah's arms a state cover. Further, Aounist reinforcement of the Hizballah-Amal bloc helped Nasrallah and Aoun to question who held the real Lebanese majority.

On the other hand, American and French determination ensured that the UN Security Council doggedly pursued fulfillment of Resolution 1559. Undeterred by the wrath of Nasrallah and other Hizballah personalities, UN envoy Terje Roed-Larsen highlighted Hizballah's denial of the right of the Lebanese state to a monopoly of force on its territory in his six monthly reports to UN Secretary General Kofi Annan. This fed into a "national dialogue" of Lebanese political leaders between March and June 2006, at which Nasrallah faced interrogation about his party's military autonomy. At the "dialogue" he had to join a consensus approving an international court to try Hariri's murderers, formal demarcation of the Lebanese/Syrian border, including the Shab'a Farms, and disarmament of Palestinian groups—Syrian allies of various flavors—outside the refugee camps. The last would be a step toward implementing the militia disbandment clause of Resolution 1559.

In April 2006, an opinion poll conducted for *al-Nahar* newspaper had three-quarters of respondents wanting Lebanese Army deployment throughout Lebanon.[33] The poll indicated that a majority of Shi'a favored Hizballah being armed, but up to 40 percent demurred. Overwhelming majorities in the other communities backed a state monopoly on force. The sectarian division between the Shi'a and other Lebanese on state integrity was disappointing, but the national result trended against Hizballah. On May 17, 2006, the UN Security Council approved Resolution 1680 in response to the infiltration of weaponry into Lebanon from Syria and American and French concern about the belligerence of Syria's rulers and its Lebanese clients toward Prime Minister Siniora. Resolution 1680 recommended that Syria establish diplomatic relations with Lebanon to prove it accepted Lebanon's existence and backed Lebanese "national dialogue" decisions. It reiterated Resolution 1559 on militia disarmament. Russia and China abstained, as they had with Resolution 1559. A few weeks later, the June 2006 Hariri murder inquiry report incorporated elements—for example, the integration of 14 other murders and bombings with the Hariri case, and reminders to Syria about Chapter VII of the UN Charter—alarming to Hizballah and Iran. It was increasingly urgent that Hizballah and Iran buttress their Syrian partner, and that Hizballah turn the tables within Lebanon.

When Hasan Nasrallah decided to make a kidnapping raid into Israel on July 12, 2006, it can be assumed that he coordinated with Damascus and Tehran. Hizballah had autonomy over disturbances near the Shab'a Farms but not over initiating a war in the Galilee. For Damascus and Tehran, the priority can only have been derailing the Hariri murder inquiry. The summoning of senior Syrians to international justice would bring down the Syrian leadership, removing Iran's chief ally in the Arab world and isolating Hizballah by eliminating its weapons source and link to Iran. Taking prisoners in exchange for Lebanese and Palestinians in Israeli jails can be interpreted as cover—offering publicity bonuses in the Arab world and servicing Hizballah's regional persona. It can hardly have been the primary reason for baiting Israel into retaliation with the prospect of transforming Lebanese politics.

As for Iran, the argument that the Hizballah-Israel conflagration was useful for diverting attention from the Iranian nuclear program is not tenable. If Iran was heading toward nuclear weapons capability, the real confrontation with the United States and others was still probably years away, and Tehran would want Hizballah to keep its powder dry. For Iran, action in July 2006 was premature, and Tehran probably only came on board with Nasrallah because of Syrian desperation. A Lebanese ally of Syria, quoted in *al-Nahar* after the outbreak of hostilities, gave a telling insight when he gloated that "the wrecking of the formation of the international tribunal" was the most important gain, "the first results of the Israeli war on Lebanon."[34]

Israel chose not to give the international community a chance to produce a draconian UN Security Council resolution that would have seriously embarrassed Hizballah. Instead, the Israelis plunged into a military offensive that closely resembled its counterproductive predecessors in the 1990s, apart from the application of greater firepower. The United States, torn between its Israeli ally and sponsorship of an emerging new Lebanon, and tempted by the chimera of a decisive blow being struck against Hizballah, held off international intervention through late July and early August 2006 while Israel wreaked damage in Lebanon.

For his part, Hasan Nasrallah made speeches from hiding places, telling the Lebanese he was only responding to a long-planned Israeli attack while issuing an ominous threat to Lebanese critics that "we might be tolerant with them, and we might not"[35] and airily dismissing infrastructural damage. In a swipe at the Hariris and Saudi Arabia, he observed: "There is no worry about reconstructing Lebanon, because we have friends who will help us with clean money."[36] Hizballah unleashed its rockets on northern Israel in a counteroffensive that was sustained but of limited effect and showed the emptiness of the party's claims to a "balance of terror."

Within Lebanon, many non-Shi'a Lebanese were furious about Hizballah's virtual coup d'état in taking the country to war with no consultation. However, Israel's assault on the international airport and roads and bridges everywhere, together with the mounting civilian deaths in the Shi'a areas, brought a general "street" coalescence with Hizballah. Fuad Siniora's government, demoralized by impotence against Israel and Hizballah's hijacking of its decision-taking, received direct encouragement from Arab foreign ministers who flew in and out of Beirut on August 7. The Arab ministers refused a Syrian proposal to commend the "Lebanese resistance,"[37] meaning Hizballah, and backed Siniora's seven-point plan already endorsed by the Lebanese government on July 27, 2006.

Siniora's plan involved deployment of the Lebanese Army throughout Lebanon, which would assert state monopoly on force. Other elements were reinforcement of the existing United Nations Interim Force in Lebanon (UNIFIL) to buttress the state, reactivation of the 1949 armistice agreement with Israel, and the UN taking charge of the Shab'a Farms until border demarcation.[38] Simultaneously, the United States and France negotiated a draft Security Council resolution that knitted together Lebanese concepts, a robust international force in southern Lebanon, and Israeli insistence on a conditional ceasefire. Syria exerted itself to nullify the international force, warning that foreign soldiers would be seen as "an occupation force, with the risk of the same fate that befell the multinational force in 1983."[39] This raised the specter of suicide bombings against such a peacekeeping contingent. Lebanon obtained adjustment of the Security Council draft, mainly to have the international force as an expansion of UNIFIL, and promised to deploy 15,000 Lebanese troops in southern Lebanon.

By the second week in August, the United States was under intense pressure from Western and Arab allies to curtail Israel's military activities and had evidently concluded that Israel was not competent to cripple Hizballah. The Lebanese death toll exceeded 1,000, almost all Shi'a, while the Israeli toll topped 100. UNSC Resolution 1701 was passed unanimously on August 11, 2006, with the ceasefire being implemented three days later. On paper, it was a setback for Hizballah and Syria. The resolution fingered Hizballah for initiating hostilities and endorsed Lebanese Army deployment along the Lebanon-Israel border, where the army had been absent for decades. The army would be stiffened by a new UNIFIL, to be increased from 2,000 to 15,000 foreign soldiers. The resolution prohibited private weapons between the Litani River and the border and sternly forbade smuggling of weapons into Lebanon. There was a clear implication that the Lebanon-Syria border should be closely monitored.

Lebanon's political balance after the August 14 ceasefire was ambiguous. On the one hand, Hizballah appeared strengthened by its "victory" in maintaining itself against the Israeli army. A poll in mid-August showed decline in the previous disapproval of Hizballah's private army. Shi'a and Sunni support for Hizballah weaponry increased substantially, though it was a majority still only for Shi'a.[40] In another poll, 69 percent of all respondents rated the United States as an enemy, compared with 26 percent in a September 2005 sample.[41] Hizballah could sidestep Resolution 1701 by concealing weaponry, and it was impossible to stop smuggling from Syria. The Lebanese Army remained infiltrated by Syria and its friends, and General Michel Aoun and his Maronite following remained estranged from the new majority. With Iranian financing, Hizballah preempted the lethargic Lebanese state with distribution of compensation for property damage.

On the other hand Hizballah's gains within Lebanon were tentative, not decisive. The new majority in the government remained viable after Hizballah and Israel suspended their fighting, and the United States, France, and Saudi Arabia determined to keep it viable. The Hariri murder inquiry ground on, and was not so easily disrupted as some may have hoped. The hostilities did not bring a political breakout for the pro-Syrian camp. Hasan Nasrallah's September 23 "victory rally" apparently fell short of the half million mobilized on March 8, 2005.[42] Earlier, scathing denunciation of the "victory" by the Shi'a chief mufti of Tyre, Ali al-Amin, perhaps rattled the Hizballah chief, who the same day asserted that he would never have launched the kidnapping if he had remotely appreciated the Israeli response.[43] This was a curious comment from a man considered for more than a decade to be a supremely realistic calculator of action and reaction between Hizballah and Israel.

THE INTERMINABLE CRISIS

In early November 2006, UN Security Council members reached consensus on the framework for a tribunal to try those to be charged with organizing and perpetrating the Hariri assassination, as well as other murders and attempted murders of Lebanese critics of Syria covered by the UNIIIC mandate. The tribunal would include a Lebanese judge to legitimatize it in Lebanon and the Arab world. The idea of a mixed international/Lebanese tribunal was originally built into UNSC Resolution 1644 of December 2005 at the request of Lebanese Prime Minister Fuad Siniora, after the murder of *al-Nahar* publisher Gebran Tueni. Resolution 1664 of March 29, 2006 authorized Secretary General Kofi Annan to negotiate an agreement with Lebanon for "a tribunal of an international character." Months of painstaking work on the framework followed, involving Lebanese and UN legal experts. Russia objected to political and security chiefs being held responsible for the actions of subordinates and to inclusion of other murder and bombing cases if there was evidence of linkage to the Hariri case, but in the end they bowed to the rest of the Security Council.[44]

On November 10, 2006, the draft protocol arrived in Beirut for approval by the Lebanese government and parliament. Sa'ad al-Hariri placed a copy of the draft on his father's grave. The determination of the Hariri-Jumblatt camp, which commanded two-thirds of the council of ministers, to proceed to an immediate government vote had an electrifying effect. Six pro-Syrian ministers, including all the Shi'a representatives, resigned to delegitimize the government before it could approve the tribunal. Prime Minister Siniora held the vote regardless, on the basis of the two-thirds quorum. President Lahoud and Hizballah declared the government illegal on the dubious argument that a major sect was absent,[45] though Siniora had not accepted the resignations. Parliamentary speaker Barri, Hizballah's Shi'a ally as leader of Amal, at first upheld the government as "constitutional"[46] but quickly fell in line with Lahoud and Hizballah Chief Hasan Nasrallah.

Hizballah and Michel Aoun's FPM had already demanded a national unity government, in which they would hold a blocking "one third plus one." For Hizballah, the new majority had declined to a fake majority, was hostile to its warfare against Israel, and was the corrupt instrument of Franco-American tutelage. Aoun, who had his own agenda to succeed Lahoud as president with Shi'a support and to reform the Lebanese state, gave Hizballah the crucial cross-sectarian buttressing without which Nasrallah and his Syrian and Iranian backers could not seriously aspire to commandeer the Beirut government. On the other side, for the March 14 camp of Sa'ad al-Hariri, Walid Jumblatt, and Prime Minister Siniora, Hizballah was Bashar al-Asad's agent, with Aoun as a fellow-traveler, and the Party of God was trying to complete the Lebanese coup d'état it had intended when it launched its July 12, 2006 surprise against Israel. The new majority, backed by the international community, upheld the democratic legitimacy of the Siniora government and had no doubt that it still enjoyed the preponderance among the Lebanese people.

From late 2006, Syria and its Lebanese allies worked relentlessly to recover supremacy in Lebanon. On November 21, 2006, political murder returned to Beirut—yet again targeting a critic of the Syrian regime—when gunmen with silencers assassinated Industry Minister Pierre Gemayel, who was a Maronite member of the Hariri-Jumblatt bloc and son of former president Amin Gemayel. On December 1, Hizballah, Amal, and Aoun launched open-ended street protests to bring down the depleted Siniora cabinet and established tent encampments adjacent to the Grand Serail (offices of the government and prime minister). The rallying-call for the protestors, mostly Shi'a with a leavening of Aounist Christians, was a national unity government—which Nasrallah and Aoun promised would inaugurate a "clean" regime and true independence, meaning independence from the United States, France, and Saudi Arabia. Hizballah made it clear to Arab League mediators in late December that it wanted the new government before any Lebanese agreement on the Hariri tribunal, which must be emasculated into impotence in line with Syrian desiderata.[47] In parallel, parliamentary speaker Barri blocked Prime Minister Siniora from transferring the UN-approved tribunal protocol to parliament for a vote that Siniora would certainly win.

Lebanon's Sunni Muslim and Druze communities overwhelmingly rejected the opposition assault on Siniora, who faced a Shi'a Muslim parliamentary speaker and a Maronite Christian president who were both associates of the Syrian-Iranian-Hizballah alignment. The siege of the Sunni prime minister was a siege of Lebanon's Sunni community, and in late January 2007 street violence between government and opposition supporters left eight dead and scores injured. Through early 2007 it became apparent that Hizballah could not so easily break the March 14 camp. In New York, the UN Security Council backed the Siniora government and took up its approval of the murder tribunal. Brushing aside Bashar al-Asad's warnings of violence to UN Secretary General Ban Ki-moon, the Security Council gave full, final international endorsement to the establishment and modalities of the tribunal in Resolution 1757 of May 30, 2007. The tribunal would operate under Chapter VII of the UN charter, potentially authorizing the use of force in case of defiance.

Another turbulent summer followed in Lebanon. From late May until September 2007, the Fath al-Islam group of Sunni extremists, including many foreigners who had infiltrated from Syria, challenged the Lebanese Army in the Nahr al-Barid Palestinian refugee camp north of Tripoli. With considerable difficulty the army slowly crushed the rebels, though Fath al-Islam leader Shakir al-Abbasi predictably managed to slip through the army cordon at the end—back to Syria. In parallel, two more opponents of Syria were assassinated—Sunni Walid Idu on June 13 and Maronite Antoine Ghanim on September 19. Both were members of the March 14 parliamentary majority.

On November 24, 2007 Emile Lahoud's extended presidential term ran out, resulting in a deadlock over the parliament's election of a successor. In a surprise move, the March 14 factions adopted Army Chief Michel Suleiman as a "consensus" candidate. Suleiman had risen to command of the Lebanese military in 1998, under Syrian hegemony, had excellent relations with Hizballah, and maintained personal contacts with the Syrian leadership. In line with his own interests, he indicated neutrality in army protection of demonstrations after 2004 and oversaw military operations against Fath al-Islam, asserting that the latter was "al-Qa'ida" and had nothing to do with the Syrian regime.[48] March 14 leaders thought he might prove serviceable cover and were in any case blocked on other options. The Syrian-aligned opposition, openly endorsed from Damascus, accepted his candidacy but refused his election. First they wanted agreement to their veto (effectively command) capability in a new government.

From November 2007 until May 2008 deadlock continued, with no president and the Siniora government technically assuming presidential functions. The drift of events now favored the Syrian regime and the Lebanese opposition. Internally, the government demonstrated little concern about socioeconomic stagnation, and its Christian personalities failed to address the persistent Christian impression of devaluation of their communities within the March 14 coalition. The latter was particularly ominous because in the Sunni/Shi'a standoff, the Christian population (35 percent) had a potentially pivotal role. Michel Aoun, Hizballah's Maronite ally, lost some ground through political grandstanding but could always claw it back. As regards the murder inquiry and tribunal, no major development transpired through the year after the supposedly groundbreaking UN Security Council Resolution 1757. The tribunal acquired a building in The Hague, but UNIIIC reports became opaque in 2007–2008, and indictments continuously receded into the distance. Given that there were identified suspects and that weighty evidence against them had been assembled by early 2006, the chain-dragging into 2008 could only fuel suspicion that international players were more interested in using the case as a bargaining chip than in truth and justice.

Bold new car bomb murders came early in the presidential "vacuum," with a shift to targeting Lebanon's military and investigative apparatus. On December 12, 2007 the victim was General François al-Hajj, an independent-minded officer and the leading candidate to replace Suleiman as army commander. The threatening message to the officer corps could not have been plainer. On January 25, 2008 the target was Captain Wissam Eid, head of communications investigations in the Hariri case.

From late 2007 onward, the Syrian regime seemed to have new international prospects. The supple Nicolas Sarkozy, anxious for a "realist" deal with Bashar al-Asad, succeeded Bashar's nemesis Jacques Chirac as president of France in May 2007. In Washington the hostile Bush administration moved into its final year, with the prospect of a similar transition to a more amenable U.S. president. The friendly Turkish government of Prime Minister Tayyip Erdogan hosted indirect Syrian-Israeli talks in Istanbul, which were conceived in Damascus as a means to compel the United States to open up again to Ba'thist Syria. In December 2007, French President Sarkozy's bid to negotiate a Lebanese presidential election with Bashar merely excited Syria's expectations about the dividends to be gained by holding out. Syria therefore refused to budge to Arab entreaties to facilitate a Lebanese settlement, even when the Saudi monarch and the Egyptian president refused to attend the March 2008 Arab summit in Damascus. Saudi fury about Syria's alliance with Iran, the deadly Syrian campaign against Saudi Arabia's friends in Lebanon, and Syrian meddling with Hamas and other radical Palestinians had no impact on Bashar—who had already scorned Saudi leaders as "half men" in an August 15, 2006 speech.[49] Given Saudi backtracking by late 2008, he plainly had their measure.

At the same time, Hizballah steadily reinforced its missile arsenal and extended its "state within the state." It constricted UN inspections south of the Litani River,[50] and to the north constructed a new network of bunkers for long-range rockets. It also had front men buy land on the southern fringe of the Druze Shuf hills, which was an activity that already deeply disturbed Druze leader Walid Jumblatt.[51] More widely, Hizballah oversaw security at Beirut airport through sympathetic army personnel and created its own landline communications system connecting Beirut, southern Lebanon, and most of the Biqa. The system even had a feeder to the vicinity of the Faraya ski resort, overlooking the Christian districts north of Beirut.[52] In early May 2008 the government challenged the creeping subversion of state authority, by transferring the Shi'a officer who headed airport security and deciding to launch a probe of Hizballah's private communications. The Party of God responded ferociously, warning that anyone questioning its communications—which were part of "the weaponry of the resistance"—was "serving the Israeli enemy."[53]

On May 8–9, 2008, Hizballah and allied militias briefly seized mainly Sunni West Beirut. In accompanying fighting, which also involved Sunni/Alawite clashes in Tripoli and a setback for Hizballah in trying to penetrate the Druze hills, about 70 died. Hizballah used heavy weapons in its "operation smashing the balance" (*amiliyat kasr al-tawazun*), and General Suleiman had the army stand aside in what he defined as "civil war."[54] Hizballah demonstrated once and for all that it would deploy its military weight against any Lebanese it viewed as problematic; the government promptly rescinded its decisions on the airport and the illicit communications system. Sunnis were deeply humiliated while Christians largely stood aloof.

The shock led to Lebanese political recalibration that proved advantageous for Syria, Hizballah, and Michel Aoun. Qatar and the Arab League sponsored a Lebanese conference in Doha, which on May 21 produced an agreement on Michel Suleiman's election, a national unity government with opposition veto capability, and a new parliamentary election law for 2009 that Aoun could represent as his achievement for Christians vis-à-vis Sunnis. Suleiman became president on May 25; he lost little time in praising "the resistance"[55] and indicated his preference for a friendly relationship with Bashar al-Asad. Siniora remained prime minister but had to endure a new indignity as Hizballah ignored the Lebanese state in arranging a prisoner swap with Israel. The parliamentary majority managed to secure a majority of cabinet members (16 out of 30), but with Druze leader Walid Jumblatt wavering in his commitment to the March 14 coalition, this had little meaning.

As for Bashar al-Asad, France has taken Syria's consent to Lebanese arrangements beneficial to Bashar's regime as justifying a full diplomatic opening to Damascus. Syria's supreme asset in enticing Western politicians remains its alignment with Iran, the fantasized sale of which is enough to attract concessions that only increase the actual potency of the Syrian-Iranian-Hizballah combine. Why Bashar should trade a supreme and appreciating asset is an interesting question, even without the Syrian leader's evident comfort and affinity with revolutionary Iran. Whatever the case President Sarkozy saw no problem with inviting Bashar al-Asad, head of a regime staffed with murder suspects fingered in UN inquiry reports, to Paris for the Mediterranean summit and the Bastille Day celebrations of July 12–14, 2008. "French sources" indicated in late June 2008 that the international murder tribunal "is the most important factor in Syrian calculations." They cited a "French conviction" that "if Damascus becomes an acceptable party that one can work with, the [murder] tribunal file can be buried in more than one way."[56] The Syrian regime therefore basked in a new respectability and had great expectations, in which France and Israel would serve as tools for restored relations with the United States and renewed command of Lebanon. With its final victory over Lebanese pluralism and international justice seemingly visible ahead, political murder took an undoubtedly calculated vacation after its work on January 25, 2008.

NOTES

1. An earlier draft of this chapter was published under the title "Crisis in the Levant: Lebanon at Risk," *Mediterranean Quarterly*, Vol. 18, No. 2, pp. 37–60. Copyright 2007, Mediterranean Affairs, Inc. All rights reserved. Used by permission of the publisher, Duke University Press.
2. Nasrallah to al-Manar television, August 16, 2006, as cited in *al-Mustaqbal* (Beirut), August 17, 2006. According to Nasrallah, Hizballah was "not just plunging into its own battle and Lebanon's battle, but the battle of the entire *umma*."
3. Lauro Martines, *April Blood: Florence and the Plot against the Medici* (London: Pimlico, 2004).
4. Fuad Da'bul in *al-Anwar* (Beirut), March 23, 1992.
5. Nicola Saikali in *al-Anwar*, August 15, 1993.
6. In November 2000, Syrian officials indicated that Jumblatt was unwelcome in Damascus when he commented on the absence of any reference to Syrian military redeployment in the new Lebanese government's policy statement (*al-Hayat*, November 7, 2000). In April 2001, the Syrians moved troops into the Druze Shuf hills, and the family of Jumblatt's close associate Akram Shuhayyib received a mail bomb. *Middle East Intelligence Bulletin*, "Dossier: Walid Jumblat," Vol. 3, No. 5 (May 2001), http//www.meib.org/articles/0105_1d1.htm.
7. *Al-Hayat* (London and Beirut), August 9, 2001.
8. Sami Nazih in *al-Ra'i al-Am*, October 15, 2005.
9. Peter Fitzgerald, *Report of the UN Fact-Finding Mission to Lebanon* (United Nations, NY: February 25–March 24, 2005), p. 5.
10. See cases of intimidation of parliamentary deputies cited in *al-Nahar* (Beirut), August 31 and September 1, 2004.
11. *Al-Hayat*, February 21, 2005.
12. *Al-Qabas* (Kuwait), October 29, 2005, on Roed-Larsen's testimony to the UN murder inquiry—which was held back from publication in the October 20, 2005 Mehlis report.
13. *The Times* (London), March 18, 2005.
14. Sunni militants with Syrian connections range from al-Qa'ida associates to their enemies in the Ahbash Sufi movement.
15. For example, comments by Aoun to the author, June 2005.
16. Author's interview with Michel Aoun, June 2005.
17. UNIIIC first report (unedited version), Beirut, October 19, 2005, paragraph 203.
18. Elias al-Murr interview with Lebanese Broadcasting Corporation (LBC) television, Beirut, September 27, 2005.
19. Sami Nazih in *al-Ra'i al-Am*, October 15, 2005.
20. Bashar al-Asad speech at Damascus University. Full Arabic text in *al-Hayat*, November 11, 2005.

21. UNIIIC second report, Beirut, December 10, 2005, paragraph 26.
22. Ba'thist Syria's belief through 2005 and 2006 that a "deal" always waits just around the corner has been almost unshakeable. See Ibrahim Hamidi, "Syria Flaunts Its Regional Cards—and the Options Are Open for a 'Deal' in Preparation for the Mehlis Report," al-Hayat, October 6, 2005 and "Damascus Receives American Indications and European Proposals for Setting-Up a Comprehensive 'Deal': Renewal of Peace Negotiations, Ending of Isolation, and [EU] Association Agreement in Exchange for Pressure on Hizballah and Hamas, and Distancing from Iran," July 25, 2006.
23. UNIIIC fourth report, Beirut, June 10, 2006, paragraph 104.
24. Ibid., paragraph 124.
25. UNIIIC fifth report, Beirut, September 25, 2006, paragraph 50.
26. Ibid., paragraphs 64 and 80.
27. Ibid., paragraph 81.
28. Barri was first to raise the claim, with Syrian endorsement. See al-Hayat, April 30 and May 7, 2000. Lebanese citizens had property titles to the area, and the French mandatory authorities had never properly demarcated the Lebanese/Syrian border that they established in 1920.
29. Report by Ibrahim Bayram, al-Wasat (London), October 23, 2000.
30. Middle-level Hizballah members in discussion with the author, March 2006.
31. For example, in August 2004 Bashar turned to Nasrallah to assist in pacifying the young Iraqi Shi'a firebrand Muqtada al-Sadr in Najaf, with the purpose of doing the Americans a "good turn" so they would tolerate the Lahoud extension in Lebanon—Walid Shuqayr in al-Hayat, September 9, 2004. Also, in November 2004 Bashar personally asked Nasrallah to persuade Walid Jumblatt to desist from his campaign against Lahoud and Syria, al-Safir (Beirut), November 27, 2004.
32. Al-Hayat, October 20, 2006. These included both ground-to-ground and anti-tank varieties.
33. Statistics Lebanon Ltd. sampled 400 respondents throughout Lebanon, April 19–24, 2006. Seventy-eight percent said yes when asked: Do you think the Lebanese Army should be the only armed forces in Lebanon? Among the three "great" communities, more than 80% of Christians and Sunnis answered affirmatively, compared with 40% of Shi'a.
34. Al-Nahar, July 18, 2006.
35. Nasrallah to al-Jazeera television, July 20, 2006, as cited by Michael Young in the New York Times, August 4, 2006.
36. Nasrallah to al-Manar television, July 16, 2006, as cited by al-Mustaqbal, July 17, 2006.
37. Al-Mustaqbal, August 8, 2006, and al-Siyyasa (Kuwait), August 8, 2006.
38. Al-Mustaqbal, July 27, 2006.
39. Syrian foreign minister Walid al-Mualim cited in al-Hayat, July 30, 2006.
40. The French research company Ipsos surveyed 600 Lebanese, August 11–17, 2006. Among Shi'a respondents, only 16% believed Hizballah should give up its weapons after the war (compared to 40% who supported a Lebanese Army monopoly of force in the April 2006 Statistics Lebanon survey). Among Sunnis, 54% believed Hizballah should not keep weapons (82% for state monopoly of force in April), and among Christians, 77% (84% in April). Mideast Monitor, September/October 2006 (citing L'Orient Le Jour, August 28, 2006), http://mideastmonitor.org.

41. Ibid. Information International for both September 2005 and August 2006 samples.
42. Interestingly, even the sympathetic *al-Safir* (September 24, 2006) merely reported "hundreds of thousands."
43. *Al-Siyyasa*, August 28, 2006; *al-Nahar*, August 28, 2006.
44. *Al-Hayat*, November 11, 2006.
45. Article 95 of the Lebanese Constitution, cited by Syria's allies, refers to "fair representation of the sects in the formation of the cabinet." It can be strongly argued that the Arabic expression *tashkil al-wizara* (creation/formation of the cabinet) refers to the initial putting-together of a cabinet rather than to its temporary balance in the event of resignations, especially resignations not accepted by the prime minister.
46. *Al-Nahar*, November 14, 2006.
47. Walid Shuqayr in *al-Hayat*, December 21, 2006, reported Nasrallah's readiness to meet Siniyora "on the basis of adjustments to the tribunal project...changing the articles relating to the responsibility of a chief for subordinates, and the connection of the other crimes to the Hariri crime." As for Damascus, Shuqayr noted: "A prominent diplomatic source has told *al-Hayat* that a top Syrian leader assured a top Arab official several days ago that Damascus will not accept the continuation of the tribunal project...in its present form" and that it is "prepared to close its borders with Lebanon, and to suspend the supervision of its border with Iraq against infiltrators crossing into Iraq, in response to the tribunal protocol."
48. *Al-Safir*, August 14, 2007. "The army commander denies any Syrian relationship with the Fath al-Islam organization, and classifies it as part of the global al-Qa'ida organization."
49. *Al-Safir*, August 16, 2006. Bashar al-Asad also condemned the March 14 camp as "an Israeli product" and described UN Security Council Resolution 1701 as "an international political salvage crane for these forces."
50. UN Security Council, *Report of the Secretary-General on the Implementation of Security Council Resolution 1701 (2006)*, New York, June 27, 2008, paragraphs 6, 21, 23, and 65. Paragraph 65 summarizes: "The presence of unidentified armed elements in the UNIFIL area of operations, coupled with incidents of restriction of the Force's movement and the monitoring of its operations, are a source of serious concern. They raise tensions and cannot but cast doubt on the motives of those involved."
51. Jumblatt expressed his concerns about this phenomenon in a discussion with the author, March 2006.
52. See May 8, 2008, Guillaume Dasquié analysis, including map of Hizballah landlines, on geopolitique.com, http://www.geopolitique.com/editorial/exclusif-la-carte-du-reseau-telecom-du-hezbollah-761.html (accessed July 11, 2008).
53. *Al-Nahar*, May 5, 2008, citing Hizballah parliamentary deputy Hasan Fadlallah.
54. *Al-Hayat*, May 14, 2008.
55. "Suleiman: The Resistance Is a Source of Strength for Lebanon," *al-Hayat*, July 8, 2008.
56. *Al-Sharq al-Awsat* (London), June 26, 2008.

5

DEMOGRAPHIC DILEMMAS

Mark Farha

Lebanon's modern history has been punctuated by periodic outbreaks of fratricidal violence, followed by political compromises that recalibrated the distribution of power and privilege among the major confessional communities. Although many factors have contributed to these cycles of conflict and compromise, recurrent phases of incongruity between demographic and political balances of power have been a major driving force in all of them—even as the pursuit of more equitable and just political representation has figured as one of the most salient justifications for communal calls to arms. The demographic question remains as much a fundamental reference point of Lebanese politics as ever before.

BACKGROUND

The Republic of Lebanon of 1926, defined by one of its chief architects as a "[c]ountry of associated (confessional) minorities,"[1] has been governed by a succession of formal and informal power-sharing arrangements that divide executive and legislative power into sectarian allotments. A large majority of Lebanese belong to one of three main sects—Sunni Muslims, Shi'a Muslims, and Maronite Christians—with Greek Orthodox, Druze, and over a dozen other groups comprising the rest.

Even prior to the Constitution of 1926, demographic and political representations never fully overlapped in the course of Lebanon's history. The first interconfessional municipal council (*diwan*) set up in Beirut in 1834 was evenly divided between six Muslim and six Christian delegates. This parity, however, was not observed in subsequent councils from which the Druze remained entirely excluded.

The executive administrative council of the *mutasarrifiyya* (retrospectively known as "Petit Liban") that governed Mount Lebanon from 1861 to World War I did not reflect its large Maronite majority, which received only 4 of the 12 seats.[2] Rather, this allotment emerged as a reflection of the international balance of powers, with the Druze, for example, now benefiting from their alliance with the Ottoman Porte and Britain in securing representation beyond their dwindling demographic weight.[3]

When the end of World War I left France as the temporary colonial master of Lebanon, the political role of its historical Maronite Catholic allies was augmented accordingly. In contrast to the *mutasarrifiyya*, the First Lebanese Republic could claim only a slim Christian majority (and Maronite plurality) within its expanded borders by way of a politicized, skewed series of censuses conducted between 1922 and 1932. The resultant findings were rejected by all Muslim political leaders, most of whom still contemplated integrating Lebanon into a larger regional order governed by a Muslim majority.[4]

Nevertheless, the 1932 census was taken as the primary benchmark and justification for the 1943 National Pact, which governed the allotment of executive and legislative power after Lebanon's independence. Under this informal arrangement, the presidency was reserved for Maronites and the premiership for Sunnis, while parliament seats were apportioned in a six-to-five ratio of Christians to Muslims (roughly corresponding to that of the census). Even so, the case could be made that demography per se played less of a role in the particular framing of the covenant than the financial and political clout each sect and constituency could marshal. The pact had emerged as a *"partage de pouvoir"* (sharing of the spoils) between Maronite and Sunni notables, represented by Bishara al-Khuri and Riad al-Sulh.[5] The Shi'a, the economically and politically weakest of the three largest sects, were not included at all until 1947, when the office of parliament speaker was tacitly reserved for them.

As the demographic balance shifted after independence, this power-sharing system was buffeted by external ideological challenges and internal political grievances. The brief 1958 civil strife pitted a pro-Western, largely Christian front against a largely Muslim coalition enamored with Egyptian President Gamal Abdel Nasser.[6] Blending together misgivings against the inordinate prerogatives of the Maronite presidency and zeal for Arab unity under Nasser, Muslim demonstrators trampled the Lebanese flag in the streets of Tyre. Such ominous signs prompted one CIA analyst to conclude that unless the United States expedited the advent of General Fuad Chehab to replace an overbearing President Camille Chamoun, "constitutional changes to make Lebanon a Moslem-governed country would become the armed rebels' minimum demand."[7] In the event, soon upon taking office, Chehab issued Decree 112, which mandated Muslim-Christian parity (*munafasa*) in all administrative positions as a provisional measure "for the sake of justice."[8]

Demands for more radical political change continued to resonate deeply. The chairman of the pan-Islamist Najjada party, Adnan al-Hakim, called for the explicit abrogation of the National Pact and a rotating Christian-Muslim presidency just prior to the outbreak of the civil war in 1975. The latter was fueled in no small part by a Sunni bid (in league with armed Palestinian groups and Kamal Jumblatt's Progressive Socialist Party) to overturn Maronite political supremacy.[9] Arguably, this domestic dispute came to increasingly reflect the interests of the external powers that armed and financed its combatants. *Al-Nahar* editor Ghassan Tueni famously dubbed it the "war of the others."

Tueni would coin a parallel phrase to describe the 1989 Ta'if Accord as the "peace of the others."[10] With the Americans largely preoccupied with winning allies for the first Gulf War, the regional external powers—chiefly the Syrians and the Saudis—acted as the godfathers of the accord's constitutionally mandated legislative Christian-Muslim parity and the stipulated reduction of the powers of the presidency. These new terms still did not correspond to demographic realities, but most major political forces came to accept them—if only at the behest of their outside patrons (including, eventually, Iran).

THE ELECTORAL SYSTEM

While the Lebanese system specifies a fixed sectarian distribution of parliamentary seats, the "fair" communal representation intended by the quota is blurred by the fact that most candidates face a multi-confessional electorate, and many must contest districts in which their sect is not a majority. Thus, for example, those who win the handful of Sunni seats in predominantly Shi'a south Lebanon are effectively beholden to Shi'a politicians, while the Sunni vote is decisive in electing the Christian and Shi'a deputies of Beirut.

To be sure, this feature of the Lebanese electoral system has been praised insofar as mixed electoral districts mandate interconfessional political alliances and, so the hope is, advance national integration.[11] A similar rationale also informed the 1989 Ta'if Accord's stipulation of large electoral districts (*muhafazat*) and the allusion to the ultimate goal of a single, national district (*da'ira muwwahhada*). In effect, however, the proverbial "politics of the notables" from the top, and the largely endogamous social segregation from below, both of which define Lebanese politics and society, stymie or exclude any non-(or multi-) confessional, grassroots movements.[12] This holds especially true within a winner-take-all election system, as opposed to a more broadly representative proportional (*nisbi*) system.

In addition, electoral districts can be gerrymandered to change how many of a given sectarian community's seats are embedded under the effective control of other communities. In the 1992 election, voters from other sects elected 36 percent of Christian deputies, whereas the vast majority of Shi'a, Sunni, and Druze deputies were elected primarily by their own confessional constituents.[13] This "appointment" of Christian deputies in south Lebanon, Ba'abda-Aley, and other districts prompted many Christian leaders to call for smaller, more homogenous voting districts.

The drafting of a new electoral law has been a matter of contentious debate. In 2006, a commission headed by former Foreign Minister Fuad Boutros proposed a hybrid system in which 77 seats are filled through first-past-the-post/winner-take-all elections in small electoral districts (*qadas*), while 51 seats are filled through a proportional electoral system at the level of governorates. Significantly, the draft law also permits Lebanese citizens residing abroad to participate in the elections, lowers the voting age from 21 to 18 years, and establishes strict monitoring and spending caps for political campaigns.

Shortly after the draft was tabled in June 2006, the three main factions of the March 14 coalition—Druze leader Walid Jumblatt, Sa'ad Hariri's Future Movement, and Samir Geagea's Lebanese Forces—all vowed to prevent its ratification.[14] Though a full-fledged public discussion never unfolded due to the ensuing paralysis of government, there has since emerged an across-the-board consensus amongst virtually all political parties toward accepting the single-district *qada*.[15]

Be that as it may, even the most creative electoral engineering can ill avert the conundrum posed by political and demographic disequilibria. How can each citizen be accorded the same measure of political rights when power is divided equally between a Muslim majority and a Christian minority? Because individual political representation is not perfectly equal even in principle, the growth of communal demographic grievances in one group or another is all but built into the system.

Current Demographic Trends

Sidestepping the surmised inconsistency between individual and communal political representation, Lebanon has not conducted a census since 1932. Tellingly, even the most aggrieved Muslim opposition parties have usually shied from demanding one. The explosive potential of the assumed demographic-political incongruity is such that calling for a measurement is tantamount to threatening civil peace. This prolonged absence of an official census has only fed the intense speculation of the country's actual demographic makeup.

Before examining some of the (often conflicting and possibly politicized) statistical data published on this matter, it is important to recall that modern states carry out censuses for a reason—indirect methods of estimating the demographic makeup of a country are necessarily imprecise. Nevertheless, two major demographic trends can be discerned.

Emigration

The first trend is a disproportionately high rate of Christian emigration from the mid- nineteenth- through the twentieth century, particularly during and after eruptions of civil strife in 1860, 1914–1918, and 1975–1990.[16]

Over 900,000 Lebanese emigrated between the outbreak of civil war in 1975 and 2001 (about 45 percent during the last decade of Syrian occupation).[17] Although it was once assumed that a majority of these recent emigrants were Christian, a 2006 study conducted by the Lebanese Emigration Research Center at NDU found that emigration is equally sought by Muslims (59.7 percent) and Christians (61.3 percent), and for virtually the same sociopolitical reasons.[18] Moreover, the percentage departure rates within each confession were 22 percent of Sunnis, 21 percent of Shi'a, 21 percent of Maronites, 23 percent of Greek Orthodox Christians, and 15 percent of Druze.[19] Given the estimated relative size of each community, one can thus deduce that the three largest denominations (the Sunni, Shi'a, and Maronites) have accounted for the bulk of total migrants. The available data thus raise questions about the longstanding assumption that the large majority of Lebanese citizens living abroad are Christians. This is politically relevant because a number of Christian politicians have called for the inclusion of absentee ballots in elections, believing that this would favorably alter the confessional profile of the electorate. Hoping to expand the prospective pool of expatriate Christian voters, MP Nimtallah Abi Nasr has gone further in campaigning for a (re)naturalization of second- and third-generation Lebanese abroad. Hizballah has actively encouraged first-generation Shi'a emigrants to register their children as citizens for much the same reason.

Fertility Rates and Household Sizes

The second major demographic trend is higher Muslim birthrates. In 1971, Shi'a showed the highest fertility rate of 3.8, followed by Sunnis (2.8), (Maronite and non-Maronite) Catholics (2), Druze (1.8), and non-Catholic Christians (1.7).[20] By 1988, the percentage of Shi'a in Lebanon had risen to 32 percent, while the number of Maronites had dwindled to 17 percent according to another study.[21] As shall further be discussed in what follows, until very recently, projected estimates of a Shi'a plurality as large as 40 percent were a staple of Western media.

Alternative sources, however, may cast doubt on the accuracy of these numbers. According to data published by Lebanon's Central Statistical Administration in 1996, average household sizes and fertility rates in largely Sunni areas of northern Lebanon (Akkar, Miniyya-Dinniyya) now outstrip those of largely Shi'a districts. Although the average household sizes of Beiruti Sunnis are lower than both, this makes Sunni-Shi'a household sizes on a national level roughly equivalent.[22]

In any event, projections based on fertility (and emigration) rates ignore a host of intervening variables. Lower infant and child mortality rates among Christians, for example, have counterbalanced higher Muslim birthrates to some extent.[23] Most significantly perhaps, the highly controversial 1994 naturalization of over 160,000 Syrians and Palestinians tipped the sectarian balance in Lebanon in favor of Sunnis[24] (which was one reason why the late Prime Minister Rafiq Hariri supported it).[25]

Proxy Measures

Analysts have pursued other methods of estimating the waxing and waning of Lebanon's sectarian communities. The most widely cited reference is the official list of registered Lebanese voters published prior to the 2005 elections, which is 26.5 percent Sunni, 26.2 percent Shi'a, and 22.1 percent Maronite.[26] However, voter registration lists, known as "check lists" (*lawaih al-shattab*), only include adults age 21 or older and thus do not take account of what may be a disproportionate Shi'a youth.[27] Moreover, Lebanese citizens are automatically counted as registered voters irrespective of whether they have emigrated or not.

A recent study by Youssef Douwayhi, based on rare privy access to birth records (*sijilat al-nufus*) since 1905, estimates Shi'a and Sunni demographic weight to be virtually equal (29.05 percent and 29.06 percent).[28] Although this method includes Lebanese under the age of 21, it also fails to exclude Lebanese citizens who have emigrated and does not account for unregistered children born to émigré families.

Although a convergence of Sunni-Shi'a birthrates is quite plausible (due to rapid Shi'a urbanization, among other things), the fact that official data showing a Sunni "baby boom" was produced at the height of the Hariri's power has been viewed with some suspicion. Similarly, prior to the civil war, public (Christian) officials had been accused of tampering with statistics to conceal the scale of Christian demographic decline.[29]

Above and beyond the methodological problems inherent in almost all these demographic studies, obvious political implications can prejudice the accuracy and interpretation of statistical data. Case in point is the CIA, which has abruptly revised its own previous demographic findings. In its 2004 edition, the CIA *World Factbook* had reported that Muslims and Christians constitute 70 percent and 30 percent of the population, respectively. Amid an intensified Israeli-American push to disarm Hizballah, these numbers were conspicuously adjusted in the 2005 edition to reflect a highly improbable, precipitous decrease in the overall Muslim population to 59.7 percent, while the Christian population rose a sudden 9 percent.[30] In fact, there is some reason to believe that these drastically adjusted estimates might be closer to the true numbers than the earlier, ostensibly inflated ones. After all, the official, published voting logs (or "registries") from 1992, 2000, 2004 all indicate a virtual Sunni Shi'a parity, as do studies by Kamal Feghali—another experienced sociologist and demographer.[31]

IMPLICATIONS

In the final analysis, available statistical levies about Lebanese demographics must be deemed inconclusive, particularly as regards the precise size of the resident population.

Nonetheless, one preliminary conclusion seems inescapable. As has been the case intermittently throughout its history, Lebanon's current power-sharing covenant is far out of step with demographic realities. Even the most conservative statistical conjectures leave Lebanese Muslims significantly underrepresented in the parliament and the council of ministers, an incongruity that will grow in the years ahead. (According to the Douwayhi study, as of 2006, Christians made up a mere 23.3 percent of Lebanese under the age of 20.)[32] Debates over the exact numbers miss the forest for the trees, as the prevalent ambiguity alone is sufficient to sustain acute perceptions of disenfranchisement among both Shi'a and Sunnis—thereby providing another seedbed for external exploitation and indigenous radicalization.

In contrast to previous phases of political-demographic imbalances, however, none of the leading Lebanese political groups today are calling for an immediate upending of the constitution. Even Hizballah, despite its official pursuit of the abolition of political sectarianism in principle,[33] has refrained from insisting on amendments to better reflect Shi'a demographic weight.

Indeed, insofar that Shi'a sociopolitical disenfranchisement contributes to popular support for Hizballah, the party's leadership may well be content with the current system for the time being. The mere insinuation of Hasan Nasrallah publicly calling for revised sectarian quotas (a demand that would be very difficult to drop once raised) sends shivers down the collective spine of the political establishment and is itself a powerful bargaining tool. Yet even though the status-quo puts an artificial cap on Shi'a representation, it has allowed Hizballah (along with the pro-Syrian Amal movement) to monopolize that representation. A deconfessionalized proportional electoral system, on the other hand, would open the doors of parliament for secular Shi'a currents.

Last but not least, the current electoral law and political alignments give Shi'a minorities in the districts of Ba'abda-Aley and Zahla a critical swing vote. Ironically, the March 14 coalition owes its much vaunted parliamentary majority to its 2005 electoral alliance with Hizballah, whose *fatwa* instructing Shi'a to vote against Michel Aoun's Free Patriotic Movement (FPM) provided its margin of victory for the 11 seats of Ba'da-Aley (the FPM and its allies narrowly won Zahla).

Branded in 2005 in a pro-Hizballah speech by Walid Jumblatt as a mortal threat to the resistance's weapons,[34] Aoun's subsequent, stunning alliance with Hizballah stems at least partly from electoral considerations, as do his repeated calls for early parliamentary and presidential elections by the popular vote. Shi'a demography, he reckons, is now on his side.

Perhaps the main reason why no one is proposing a revision of Ta'if is that Lebanese Christians are split between the Sunni-led March 14 coalition and the Shi'a opposition, and both sides know that raising the issue of political-demographic incongruity would antagonize their allies. Ironically, then, any initiative for an overhaul of Ta'if would have to be initiated by leaders of the Christian community—the very confession destined to lose the most from such a reform.[35] With rival Christian leaders vying for the loyalty of their community, however, they cannot afford to be seen as chipping away at the last remnants of Christian privileges in the system. Even Aoun has put his own party's progressive, comprehensive deconfessionalization agenda on ice and instead cast himself as the communal guardian of a Christian community divested of its rights due in the post-Ta'if era.

Christian fears of Muslim demographic strength are reinforced by trepidation about radical Islamism (a sentiment shared by a great many secular Muslims in and beyond Lebanon). One reason why the political empowerment of Shi'a is conflated with Hizballah is that the latter has imposed a startling degree of conformity on the Shi'a electorate. This was evident during the two-month Hizballah-led boycott of the cabinet in the winter of 2005–2006, when prominent Shi'a cleric Afif Nabulsi issued a fatwa prohibiting Shi'a not part of Hizballah and Amal from joining the government.[36] Both Hasan Nasrallah and the purportedly secular Nabih Barri vociferously defended the fatwa and denounced any criticism as an "attack on the scholars of Islam."[37]

This raises questions about whether Shi'a empowerment attained through the agency of religious fundamentalists is healthy for democracy. Although Sunni Islamism (on display when demonstrators rampaged through the Christian neighborhood of Ashrafiyya during the Danish cartoon controversy in February 2006 and more recently with the terrorism and revolt by Fath al-Islam) is viewed with at least as much apprehension, the inchoate, dispersed makeup of militant Sunni movements in Lebanon renders them less likely to sweep to power through elections.

CONCLUSION

In view of the growing disequilibrium between demographic and political representation in Lebanon (and all of its associated pathologies), a recalibration of the Ta'if power-sharing formula along the lines of a tripartite division of power (*muthalatha*) among Christians, Sunnis, and Shi'a is all but inevitable in the coming years. Although deconfessionalization may be a better cure for Lebanon's ailments in principle, in practice those who hold positions of power under the sectarian system are not likely to promulgate its abrogation (even if they pay lip service to the idea as a long-term goal).

While a tripartite division of power may not correspond precisely with Lebanon's demographic balance, it is the closest possible approximation in the absence of a census (few dispute that Christian, Sunnis, and Shi'a each constitute somewhere in the range of 25–35 percent of the population) and the only recalibration formula that could conceivably win the support of all three. So long as no one sect comprises a demographic majority (a situation that, barring a major cataclysm, is not likely to change even in the long term),[38] few Lebanese would feel themselves egregiously underrepresented by a tripartite division of power.

However, while proposals to this effect have circulated for over two decades,[39] a sweeping revision of the Constitution is highly unlikely in the short term. Indeed, the main leaders of both March 14 and the opposition have explicitly rejected Sunni-Shi'a-Christian tripartism as an alternative to Muslim-Christian parity[40]—a position that perhaps has less to do with innate preferences than with the political exigencies of appealing to a deeply divided and anxious Christian community.

Trust between Sunnis and Shi'a and between rival Christian political blocs—a sine qua non for any prospective reform of constitutional scope—has steadily eroded as a result of Lebanon's prolonged political standoff. Although the opposition controls 45 percent of parliament, March 14 leaders have balked at accepting a national unity cabinet in which they would lack the two-thirds majority needed to unilaterally make decisions.[41] The exclusion from government of Lebanon's two leading Shi'a parties and most popular Christian party left the country's main political institutions in limbo.

In this interim period, the ruling coalition and the opposition both looked to the street as an arena and force majeure arbiter of their contending claims. Whereas the massive March 14, 2005 demonstration succeeded in prompting the Syrian withdrawal from Lebanon, subsequent shows of people power have only served to replicate deepening demographic and political bifurcations. Wagering on the street in the present context predictably pushed the country toward the precipice of open civil strife after Hizballah's armed militia succeeded in seizing control of West Beirut.

Until this critical point, the framing of a consensus in Lebanon had been hampered by external conditions, such as the bloody sectarian conflict between Sunnis and Shi'a in Iraq and—most importantly—the regional showdown between the U.S./Israeli/Saudi and Iranian/Syrian axes. Just as the Ta'if Accord was made possible by a Saudi-Syrian-American rapprochement, a more unlikely and involuntary regional détente paved the way to a new domestic consensus. Against all odds external mediation, this time led by Qatar, yielded a truce agreement signed in Doha on May 21, 2008.

The Bush administration, which had repeatedly prodded March 14 to ignore opposition demands and go ahead with a unilateral "50 plus 1" election of the president, now grudgingly lent their support to the Doha Accord, which granted the Hizballah-led opposition the veto powers it had sought all along. The Syrians and Iranians too may have sensed that a further encouragement of political brinksmanship on the part of their allies in Lebanon might turn a domestic deadlock into a civil war, which in turn could quickly inflame the region at large.

Ultimately, the looming threat of civil war and/or external domination[42] was once again averted by ways of concessions made by both sides. The Doha Accord merely reconfirmed the truism that a consociational democracy cannot function without a coalition government taking account of the vital interests and core concerns of the three major constituent communities of the country, each of which enjoys mutual veto powers—if not invariably de jure, then indubitably de facto.

Yet such a traditional, sect-focused analysis of the Lebanese predicament may omit perhaps the most critical segment of Lebanese society. For a case can be made that the most underrepresented constituency in Lebanon is not the Shi'a, Sunnis, or Christians, but the considerable number of Lebanese who do not identify primarily with the sect or creed into which they are born. Interestingly, the proportion of Lebanese who privilege their national identity over their confessional identity (34 percent, according to a 2005 survey)[43] compares positively with virtually all Arab and Middle Eastern countries.[44] If the strengthening of an intercommunal civic identity is the only exit out of the vicious cycles of confessional conflict,[45] temporary compromise, and renewed contestation, then finally[46] lending a voice and official,

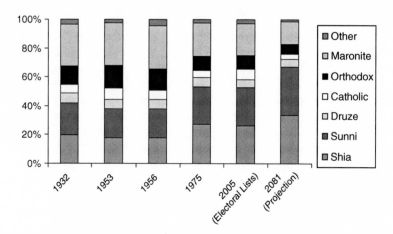

Figure 5.1:   Historical Evolution of Demography in Lebanon

Sources: Population Registry of December 31, 1953, Published in Klaus-Peter Hartmann, Untersuchungen Zur Sozialgeographie Christlicher Minderheiten Im Vorderen Orient, Vol. 43 (Wiesbaden: Beihilfe zum Tübinger Atlas des Vorderen Orients, 1980), p. 126. *Estimates by al-Nahar, April 26, 1956; 1975: Fiches du Monde Arabe,* Lebanon-Economy: Population Data, IL-17 (September 24, 1980); *2005: List of Eligible Voters as Published by the Lebanese Interior Ministry in Al-Safir and* Al-Nahar, February 11, 2005. These latter official numbers fall within the margin of error (3 percent) of those presented by the statistician Youssef al-Duweihi in *al-Nahar,* November 12, 2006. Pollster Abdo Sa'ad has estimated a slightly higher percentage of Muslims. See http://www.beirutcenter.info/default.asp?contentid=692&MenuID=46 (last accessed December 23, 2006). The projections for 2081 were published based on a study by Ibrahim Muhanna and Information International in "End of Lebanon as We Know It," *The Monthly,* No. 62 (September 2007), p. 8.

constitutional recognition to what Jawad Adra calls the "hidden third" of Lebanese society is one of the most sensible steps to secure Lebanon's future stability and prosperity (see figure 5.1).[47]

NOTES

1. Michel Chiha, *"Un pays de minoritiés associées,"* *Politique Intérieure* (Beirut: Editions du Trident, 1964), p. 232.
2. The Druze received three seats, Greek Orthodox Christians two, and the Greek Catholics, Shi'a, and Sunni Muslims one each. *Règlement Organique* as published in al-Aziz Nawwar, *Watha'iq asasiyya min tarikh Lubnan al-hadith, 1517–1920* (Beirut: Arab University of Beirut, 1974). On June 5, 1915, the last Christian governor, Ohannes Pasha, saw his term prematurely terminated by the Porte, and in August of the same year Cemal Pasha replaced the Armenian with a Turkish Sunni, Munif Bey, and officially abolished Lebanon's semiautonomous status and elected representative bodies.
3. Previously, the so-called protocol of Shakib Efendi, drawn up after the clashes of 1840, heralded the spirit of equality by instituting an even confessional division with the creation of the "dual districts" (*qa'im maqamayn*), one Christian and one Druze (1842–1860). The governing councils of each district were composed of one Sunni, Maronite, Druze, Orthodox and Melkite member, the Shi'a notably being left out prior to the revised *nizam* of 1845 when the *Matawila* (Shi'a) were allowed to nominate one qadi as their representative on the council. To be sure,

throughout the mutasarrifiyya the Shi'a did not constitute more than 5% of the population. Caesar Farah, *The Problem of the Ottoman Administration in the Lebanon. 1840–1861* (Ann Arbor: 1977), p. 453.

4. Basim al-Jisr, *Al-Sira'at al-Lubnaniyya* (Beirut: Dar al-Nahar, 1981), p. 30. Decree 8837, which set forth the guidelines for naturalization in Lebanon, favored Christian rather than Muslim refugees. Thus Armenian and Syrian refugees were specifically mentioned, while Kurdish refugees and Bedouins were excluded. See Rania Maktabi, "The Lebanese Census of 1932 Revisited. Who Are the Lebanese?" *British Journal of Middle Eastern Studies*, Vol. 26, No. 2 (November 1999), p. 227.

5. It should be noted that some members of the Maronite elite opposed the pact, amongst them Yusuf al-Sawda, MP Yusuf Karam, and Bishop Mubarak, the latter calling for a petit Lebanon with a decisive Christian majority. See al-Jisr, *As-Sira'at al-Lubnaniya*, p. 91. Ibrahim Yazbak, a confidante of Riad al-Sulh, says that the terms of the National Pact with Bishara al-Khuri did not remain secret but were disclosed by Sulh to Lebanese notables and to Shukri al-Quwatli and Jamil Mardam Bey. See Saffiye Saadeh, *The Social Structure of Lebanon* (Beirut: Dar al-Nahar, 1993), p. 60.

6. This was particularly evident among Sunnis, but even Shi'a parliament speaker Adil Usayran declared that "Lebanon will march with the Arab caravan" and that "anyone who thinks of working for interests other than those of the Arabs will have no room in Lebanon." *Egyptian Gazette*, March 5, 1958, cited in Fawaz Gerges, "The Lebanese Crisis of 1958: The Risks of Inflated Self-Importance," *Beirut Review*, 5 (Spring 1993), p. 85.

7. Wilbur Crane Eveland, *Ropes of Sand* (London: W. W. Norton, 1980), p. 301.

8. Thus reaffirming the principle enunciated in Article 95 of the Constitution and prefiguring the 1990 Ta'if Accord's extension of confessional parity to the parliament. See Basim al-Jisr, *Mithaq 1943* (Beirut: Dar al-Nahar, 1979), p. 239.

9. Muhammad Bayhum has argued that the 1975 war arose as a result of Sunni dissatisfaction with the terms of the National Pact. See *Al-Naz'at As-Siyyassiyya fi Lubnan* (Beirut: Jamiyat Bayrut al-Arabiyya, 1977), p. 7.

10. In Hanan Aad, "Hadirat bi-Da'wa Min Markaz Al-Tawthiq Wa Al-Abhath," *al-Nahar*, March 6, 2004.

11. Despite the alleged pro-Christian bias of the census and elaboration of the 1926 Constitution, the adoption of the single electoral college meant that in five out of six voting constituencies Christian candidates could be vetoed by Muslim voters in post-1926 elections. Pierre Rondot, "Lebanese Institutions and Arab Nationalism," *Journal of Contemporary History*, Vol. 3, No. 3 (1968), p. 44.

12. It is thus not fortuitous that the Communist party, which enjoyed no single confessional constituency, remains the only major party never to win a parliamentary seat in the Lebanese parliament.

13. Farid al-Khazen, *Lebanon's First Postwar Parliamentary Election* (Oxford: Center For Lebanese Studies, February 1998), pp. 44 ff.

14. Walid Jumblatt was most forthright and unwavering in his outright rejection of the Butrus law. His right-hand MP Marwan Hamada reaffirmed his concern for an electoral system based on the *qada*, or a "smaller district to satisfy the small sects in Lebanon." *Al-Balad*, December 10, 2007, p. 5.

15. Patriarch Sfeir has repeatedly called for the 64 Christian deputies to be elected by Christian constituents and deemed the "law proposed by the commission difficult to implement." *Al-Safir* (Beirut), May 19, 2007. Nabih Barri was

quoted on March 27, 2007 by Ghassan Tueni as grudgingly accepting the *qada* even though it "does not serve (his) interests." Hasan Nasrallah, like Michel Aoun, has expressed his willingness to accept either system.

16. The Allied sea blockade of 1915 triggered a famine that claimed the lives of at least 150,000 Lebanese, mainly, though not exclusively, Maronite Christians in North Lebanon. Elisabeth Thompson has estimated that (mostly Christian) Mount Lebanon lost as much as 18% of its population to conscription and famine in World War I, far outstripping the human toll of 5% in France and Germany. See Elisabeth Thompson, *Colonial Citizens* (New York: Columbia University Press, 2000), p. 38. Suleyman Dahir has noted that the Shi'a of Jabal Amil also suffered exacting casualties and severe economic dislocation as vital grain supplies from Hawran were being siphoned off to Beirut, with war profiteering running rampant. See Youssef Moawad, *Al-Nahar* (Beirut), May 6, 2004. The most complete treatment to date of this era is: Nicholas Ajay, *Mount Lebanon and the Wilayah of Beirut, 1914–1918: The War Years*, Ph.D. Dissertation, Georgetown University, 1973.

17. Of the 900,000 refuges, 54.4% left between 1975 and 1990, while 18.4% between 1991 and 1995, and 26.6% between 1996 and 2001. C. Kasparian, *L'Entrée des Jeunes Libanais dans la Vie Active et l'Émigration des Libanais depuis 1975*, Vol. 3 (Presses de l'Université Saint Joseph, 2003), p. 14.

18. "31.1% of the migrants surveyed said that their reason for not returning was the instability of Lebanon, 24.4% said the reason was the political situation while 17.8% preferred to stay abroad to secure their future." "Insecurity and Migration Report," published at http://www.ndu.edu.lb/lerc/index.htm (accessed October 27, 2007).

19. Anis Abi Farah, "Al Mughtaribun bayna 1975 wa 2001," *As-Safir*, December 3, 2001, p. 6. The author thanks Guita Hourani for alerting him to these sources.

20. Joseph Chamie, *Religion and Fertility* (New York: Cambridge University Press, 1981), p. 85. It should be noted that the high Shi'a and Sunni birthrates have decreased slightly in the 1990s and that rural Christian families tend to have more children.

21. Majed Halawi, *A Lebanon Defined: Musa Al-Sadr and the Shi'a Community* (Boulder: Westview Press, 1992), p. 50. Halawi estimates the number of Shi'a at 1,325,499 out of a population of 4,044,784 in 1988.

22. In 1996, the *qada* of Akkar was estimated to have the highest average household size of 6.0, followed by Miniyya-Diniyya at 5.7 and Hermel at 5.8. The average family in Bint Jbayl counted 4.8 members and in Nabatiyya 4.7. *State of the Environment Report* (Beirut: Central Statistical Administration, 1996). The average number of children born to married women from the Muhafaza of North Lebanon was reported as 4.2 as opposed to 2.8 in Beirut, 3.6 in Nabatiyya, and 3.9 in the Biqa in 1996. These numbers are from the Lebanese Ministry of Public Health as cited in Muhammad Faour, "Religion, Demography and Politics in Lebanon," *Middle Eastern Studies*, Vol. 43, No. 6 (2007), p. 914.

23. See, e.g., Robert B. Betts, *Christians in the Arab East: A Political Study* (Athens: Layacabettus Press, 1975), p. 85. Another regression analysis focusing on fertility differentials in Greater Beirut concluded that differentials between Muslim and Christian fertility rates "persisted after control for social class," even though they were given to "taper off progressively in the capital Beirut." See M. Khlat, M. Deeb, and Y. Courbage, "Fertility Levels and Differentials in Beirut during

Wartime: An Indirect Estimation Based on Maternity Registers," *Population Studies*, Vol. 51, No. 1 (March 1997), pp. 85–92.

24. Government decree 5247, published in its full length of 1,279 pages in the *Official Gazette*, No. 26, Supplement 2, June 30, 1994. Interior Minister Michel Murr stated that 110,000 Muslims and 50,000 Christians were granted Lebanese citizenship, but the exact number is in dispute—with some members of the Christian opposition putting the number at 300,000 and upward. One detailed study of the decree arrives at an estimate of 222,730 based on an average family size of six members. See Tony George Atallah, "al-Mujanisun fi Lubnan ma b'ad al-Harb," *al-Abhath*, Beirut 45 (1997), pp. 100–102. Sixty-two percent of the naturalized citizens were foreigners—mainly Sunni Syrian (Bedouins) from Wadi Khalid near Akkar and Palestinians living in Lebanon, while 15% hailed from the so-called seven villages, a border region ceded to Palestine by the French after they concluded the Paulet-Newcombe agreement with the English in February 1922. The issue was put to rest until it flared up again in wake of Emile Lahoud's presidential extension campaign in 2004 when the Maronite League won its case before the highest constitutional supervisory body, the *Majlis al-Shura*, to revoke 4,000 of the previously bestowed naturalizations. Hariri was in no mood to hurry the implementation of this decree and decided to form yet another additional committee to once again probe the retraction before any eventual ratification. See a*l-Safir*, April 22, 2004.

25. Hariri disclosed as much when he attempted to allay the concerns of Maronite Patriarch Nasrallah Boutros Sfeir, who had complained of a loss of Lebanese identity, by telling him that at least the decree reportedly "bestowed the nationality on Sunnis more so than it did on Shiites." Antoine Sa'ad, *as-Sadis wa'l Saba'un, Mar Nasr Allah Butrus Sfeir, al-Jamia al-Lubnani ya lil thaqafa*, Vol. 2 (Beirut: al-Jamiyat al-Taawuniyya lil-Thaqafat wa al-Iman, 2005), p. 161.

26. These are official numbers published in *Al-Safir and Al-Nahar*, February 11, 2005.

27. According to Duwayhi's investigation of the birth records, of those under the age of 20, only 23.31% are Christian, and the remainder (76.59%), Muslims. *Al-Nahar*, November 16, 2006.

28. See Yusuf Duwayhi, *Al-Nahar*, November 16, 2006.

29. Muhammad Faour, "The Demography of Lebanon; A Reappraisal," *Middle Eastern Studies* Vol. 27, No. 4 (October 1991), p. 632.

30. See https://www.cia.gov/library/publications/the-world-factbook/print/le.html (accessed March 3, 2006). *CIA: The World Factbook: Lebanon*, CIA World Fact Book, 2006.

31. *Lebanon in an Encyclopedia, by Kamal Feghali* (Beirut: International Publisher, 2002), p. 26. The earlier 1932, 1943, 1951, and 1956 electoral lists showed a 2–5% Sunni plurality.

32. Duwayhi, *Al-Nahar*, November 13, 2006, p. 14.

33. See the party's 1992 Electoral Program as published in Naim Qasim, *Hizballah: The Story from Within* (London: Saqi Books, 2005), pp. 273 ff., p. 31.

34. "The Syrians brought Aoun as a tool to confront Hizbollah specifically...we, Hizbollah and the forces of Christian moderation (the LF) however shall persevere." Walid Jumblatt cited in *Al-Safir*, June 13, 2005.

35. Thus runs the reasoning of Michael Young in "Lebanon's Pact: Prelude to a Postmortem," *The Daily Star* (Beirut), December 19, 2007.

36. Nabulsi's fatwa was published in Lebanese papers on December 21, 2005. A court case was subsequently raised by the plaintiffs Yusuf al-Zayn, Talal al-Husayni, Fares Sassin, Dr. Fahmiyya Sharaf al-Din, Nada Sehnaoui, Mona Fayyad, Ghassan Mukhaybar, and Muhammad Farid Matar. A separate suit was filed by Adnan al-Amin. The plaintiffs focused on the fact that Nabulsi was not a member of the higher Shi'a council and thus had no right to issue the fatwa. The constitutional right of Shi'a, however, should be to vote irrespective of religious edicts, officially "recognized" or not.

37. Nasrallah, cited in Hazim Saghieh, "Hizballah: A Constructive Ambiguity," *al-Hayat*, January 25, 2006.

38. Depending on the underlying assumptions of mortality- and birthrates, the Shi'a in 2081 will constitute between 33.69 and 44.83%, the Sunnis between 33.38 and 36.60%, and the Christians between 26.8 and 11.04%. See Ibrahim Muhanna and Information International, "End of Lebanon as We Know It," *The Monthly*, No. 62 (September 2007), pp. 8–9.

39. See the discussion on "triple parity" (*muthalatha*) in Antoine Messara, "Partage du Pouvoir: Le Cas de Liban," in Nadim Shehadi (ed.), *Lebanon: A History of Conflict and Consensus* (Oxford: CLS, 1987), p. 254.

40. Nevertheless Hizballah and the FPM have been accused by some in the ruling coalition of harboring such intentions. For example, Interior Minister Ahmad Fatfat, MP Hadi Hobaysh, and Amine Gemayel have associated the proposed 10–10-10 ministerial division between the president, March 14, and the opposition with a covert attempt to institutionalize sectarian tripartism. See *Al-Nahar*, January 21, 2008.

41. The major concern of the opposition is the disarmament of Hizballah, while March 14 fears a foiling of the international tribunal for the Hariri and subsequent political assassinations in Lebanon.

42. Opposition spokesmen Wiam Wahhab and Nasir Qandil have predicted the return of Syrian troops to "safeguard security." *Al-Nahar*, February 12, 2008. In response to the prospect of a Syrian intervention, Cardinal Sfeir has raised the possibility of a UN-appointed governor for Lebanon. See *al-Nahar*, February 9, 2008.

43. Jawad Adra, "Corruption: The Lebanese Syndrome: Maintaining the System, Depleting the Resources," *I-Monthly* (Beirut), October 25, 2005, p. 4.

44. Only 29% of Turkish, 23% of Jordanian, and 7% of Moroccan Muslims privilege their national- over communal identity. *Six Arab Nation Survey Report*, Zogby International, WEF, Davos, November 2005. A survey conducted by the Pew Research Center revealed that a whopping 81% of British, 69% of Spanish, 66% of German, and 46% of French Muslims consider themselves as Muslim first (rather than a citizen of their country). Forty-two percent of U.S. Christians and only 14% of French and Spanish Christians think of themselves as Christians (rather than citizens) first. See "Muslims and Europe: Survey Finds Positive Attitudes," *International Herald Tribune*, July 7, 2006, p. 4.

45. Despite the looming danger of sectarian animosities, polling also shows that most Lebanese are aware that politicians use religious rhetoric to camouflage their selfish ends. See the survey conducted by Abdo Sa'ad published in *Al-Akhbar* (Beirut), August 20, 2007, which shows that 72% of Lebanese consider the countries' politicians to be utilizing religion for their own interests.

46. Even prior to independent Lebanese initiatives to create a secular sect, the first attempt to recognize a "secular community" (*une communauté de droit commun*) stretches back to the French Mandate, namely *Arrêté no. 60* of 1936,

which was brought to fall by the fierce opposition of the *ulama* of Damascus, Beirut, and Tripoli.

47. It is the hidden third that would have had a major impact had the media been independent within an environment conducive to change. It is the hidden third that has never surrendered to foreign forces or to religious leaders even when facing the hardest challenges.... Neglected by both the government and the opposition, this hidden third, once discovered, would be recognized as the guardian and the cornerstone of this country. (Editorial by Jawad Adra, *Informational International Monthly*, No. 59 [May–June 2007], p. 2.

6

LEBANON'S CULTURE: POPULAR MUSIC AS A CASE STUDY

Charles Paul Freund

At the height of Lebanon's Cedar Revolution in 2005, when Beirut's streets were packed with demonstrators protesting the murder of Rafiq Hariri and demanding an end to three decades of Syrian occupation, a striking music video hovered near the top of the region's pop music charts: Issa Ghandour's *Min Safer*. Ghandour's song was a moody evocation of the meaning of place and of the spiritual costs of exile from that place. According to the lyrics the singer, in losing forever his country, had been exiled as well from his soul.

Neither Ghandour's lyrics nor the video's images made specific reference to Lebanon, but no one who saw the video was likely to miss the obvious connection, and not only because Ghandour sang in the unmistakable Lebanese accent. The video—artfully directed by Leila Kanaan—evoked in miniature Lebanon's violent recent history and presented Ghandour (portrayed as an exile longing to return) with the untrusting wariness of those who stayed behind and with the taunting ghosts of his unlived, might-have-been Lebanese life.

Ghandour's personal tragedy of exile, suggested the video, was also Lebanon's national tragedy of loss. In the sense that Lebanon's anti-Syrian demonstrators wanted their country not only to resume its full independence but also to resume its interrupted history, the Ghandour video drew on the same cultural sources as did Lebanon's independence movement. They were both manifestations of a national exceptionalism that has been called "Lebanonism."

"Lebanonism" is a term that has been used by different people to mean quite different things. To such thinkers as the American academic Benjamin Barber, it describes an ongoing state of tribal friction. To some economists, it describes the economic policies that once allowed Lebanon to achieve impressive prosperity in a limited time and which resulted in the mid-century "boom." To some pan-Arabists, it has described an objectionable formula for Christian domination. However, to certain Lebanese, the word describes an embrace of social pluralism and of difference from Lebanon's neighboring cultures.

Thus, when demonstrations broke out in the immediate wake of the Hariri assassination, some observers claimed that the phenomenon of Christians, Druze, Sunnis, and others linking arms in the streets was a manifestation of a "new Arab nationalism." Not so, wrote Lebanese analyst Tony Badran. "This is *not* an Arab nationalist revolution. This is a 'Lebanonist' revolution! This is about the coming together of the Lebanese (Druze, Maronite, Sunni, Shiite, etc.) for Lebanon and the idea of Lebanon as a plural society."[1]

In recent years, pop music videos have become a prime medium—perhaps *the* prime medium—for the cultural expression of this modernist "Lebanonism." Although numerous Lebanese videos have become notorious in the Middle East and beyond for their pictorial sensualism, many others address a far-ranging mix of modernist issues (including eroticism) within a Lebanese context.

Exile and separation are among them. Lebanon has been an emigrant culture for generations, and as a result many of its cultural artifacts reflect the widespread wounds of familial separation. Ghandour's video reflects one aspect of that emigrant vein. So did Fadl Shaker's 2003 production, *Ya Ghayab*, a song addressed longingly to one who is far away. Shaker's popular video consisted of a straightforward recording of him singing before a live club audience. What makes the video visually noteworthy is the crowd: an apparent mix of Christians and some Muslims who clearly know the song well and who seemingly share an identification with the transcending national experience of separation. It is a Lebanonist crowd.

Shaker's 2003 video expressing longing for the absent emigrant and Ghandour's 2005 video expressing the frustration of the exile who can never fully return are of course only two aspects of this complex and continuing Lebanese story. Jad Nakhle's 2008 video, *Libnan al-Helou*, completes a video triptych, so to speak: Nakhle is, in this production, a Lebanese who is considering abandoning Lebanon.

Nakhle's video was released in the wake of Lebanon's extended presidential crisis, which finally ended with the Shi'a Islamist militia Hizballah turning its weapons on its fellow Lebanese and later gaining veto power in the government—an arrangement that undercut the hopes of the 2005 independence movement. *Libnan al-Helou* seems to express that embitterment. "Oh mother," Nakhle apostrophizes over footage of war, invasion, and fleeing crowds that had gathered at Beirut's port, "you've told me about the good times, but all I've known is war." Should I stay, he asks, or should I too leave?

Nakhle's evocation of the lost "good times" would resonate with many Lebanese; their memories of the prosperity and relative liberalism of the period prior to the country's extended civil war is deeply ingrained in the consciousness of those groups who benefited from that era's social and economic liberalism. Indeed, the end of that period represents precisely that interruption of Lebanese history that helped shape the pro-independence movement and the cultural artifacts (such as Ghandour's *Min Safer*) that reflect it.

Lebanon, Fouad Ajami wrote in the *Wall Street Journal*, "was where Arab modernism made a stand." Perhaps contemporary Lebanonism can best be understood as a self-conscious embrace of that fact. That modernism continues to assert itself in the face of its challenges, especially in cultural terms.

In 2002, for example, one of the more interesting videos watched by Arab audiences featured an attractive brunette who, according to the video's tale, was involved in a liaison taking place in a Paris hotel room. The visual narrative offered the woman's often disconnected impressions of this apparently illicit relationship: Sometimes a man with a calculating smile was in the room with her; sometimes she was there alone, as if waiting for him. Naturally, the video is drenched in images of desire, especially the woman's erotic perceptions of the liaison and of herself.

In one imagined sequence she was not wearing much more than a revealing bustier; in another she was lying suggestively prone, apparently thinking about the mysterious smiling man. Several times the camera invited the viewer to assume the role of the man, with the woman gazing at the viewer with all the erotic intensity she could muster. As is usual in music videos, many shots feature the same woman in the role of singer—appearing onstage and performing the song we are hearing.

Eroticism that seems as if it has emerged from the pages of a Victoria's Secret catalog, as was the case with this video, is not usually noteworthy. Indeed, the video's assumption that there was something "forbidden" about its subject matter, something that had to be approached in an "artistic" fashion, may have seemed outdated to international viewers. However, in this case it is exactly such elements that made the production compelling. Had the video been American or European or Japanese, it would not have attracted much interest. Yet the point was that it was an Arab artifact. The woman was a singer named Elissa; her song, which helped make her a leading celebrity in the Middle East, was entitled *Aychaylak*, and both her song and her video were among the year's biggest music hits in the Arabic-speaking world.

Elissa's video helped establish a new boundary of what was visually permissible in contemporary Arab media; she herself said that some of its sequences embarrassed her, though as the video was embraced by an enthusiastic audience she also took credit for what she calls her "daring."

While Elissa's imagery may have been especially bold, the suggestiveness of her video was typical of what was then happening in the Middle Eastern music scene. More and more Arab women singers presented themselves in such provocative terms, as figures who expressed and even asserted themselves erotically through fashion, movement, expression, and voice. Nawal Zoghbi, one of the region's biggest stars (she has been Pepsi's spokeswoman there), appeared at the about the same time in a hip-shaking video dressed in a tight and, by Middle Eastern standards, revealing leather outfit. She was backed up by a trio of black women singers in leather who were even more provocative.

Shortly afterward came a notorious video featuring singer Hayfa Wahbi, whom nobody in the region took seriously as a singer at all. (She claimed only to be an "entertainer.") The whole point of Wehbe's video was to show her dancing in a rain-soaked outfit (much like the "wet sari" sequences of popular Bollywood movies) while staring into the camera with her sultriest expression. The most popular of the stars to emerge from this period was Nancy Ajram, who debuted as a dancer whose provocative moves inspire a café brawl.

These singers are all Lebanese, but the model they established soon included women performers from other counties as well—most notably the controversial Egyptian singer Ruby. For that matter, the world of Arab videos is in many ways a pan-Arab project. The recording label for many of the leading Lebanese acts, Rotana, is based in Dubai—the Gulf state with the region's most open economy. Rotana's acts can be seen throughout the Arab world but are showcased via such channels as ART-TV, which is a multi-format Arabic-language satellite service established by Saudi investors, based in Jordan, and with studios in Cairo, Beirut, and elsewhere in the region. Most of the video production houses, however, are in Lebanon, and they have established a highly polished "look" that has quickly become recognizable. The videos' credits (often in English) reflect diverse crews of Muslim and Christian Arabs, along with a smattering of Turkish names. The most notable director of these videos is Said al-Marouk, a filmmaker based in Germany whose work stands out because of its scale, spectacle, and excess. (He is the Ken Russell of the genre.)

In short, there has been a revolution going on in popular Arabic music videos (known in the Middle East as "clips")—one that is substantially led and shaped by Lebanese sensibilities, and the obvious question it invites is whether an upheaval has been taking place as well among the videos' consumers. Although dramatic social and cultural changes are particularly visible in songs and videos by women, they involve the songs and performances of Arab men too. Sex may have become the most immediately striking aspect of these productions, but it is the least important dimension of their revolutionary potential.

Certainly, the videos' critics have focused on the eroticism. Not only do such critics make the obvious charge that the videos are merely exploitive (a charge that in some cases is entirely justified), but some critics go much father. To them, the contemporary videos are socially destructive; a popular singer in a swimsuit, they argue, is no more desirable a model for the region than is a woman suicide bomber strapped in an explosives' vest. Lebanese libertinism, they suggest, is as dangerous in its own way as is Saudi fundamentalism.

Of course, eroticism—even blatant eroticism—is not new in contemporary Arab culture. As students of the Arab world's popular entertainment have noted, Egypt generated erotic images of female singers and actresses much earlier in the twentieth century. Eroticism is currently a well-known element of the region's feminist fiction, used by such authors as Lebanon's Hanan al-Shaykh and Egypt's pioneer feminist author, Nawal Sawadi. Nevertheless, avant-garde fiction like theirs tends to remain within a limited, sympathetic subculture. Arabic pop videos, on the other hand, are pro-duced for pleasure (not to speak of profit) and consumed by an immense audience that can turn such works into social and political artifacts on a grand scale.

Indeed, it is the social and political implications of these videos, rather than the eroticism per se, that make them interesting. What these videos offer their audience is not merely an outlet for repressed desire but an imag-ined world in which Arabs can shape and assert their identities in any way they please. The question is whether the videos are a leading cultural indi-cator of social and political change that enables Arabs to do the same in the real world.

The imagined Arabs in these often handsomely mounted productions stretch from the plausible to the fantastic: not only Arab femmes fatales in designer lingerie but cool Arab race car drivers, Arab cowboys, and Arab motorcyclists decked out in Harley-Davidson paraphernalia. There are Arab football players; Arab lovers driving pickup trucks through the American desert; Arab heroes of Gothic vampire melodramas being stalked by beau-tiful ghouls; veiled Arab women of the Islamic golden age; Arab couples searching for each other in a chromed, retro 1950s universe; Arabs haunted by mysterious desert symbols that hold the key to forgotten identities; medi-eval Arab countesses in their Spanish castles; and even science-fiction Arabs confronted by mustachioed alien children from outer space.

Some of these subgenres, such as the Gothic and science fiction, have until now made little headway in Arabic popular culture; so the videos may even be stretching pop cultural boundaries. Their greater potential value, however, lies in their power to stretch the boundaries of their viewers' imag-ined selves.

Thus, while these videos are entertaining and titillating viewers, they are also transmitting new ways of being to an apparently receptive audience, new and multiplying approaches to being an "Arab" that combine traditional forms of cultural self-presentation with forms borrowed from an array of other sources. The combinations that promise to emerge would not be mere copies of borrowed foreign models; they would be new and indigenous cul-tural creations, just as is the case in cultures around the world. This syncre-tism is already true of the music itself, which not only uses traditional Arabic instrumentation (such as the nye, oud, qanun, and the like) in new ways but also borrows instruments and rhythms from the Caribbean, Europe, India, rock, rap (including rap in Spanish), and numerous other sources.

What this low, "vulgar" genre is offering, in sum, is a glimpse of a latent Arab world that is both liberal and "modernized." Why? Because the foun-dation of cultural modernity is the freedom to achieve a self-fashioned and fluid identity, the freedom to imagine yourself on your own terms, and the videos offer a route to that process. By contrast, much of Arab culture remains a place of constricted, traditional, and narrowly defined identities, often subsumed in group identities that hinge on differences with, and antagonism toward, other groups.

For nearly a century, a series of utopian political systems has been advanced in the region to attempt to break this cycle of conflict and stagnation: pan-Arabism, Ba'thism, Nasserism, Islamism, and so forth. These have all failed, sometimes disastrously. What may yet work in the region is what has worked elsewhere for centuries: commercialism that does not transmit a regime's utopian dreams but addresses the personal dreams of the audience.

If the audience for these videos uses them to foment a long-term cultural revolution, it would hardly be the first time that "vulgar" forms were at the center of significant social change. In fact, "low" culture has almost certainly done more to transform the modern world than has "high" culture. That is because, as communications professor Joli Jensen argues in the recent *Is Art Good For Us?*, people often use the low, "expressive" forms of art to engage with and understand the world around them, and not only the high, "instrumental" cultural forms that are collected in museums because they are supposed to be good for a public that needs uplifting.[2]

Cultural history is replete with examples of this process, despite critics' traditional focus on aesthetic achievement. The most popular literature in France in the years leading up to the revolution was not necessarily by the likes of Jean-Jacques Rousseau but involved erotic dialogues and utopian fantasy that have been almost entirely forgotten. The most influential Russian novel, arguably, was written not by Tolstoy or Turgenev but by the forgotten journalist Nikolai Chernyshevsky. His wooden nineteenth-century tale *What Is to Be Done?* was one of a series of popular novels at the center of an intense late-czarist cultural controversy (it, too, was colored by eroticism) that accompanied liberalization and was instrumental in setting the stage for the Leninist enterprise that was to follow. Tolstoy's own most influential work was not *War and Peace* but a populist spiritual work entitled *The Kingdom of God Is Within You*. Its lesson of returning good for evil was to inspire Gandhi and, eventually, Martin Luther King, Jr.

The most effective literary expressions of eighteenth-century British feminism were not the period's eloquent tracts but the "cheap" Gothic novels that dramatized virtue in distress. The modern American character was shaped far less by celebrated transcendentalist and realist works than by such yarns as Owen Wister's *The Virginian*, which offered a powerful model of quiet masculine strength. Furthermore, mid-century Eastern Europeans living under Communism who sought cultural expressions of personal liberty found them in jazz, jeans, rock music, and Hollywood.

A scholar named Samia Mehrez at the American University in Cairo discovered something quite interesting about the direction of the Arab novel. Reading through the major works of the 1990s from Egypt's younger novelists—and Cairo remains the center of the Arab literary world—Mehrez realized that, in literary terms, the Arab family was not what it used to be. That is, it was playing a much smaller role in these works than had been the case in earlier such works. The family, as she put it in an article for the *Arab Studies Journal*, was receding from the Arab imagination.[3]

This is no small matter. Arab storytelling about the contemporary world has revolved around the family. No matter what kind of story one was telling, or what kind of characters one was presenting, no matter whether one was addressing a readership that included elite elements, as in the case of the Nobel Prize–winning writer Naguib Mahfouz, or a more popular readership, the narrative frequently turned on the impact that events have on a family.

Many stories were essentially family sagas to begin with, but even genre stories—crime or cop stories, romantic stories, even the relatively rare work of horror—tended to turn into family stories. This is all quite natural; Arab society has been very tight-knit, very much centered around the family. That the stories most interesting to an Arab audience would focus on families is not surprising. It remains true of stories in many popular media, especially movies and the region's month-long television serial melodramas.

However, in the 1990s, it seems, it stopped being true in literary fiction. What, then, were such novels about, if they were not about families? They were about characters who were presented as being separate from the groups they belonged to, "cut loose," as Samia Mehrez puts it, "from conventional icons of family and nation."[4] In short, they were about individuals. More than that, they were in many cases about the struggle of these characters to *become* individuals.

These new Arab authors were pessimistic about the kind of emotional and psychological effort involved. Indeed, they appear to have concluded that the effort was futile. Purportedly speaking on behalf of a generation of Arabs that had been supposedly disempowered both personally and collectively, the major theme that was running through these works was, to quote from Mehrez's essay, "the impossibility of becoming what you want."

A depressing picture: disempowerment, isolation, futility, frustration. Yet had Mehrez put aside her avant-garde reading on any given evening and turned on her television instead, she would have seen a very different Arab world.

She would have seen a world that celebrates Arab individuality, provides an ever-increasing number of models for Arab identity, subverts state power, challenges restrictive social and moral norms, portrays socially marginalized groups in sympathetic terms, seeks solutions to societal problems, portrays women in roles of power, and ultimately increases social tolerance. She would have seen a world, in other words, that reflects an increasing degree of dynamism and innovation. That is the world reflected in popular Arab culture.

Almost all of these attributes can be found in the remarkable world of the Arab music video, particularly its Lebanese version, which also took shape in the 1990s. That is, at the very same time that the pessimistic elite Arab novel was beginning to appear, an alternative arose as well—one that offered a very different version of the Arab imagination. Thus there is a case in which two centers of culture recognize what appears to be a vitally important shift in Arab identity and react to it. One of them becomes depressed at the prospect of greater Arab individuality, which it sees in terms of isolation and futility. The other celebrates that individuality and in fact is providing the tools for intensifying individuation because that is how the consumers of pop artifacts everywhere else in the world use these artifacts.

The fact is that the region's pop culture continues to be the source of much contention among Arabs. The Egyptian singer Ruby, for example, has been sued by the same Islamist lawyer, Nabih al-Wahsh, who had earlier sued to end the marriage of the Arab world's leading feminist, Nawal Sadawi, on the grounds of her alleged blasphemy. He failed in that effort, and he attempted to end Ruby's career on the grounds that she is a threat to the moral order. When Lebanon's Nancy Ajram staged a concert in Kuwait in 2003, her fans were attacked by rock-throwing Kuwaitis who did not approve of the music.

Of course, it is not only Islamists who are unhappy with suggestive videos. The region's secular talk shows have also been debating whether to censor Ruby's unabashedly suggestive music videos, or those of Tunisia's Najla, or Lebanon's Elissa. It is probably not surprising that there are many voices in the region objecting to the explosion of public eroticism. However, it may be surprising how many voices have been raised in defense of these controversial performers on a variety of grounds. These include arguments that erotic material does no lasting harm and that far more erotic material is in any event now available on the Internet.

A serial melodrama presented throughout the Middle East during one recent Ramadan suggested that Arab culture might have something to learn from America's approach to domestic problem solving. Titled "Aunt Noor," the series centered on an Arab-American emigrant who returns for a visit home, encounters a family in disarray, and applies the directness and therapeutic techniques she has learned in the United States to resolve her family's dysfunctions. (Arab culture can be quite circumspect.) The family lived happily after but not the audience. It too was the subject of heated debate, as Arabist critics objected to what they perceived as a yet another cultural humiliation.

A series scheduled to be shown in 2008, during Ramadan, was pulled after only a few episodes. *The Road to Kabul*, as it was called, was about an Arab woman who marries an Afghan man and who ends up living through the brutal Taliban regime. There had been some anticipation in the region that the series would spark a popular debate about the role of women under Koranic law. It never happened. A threat to the lives of everyone involved in the series, including its cast and crew, was posted on an Islamist Internet site, and the Qatar-based producers of the series suddenly discovered fatal technical flaws in the series and canceled the airing.

Years ago, political satire was rare in the Arab world; a well-known rule that governed the relation between culture and politics was that nothing should be allowed to distract from major pan-Arabist aims, especially the confrontation with Israel. In the 1960s, a Syrian comedian named Durayd Laham—sort of a cross between Woody Allen and Groucho Marx—was famous for what were then considered to be daring comedy films, which were understood to be poking indirect fun at the Syrian regime. However, he would deal with such subjects as substandard housing and other daily-life frustrations for which the regime might be responsible, not with politics directly.

Today, the corruption, hypocrisy, and even legitimacy of the Arab political leadership are regularly under attack in a variety of television comedy
programs. Examples include a franchise of *Saturday Night Live*, broadcast
weekly on the Emirates-based MBC. (It is called *CBM*, which is merely MBC
backward.) The show, staged in Lebanon, mixes music and satire in a familiar
manner and frequently does so at the expense of the region's political players.
A second source of subversion is a Syrian genius named Yasir al-Azmeh, who
in his occasional television series has skewered the Ba'th party, the complicity
of the Syrian populace in their own political frustrations, the region's hypo-
critical exploitation of the Palestinian issue, the often insincere anti-American
posturing in the Middle East, and a great deal more.

Cultural conflict is a daily enterprise in the region. Movie posters are torn
down because people do not like the images on them. Controversial television formats are introduced to *Big Brother*, the European television enterprise that sets up a house filled with people and trains cameras on them week
after week, and attempts were made to do a version of this format in Bahrain.
Despite making adjustments for the culture—the men and women inhabitants did not have to sleep under the same roof—the attempt sparked widespread outrage, and the show was soon canceled.

These are only a few instances of what is a sustained conflict between Arab
commercial pop culture and various portions of Arab societies. The new pop
culture is obviously appealing to huge segments of these societies; they are
supporting it with their money, time, attention, and energy. It is also obviously discomfiting a lot of other people. Some of the people critical of the
popular culture are reasonable people steeped in traditions that are important
to them and who are unhappy to see these familiar patterns and norms threatened. Others, however, are the region's ideologues and authoritarians, specifically the entrenched remnants of Arabism and the rising Islamists.

The war between ideologues and popular culture is an old story and a very
interesting one. Some of the arguments taking place in the region about
music echo the debates over jazz, movies, and rock music that took place
under Communism and fascism.

For example, the first music video to emerge from post-Ba'thist Iraq was
a very sexy presentation called "Bortugala." It featured some attractive
women dancing in an eye-catching fashion. The reaction at al-Jazeera's website was striking; the video was called an example of "U.S. occupation culture," which was degrading to Iraqis and Arabs alike. There is a sense that a
lot of Arabs quite liked it, but what was notable about the Arabist criticism is
that it sounded like the sort of thing that Communists used to say about
jazz, or later rock music; that is, they were decadent and degrading forms.

Authoritarian systems have managed to control both traditional folk culture and even high culture either by harnessing them to their own purposes
or destroying the types of high culture they have not liked. Yet no authoritarian system has ever been able to deal effectively with pop culture. Not the
fascists, not the Communists (who tried to create socialist dance music and
indeed a whole alternative socialist "pop" establishment), not even the

Taliban, which banned everything associated with pop culture, including its content and its technology and still ended up with a fad for Leonardo diCaprio haircuts in Kabul.

These videos are fun, they are titillating, and they are pretty good examples of the cultural syncretism that Tyler Cowen discusses in his book, *Creative Destruction*.[5] That is, they involve cultures borrowing elements from one another in a process that results not in the destruction of either culture, but in new forms emerging in both. There are a lot of foreign influences apparent in these videos, but they remain unmistakably Arab.

Numerous videos present women in roles of power and play around in other ways with gender types. At least three of Nancy Ajram's videos feature male characters who are probably intended to be understood as gay. They are treated in either neutral terms or positively. Several videos confront the nature of Arab identity directly, especially in encounters with non-Arab "others."

Yet it is the issue of individuals versus groups that is really central here. Lebanon is the Arabic-speaking country most affected by these changes, but cultures that have been transformed by individualist, consumerist self-fashioning all share important things in common. Most of the members of these cultures are far less tied to the groups they were born into than are traditional cultures. As a result, they tend to be far more willing to tolerate each other than is the case in many traditional societies. Those who like this phenomenon call it liberationist. Those who do not call it social atomization, a charge that has been made for two centuries.

Gilles Lipovetsky is ambivalent about this process.[6] He is a Swiss academic who studies ephemeral culture. He is not sure he likes all the results, but he is sure he likes some of them. His formulation is that the less we care about each other, the more likely we are to put up with each other and cooperate. Lebanon may not have reached that stage in its politics or society, but its popular culture products have certainly raised these issues.

NOTES

1. Tony Badran, "The Wrong Nationalism," February 20, 2005, Across the Bay, http://beirut2bayside.blogspot.com/2005/02/wrong-nationalism.html.
2. Joli Jensen, *Is Art Good for U.S.?* (Lanham, MD: Rowman & Littlefield Publishers, Inc., 2002).
3. Samia Mehrez, "Where Have All the Families Gone? Egyptian Literary Texts of the 1990s," *Arab Studies Journal*, Vol. IX, No. 2/Vol. X, No. 1 (Fall 2001/Spring 2002), pp. 31–50.
4. Ibid., p. 47.
5. Tyler Cowen, *Creative Destruction: How Globalization Is Changing the World's Cultures* (Princeton: Princeton University Press, 2002).
6. Gilles Lipovetsky, *The Empire of Fashion: Dressing Modern Democracy* (Princeton: Princeton University Press, 1994).

7

LEBANESE ECONOMY BETWEEN VIOLENCE AND POLITICAL STALEMATE

Nimrod Raphaeli

Lebanon is a small country, unique in its economic framework and singularly complex in its political and cultural composition. It has a genuine laissez-faire commercial economy, but its economy is forced to embrace not only free enterprise but a large measure of political feudalism and sectarianism as well. The country is small in area—4,000 square miles—and poor in natural resources, yet it has a world-class international banking system that has remained stable and resilient through conflicts of differing degrees of severity. Geography has also been generous to Lebanon, providing it with scenery and natural beauty that give it the potential to be one of the largest tourist attractions in the Middle East.

In referring to Lebanon as the "Merchant Republic," Carolyn Gates underscores the economy's "outward orientation," which was not the result of "a theoretical construct" devised by policy-makers and intellectuals but rather a result of evolution and its capacity to respond and adjust to both internal and external challenges and shocks.[1] Lebanon's economic evolution was prompted, after World War II, by the efforts of "Christians and Beirut merchants, bankers and economists"—which Gates characterizes as "the New Phoenicians," dedicated to promoting laissez-faire in Lebanon. The group was looking at the pre-Arab and pre-Muslim commercial city-state of ancient Phoenicia as "the model for Lebanon's independent future."[2] It was looking to the United States for capitalist ideas and encouragement. In short, they were to establish "a minimalist state with few interventionist powers."[3]

Yet there is also another side of Lebanon. According to Lebanese sociologist Samir Khalaf: "Lebanon, from all observable indicators, embodies the phenomenon of schism in the political and cultural realms.... It is a society without foundation, fragile, divided, disjointed and torn." Dr. Khalaf goes on to say that Lebanon is "a home so divided by ethnic, religious and sectarian conflicts that it is almost impossible to put its parts back together anew."[4] The Lebanese political analyst Nasri al-Sayigh adds: "No one can predict the return anytime soon of the military violence to Lebanon." Sayigh points out, however, that "the Lebanese live under the weight of permanent violence arising from standing in sectarian and political formations and media violence. These phenomena provide ammunition for a future battle which would be postponed pending the calculations of politicians about the gains and losses from unleashing the latent violence."[5] The London daily *al-Hayat*, formerly the leading Lebanese newspaper, opined that Lebanon was burdened by "a confrontational atmosphere." As a result, the country is unable to rise above the political and sectarian conflicts that will be a drag on its economy.[6] In the words of a Lebanese economist: "We have good weather, beautiful mountains, a multilingual population and a free economy. But what is missing are wise politicians."[7]

DEMOGRAPHIC CHANGES: A NEW POLITICAL FORMULA

Ever since it attained independence from the French in 1943, Lebanon's political system has been based on the National Charter (*al-mithaq al-watani*)—an unwritten but enforced pact that recognizes the division of the country into religious communities. As determined by this charter, the president of the republic is a Maronite Christian, the prime minister is Sunni Muslim, and the speaker of parliament is a Shi'a Muslim.

The charter's distribution of power among the various religious communities reflects the fact that in the 1940s, Christians (Maronites, Greek Orthodox, Roman Catholics, Armenians, and others) represented 60 percent of the population and the various Muslim communities (primarily Sunni, Shi'a, Druze, and others) occupied the remaining 40 percent. By 2006, after waves of emigration caused by civil war and rising Arab nationalism, the size of the Christian community was reduced to 30 percent of the total Lebanese population of 3.75 million and is likely to be reduced further to 27 percent by 2011. Apart from emigration, fertility favors the Shi'a of Lebanon in particular and the Muslims in general.

The resident Lebanese population is young, with approximately 37.4 percent under 20 years of age, but 69 percent of the Shi'a and 51 percent of the Maronites are in this group.[8] The labor force, estimated at 1.2 million, is roughly 50 percent of the working-age population (15–64 years). The International Labor Organization (ILO) interprets the population structure to mean that while two-thirds of the resident Lebanese population is of working age, only one-third is actually working, which is low when compared with OECD countries. This continuing trend is primarily due to the weak participation of women in the labor force (although there may be a certain degree of undeclared participation of women in agriculture and other informal sectors' activities). From 1997 to 2004, female participation in the labor force increased by less than one percentage point (from 21.7 percent to 22.33 percent).

The employment-to-population ratio improved to 35.7 percent in 2004, as compared to 31.1 percent in 1997. This ratio is still relatively weak, compared to an average ratio of 47.8 percent for the Middle East, and an average ratio ranging from 45 percent to 60 percent in developed countries, implying, according to the ILO, a particularly high rate of economic dependency in Lebanon. Of course, one must recognize the possibility that many Lebanese are engaged in the informal sector, such as trading activities, which cannot be easily traced if—to avoid paying taxes—people choose not to report them. In fact, by ILO's own assessment, micro-, small-, and medium-sized enterprises have historically been among the most important sources of employment and income in Lebanon and are expected to continue to be central to the provision of livelihoods and sustainable employment opportunities for the various population segments most in need of support. Micro- and small-sized enterprises do not normally keep good records of employment, and it is not uncommon for members of a family to work on a micro-project on a part-time basis; they are often not included in employment surveys or employment data.

Of course, it is a political reality that no government in Lebanon will carry out, for example, a household survey. Prior to the July 2006 war, the ILO agreed to help the Central Administration of Statistics (CAS) design a regular labor market survey to be tentatively launched in 2007, but such a survey was never carried out. The head of the Lebanese Center for Policy Studies, Oussama Safa, expressed doubts that any government agency will ever conduct a labor market survey based on new data collected from households across the country. In the words of a former minister of labor: "We can't do any statistics on Lebanon, because any statistics you do will show the sectarian makeup of the country and how the salary is divided among the sects."[9]

Not surprisingly, the head of the executive council of Hizballah, Hashem Safi al-Din declared: "We in Lebanon are facing three choices: partnership, political system on hold, or partition." By partnership, Hizballah means that the selection of a president, while Maronite, must be acceptable to it and, by extension, to Syria. In economic terms, the political stalemate has had three adverse consequences: First, a large decline of investment due to heightened risk spread; second, the inability of the government to promote legislation in parliament on such key issues as privatization because the speaker of parliament, Nabih Barri, a pro-Syrian Shi'a politician, had for many months put parliament on hold pending the election in May 2008 of a so-called consensus president—meaning a president acceptable to Hizballah and his Syrian sponsors; and third, large-scale emigration of Lebanese endowed with relatively high levels of human capital. This time the loss is particularly significant because many of the emigrants come from the tourism and banking sectors where they find expanding opportunities in the Gulf oil countries. It would also mean that revival, particularly in the tourism sector if things were to go back to normal, would be extremely difficult.[10]

KEY CHARACTERISTICS OF THE LEBANESE ECONOMY

The Lebanese economy is based primarily on the service sector. Between 1994 and 2004, the contribution of the sector increased from 61 to

72 percent of GDP. Major subsectors are commerce, tourism, and financial services. The industry and manufacturing sector accounts for 21 percent of GDP. The majority of industrial enterprises are of small- and medium size, with the food industry as the largest component (forming 23 percent of the industrial enterprises and almost 26 percent of the total industrial output according to a 1998 industrial survey). Agriculture plays only a minor role in the economy. In 2004, it contributed less than 7 percent of GDP (12 percent in 1994).[11] The proportion of the total national product that arises from goods-producing sectors, namely agriculture, industry, and construction, does not, as a rule, exceed 35 percent.[12] Table 7.1 provides a useful summary of Lebanon's economic and social indicators.

The weight of the various economic sectors is correspondingly reflected in the distribution of the labor force. According to a survey by the ILO, the majority of workers in Lebanon is employed in services (37.4 percent) and trade (22.1 percent). Industry accounts for a further 15 percent of employment, 8.7 percent in construction, and 7.6 percent in agriculture.[13]

THE CIVIL WAR AND ITS AFTERMATH

Prior to the outbreak of the civil war of 1975–1990 Lebanon was a democratic upper middle-income country prospering as a regional service center on the crossroads between Europe and the Middle East. According to a document submitted by the Lebanese government to a conference of donors in Paris in January 2007 (known as Paris III), Lebanon barely had any debt. It enjoyed prudent economic management and an economy driven mainly by a dynamic private sector and supported by a small public sector. It enjoyed low inflation, high rates of economic growth, large balance of payments surpluses, small fiscal deficits, and a floating, stable, and fully convertible domestic currency pegged to the U.S. dollar. By May 2008 dollarization covered 77.5 percent of economic activities.[14]

A combination of a stable macroeconomic environment, liberal economics, and its role as a regional intermediary gave Lebanon a strong comparative advantage in the services sector of its economy, particularly in banking and finance, tourism, insurance, and trade-related services.[15] However, this blissful situation was quickly to turn upside down as a result of the civil war, which extracted a heavy toll in human and material terms. The economy suffered from the destruction of infrastructure and industrial facilities while the reluctance to invest resulted in the obsolescence of remaining production capacity. There was mass emigration, which repeated itself after the July 2006 war between Hizballah (Party of God) and Israel, with an unmitigated loss in professional and entrepreneurial skills. The emigration of workers was also accompanied by the flight of capital as investment opportunities became both limited and risky. The massive destruction of infrastructure was estimated by the United Nations to have cost Lebanon $25 billion, equivalent to about six to seven times the GDP in 1990.

Upon the ending of the civil war, the government undertook the rehabilitation and reconstruction of the public infrastructure, investing in what was termed "social peace," including the incorporation of the militias, and providing for resettlement and social assistance to the displaced. The civil war caused the erosion of the revenue base that forced the government to resort to market borrowing, often at high interest rates. By 2000 gross public debt spiked to $25 billion from $2 billion a decade earlier, equivalent to 150 percent of GDP, while the economy was stagnating.[16]

Against the background of a stagnating economy, the government of Prime Minister Rafiq al-Hariri, who came to office in late 2000, developed an economic reform program aimed at rapidly rehabilitating and enhancing the country's severely damaged infrastructure in preparation for private sector–led growth over the medium term. To assist in implementing its reconstruction program the government sought external support in the context of the Paris II meeting in 2002. The donor community responded by granting Lebanon $2.4 billion in direct fiscal support (non-project financing) on concessionary terms—a maturity of 15 years with an extended grace period and an interest rate of 5 percent.[17]

The aid package approved at the meeting of Paris II improved the structure of the public debt and sharply reduced its cost. As a result, interest payments on the debt fell sharply from 17 percent of GDP in 2002 to about 10 percent of GDP in 2005. Macroeconomic performance was equally commendable as real growth registered more than 7 percent, and the overall budget deficit declined to less than 8 percent of GDP (from 25 percent in 2000). The introduction of the value-added tax (VAT) in 2002 made a contribution to the fiscal sector although the VAT program has never been fully implemented.[18]

THE DERAILMENT OF THE ECONOMY: THE SYRIAN FACTOR

In late 2004 Lebanon entered into a political spiral as a result of a Syrian demand that the single six-year term constitutional limit of President Emile Lahoud, a "Syrian puppet,"[19] be extended by two years through the end of November 2007, sanctioned by a hasty constitutional amendment. Under Syrian threats to his persona, Prime Minister al-Hariri succumbed to the Syrian pressure and supported the extension. Hariri, wealthy and well connected with the Saudi regime, sought to maintain his dignity and a modicum of independence, but he was summarily disposed of on February 14, 2005, assassinated by a massive car bomb while he was on his way from a meeting in parliament to the government building.[20]

The assassination of Hariri spurred massive protests in Beirut and international pressure that led to the expulsion from Lebanon of the Syrian army, which had earned money for the regime in Syria by controlling the drug trade in Lebanon and engaging in massive smuggling. In December 2006, the Lebanese government approved an agreement with the UN Security Council to create a special tribunal of international character, which would be responsible for trying those who might be indicted as a result of the investigation of the assassination of Hariri. Syrian proxies in Lebanon— including President Emile Lahoud while he was still in office through November 2007, parliament speaker Nabih Barri, and the Shi'a ministers representing Hizballah in the cabinet—had refused to recognize the decision by the majority in government to welcome the international investigation of the assassination and had sought assiduously to delegitimize the entire government. In the meantime, the assassinations of anti-Syrian Lebanese politicians continued, one at a time, to prevent an anti-Syrian majority in parliament from electing a president not to Syria's taste. Syria has never resigned itself to accept Lebanon as an independent country and, apart from Israel, Lebanon is the only other country in the Middle East with which Syria has no formal diplomatic relations.

POST-HARIRI ECONOMIC REVIVAL

The resilient Lebanese economy showed signs of revival following the mid-2005 parliamentary elections and the formation of a new cabinet under Prime Minister Fuad Siniora, who served as minister of finance in the Hariri government. The Siniora government prepared a comprehensive reform program that was about to be adopted before another war was invited upon Lebanon by Hizballah, which is backed by the Shi'a community under Sayyid Hasan Nasrallah, with its militia trained, financed, and armed by Iran, operating through the client regime of Bashar al-Asad in Syria.[21] Acting as a proxy for Iran and Syria, Nasrallah provoked a war with Israel in the summer of 2006, after which the Hizballah movement tried using its own street revolt to topple the Siniora government. The Lebanese economy came under new shocks once more. The reform program prepared by the Siniora government was put on hold. One of the most immediate and serious outcomes of the suspension of the activities of parliament by its pro-Syrian speaker Barri was the inability of government to seek approval of the national budget or approval of reform-related legislation.

As a result of these events, the performance of the Lebanese economy has remained below potential despite having recovered from the shocks of 2005 and 2006. Output remains depressed, impacted by political turmoil that has adversely affected consumer and investor confidence, deterring tourists, encouraging the departure of skilled workers, and hindering the implementation of much needed structural reforms.

THE COST OF THE JULY WAR

The war's economic cost, both direct and indirect, was substantial. Lebanon's infrastructure, particularly in the southern region of the country, where Hizballah conducted its war with Israel, sustained heavy damage.[22] Thousands of houses were destroyed or damaged, bridges and roads were destroyed, and a promising tourism season suffered a major setback (see table 7.1).

Table 7.1   Lebanon: Conflict-Related Damages[23]

	Total Damages (U.S. $ Millions)
Transport	484
Electricity	244
Telecommunications	116
Water	80
Health and education	34
Housing and commercial spaces	2406
Industry	220
Military	16
Fuel distribution stations	12
Total	3612

While agriculture is a small sector in Lebanon, half the working population in south Lebanon relies wholly on agriculture for a living—with the sector providing nearly 70 percent of total household incomes. Some 50,000 families have been financially affected by the war.[24]

Table 7.1 does not include the damage to agriculture, forestry, and fishing, which the UN Food and Agriculture Organization (FAO) has estimated at $280 million. Moreover, with the loss of income from harvests and lost animal produce, many farmers have become heavily indebted, as it is during the May to October harvest period that they usually repay their debts to secure credit for the following production season. The start of the new cropping cycle has been disrupted due to the lack of working capital.[25]

The indirect cost of the war is even more significant, particularly on the fiscal sector. Real GDP growth, which achieved a respectable rate of 5–6 percent in the first half of 2006, ended the year on the negative side with a decline of 5 percent. According to a government report to the IMF, the decline in the GDP represented "a loss of output and income in 2006 in the order of $2.2 billion (at 2005 prices). The loss of output in the medium term (as compared to the levels that were envisaged) is a multiple of this amount."[26] Moreover, after four consecutive years—including the first half of 2006—of budget surplus, the year ended with budget deficit of 0.4 percent of GDP but the government projected it to grow to 14 percent in 2007.

Far more serious is the growth of the gross public debt, which totaled $39.8 billion at the end of June 2007—equivalent to 180 percent of estimated postwar 2006 GDP.[27] By the end of May 2008, the size of the gross public debt reached $43.2 billion, registering an increase of 2.74 percent over the level at the end of December 2007.[28]

To shore up the Lebanese currency and as a demonstration of support, Saudi Arabia and Kuwait deposited with Banque du Liban (BdL or Central Bank) $1 billion and $500 million, respectively. The Lebanese government has declared its commitment to honoring debt obligations—a courageous act, given the government's own estimate that by 2010 debt-to-GDP ratio would increase to about 21.5 percent.[29]

The balance of payment was another casualty of the war. Against a surplus of $2.562 billion in the first half of 2006 the balance of payment recorded a deficit of $207 million for the comparable period of 2007. Banque du Liban did not expect the balance of payment to be in a surplus mode for the remainder of 2007 due to shortfall in income from the tourism sector and the reluctance of investors to risk their money in what obviously was a highly volatile political situation. The month of June 2006 recorded the highest deficit ever in Lebanon's balance of payment.[30] In the first quarter of 2008 the balance of payment registered a deficit of $213.9 million.[31] For all of 2007, the balance of payment, contrary to earlier projections, registered a surplus of 2,036.6 million, which could be attributed to two factors: the Saudi and Kuwaiti deposits of $1.5 billion and the spike in the price of gold held by the Central Bank.[32]

Perhaps the most dramatic decline was in the activities of Beirut's stock exchange. During the first half of 2007 the number of shares traded was 22 million, compared with 106 million shares the year before, a decline of 80 percent, while the value of the share traded declined to $334 million from $1.575 million during the first half of 2006, a decline of 79 percent. During the same time frame, construction permits declined by 26.2 percent and real estate taxes declined by another 10.4 percent.[33]

Summarizing the economic situation in Lebanon in the three years 2005 through 2007 Riyadh Salameh, the governor of the Central Bank, said in a newspaper interview that the economic situation "paid the cost of the political crisis." For example, the accumulated economic growth in the last three years combined did not exceed 5 percent while the country should have grown by 20 percent, which would have raised the GDP to $30 billion instead of the current level of $24 billion. This situation "has caused the contraction of the Lebanese wealth as well as the prices of shares on the stock market." These circumstances have meant the absence of work opportunities which caused a massive emigration among Lebanese youth. While the commitments under Paris III remained solid, actual disbursements of funds have been lagging because the government was not in a position to carry out the reforms that Paris III was meant to finance. The only positive development was the increase in the remittances by Lebanese (see table 7.2), which support the balance of payment.[34]

The seemingly endless debate over the presidency and the government, coupled with sporadic assassinations, has left deep marks on the already fragile economy. In 2007 Lebanon, which saw impressive growth in 2004 and 2005, failed to take advantage of the oil boom in the region as Gulf investors sought other suitable places to put their money.

THE IMPACT OF THE WAR ON TOURISM

The tourism and hospitality industry in Lebanon, which normally accounts for 10–12 percent of GDP, had been expected by the Ministry of Tourism to witness a remarkable year in 2006 with an anticipated 1.6 million tourists.[35]

The Ministry of Tourism estimated that direct and indirect losses to the tourism industry amounted to $2 billion from hotels, furnished apartments, restaurants, rental car businesses, and travel agencies. Direct losses were experienced in the war-affected areas, namely in the south, the Biqa, Akkad, and the Beirut suburbs and the airport.

Heavy indirect losses had affected the entire tourism industry. While large hotels and resorts in Beirut and other cities were not directly hit, the war had led many businesses to revert to dismissing their employees due to cancellation of reservations, weddings, and events they prepared for in light of high expectations for the summer of 2006. The situation appreciably worsened in 2007 as the political stalemate in Lebanon with the potential risk of another internal strife continued to deter tourists from visiting Lebanon.

It was reported, for example, that political and security uncertainty reduced passenger traffic in Beirut Al-Hariri International Airport by as much as 11.5 percent through June 2007 compared with 2006, which, as already noted, was not a good year for tourism. Likewise, cargo shipment declined by 11 percent. Fortunately for the tourism industry in Lebanon, "the backbone of Lebanon's tourism" consists of Lebanese expatriates who continue to travel to the country regardless of the security situation—which mitigates the level of loss.[36]

One fascinating bit of detail is that the volume of incoming mail had declined by 5 percent, to 38 tons, while outgoing mail has increased by 55 percent to 48 tons.[37] The best explanation for this phenomenon is that Lebanese families are writing to relatives abroad either to assure them of their well-being or to seek financial assistance.

It is perhaps somewhat of a curiosity that Iran accounted for the largest number of foreign tourists in the first quarter of 2008, with 24,145 visitors, or 12.3 percent of the total.[38] Since Hizballah has insisted that a Hizballah-affiliated military officer keep his post as chief security officer at the Rafiq al-Hariri International Airport in Beirut there is no way of determining with any degree of certainty the reason behind this large inflow of Iranian tourists and how many of them are bona fide tourists at a time of great uncertainty in the country.

LOSSES AT THE PERSONAL LEVEL

At the personal level, the loss of life, loss of crops and livelihoods, destruction or damage of housing, and the displacement of family members have aggravated the living conditions of the most vulnerable segments of the population and increased their threshold of deprivation. In fact, according to the FAO mission, between 1998 and 2004, or two years prior to the July 2006 war, income-related indicators, mainly in employment and economic dependency, worsened from 43 to 52 percent for the entire population. Prior to the conflict, around 7 percent of the population lived in absolute poverty and another 28 percent in relative poverty. In the aftermath of the conflict, income-related indicators were expected to worsen and the economic dependency ratio was expected to grow. The FAO mission concludes its analysis of the social impact of the conflict with this sobering note:

> *The war has increased the numbers of the most vulnerable populations at risk of falling into the poverty trap. These include women heads of households, children, elderly living alone and the disabled, as well as unskilled labor, farmers and those employed in the informal sector.... Limited resources, no social/employment protection and weak state forms of social protection mechanisms render their lives and those of their dependants at stake.* Traditionally, family remittances and the other such communal support compensated for the absence of formal safety net programs. With more families facing socio-economic hardships, these forms of support may also dwindle. More critically, falling into the poverty cycle also means a potential increase in child labor as more families may pull children out of school so as to augment family income.[39]

INTERNATIONAL AID EFFORT

On August 31, 2006, shortly after cessation of hostilities, the Swedish government hosted a conference for Lebanon's Early Recovery in Stockholm. At the conference Lebanon received indications of support amounting to about $900 million for humanitarian assistance needs and early recovery efforts. Hizballah, acting upon financial promises from Iran, offered to compensate everyone whose house had been damaged or destroyed. Some money was indeed offered in front of blazing TV cameras, but the promises of large-scale financial support from Iran appear to have fizzled. Amid another fanfare, a couple of small bridges were reconstructed by the "Iranian Authority for the Reconstruction of Lebanon," which apparently operates from inside the Iranian embassy in Beirut. At a ceremony marking the opening of the bridges a spokesman for Hizballah declared that "the response of Iran's Islamic Republic was equal to the damage caused by the Israeli aggression."[40] It is noteworthy, however, that in all its reports to the international community the government of Lebanon never mentioned Hizballah by name or hinted at its existence.

REVISED REFORM PROGRAM

Toward the Paris III conference in January 2007, the government of Lebanon submitted a revised, and perhaps overly optimistic, reform program to stimulate growth, create employment, reduce poverty, and maintain social and political stability. The program included a host of reform measures, including improvement of governance, privatization of telecommunication, reform of the social sector (including health and social security), and reform of the power sector, including the unbundling of generation, transmission, and distribution functions of Electricity du Libran (EdL, Lebanon's power company), reducing illegal connections in the national grid, and raising the VAT from 10 percent to 12 percent.[41] The donors adopted the program and approved a package of aid worth $7.4 billion as grants and loans to help revive the Lebanese economy.

FAILURE IN IMPLEMENTING REFORMS
SUBMITTED TO PARIS III

Caught in a daily struggle for survival, the government has not done much in implementing its reform program. Not satisfied with the government's performance the donors withheld funds promised at Paris III. As their total disbursement reached the relatively insignificant amount of $277 million by the end of September, it comprised $77 million from the IMF for Banquet du Libran; $100 million from the World Bank for reforms of the social sectors; and $100 million by Saudi Arabia for reform of the budgetary system. The government claims that it has implemented 123 of the 300 reform initiatives, but representatives of the main donors, meeting in Beirut on October 1, 2007, noted that the initiatives implemented were of a procedural nature and that the government had taken no action on key initiatives, even those that required no parliamentary approval such as raising the excise on gasoline, privatizing the wireless phone company, and curbing subsidies to the power company, which has been a drain on national resources for years.[42]

During the annual meetings of the World Bank and the IMF in Washington, DC, in October 2007 the Lebanese delegation met with the "Core Group" established by Paris III to follow up on the implementation of the reform program. Aside from a promise by the Arab Monetary Fund to make a loan to Lebanon for $150 million (the following month) and a statement by the French delegate that France would release the first tranche of its 500 million euros it pledged to Lebanon at the end of calendar year 2007 there was no real loosening of the coffers by other donors.

In its evaluation of Lebanon's performance under the program supported by the Emergency Post-Conflict Assistance the IMF noted that the primary balance and net debt targets for end-December 2007 were met with significant margins, as the government achieved a primary surplus excluding grants of 0.5 percent of GDP, compared to a target of minus 3.7 percent. This substantial over-performance reflected strong overall revenues, which more than counterbalanced the loss from gasoline excises that were reduced to zero, and expenditures savings, derived mainly from a slower pace of foreign-financed spending, lower than expected transfers to municipalities and the electric company (EdL).

According to the fifth Paris III progress report released by the Lebanese Ministry of Finance, total agreements signed with international donors until March 2008 reached $4.408 billion out of a revised $7.533 billion of total pledges secured in the aftermath of the Paris III summit. It is worth noting that the $7.533 billion figure is a revision of an earlier $7.61 billion figure, following MOF reclassification and elimination of overlapping pledges.

The IMF also noted that the government's net debt declined from 173 percent to 165 percent of GDP in 2007, in part because the primary surplus rose above its debt-stabilizing level. However, most of the decline resulted from the transfer of unrealized gold valuation gains from the Central Bank to the government, which weakened the Central Bank's balance sheet.

Remittances from Expatriate Lebanese

One of the major sources of funding that keep many Lebanese above the poverty line is the volume of remittances by expatriate Lebanese to their home countries. The United Nations Conference on Trade and Development's (UNCTAD) report entitled "Development and Globalization: Facts and Figures 2008," which sheds the light on the role of developed countries in providing capital for the rest of the world, ranks the developing countries according to two criteria—remittances received (in volume) and remittances received as a percent of GDP. Out of 168 developing countries, Lebanon came in ninth in terms of remittances received and second in terms of the percentage of GDP. UNCTAD offered a table of the 20 countries that receive the largest amount of remittances, with India receiving the most and Ecuador the least. The following table, adapted from the original one published by UNCTAD, shows how Lebanon is ranked both internationally and in the context of other Arab countries that are also included among the top 20 recipients of remittances (see table 7.2).

In 2006, Lebanon received $4,924 million in remittances, placing it in the ninth spot in the ranking of developing countries according to remittances received but below Morocco and Egypt, both countries with much larger populations. It is also worth noting that incoming remittances to Lebanon have been on a continuously upward trend, as they went up by a significant 211 percent from their value in 2000, which was at $1,582 million, and by a higher 301.9 percent from $1,225 million in 1995. The marked increase in slope over the years may be attributed to the rising number of Lebanese expatriates—a reflection of the deteriorating security situation in Lebanon, which is impelling many of its citizens, primarily the entrepreneurial and professional people, particularly among the Christians, to seek a better future elsewhere.

The importance of remittances to the Lebanese economy is clear: In 2006, remittances to Lebanon accounted for 22.3 percent of its GDP, making it the developing country with the second highest remittances-to-GDP ratio, following the land-closed country of Lesotho in southern Africa.

Table 7.2   Remittance-Receiving Developing Countries (Adapted Table)

Country	Rank	Remittances ($U.S., 2006 in Billions)	% Remittances to GDP (2006)	Growth in Remittances (2006/2000)
India	1	25,700	2.9	99
Morocco	7	5,4048	7.7	134
Egypt	8	5,017	4.6	76
Lebanon	9	4,924	22.3	211
Algeria	17	2,527	2.2	220
Jordan	19	2,500	17.4	36
Ecuador	20	2,038	5.0	54

Source: UNCTAD, "Development and Globalization: Facts and Figures 2008."

On the other hand, the UNCTAD report also provides a list of top 20 remittances-paying countries, ranked by remittances paid in 2006. Lebanon ranks thirteenth, with a total of $4,018 billion in remittances paid. UNCTAD suggests that the volume of outward remittances indicates that there is a relatively high number of foreign workers within the whole labor force in Lebanon, as those are the contributors of outward remittances.[43] The ILO has confirmed this point in its mission report referred to earlier. The ILO indicates that the presence of foreign workers in Lebanon is quite substantial. The report identifies the majority of these migrant workers as "unskilled, performing strenuous, labour-intensive and often dangerous jobs that do not require specific education or skills qualifications."[44]

THE BANKING SECTOR: SUSTAINABLE PERFORMANCE AMID ECONOMIC STAGNATION

As noted earlier, the Lebanese economy is a service economy, with the banking sector often playing a key role during periods of political turmoil. Indeed, figures released by the Central Bank indicate that the consolidated balance sheet of commercial banks continued to exhibit resilience over the first eight months of 2007, as the aggregate activity, measured by the consolidated assets of banks operating in Lebanon, grew by 6.9 percent at the end of August, the equivalent of LP [Lebanese pound or lira] 7.962 billion, or $5.281 million, to reach LP 122,801.9 billion, or $81,460.6 million. During the month of August 2006 alone consolidated assets grew by 2.4 percent, indicating that the banks "weathered away the unfavorable effects of the unstable prevailing political and security conditions."[45]

Asset growth was greatly driven by the 6.5 percent growth in customer deposits in the eight months between end-2006 and end of August 2007. This translates, according to Bank Audi, into an increase of LP 5,929.2 billion, or $3,933.1 million, bringing the total deposits to LP 97,423.3 billion or $64,625.7 million.[46] In this context, Francois Basil, the president of the Banking Association of Lebanon, made an emotional appeal to the political leaders "to resort to their conscience and their wisdom to find the proper solution for electing a new president [of the republic] and to think of the future of their children, the future of the Lebanese people, the future of the new generation and the future of the homeland."

He coupled his call with a warning that the emigration of so many talented people will affect the profitability and growth of the banking sector and the classification of Lebanese banks by the international institutions.[47]

While the loss of human capital in the banking sector has long-term serious consequences, the Lebanese have not been sitting waiting for the political drama to run its course. According to a report prepared by Lebanon's Banking Association, foreign banking activity represents 6–7 percent of Lebanese banks' total activity while generating as much as 35 percent of their total earnings in 18 countries. Jordan and Syria each attracts

30 branches of Lebanese banks, or 23 percent of the total number of branches, followed by Egypt with 17 branches, Cyprus 10 branches, and the UAE with eight branches.[48]

The Lebanese banks have discovered fertile ground for their activities in Iraqi Kurdistan, perhaps the most secure and stable part of Iraq. Taking advantage of incentives offered to investors by the Kurdistan Regional Government, Lebanese companies are investing heavily in building a refinery and four cement factories. These activities are followed closely by Lebanese banks. For example, Byblos Bank, the largest in Lebanon, has opened a branch in Erbil—the capital of the Kurdish region—and Bank Intercontinental has also established a presence in Erbil.[49]

CREDIT RATING

In its semiannual survey on the creditworthiness of 174 countries, the *Institutional Investor Magazine* ranked Lebanon in the 115th position worldwide and 19th among 20 countries in the Middle East and North Africa region. The survey measures the creditworthiness of countries on a scale of 0 to 100, with 100 representing countries with the least chance of debt default. The ratings are based on input provided by senior economists and sovereign risk analysts at leading financial institutions.[50] The rating suggests that the position of Lebanon is relatively weak globally and even more so regionally. As a result, the rating agency Standard & Poor's lowered its long-term credit rating for Lebanon's state (sovereign) debt from B– to CCC+, attributing its lower rating to feuding political factions.[51]

EXTERNAL SECTOR

Apart from the banking sector, the external sector, measured by the total of exports and imports, demonstrated a favorable performance in the first quarter of 2008 relative to the first quarter of 2007, with the latter period being marked by a healthy import and export activity as well. Figures released by the Higher Customs Council show that the aggregate value of imports and exports totaled $4,373 million in the first quarter of 2008, up by as much as 31.6 percent from $3,323 million in the same quarter of 2007. However, despite the advancement in activity and the fact that it is characterized by a higher export growth, the trade deficit continued to pose a constraint on the sector, as it is widened by 26.1 percent from $2,081 million in the first quarter of 2007 to $2,623 million in the same period of 2008. The growing gap is a result of the appreciation of the euro since Lebanon's imports originate from countries with the euro as their currency.[52]

ELECTRICITY: THE BIGGEST DRAIN ON BUDGET

The government's transfer to the loss-making electric company EdL represents a big drain on the government budget. According to the minister of finance, these transfers between 1993 and 2006 amounted to $3.8 billion, with an additional accumulated interest payment of $7.5 billion, bringing the total to $11.3 billion. All of Lebanon's power plants run on fuel oil, despite some attempts to shift to natural gas. Lebanon's electricity sector, which suffers from serious technical and financial problems, operates with a big loss, thereby necessitating an annual subsidy of about $1 billion. In fact, based on the level of transfer to EdL in the first half of 2007, the minister of finance projects that the level of subsidy to EdL for the whole year will be in the range of $1.2 billion.[53]

In an effort to move toward privatizing the power sector, the Lebanese government and the International Finance Corporation (IFC)—the private sector arm of the World Bank—signed an agreement on July 16, 2007 under which the IFC will assist Lebanon in launching the first independent power project (IPP) at the Badawi (Dir Ammar) power plant. The IFC will advise the government on finding private sector investors for the construction of a 450-megawatt plant, which is expected to meet a large part of the projected 550-megawatt increase in electricity consumption in Lebanon by 2010. By signing the agreement with the IFC, the government of Lebanon may have been able to wiggle itself out of a commitment made to the donors at Paris III to privatize the power sector. In all fairness, however, it is not clear that under the current political uncertainties there are many potential private investors who are ready to buy a deficit-ridden public utility with no guarantee that the government is capable of enforcing rate adjustments upward.

POST-DOHA ECONOMIC DEVELOPMENT

After months of political squabbling that led the country to the verge of civil war, the Lebanese fractious political forces met in Doha, Qatar, on May 16–21, 2008, under the auspices of the Emir of Qatar Shaykh Hamad bin Khalifa al-Thani. The Lebanese leaders, taking part at the meeting, signed a document calling for the immediate election of a president and formation of a national unity government.[54] A new president, Michel Suleiman, was elected on May 25 but as of the end of June 2008 there was still no government of national unity.

The agreement generated considerable enthusiasm about the economic prospects of the country. The first post-Doha event of economic consequence was the immediate dismantling of the "protest tents" put up by the opposition forces under the leadership of Hizballah in the center of Beirut, which were meant to paralyze the government activities. With the dismantling of the tents, businesses and restaurants were opened again after 18 months of closure. The daily *al-Mustaqbal*, which speaks for the Hariri movement, quoted economic organizations that spoke of "profound transformation" to achieve growth and development. Real estate prices in central Beirut spiked by 15–20 percent, and the biggest beneficiary was Solidaire International— which is largely owned by the Hariri family and controls vast tracks of land and buildings in the center of Beirut. The market value of Solidaire at the

Beirut Stock Exchange went up more than 30 percent overnight.[55] In fact, the stock price of Solidaire was $70 in May 2007 but reached $240 a year later.[56]

The leading daily *al-Nahar* was even more enthusiastic about the future. It wrote that as soon the "white smoke" was observed at the Sheraton Doha, the "general mood" in Beirut has changed overnight from overly pessimistic to overly optimistic. The governor of the Central Bank, Riyadh Salameh, was quoted as saying that the agreement will have an impact on the market, foreign exchange, and the pricing of Lebanese sovereign bonds.[57]

One of the immediate results of the Doha agreement is the revival of tourism. According to data made available by Al-Hariri International Airport, seats on incoming flights are fully booked for the next three months by Gulf tourists and expatriate Lebanese. The number of arrivals has reached 7,000 passengers daily, compared with 4,000 the year before.[58] The demand for workers in the tourism and entertainment sector will not be far behind.

The challenges facing a new government are enormous: sluggish growth, rising national debt, budget deficits, and reforms to be undertaken under Paris III to unlock the promised aid money by key donors. Most importantly, it must assure potential investors, particularly those from the oil-rich countries, that stability has been restored to the country.

CONCLUSION

A combination of tragic events, including 15 years of civil war, 16 years of Syrian military and intelligence presence, the assassination of Prime Minister al-Hariri and other key figures in the government and parliament, and the July 2006 conflict with Israel instigated by Hizballah acting as a proxy for Syria and Iran, has deprived Lebanon of three decades of human capital, technical capacity, and economic growth and has launched the country into a path of political and economic uncertainty.

This essay has alluded to the issue of political stalemate, which could restrict the government's ability to carry out its reform program in part or in full. A similar conclusion was reached by the IMF, whose report refers to Lebanon being "highly vulnerable to swings in confidence." While "the international reserve buffer and expected donor inflows should mitigate the risks to financial stability," the increase in the government's financial imbalance in 2007, "even if temporary, poses additional strains on the system."[59]

As always, Lebanese economic dysfunctions cannot be divorced from the regional context given the heavy influence exerted by outside powers on Lebanon's various political parties and sectarian groups. Iran and Syria remain destabilizing forces, with each pursuing different strategic objectives. Syria wants to restore its hegemony over Lebanon, and Iran wants to extend its power in the Middle East and to serve as an immediate threat to Israel through its Lebanese proxy—Hizballah.

In the meantime, the most probable scenario is that the current stalemate between Lebanon's factions will endure until parliamentary elections are held in 2009. However, there is a significant risk of further deterioration and more violence given the uncertainty inherent in such a tense atmosphere that led the recently elected president of Lebanon, Michel Suleiman, to lament that the "disagreements between the Lebanese have reached the suicide level," which could only serve "the interests of the Israeli enemy."[60] The political stalemate has also meant that the reforms envisaged under Paris III are shelved for now, and shelved with them is the aid money that was committed but not disbursed—aid money so vital to regenerating the Lebanese economy.

If there is one lesson to be drawn about Lebanon it is that the country's "resilient financial markets...persistently and stoutly face any type of internal and external turmoil at the horizon...despite its large debt overhang and significant external vulnerabilities."[61]

APPENDIX

Table 7.3   Lebanon Data Profile

People	2000	2005	2006
Population, total (million)	3.8	4.0	4.1
Population growth (annual %)	1.2	1.2	1.1
Life Expectancy at birth, total (years)	71.3	72.5	—
Fertility rate, total (births per woman)	2.5	2.3	—
School enrollment, primary (% gross)	110.9	106.3	—
School enrollment, secondary (% gross)	82.1	89.1	—
School enrollment, tertiary (% gross)	37.0	50.7	—
Ratio of girls to boys in primary and secondary education (%)	101.9	102.2	—

Environment	2000	2005	2006
Surface area (sq. km.)	10,400.0	10,400.0	10,400.0
Agricultural land (% of land area)	34.0	—	—
Improved water source (% of population with access)	100.0	—	—
Energy use (kg of oil equivalent per capita)	1,340.8	—	—
Energy imports, net (% of energy use)	96.6	—	—
Electric power consumption (kWh per capita)	2,081	—	—

Economy	2000	2005	2006
GNI, Atlas method (current $U.S., billions)	17.3	22.1	22.3
GNI per capita, Atlas method ($U.S.)	4,590.0	5,510.0	5,490.0
GDP (current $U.S., billions)	16.8	21.5	22.7
GDP growth (annual %)	1.7	1.0	0.0
Inflation, GDP deflator (annual %)	–2.8	–0.7	5.6

Continued

Table 7.3 Continued

Economy	2000	2005	2006
Agriculture, value added (% of GDP)	7.3	6.5	—
Industry, value added (% of GDP)	23.7	22.3	—
Services etc., value added (% of GDP)	69.0	71.2	—
Exports of goods and services (% of GDP)	13.8	19.7	—
Imports of goods and services (% of GDP)	36.8	45.1	—
Gross capital formation (% of GDP)	20.1	20.7	—
Revenue, excluding grants (% of GDP)	16.4	—	—
Cash surplus/deficit (% of GDP)	−18.9	—	—

Global Links	2000	2005	2006
Merchandize trade (% of GDP)	41.3	55.6	54.8
Foreign direct investment, net inflows (BoP, current $U.S.)	964.1 million	2.6 billion	—
Total debt service (% of exports of goods, services, and income)	—	17.7	—
Official development assistance and official aid (current $U.S.)	199.3 million	243.0 million	—
Workers' remittances and compensation of employees, received ($U.S., billions)	1.6	4.9	4.9

Source: World Development Indicators Database, April 2007.

Table 7.4 Agriculture and Industry.

	2006	2007					2008	Variation	
		Q1	Q2	Q3	Q4	2007	Q1	Q1/Q1	2007/2006
Agricultural exports ($U.S., millions)	104	27	36	36	35	134	31	14.8%	28.8%
Industrial exports ($U.S., millions)	2,178	594	655	676	757	2,682	844	42.1%	23.1%
Electricity production (KWh, millions)	10,214	2,520	2,563	2,829	2,636	10,548	2,727	8.2%	3.3%
Imports of industrial equipments ($U.S., millions)	130	39	40	44	39	163	36	-8.9%	25.4%
Imports of oil derivatives (metric tons, thousands)	4,123	861	700	1,036	1,018	3,614	991	15.5%	−12.3%

Source: Bank Audi, "Lebanon Economic Report," Lebanon. First Quarter, 2008, p. 3.

Table 7.5 Construction

	2006	2007 Q1	2007 Q2	2007 Q3	2007 Q4	2007	2008 Q1	Variation Q1/Q1	Variation 2007/2006
Construction permits (square meters, thousands)	8,693	1,610	2,457	2,306	2,665	9,038	2,148	33.4%	4.0%
Delivery of cement (in tons)	3,422,927	802,266	1,032,145	1,132,681	977,853	3,944,945	863,837	7.7%	15.3%
Number of property transactions	127,016	36,721	37,351	37,080	43,006	154,158	—	—	21.4%
Value of property transactions (LP million)	4,732,622	865,119	1,323,644	1,550,493	2,589,800	6,329,056	—	—	33.7%
Average transaction value (LP millions)	37	24	35	42	60	41	—	—	11.0%
Property taxes (LP billions)	348	71	93	105	191	460	—	—	32.2%

Source: Bank Audi, "Lebanon Economic Report," Lebanon, First Quarter, 2008, p. 4.

1 LP = 0.000663 U.S.D (June 27, 2008).

Table 7.6 Trade and Services

	2006	2007					2008	Variation	
		Q1	Q2	Q3	Q4	2007	Q1	Q1/Q1	2007/2006
Number of ships at Beirut Port (thousands)	1,829	614	545	519	509	2,187	527	-14.2%	19.6%
Number of containers at Beirut Port (thousands)	339	100	111	112	122	444	114	14.6%	31.0%
Merchandise at Beirut Port (tons, thousands)	4,227	1,298	1,247	1,365	1,407	5,318	1,425	9.8%	25.8%
Planes at airport	32,980	8,810	9,528	10,965	29,749	39,052	9,403	6.7%	18.4%
Number of passengers at airport	2,739,606	660,626	772,141	1,072,989	820,677	3,326,433	749,562	13.5%	21.4%
Number of tourists	1,062,635	180,523	231,518	354,639	250,392	1,017,072	193,778	7.3%	-4.3%

Source: Bank Audi, "Lebanon Economic Report," Lebanon. First Quarter, 2008, p. 5.

NOTES

1. Carolyn L. Gates, *The Merchant Republic of Lebanon: Rise of an Open Economy* (London: The Center for Lebanese Studies with I. B. Tauris Publishers, 1998), p. 2.

2. Ibid., p. 82.

3. Ibid., p. 88.

4. *Al-Sharq Al-Awsat* (London), November 16, 2007. The quotation is taken from Dr.Samir Khalaf's book *Lubnan fi madar al-unf* [Lebanon in the Cycle of Violence] (Beirut: Dar al-Nahar, 2002).

5. Ibid.

6. *Al-Hayat* (London), September 3, 2007.

7. *BusinessIntelligence Middle East* (Dubai), January 3, 2008.

8. An ILO Post Conflict Recent Work Programme for Lebanon. Report of the September 2006 Mission to Lebanon, October 2006.

9. www.reuildlebanon.gov.lb.

10. *Al-Sharq al-Awsat*, August 30, 2007.

11. Food and Agriculture Organization of the United Nations, *Lebanon: Damage and Early Recovery Needs Assessment of the Agriculture, Fisheries and Forestry* (Rome: November 2006).

12. Embassy of Lebanon, "Profile of Lebanon—The Economy" (Washington, DC), www.lebanonembassyus.org/country_lebaonon/economy.html.

13. ILO Report of the September 2006 Multi-Disciplinary Mission to Lebanon, October 2006.

14. *Al-Sharq Al-Awsat*, May 16, 2008.

15. The Lebanese Republic, "Recovery, Reconstruction, and Reform," submitted to the International Conference for Support of Lebanon, Paris, January 25, 2007. The program was eventually expanded and submitted as an appendix "Lebanon: Letter of Intent," on March 30, 2007, to a letter addressed to Mr. Rodrigo de Rato, the managing director of the International Monetary Fund, requesting "Emergency Post-Conflict Assistance." The document is attached to IMF Country Report No. 07/177, dated May 2007.

16. The Lebanese Republic, "Recovery, Reconstruction, and Reform," pp. 45–46.

17. Ibid., p. 47.

18. Ibid., p. 47.

19. Jackson Diehl, "As Lebanon Goes," *The Washington Post*, October 8, 2007.

20. See Talal Nizameddin, "The Political Economy of Lebanon under Rafiq Hariri: An Interpretation," *Middle East Journal*, Vol. 60, No. 1 (Winter 2006), pp. 95–114.

21. In a statement to France Press, the assistant to the head of the executive council of Hizballah, Bilal Na'im, said that Hizballah's institutions are financed by the Shari'a-based fund under Iran's supreme leader Ali Khamene'i, *al-Hayat*, December 15, 2006. In a two-part interview, Mohammad Hasan Akhteri— former Iranian ambassador to Syria for 14 years (through February 2008)— relates in detail the Iranian role in building, arming, and training Hizballah, which was made possible by the support of the Syrian regime. See *al-Sharq Al-Awsat*, May 14 and 15, 2008, and Nimrod Raphaeli, "The Iranian Roots of Hizballah," MEMRI Inquiry & Analysis No. 408, June 17, 2008.

22. One of the 2006 postwar ironies is the stationing of UN peacekeepers who brought "baraka" [blissful plenty] to the bazaars of southern Lebanon, http://afp.google.com/article/ALeqM5hy3bpQ0-8jjhZD1fD9BEwN9DamPQ.

23. ILO Report, October 2006, p. 35.
24. www.fao.org/newsroom/en/news/2007/1000647/index.html (August 8, 2007).
25. www.fao.org/newsroom/en/news/2006/1000445/index.html.
26. The Republic of Lebanon, "Recovery, Reconstruction and Reform," International Conference for Support to Lebanon, Republic of Lebanon, Paris, January 2007, http://www.rebuildlebanon.gov.lb/imagesgallery/ParisIIdocumentFinalEngVersion.pdf, p. 40.
27. "Debt and Debt Markets" (second quarter 2007), www.finance.gov.lb.
28. *BusinessIntelligence Middle East*, June 4, 2008.
29. The Republic of Lebanon, "Reconstruction, Recovery and Reform," p. 52.
30. *Al-Sharq al-Awsat*, September 1, 2007.
31. Bank Audi, *The Lebanon Weekly Monitor*, "Balance of Payment Registers a Deficit," No. 19 (May 5–10, 2008), p. 3.
32. http://www.bdl.gov.lb/pub/mb/mb163/MB163.
33. *Al-Sharq al-Awsat*, September 7, 2007.
34. *Al-Hayat*, January 4, 2008.
35. ILO Report, October 2006, p. 10.
36. FAO, "Lebanon," p. 4.
37. *Al-Mustaqbal* (Beirut), August 1, 2007.
38. Bank Audi, *The Lebanon Weekly Monitor*, No. 18 (April 28–May 3, 2008).
39. FAO, "Lebanon," pp. 8–9; italics in the original.
40. *Al-Mustaqbal*, August 12, 2007.
41. The Republic of Lebanon, "Reconstruction, Recovery and Reform" pp. 53–60. The case of the Electricite du Liban is quite disturbing since by government's own admission the company loses approximately 35% of its generated power to "significant technical and non-technical losses" and another 6% to loss on collection.
42. Huda al-Hussein in *al-Sharq al-Awsat*, August 30, 2007. The population figure is taken from a study published in August 2007 by Information International.
42. *Al-Qabas* (Kuwait), October 9, 2007.
43. Bank Audi, *The Lebanon Weekly Monitor*, No. 17 (April 21–26, 2008).
44. ILO Report, October 2006, p. 6.
45. Banque du Liban, Department of Statistics and Economic Research, Monthly Bulletin, No. 163 (December 2007).
46. Bank Audi, *The Lebanon Weekly Monitor*, No. 40 (October 1–6, 2007).
47. *Al-Nahar* (Beirut), September 26, 2007.
48. *Al-Hayat*, October 9, 2007.
49. *Al-Sharq al-Awsat*, August 10, 2007.
50. *Institutional Investment Magazine*, March 2008.
51. *The Daily Star* (Beirut), February 7, 2008.
52. Bank Audi, *The Lebanon Weekly Monitor*, No. 17 (April 21–26, 2008).
53. *Al-Mustaqbal*, August 14, 2007.
54. The full text of the agreement was published in *al-Sharq al-Awsat*, May 22, 2008.
55. *Al-Mustaqbal*, May 22, 2008.
56. *Al-Nahar*, June 27, 2008.
57. *Al-Nahar*, May 22, 2008.
58. *Al-Sharq al-Awsat*, June 27, 2008.
59. IMF Country Report No. 07/177, p. 21.
60. *Al-Nahar*, June 25, 2008.
61. Bank Audi, *Lebanon Economic Report*, 1st Quarter 2008.

8

ISLAMIST GROUPS IN LEBANON

Gary C. Gambill

Although Lebanon's ethno-sectarian demography is manifestly unsuitable for the establishment of an Islamic state, the salience of militant Islamist movements in this tiny Mediterranean country has few parallels. Above and beyond the regional conditions fueling Islamic revivalism, Lebanon's weak state, acute socioeconomic and political inequities, and experience of pervasive external intervention converged to create an unusually permissive environment for Islamists. Under these circumstances, radical Islamism has become a powerful instrument of communitarian social mobilization and an effective vehicle for drawing resources from the outside world.

BACKGROUND

The modern state of Lebanon is a unique amalgam of 18 officially recognized religious sects, the product of over a millennium of immigration by Christians and heterodox Muslims from the surrounding Sunni Islamic world and deliberate colonial border demarcation following the collapse of the Ottoman Empire. Political offices in Lebanon have been distributed among its sectarian communities by fixed quotas. Under the terms of the 1943 National Pact, the presidency is reserved for Maronite Christians, the office of prime minister for Sunni Muslims, and the office of parliament speaker for Shi'a Muslims. Parliament seats were divided among Christian and Muslim sects by a 6:5 ratio until 1989, then evenly afterward. In addition, the Lebanese Constitution and subsequent laws grant the religious establishment of each sectarian community authority over matters pertaining to personal status (e.g., marriage, divorce, child custody, and inheritance).

Lebanon's sectarian system (*al-nizam al-ta'ifiyya*) proved to be an effective barrier against the rise of an authoritarian state (which, in the Arab world, invariably entails the monopolization of power by one ethno-sectarian group), but it also reified patron-client relationships *within* the country's confessional communities and inhibited the growth of a common national identity. This paved the way for outside intervention from multiple quarters, the breakdown of the state, a long civil war, and an internationally sanctioned

Syrian occupation. These crisis conditions have heavily shaped the evolution of radical Islamist groups.

While any explicit taxonomy of actors in the highly idiosyncratic and fluid sociopolitical environment of modern Lebanon is necessarily imprecise, three poles of Islamic fundamentalism are readily discernable. Shi'a Islamism in Lebanon has evolved along one broad institutionalized trajectory under the guidance of clerics; this is a distinct hallmark reflecting the exalted spiritual status of the *ulama* (religious scholars) in Shi'a Islam and the communitarian solidarity of Lebanese Shi'a. Sunni Islamism in Lebanon has been much more fluid and fragmented, with two distinct ideological currents— political Islamism and Salafism.

SHI'A ISLAMISM IN LEBANON

The emergence of radical Islamism among Lebanese Shi'a is rooted in the community's longstanding political and socioeconomic deprivation.[1] Despite constituting the country's largest single sectarian group, Shi'a were awarded the third-largest share of parliamentary seats in Lebanon's First Republic and were barred from the two highest government offices. Moreover, Shi'a political representation was dominated by feudal landlords who had little interest in the socioeconomic advancement of their constituents.

By the mid-1970s, Shi'a parochial allegiances were steadily eroding as a result of rising education levels, the influx of new wealth from Shi'a emigrants, and rapid urbanization owing to the state's neglect of the agricultural sector and increasingly destructive Israeli reprisals against the Palestinian Liberation Organization (PLO) in south Lebanon.[2] Most politicized Shi'a gravitated toward leftist or Arab nationalist parties that challenged the legitimacy of Lebanon's confessional power-sharing system until the late 1960s, when Sayyid Musa al-Sadr's Harakat al-Mahrumin (Movement of the Deprived) emerged as a moderate force focused on advancing Shi'a communal interests within the Lebanese system. Although Sadr was committed to the peaceful pursuit of modest social, economic, and political change, his movement's religious idiom resonated deeply. Whereas Sunni theology is centered on the prerogatives of rulers, Shi'ism is imbued with the ethos of resistance to tyranny and oppression.

Revolutionary Shi'a Islamism emerged as a third pole of identification after the outbreak of civil war in 1975, espoused by a younger generation of clerics who were radicalized during their studies in the Shi'a seminaries of Ba'thist Iraq. The most prominent, Sayyid Husayn Fadlallah, called for the impoverished and dispossessed Shi'a of Lebanon to take up arms not in defense of their class or sect (as the Amal militia of Sadr's successor, Nabih Barri, claimed to do) but in defense of the Islamic faith[3]—a seemingly quixotic vision that suddenly gained credibility after the 1979 revolution in Shi'a Iran. Following Israel's 1982 invasion of Lebanon, contingents of Iran's Islamic Revolutionary Guards Corps (IRGC) entered the Syrian-controlled Biqa Valley of eastern Lebanon with plentiful cash, weapons, and a proven model for revolutionary action.

Although Fadlallah maintained his independence (and later came to dismiss publicly the religious qualifications of Iran's clerical leadership),[4] a host of younger and lesser-known Lebanese clerics in the Biqa readily accepted Iranian patronage—most notably Subhi al-Tufayli and Abbas al-Musawi. Loosely organized under the name Hizballah (Party of God), they embraced Ayatollah Ruhollah Khomeini's doctrine of *wilayet al-faqih* (the theological basis for clerical rule enshrined in Iran's constitution) and formally vowed to establish an Islamic Republic in Lebanon (to this day, Hizballah's flag bears the inscription "the Islamic Revolution in Lebanon") through peaceful means. In practice, however, this aspiration has always been subordinate to the pursuit of armed struggle against Israeli and Western "oppressors." While few Lebanese Shi'a harbored the kind of deep historical grievances against Israel and the West felt by most Sunni Arabs, they had borne the brunt of the Israeli invasion and feared that the entry of an American and European multi-national force (MNF) into Beirut months later would empower Lebanon's governing alliance of Christian Phalangists and Sunni Beiruti notables at their expense.

From the spring of 1983 to the summer of 1985, underground Lebanese Shi'a terrorist cells linked to Hizballah (or, more precisely, spawned by the same Iranian patronage network) carried out a spectacular wave of suicide bombings against Western and Israeli military and diplomatic targets that resulted in the withdrawal of the MNF and the redeployment of the Israel Defense Forces (IDF) to a thin "security zone" in the south. The June 1985 hijacking of TWA Flight 847 by Shi'a Islamists forced Israel to release over 700 Lebanese and Palestinian detainees captured during the war. These astonishing successes salved the Lebanese Shi'a community's intense feelings of victimization and demonstrated that religious devotion could compensate for its material weaknesses.[5] For a minority sect traditionally viewed with disdain by religious Sunnis and with distrust by Arab nationalists, it also brought a powerful dose of collective vindication.

For all of its relentless violence against the West and Israel, Hizballah rarely engaged in the kind of indiscriminate bloodletting characteristic of other wartime militias (a "purity of arms" that remains integral to its public image in Lebanon today). Shi'a suicide bombings against Western peacekeepers and diplomats, while abhorrent, "achieved pinpoint precision—an unusual technique for Beirut, where exploding cars usually killed indiscriminately," notes Martin Kramer.[6] Similarly, Hizballah's kidnapping of dozens of Western nationals contrasted sharply with the thousands of indiscriminate abductions and summary executions perpetrated by other militias during the war. At any rate, Hizballah gradually phased out such methods as it built its conventional military strength and developed a formal leadership structure.[7]

As Hizballah racked up victories against foreign "oppressors," Iranian funding enabled it to build a vast network of schools, hospitals, and other social welfare institutions. By the latter half of the decade, Shi'a living standards in areas of the Biqa and southern Beirut under its control were higher in most respects than they were *before* the war. This combination of "resistance" and relief has remained central to Hizballah's popular appeal.

Notwithstanding the strategic alliance that emerged between Tehran and Damascus in the 1980s, Hizballah bitterly fought the Syrians[8] and their local proxies at times (particularly the rival Shi'a Amal militia), in part because it recognized that Syrian hegemony would constrain its freedom of action in fighting Israel and restore Lebanon's antebellum power-sharing system.[9] After Syrian forces completed their conquest of Lebanon in October 1990, however, Hizballah accepted the legitimacy of Lebanon's Second Republic in return for a virtually exclusive right to organize "resistance" to the IDF in south Lebanon (other Lebanese and Palestinian groups were allowed only subordinate token participation).[10]

Massive Iranian arms shipments, airlifted to Damascus and driven overland to the Biqa, enabled the organization to build one of the best-equipped paramilitary forces in the world. Following the 1992 ascension of Secretary General Hasan Nasrallah, Hizballah introduced a much more rigorous level of training, sophisticated new tactics, and a sweeping reorientation from religious to nationalist discourse more acceptable to the broader Lebanese public (and the Syrians). Although the ebb and flow of its operations were carefully regulated by Damascus in accordance with the climate of Syrian relations with Israel, Hizballah was clearly in charge of the campaign and reaped the political benefits of its success.

In return for these prerogatives, Hizballah accepted a postwar political order that perpetuated Shi'a deprivation.[11] While the 1989 Ta'if Accord transferred the lion's share of executive power from the Christian presidency to the Sunni premiership, the Shi'a received only a slight strengthening of the parliamentary speakership and a marginal increase in parliamentary representation. Moreover, the Syrians prohibited Hizballah from freely competing for this meager allotment of seats, forcing it to form electoral coalitions with Amal and other favored (and therefore unpopular) Syrian clients.[12]

In addition, Hizballah was obliged to live with socioeconomic policies that privileged the postwar commercial elite. The unregulated influx of unskilled Syrian workers into Lebanon (critical both to Damascus and to the Lebanese construction tycoons who made fortunes rebuilding the country) pushed the predominantly Shi'a urban poor out of the workforce,[13] while Syrian produce smugglers and government's neglect of the countryside drove destitute Shi'a farmers into bankruptcy.[14] Income inequality steadily increased[15] as Prime Minister Rafiq Hariri cut income and corporate taxes to a flat 10 percent, while raising indirect taxes (e.g., gasoline) on the public at large, slashing social expenditures, and freezing public sector wages.

Ironically, these inequities *strengthened* Hizballah by perpetuating the Shi'a community's dependence on its social welfare institutions and discrediting rival political forces. By excluding itself from government and delivering both resistance and social services with amazing efficiency, Hizballah projected an image of incorruptibility that contrasted starkly with the legendary excesses of the governing elite. This was critical to its success in raising funds from the Lebanese Shi'a diaspora, both through donations and through a

variety of illicit enterprises (e.g., the blood diamond trade in West Africa, cig-
arette smuggling, and audiovisual bootlegging in the Americas) that required
its supporters to take great risks.[16] By the end of the 1990s, Hizballah's own
financial resources substantially exceeded its handouts from Iran.

As Hizballah recast itself as a national liberation movement, it effectively
abandoned the pursuit of an Islamic state in Lebanon.[17] Although Hizballah
leaders called for ending the political system organized along the lines of
religious community (a step that arguably could pave the way for an Islamic
state down the road by first enshrining majority rule), they displayed far less
inclination to root out "un-Islamic" influences in Lebanese society than
even the most mainstream Sunni clerics (see later).[18]

While Hizballah's "Lebanonization" (and Nasrallah's Clintonesque public
statements)[19] led many outside observers to predict that it would promptly
lay down its arms and become a "normal" political party once Israeli troops
withdrew from south Lebanon,[20] such forecasts failed to recognize that
these choices revealed little about the underlying intentions of Hizballah
leaders—beyond a concern with attracting as large a popular base of support
as possible within the Shi'a community and Lebanon as a whole. Since reli-
giosity has not been a primary determinant of Shi'a popular support for
Hizballah (as shown by Judith Palmer Harik's survey of Shi'a public opinion
at the end of the civil war),[21] secular discourse was favored to win non-Shi'a
support. Since the goal of "national liberation" garnered broader appeal than
other rationales for fighting Israel, nationalist discourse was favored.

While the expectation that pursuit of Shi'a political hegemony would lead
Hizballah to "normalize" seemed plausible to many, it presupposed a
"normal" Lebanese public sphere in which government policies derive from
a competitive political process (democratic or not). Nothing of the sort
existed in Syrian-occupied Lebanon, where the main parameters of foreign
and domestic policy were inviolable (especially with respect to Shi'a
empowerment).[22] Consequently, giving up the enormous reputational benefits derived from projecting itself as the vanguard of the Arab-Islamic
struggle against Zionism would have condemned Hizballah to political
oblivion.

This is not to say that Nasrallah would have rushed to convert swords into
ploughshares after Israel's May 2000 withdrawal had the system been receptive to Shi'a empowerment, but lack of opportunities to effect domestic
change made it easier for him to ignore normalization advocates within both
Hizballah (particularly its parliamentary bloc) and the Shi'a community at
large.[23] Most Shi'a Muslims see the "resistance" as a form of compensation
for their political and economic deprivation and a critical instrument of communal leverage. They will not be willing to fully discard it until Shi'a Muslims
are given pride of place alongside Sunnis and Christians in setting the political and economic parameters of state policy.

The outbreak of the al-Aqsa Intifada in September 2000 provided a conducive strategic climate for continued "resistance," as Israel was too preoccupied with Palestinian violence on its doorstep to undertake a major military

campaign in Lebanon. After resuming sporadic cross-border attacks against Israeli forces in the fall of 2000, Hizballah steadily expanded its rocket arsenal (further deterring a major Israeli incursion) and played a more direct role in financing, training, and equipping Palestinian terrorists (ensuring that the violence in the West Bank and Gaza did not recede sufficiently for Israel to risk a war in Lebanon). Hizballah's television station, al-Manar, began broadcasting by satellite and introduced a tidal wave of new programming intended to incite violence against Israel.[24] Although Nasrallah repeatedly insisted that Hizballah would not stand in the way of a peace settlement acceptable to the Palestinian people,[25] his slippery disclaimers implied a virtually unreachable threshold of consensus.

Although the withdrawal of Israeli forces from south Lebanon led to a spike in public admiration for Hizballah, the recession of this external threat also gave others in the Shi'a community more freedom to assert themselves. The outwardly amicable relationship between Nasrallah and Fadlallah grew more contentious and occasionally erupted into public acrimony,[26] while recurrent clashes between members of Hizballah and Amal sent dozens to the hospital (and a few to the morgue).

However, as mounting pressure on Syria to withdraw from Lebanon merged seamlessly into pressure for the disarmament of Hizballah, the Shi'a community rallied behind Nasrallah. Whatever misgivings they may have had about Hizballah, the vast majority of Lebanese Shi'a remained unwilling to entrust their security to the state and fearful of being marginalized after disarmament. In light of the Lebanese Army's brutal slaying of five unarmed Shi'a Muslims who were protesting fuel price increases in May 2004, it is not difficult to understand why.

SUNNI ISLAMISM IN LEBANON

While Sunni Islamism in Lebanon evolved against the same backdrop of "macro" crisis conditions (e.g., Maronite Christian political hegemony, the collapse of the state, pervasive foreign intervention), it derives from a different theological tradition and has been heavily conditioned by the historical experience of Sunnis in Lebanon.

In contrast to Shi'a *ulama*, Sunni clerics in Lebanon (and elsewhere) have historically been little more than "religious functionaries" of the state,[27] more often than not finding themselves in opposition to Islamist movements. Consequently, Sunni Islamism has been less institutionalized and highly diffuse.

In sharp contrast to the Shi'a, Lebanese Sunni have been overwhelmingly urban since the establishment of Lebanon (concentrated in the northern port of Tripoli, the southern port of Sidon, and Beirut) and occupy no broad swathes of geographically contiguous territory. They are also unique among Lebanon's major sectarian communities in not having developed a minoritarian outlook. Whereas Shi'a, Maronites, and Druze have traditionally seen themselves as islands in a vast Sunni Islamic sea, Lebanese Sunnis were part of that sea until the fall of the Ottoman Empire and deeply resented their absorption into a Greater Lebanon in the early 1920s (Shi'a were much more ambivalent). All of this makes them highly receptive to a multiplicity of influences from the surrounding Arab world.

While the Sunni elites who agreed to the 1943 National Pact had concrete interests in common with their Christian counterparts that were best preserved in an independent Lebanon (evident in the subsequent domination of Sunni politics by a very small number of prominent families),[28] the formation of Lebanon hurt the interests of most Sunnis. Tripoli, once equal in economic weight to Beirut, was cut off from its traditional trade relations with the Syrian interior and declined in relative prosperity (which is one reason why all major currents of Lebanese Sunni Islamism have been centered in the city)—as did Sidon after its trade routes to Palestine were cut in 1948. While socioeconomic deprivation has served to unite the Shi'a community, it has been a source of division among Sunnis.

Adding to the diffuse nature of Sunni Islamism in Lebanon is its development along two distinct doctrinal axes—political Islamism, as embodied by the Muslim Brotherhood and its offshoots, and Salafi Islamism—neither of which has found a charismatic leader on par with Nasrallah or a state sponsor wholly committed to its propagation.

The Political Islamists

In spite of the Sunni notability's acceptance of the 1943 National Pact, the first decade of Lebanon's independence witnessed a number of Sunni religious movements that publicly embraced the *idea* of an Islamic state, most notably Ibad al-Rahman (Worshipers of the Merciful). However, the 1964 establishment of the Lebanese branch of the Muslim Brotherhood, known as al-Jama'a al-Islamiyya (the Islamic Association), marked a watershed in several respects. Led by Tripoli natives Fathi Yakan and Faysal Mawlawi, al-Jama'a saw the pursuit of an Islamic state as a viable (if long-term and incremental) political project and a counter to the burgeoning appeal of secular Arab nationalism as the ideology of choice for disaffected young Sunnis.

Al-Jama'a was fiercely opposed to both Sunni political elites and the Sunni religious establishment, known as Dar al-Fatwa. Although Dar al-Fatwa administered a vast network of mosques, schools, civil courts, and other social institutions, politicians exerted enormous influence over it by manipulating the (predominantly nonclerical) electoral college that selects the Sunni grand mufti, who in turn controls subordinate appointments. This was especially intolerable to Yakan and Mawlawi, because it contrasted so sharply with the Maronite church (as they saw it)—a religious establishment that not only does not answer to political elites but has the moral authority and social "imbeddedness" to exert influence over them. Al-Jama'a began building its own network of schools and charities to compete with those of Dar al-Fatwa (and with the Maqasid Foundation, which is a charitable network then controlled by the Salam family).

The outbreak of civil war and the breakdown of the state effectively sev-
ered the political elite's hold over Dar al-Fatwa, creating a free for all in
which prominent Sunni clerics fell under the influence of whichever armed
forces were ascendant.[29] Although al-Jama'a fielded a modest militia that
fought alongside Palestinian and Lebanese leftist groups against Christian
forces early in the war, it became fragmented as the fault lines of the war
shifted. In 1976 Syrian military forces entered Lebanon to stave off the
defeat of the Christians, which is an intervention seen by most radical Sunni
Islamists in both countries as a nefarious power play by Alawites (the heterodox Islamic minority sect that dominates Syria's Ba'thist regime) to subvert Sunni influence. However, while Sunni Islamists in Sidon largely
acquiesced to Syria's tightening grip over most of the country, a host of radical splinters of al-Jama'a sprouted up in and around Tripoli to combat Syrian-
backed militia forces—most notably Ismat Murad's Harakat Lubnan al-Arabi
(Arab Lebanon Movement), Kana'an Naji's Jundallah (Soldiers of God), and
Khalil Akkawi's al-Muqawama al-Sha'biyya (Popular Resistance). In 1982,
these factions formed Harakat al-Tawhid al-Islami (the Islamic Unification
Movement, IUM) under the leadership of the charismatic preacher Sa'id
Sha'ban (who famously lamented that Lebanese Christians would have emi-
grated to Cyprus or Latin America had the Syrians not intervened).[30]

Taking advantage of Syria's weakness in the aftermath of Israel's invasion
of Lebanon, Tawhid forces (swelled by an influx of Syrian Islamists who
escaped the Asad regime's apocalyptic showdown with the Muslim
Brotherhood) seized control over much of Tripoli and forged an alliance with
the PLO. For two years, they imposed Islamic law at gunpoint in neighborhoods they controlled (e.g., banning alcohol and forcing women to veil) and
executed dozens of political opponents (mostly Communists). The shrinking
of Tripoli's Christian minority from 20 percent of the population before the
war to 5 percent today was largely the result of this brief interlude.[31]

In the autumn of 1985, Syrian forces swept into the city and brought
Tawhid's mini-state to an end. Sha'ban's close relations with Iran and recognition of Syria's resolve ("Tripoli is not dearer to us than Hama," Vice-
President Abd al-Halim Khaddam reportedly told him at the time, referring
to the Syrian city razed by his government a few years earlier)[32] led him to
reach an accommodation with Damascus, but other Tawhid "emirs" fought
on until they were physically eliminated (such as Akkawi) or captured (such
as Minqara and hundreds of others).

Although armed Sunni Islamist resistance to Syrian forces in Lebanon
disappeared after 1986, the Syrians took no chances, brutally eliminating
Sunni public figures who expressed even the faintest hint of anti-Syrian
dissent.[33] While a large majority of Lebanese Sunnis opposed Lebanon's separation from Syria in the 1920s, at the end of the civil war just 3 percent
favored unification.[34]

In conjunction with its suppression of radical Sunni Islamists, Syria supported the growth of a hitherto obscure movement known as al-Ahbash.
Founded by Shaykh Abdallah al-Hirari, an Islamic scholar of East African

origins (al-Ahbash literally means "the Ethiopians") who immigrated to Lebanon in 1950, the movement blended Sunni and Shi'a theology with Sufi spiritualism into a doctrinal eclecticism that preached nonviolence and political quietism.[35] However, the institutional arm of the movement, Jam'iyyat al-Mashari al-Khayriyya al-Islamiyya (Association of the Islamic Philanthropic Projects), underwent a bizarre metamorphosis as Damascus expanded its grip on the country, forcibly seizing control over prominent mosques and hiring ex-members of the defunct Sunni Murabitun militia to defend them. After Syria completed its conquest of Lebanon in 1990, al-Ahbash grew into the country's largest Sunni religious organization. By the middle of the decade, al-Ahbash leader Nizar al-Halabi was reportedly being groomed by the Syrians to become grand mufti.

Sunni preachers had to contend with very restrictive Syrian "red lines" if they wished to play any part in Lebanese public life during the occupation. Religious mobilization on political issues was permissible only if the target of opprobrium was Israel, moderate Arab regimes, or Lebanese critics of the Syrian occupation—particularly those who held official positions in Dar al-Fatwa. The Union of Akkar Ulama became a virtual mouthpiece of Syrian intelligence, known for its inflammatory denunciations of those who criticized the Syrian occupation.[36] Even Grand Mufti Muhammad Rashid Qabbani routinely offered obsequious praise of the Syrians.[37]

Al-Jama'a and Tawhid courted the Syrians in hopes of gaining influence in government, but the payoffs of their cooperation were meager to begin with and steadily diminished as Syria consolidated its control over Lebanon. Al-Jama'a participated in the heavily Syrian-orchestrated electoral process and saw three of its candidates elected in 1992 (Yakan and Asad Harmush in north Lebanon, Zuhayr al-Ubaydi in Beirut), but this dropped to one in 1996 and none in 2000. After al-Tawhid experienced a resurgence in the late 1990s, the Syrians released Minqara from prison in a transparent (and successful) attempt to splinter the movement ahead of the 2000 elections.

A critical element of Syria's campaign to defuse Sunni militancy was its support for Hariri's ambitious drive to break the political power of traditional Beirut Sunni families. The prime minister's well-funded electoral machine replaced the scions of these families with colorless businessmen interested only in reaping as big a windfall as possible from the country's reconstruction. After the 1996 elections Hariri passed controversial legislation removing most sitting *ulama* from the electoral college that appoints the grand mufti, thereby increasing the subordination of Dar al-Fatwa to the governing elite even further. By eliminating political pluralism within the Sunni community, the Syrians ensured that political Islamists would find few receptive allies within government.

Denied the freedom to criticize substantive aspects of governance, mainstream Sunni clerics and Islamists alike crusaded against un-Islamic cultural influences in Lebanon. In sharp contrast to Hizballah, the political platform of al-Jama'a in the 1998 municipal elections (where the absence of fixed sectarian quotas obviates the need to attract non-Muslim voters) called for banning alcohol, horse racing, and other immoralities (an effective pitch that netted one-third of the seats in Sidon and Tripoli).[38] Dar al-Fatwa crusaded against books, films, and music that were ostensibly offensive to Islam. Qabbani was largely responsible for the 1999 indictment on blasphemy charges of Lebanese Christian singer Marcel Khalife (who was publicly defended by Fadlallah and most other top Shi'a clerics).[39]

By heavily curtailing the ability of political Islamists to exert influence in national government and indirectly encouraging clerical assaults on secularism and non-Islamic culture, the Syrians unwittingly facilitated the expansion of a more deeply puritanical strand of Sunni Islamism.

The Salafists

Salafism is a puritanical Sunni current that seeks to emulate the "righteous ancestors" (*al-salaf al-salih*) of early Islamic history and to purge the faith of fallacious innovations (*bid'a*). While most Salafists pursue this goal nonviolently through missionary and educational activity, others (commonly dubbed Salafi-jihadists) embrace violence to achieve its aims. "Both have the same objective...to convert society into an Islamic society," explains Lebanese journalist Hazim al-Amin, but "vary in the method of achieving it."[40] The Salafi current in Tripoli, founded by Shaykh Salim al-Shahal in the mid-1970s, largely confined itself to religious education and charity work for two decades.

In sharp contrast to the political Islamist currents, Salafists and Salafi-jihadists are largely apolitical. The former eschew involvement in local politics so as to maintain the freedom to disseminate their message to the people with minimal interference from the state, while the latter do so to maintain freedom of action in fighting the enemies of Islam abroad. Both abjure any national identity, and claim allegiance to the universal community of Muslim believers (*umma*).

A second distinguishing feature of Salafi currents is intolerance of heterodox Muslims. Although Tawhid's aggressive imposition of Islamic law in Tripoli may have appealed to Salafists, Shahal viewed Sha'ban's close relations with Iran (and, later on, with Syria) as an abomination.

A third important characteristic of the Salafi current in Lebanon is the prominent role of preachers who studied theology in Saudi Arabia, where the ultraorthodox Wahhabi sect dominates. Salim al-Shahal had very close ties with the late head of Saudi Arabia's Council of Senior Islamic Scholars (and future grand mufti), Shaykh Abd al-Aziz ibn Abdallah ibn Baz, who arranged for hundreds of Lebanese and Palestinian students to enroll in Islamic studies programs at Saudi universities during the civil war (including Shahal's son, Dai al-Islam). Fueled by funding from wealthy Saudi donors (and enjoying a measure of immunity from state interference because of close Syrian-Saudi relations), the Salafi current quietly established a strong social foundation in Tripoli and in the nearby Badawi and Nahr al-Barid Palestinian refugee camps during the early 1990s.[41]

However, the emergence of the Salafi-jihadi current in Lebanon began not in the north but in the Palestinian refugee camp of Ayn al-Hilwa, on the outskirts of the southern Lebanese port of Sidon. Until the early 1990s, Islamist currents in the camp were predominantly Iranian-backed and operated in conjunction with Hizballah, prime among them an armed network known as Ansarallah (Partisans of God), established by Hisham Shraydi. After Shraydi was assassinated in 1991, his successor, Abd al-Karim al-Sa'adi (aka Abu Muhjin), initiated a sweeping reorientation in the group's religious identification and renamed it Asbat al-Ansar (League of Partisans).

This transformation was partly due to the fact that the Syrians severely curtailed Palestinian attacks against the Israelis from Lebanese soil after 1990 (so as to portray the violence in south Lebanon as strictly Lebanese national resistance) and effectively banned operations by Sunni Islamists, whether Palestinian or Lebanese (for fear that battle-hardened Sunni jihadists might one day turn their guns on Damascus). The fact that the Syrians pulled out all the stops in inflaming Sunni hatred toward Israel, while allowing only Shi'as the privilege of actually fighting the Jewish state, created enormous anti-Shi'a resentment.

In order to mobilize Islamists in Ayn al-Hilwa, Shraydi's successors were forced to find an alternative form of identification that deemphasized the struggle to regain Palestine. As Bernard Rougier explains, "they put an end to Iranian tutelage for reasons of sectarian incompatibility and reoriented the group's operations far from the Lebanese-Israeli border," while "stamping it with a salafist character it did not originally have."[42] Toward this end, in 1994 Asbat al-Ansar invited Shahal's charitable group, Jam'iyyat al-Hidaya wal-Ihsan (Association for Guidance and Charity), to teach religious classes in the camp, effectively imbuing the group with a theological validation of its stances.

The following year, in a fairly self-evident bid to attract broader Sunni support in Lebanon, Asbat al-Ansar assassinated Ahbash leader Nizar al-Halabi. Although there is no evidence that Salafi leaders in Tripoli were informed of the audacious killing, this hardly mattered in view of their constant denunciations of the Ahbash over the years. In the weeks that followed, the Lebanese authorities arrested scores of Sunni fundamentalists in north Lebanon on charges of plotting terrorist attacks (most of them subsequently released after robust interrogation), banned Shahal's charity, and charged eight Salafists (including two members of the Shahal family) with publishing seditious material.[43]

The heavy-handed Syrian response to the killing of Halabi—culminating in the gruesome public execution of his assassins in 1997—only served to further radicalize Lebanese Salafists and inspire them to follow Asbat's example. In 1998, a Lebanese veteran of the Afghan war, Basam Ahmad al-Kanj (aka Abu Aisha), arrived in Tripoli and began recruiting disaffected Lebanese (and some non-Lebanese Arab) Sunnis into a guerrilla force in the mountainous Dinniyya region east of the city. On New Year's Eve 1999, a group of the militants ambushed a Lebanese Army patrol that had been sent to investigate, touching off six days of fighting that left 11 soldiers and

20 rebels dead. Around 15 of the Dinniyya militants managed to escape by boat and take refuge in Ayn al-Hilwa.

Although officials in Beirut accused Asbat and the Dinniyya militants of seeking to establish an Islamic state, there is little evidence that either entertained such ambitions. Asbat al-Ansar focused its resources on consolidating its enclaves in Ayn al-Hilwa against encroachments by Fatah and on training militants to fight abroad (mostly in Chechnya). Apart from its murder of four Lebanese judges in 1999 (in retaliation for the execution of Halabi's assassins), the closest it came to attacking the Lebanese state was shooting a policeman who tried to obstruct its January 2000 rocket attack on the Russian embassy. Asbat militants also carried out small-scale bombings of churches and bars, but most of these attacks caused only material damage and did not pose a threat to the state (if anything, they legitimized official claims about the dangers of sectarian violence if Syrian troops were to depart). Had it been otherwise, the Syrians would never have tolerated the "island of insecurity" in Ayn al-Hilwa.

The Dinniyya crackdown simply reflected Syria's refusal to allow an armed Sunni Islamist presence to develop outside of this tiny enclave (where the comings and goings of Salafi-jihadists can be closely monitored), irrespective of its intent. Those who crossed this line disappeared into a murky "state within a state" of Syria's making, one in which Islamists were held without trial for years on end or brought before military tribunals that habitually dismiss allegations of routine torture by Lebanese and Syrian security forces.[44] Dai al-Islam al-Shahal went into hiding rather than taking the risk of answering a summons.[45]

Inside Ayn al-Hilwa, the Salafi-jihadist current continued to grow in strength, fueled by an influx of new external funding after the September 11 attacks. Initially, Asbat al-Ansar relied on donations funneled through Salafi charities in the camp affiliated with the imam of the al-Nur mosque in Ayn al-Hilwa, Jamal Khattab, or on those funds that were transported directly by al-Qa'ida couriers.[46] Increasingly, however, Asbat has received money directly wired by supporters abroad—a simple process in Lebanon, which has one of the world's most protective bank secrecy laws and little record of investigating terrorist financing.[47] In its eagerness to draw support from the global jihadi movement, Asbat began targeting Americans in Lebanon. In addition to several bombing attacks on American commercial franchises, it is alleged to have been behind the killing of an American missionary in 2002 and a failed plot to assassinate American Ambassador Vincent Battle the following year.

As Asbat expanded, its transnational jihadist ambitions necessitated a minimal level of accommodation with the Lebanese authorities. This became evident in July 2002, when it turned over to the authorities a Dinniyya militant who fled into the camp after killing three Lebanese soldiers who tried to apprehend him. This controversial decision led a faction of Asbat, headed by Abdallah Shraydi (the son of Hisham Shraydi), to break away and operate independently as Asbat al-Nur (which eventually dissolved after he was killed the following year). Another Salafi-jihadi faction, calling itself Jama'at al-Nur, emerged under the leadership of Ahmad al-Miqati and other Dinniyya militants in the camp.

The Salafi-jihadists temporarily overcame their differences following the U.S.-led ouster of Saddam Hussein in 2003, as all agreed that recruiting and training operatives to fight in Iraq was the highest priority. Moreover, since the Syrians were anxious to undermine the American presence in Iraq, the Lebanese authorities were now willing to turn a blind eye to terrorist recruitment outside of Ayn al-Hilwa, and non-Salafi Islamists were eager to offer support. Scores of local volunteers were sent to Iraq,[48] a few playing important leadership roles in the Arab jihadi wing of the insurgency.[49] If the tally displayed on banners plastered throughout Tripoli is reasonably accurate, the Lebanese Sunni community's per capita contribution of "martyrs" has been rivaled only by that of the Saudis.[50] Lebanon became a critical conduit for non-Lebanese Arab (particularly Saudi) jihadists traveling to and from Iraq—and then very quickly became a port of call for jihadists headed everywhere else under the sun.[51]

The participation of many Lebanese Sunni Islamists in Iraq paved the way for the emergence in Lebanon of Salafi-jihadi networks that adhere to the zealous takfirism (declaring other Muslims to be unbelievers) of Abu Mus'ab Zarqawi, the Jordanian-born leader of al-Qa'ida in Iraq. In 2004, dissident Asbat members and Dinniyya militants[52] formed a new movement calling itself Jund al-Sham (Soldiers of the Levant),[53] a name previously used by Zarqawi's followers before he arrived in Iraq. In a series of public statements, Jund al-Sham declared Shi'a and Christians to be "infidels."[54] By allowing jihadists to infiltrate Iraq and kill both by the thousands, however, the Syrian and Lebanese governments gained a measure of immunity for their own "infidel" constituents.

In September 2004, the Lebanese authorities carried out a wave of arrests in the predominantly Sunni town of Majdal Anjar in the Biqa (a critical logistical hub of jihadists going to Iraq), claiming to have uncovered imminent terror attacks against the embassy of Italy and other targets in Lebanon. However, most Lebanese Sunnis were convinced that the plots were fabricated by the Syrians to deflect American pressure after the UN Security Council passed Resolution 1559 that called for a Syrian withdrawal weeks earlier. When the 35-year-old Lebanese mastermind of the plot, Isma'il Khatib, died of "heart failure" in custody, thousands of Sunnis protested in the streets of Majdal Anjar.[55]

The last year of the Syrian occupation witnessed the public reemergence of Hizb al-Tahrir al-Islami (Islamic Liberation Party), an international Islamist movement that defies the political/Salafi dichotomy. Although al-Tahrir aspires to bring about the unification of the Islamic world under a restored caliphate, it is committed to achieving this goal nonviolently through persuasion of elites in each country. While some chapters of al-Tahrir in Europe and the former Soviet republics of Central Asia have been linked to violence, the Lebanese chapter has been nonviolent.[56]

LEBANESE ISLAMISM AFTER
THE SYRIAN WITHDRAWAL

The withdrawal of Syrian forces from Lebanon gave Shi'a and Sunni Islamists unmitigated freedom to participate in public life for the first time in decades—at a time when public disillusionment with the political establishment was at an all-time high and parliamentary elections were just weeks away. Both took the opportunity to renegotiate their relationships with other political forces from a position of strength.

For Hizballah, the Syrian withdrawal removed the glass ceiling blocking its pursuit of absolute Shi'a political hegemony. Barri saw the writing on the wall and effectively subordinated Amal to Nasrallah, who graciously granted it equal billing on "steamroller slates" that easily swept majority Shi'a districts in the May–June 2005 parliamentary elections. Moreover, it so happened that the "March 14 coalition," led by the late Hariri's son and political heir, Sa'ad, and Druze leader Walid Jumblatt, needed Hizballah to defeat Michel Aoun's secular nationalist Free Patriotic Movement (FPM) in hotly contested Christian-Druze districts with Shi'a minorities.[57] Nasrallah's price for his endorsement was continued government sanction of Hizballah's "resistance" to Israel, effectively formalizing the quid pro quo that evolved under the Syrian occupation. In order to ensure that the coalition did not renege on this commitment, Hizballah joined the cabinet for the first time, with two ministers. Consequently, the new government of Prime Minister Fuad Siniora (a stand-in for Sa'ad Hariri) declined to interfere with its arms shipments from Iran[58] and refused to obstruct (or even publicly criticize) its periodic cross-border raids.

The March 14 coalition also courted Sunni Islamists in its bid to defeat the FPM in mixed Sunni-Christian districts of north Lebanon, where victory hinged on mobilizing high turnout among Sunnis (which had been very low in the first round of the elections in Beirut). Having endured relentless harassment by Syrian-backed governments for years, Salafi preachers in Tripoli and Akkar suspended their traditional aversion to electoral politics and mobilized their followers to go to the polls. Preachers on the payroll of Dar al-Fatwa needed much less enticement (for obvious reasons), many of them going beyond "get out the vote" campaigning to explicitly endorse March 14. Although al-Jama'a joined most traditional Sunni politicians in boycotting the elections, few Sunnis in north Lebanon took notice—thereby underscoring how much credibility on the street it had lost to the Salafi current.

After the elections, the newly elected parliament rewarded the Salafists with an amnesty law that freed 26 Dinniyya militants and 7 of the Majdal Anjar detainees still in custody awaiting trial.[59] In addition, the government established a quid pro quo with Salafi-jihadists, allowing them to operate with minimal interference by the state so long as they did not carry out attacks in Lebanon itself—an arrangement openly acknowledged by pro-March 14 Lebanese and Saudi media.[60]

Although the ruling coalition came under considerable outside pressure to abandon or revise these understandings, its tenuous electoral mandate gave it little room for maneuver. Any attempt to renege on the agreement with Hizballah would have led Nasrallah to declare a boycott of the government that few credible Shi'a public figures would be willing to defy. Moreover, a substantial majority of Sunnis (and significant minorities of Christians and Druze) remained supportive of Hizballah's armed presence.[61] Confronting the Salafi-jihadi current (absent a major provocation) was also untenable, as it would alienate mainstream Salafists—the segment of the Sunni community *least* sympathetic (indeed, outright hostile) to Hizballah. In both cases, disunity within Hariri's core Sunni constituency limited the coalition's leverage with severe consequences.

Hariri's top priority has been to unify Sunni ranks under his leadership and to replicate the *assabiyya* (group solidarity) of the Shi'a community by relying heavily on his massive financial resources. The charitable arm of his Future Movement began providing subsidies to poor Sunnis in many areas of the country. He reportedly lavished money on al-Jama'a, leading many of its top leaders to back the coalition publicly. The fact that the Syrian Muslim Brotherhood came out strongly against Syrian President Bashar Asad after 2005 facilitated this transition. The Siniora government legalized al-Tahrir, making Lebanon the only Arab state to do so.

During the uproar over a Danish newspaper's publication of cartoons lampooning Muhammad in February 2006, Hariri provided transportation for Sunnis in north Lebanon to attend a demonstration in Beirut[62]—an initiative that backfired horribly when the protesters went on a rampage, setting fire to a building housing the Danish embassy and vandalizing two nearby churches in full view of Internal Security Forces (ISF) riot police.

The Israel-Hizballah War

Hizballah's overriding goal after the withdrawal of Syrian forces was to preserve and legitimate its paramilitary forces. However, as international pressure for its disarmament mounted steadily, Nasrallah faced a vexing catch-22. While avoiding major provocations against Israel would help counteract *international* pressure, a conspicuous lull threatened to fuel the growth of *domestic* pressure—not from Shi'a (who assume most of the risks incurred by the attacks and do not strongly identify with the Palestinian struggle) but from Sunnis (who assume little risk, strongly identify with the Palestinian struggle, and would otherwise have strong reservations about an armed Shi'a presence).

It is no accident that Hizballah's initial failure to respond to the massive upswing of Israeli-Palestinian violence in June 2006 led Zarqawi to issue a rambling tirade against the group for "raising false banners regarding the liberation of Palestine" and "stand[ing] guard against Sunnis who want to cross the border."[63] Nasrallah may have been chomping at the bit to join the fray, but the intensification of Salafi hostility toward Hizballah (in April 2006, the authorities arrested nine Lebanese and Palestinian Salafi-jihadists who were allegedly plotting to assassinate Nasrallah)[64] made it virtually imperative to act. Hizballah's kidnapping of two Israeli soldiers in a bloody cross-border raid on July 12, 2006 was perhaps less an act of solidarity than an attempt to upstage Palestinian Islamists and relegitimate itself in Sunni eyes.[65]

The 33-day American-backed Israeli military campaign that followed was largely designed to prevent this from happening. While the Israelis presumably recognized the futility of trying to change Lebanese Shi'a public opinion by force of arms (they had been down that road before), there was clearly an expectation that targeting Lebanon's economic infrastructure would turn Sunnis (and Christians) against Hizballah. However, despite the immense destruction visited upon Lebanon, the war failed to significantly diminish support for Hizballah among Lebanese Sunnis[66] and greatly *increased* support for Hizballah among Arab Sunnis outside of Lebanon.[67]

Nevertheless, the scale of destruction rendered Hizballah provocations against Israel politically unthinkable for the foreseeable future and the subsequent deployment of an expanded UNIFIL (United Nations Interim Force in Lebanon) force sealed off its access to the border. Deprived of an outlet for confronting Israel, Hizballah turned its attention to domestic affairs after the war, forging a united opposition front with the FPM and leading a Shi'a boycott of the government. This reorientation alienated many Sunni political Islamists who had been staunch supporters of the "resistance" during the war,[68] for Hizballah was now committing the double sin of mobilizing Shi'as against a Sunni prime minister in league with secular Christians. Al-Jama'a quickly splintered, as Mawlawi and most of its senior leadership lined up behind the government while Yakan and a substantial minority of its rank and file joined the opposition under the umbrella group Jabhat al-Amal al-Islami (Islamic Action Front). Although the two rival factions of Tawhid (led by Minqara and Bilal Sha'ban) both reaffirmed their support for Hizballah and joined the IAF, a few former Tawhid "emirs" (e.g., Kana'an Naji) came out in support of March 14. On the other hand, Shahal and the vast majority of Salafi preachers now backed the government more firmly than ever.

The Rise of Fath al-Islam

The March 14 coalition's struggle to preserve Sunni unity amid Lebanon's escalating postwar political crisis widened the latitude enjoyed by Salafi-jihadists, as Hariri was understandably reluctant to enter into a confrontation with fellow Sunnis. The Siniora government therefore did nothing to reverse Jund al-Sham's prewar seizure of the neighborhood of Ta'mir adjacent to Ayn al-Hilwa or to prevent it from terrorizing the inhabitants. The militants finally allowed the army to deploy in Ta'mir only after Bahiya Hariri (Sa'ad's aunt) paid them off in early 2007.[69]

The Syrians exploited this weakness by allowing Arab jihadists to cross into Lebanon, most notably Shakir al-Abbasi—a Jordanian-Palestinian associate of Zarqawi best known for organizing the 2002 assassination of U.S. diplomat Lawrence Foley in Amman. During the summer and fall of 2006, Abbasi quietly recruited a small force of several dozen militant Sunni Islamists and trained them at facilities made available by pro-Syrian Palestinian organizations. After operating underground for several months, however, his men apparently "went native" in late November 2006 by seizing control of three Fath al-Intifada compounds in the Nahr al-Barid refugee camp near Tripoli and issuing a statement denouncing the "corruption and deviation" of the sclerotic Syrian proxy and the "intelligence agencies" it serves. Calling themselves a "Palestinian national liberation movement" and adopting the moniker Fath al-Islam, they declared a holy war to liberate Palestine.[70]

While Abbasi presented Fath al-Islam as an all-Palestinian movement,[71] most of the hundreds of volunteers who answered his call over the next six months were Lebanese[72] and a substantial minority were Saudis,[73] Syrians, and nationals of various other Arab and Islamic countries. Astonishingly, this massive expansion took place with little interference from the government.[74] Despite having been convicted in absentia for the Foley murder, Abbasi operated in the open—even playing host to journalists from the New York Times (which noted obliquely that "because of Lebanese politics" he was "largely shielded from the government").[75]

While there is little evidence to support claims by investigative journalist Seymour Hersh and others that March 14 leaders encouraged the growth of Fath al-Islam and other *armed* Islamist groups as counterweights to Hizballah,[76] the coalition was clearly reluctant to pay the hefty political premium of confronting a well-financed and provisioned Sunni jihadi group operating within the protection of a Palestinian refugee camp. It was not until Fath al-Islam robbed its third bank in the Tripoli area and U.S. Assistant Secretary of State David Welch visited Beirut to press the issue in May 2007 that Siniora finally sent the ISF into action with a predawn raid on a Fath al-Islam safehouse.

Siniora's failure to inform the army beforehand left Lebanese soldiers stationed outside Nahr al-Barid vulnerable to a withering reprisal hours later while most were asleep in their barracks (nine were found with their throats slit). Ironically, however, the deaths of 22 soldiers that day diminished the political expense of taking the group down by collectively horrifying the vast majority of Lebanese. Although a number of terror attacks outside the camp were carried out by sleeper cells established by Fath al-Islam or under the direction of outsiders (culminating in the June 24 bomb attack in south Lebanon that killed six UNIFIL peacekeepers) as the army methodically isolated and destroyed Fath al-Islam over the next three months, few Lebanese voiced objections. Even Asbat al-Ansar distanced itself from Fath al-Islam and extinguished an abortive attempt to join the revolt by Jund al-Sham (which appears to have since disbanded and returned to the fold). Al-Qa'ida leaders abroad wisely chose not to endorse the ill-fated rebellion.

The Lebanese Army's victory over Fath al-Islam undoubtedly strengthened the coalition's leverage vis-à-vis other Salafi-jihadist groups. However, so long as the coalition relies primarily on support from the Sunni community, there will be political impediments to constraining their growth. It is telling that Dai al-Islam al-Shahal can beam with praise for Hariri[77] even as he acknowledges having met twice with Abbasi prior to his apocalyptic confrontation with the state.[78] There is a code of understanding among Salafists in Lebanon that accepts the formation of underground armed networks so long as they do not antagonize the authorities. Persuading them otherwise will be virtually impossible so long as Hizballah remains armed, which clearly will be the case for the foreseeable future.

NOTES

1. For a good overview of Lebanese Shi'a history, see Fouad Ajami, *The Vanished Imam: Musa al Sadr and the Shia of Lebanon* (Ithaca: Cornell University Press, 1986).
2. An estimated 60% of the rural population of southern Lebanon had migrated into the slums of Beirut by 1975. Salim Nasr, "Roots of the Shi'i Movement," *Middle East Research and Information Project (MERIP) Reports*, No. 133 (June 1985), p. 11.
3. Sayyid Muhammad Husayn Fadlallah, *Al-Islam wa Mantiq al-Quwwa*, 2nd ed. (Beirut: al-Mu'assasa al-jam'iyya lil-dirasa wal-nashr, 1981).
4. "The Iranians believe that all decisions regarding Shi'a Islam must come from Iran," Fadlallah said in 2003. *L'Orient-Le Jour* (Beirut), January 25, 2003. See Roschanack Shaery-Eisenlohr, "Iran, the Vatican of Shi'ism?" *Middle East Report*, No. 233 (Winter 2004), http://www.merip.org/mer/mer233/Shaery-eisenlohr.html
5. See Martin Kramer, "The Moral Logic of Hizballah," in Walter Reich (ed.), *Origins of Terrorism: Psychologies, Ideologies, Theologies, States of Mind* (Cambridge: Cambridge University Press, 1990), pp. 131–157.
6. Martin Kramer, "Hizbullah: The Calculus of Jihad," in Martin E. Marty and R. Scott Appleby (eds.), *Fundamentalisms and the State* (Chicago: University of Chicago Press, 1993), pp. 539–556.
7. While Fadlallah acknowledged the efficacy of suicide bombings under some circumstances, he declined to issue religious edicts explicitly sanctioning (or forbidding) them and, from the mid-1980s onward, argued that these circumstances no longer applied. He ruled that hijackings and kidnappings of innocents are always "inhumane and irreligious." Kramer, "The Moral Logic of Hizballah."
8. Hezbollah bitterly contested Syria's 1987 occupation of West Beirut, prompting the Syrians to execute 23 of its fighters in retaliation, upon which it organized one of the largest anti-Syrian demonstrations of the war. See "7,000 Shia Mourners Call for Revenge," *The Times* (London), February 26, 1987. It also allowed "large amounts of vital materials" to pass through its stronghold in the southern suburbs of Beirut to General Michel Aoun's besieged Lebanese Army units during his 1989–1990 rebellion against Syrian forces. See "Syria Summons Druze Leader over Disputes in Pro-Syrian Camp," United Press International (UPI), October 9, 1990.
9. It is important to bear in mind that few Shi'a held favorable views of Syria during this period. A 1987 survey of Shi'a college students found that more blamed Syria for Lebanon's civil war than Israel or the United States. See Hilal Khashan, "Do Lebanese Shi'is Hate the West?" *Orbis*, Vol. 33, No. 4 (1989), pp. 583–590.

ISLAMIST GROUPS IN LEBANON

10. See Nizar Hamzeh, "Lebanon's Hizballah: From Revolution to Parliamentary Accommodation," *Third World Quarterly*, Vol. 14, No. 2 (1993), pp. 321–337.

11. While Hezbollah was free to criticize such inequities, it was not allowed to mobilize the Shi'a community in ways that might undermine political stability of occupied Lebanon (e.g., by organizing mass protests or openly coordinating with the Christian opposition). When Tufayli split from the movement to lead a "revolution of the hungry" in the late 1990s, his followers were hunted down by Lebanese Army troops.

12. During the 2000 elections, one Hezbollah candidate estimated that the party would have won 20 seats (twice its allotment) had it been allowed to run head-to-head against Amal. See "Victorious Hezbollah Faces Compulsory Alliances," UPI, September 2, 2000.

13. See Gary C. Gambill, "Syrian Workers in Lebanon: The Other Occupation," *Middle East Intelligence Bulletin*, Vol. 3, No. 2 (February 2001), http://www.meib.org/articles/0102_l1.htm.

14. See Gary C. Gambill, "Lebanese Farmers and the Syrian Occupation," *Middle East Intelligence Bulletin*, Vol. 5, No. 10 (October 2003), http://www.meib.org/articles/0310_l1.htm.

15. Although there are few reliable statistics on this, according to the World Bank "income inequality is generally believed to have increased" during the 1990s. See World Bank, *Lebanon: Country Brief* (Washington, DC: World Bank, September 2005), http://lnweb18.worldbank.org/mna/mena.nsf/Countries/Lebanon/DD01F4FEEFA05C2A85256CC9006C6A80?OpenDocument.

16. See Blanca Madani, "Hezbollah's Global Finance Network: The Triple Frontier," *Middle East Intelligence Bulletin*, Vol. 4, No. 1 (January 2002), http://www.meib.org/articles/0201_l2.htm; "Hezbollah and the West African Diamond Trade," *Middle East Intelligence Bulletin*, Vol. 6, Nos. 6–7 (June/July 2004), http://www.meib.org/articles/0407_l2.htm.

17. "We believe the requirement for an Islamic state is to have an overwhelming popular desire, and we're not talking about fifty percent plus one, but a large majority. And this is not available in Lebanon and probably never will be," Nasrallah said in 2004. See Adam Shatz, "In Search of Hezbollah," *New York Review of Books*, April 29, 2004.

18. See May Chartouni-Dubarry, "Hizballah: From Militia to Political Party," in R. Hollis and N. Shebadi (eds.), *Lebanon on Hold: Implications for Middle East Peace* (London: Royal Institute of International Affairs, 1996), pp. 59–62.

19. In 1993, e.g., Robert Fisk published an article entitled "Hizbollah Vows Peace When the Troops Pull Out" on the basis of Nasrallah having told him that the group would "close the file concerning the occupation of Lebanese land" after an Israeli withdrawal (he did not say whether there were other files and Fisk did not ask). See Robert Fisk, "Hizbollah Vows Peace When the Troops Pull Out: 'Party of God' Will Concentrate on Lebanese Politics and Leave Palestinians to Fight Own Battles, Leader Tells Robert Fisk in Beirut," *The Independent* (London), November 10, 1993.

20. See, e.g., Augustus Richard Norton, "Hizbullah: From Radicalism to Pragmatism," *Middle East Policy*, Vol. 5, No. 4 (January 1998).

21. Judith Palmer Harik, "Between Islam and the System: Sources and Implications of Popular Support for Lebanon's Hizballah," *The Journal of Conflict Resolution*, Vol. 40, No. 1 (March 1996), pp. 41–67.

22. The Syrians underscored this shortly after the Israeli withdrawal by calling a halt to President Emile Lahoud's anticorruption campaign, facilitating Hariri's return to office after a two-year hiatus and manipulating Shi'a electoral lists in the fall 2000 elections.

23. According to Emile al-Hokayem, there has been a rift within Hizballah "between a powerful core committed to permanent resistance and the mid-level political cadre willing to focus exclusively on political participation." See Emile al-Hokayem, "Hizballah and Syria: Outgrowing the Proxy Relationship," *The Washington Quarterly*, Vol. 30, No. 2 (Spring 2007).

24. See Avi Jorisch, *Beacon of Hatred: Inside Hizballah's Al-Manar Television* (Washington, DC: Washington Institute for Near East Policy, 2004).

25. Seymour Hersh, "The Syrian Bet," *New Yorker*, July 28, 2003; Adam Shatz, "In Search of Hezbollah," *New York Review of Books*, April 29, 2004.

26. After being fired as director of al-Manar TV in 2003, Nayef Krayem wrote in a public reply that he had been unjustly accused of "being with Fadlallah." In August 2004, Hezbollah activists broke into a mosque controlled by followers of Fadlallah and plastered posters of Khomeini inside. *Al-Nahar* (Beirut), May 12, 2003; *al-Balad* (Beirut), August 23, 2004.

27. Vali Nasr, *The Shiite Revival: How Conflicts within Islam Will Shape the Future* (New York: W. W. Norton, 2006), p. 68.

28. Members of four prominent Sunni families (Sulh, Karama, Yafi, and Salam) held the premiership in 40 of the 53 Lebanese cabinets that served from 1943 to 1982. See Samir Khalaf, *Lebanon's Predicament* (New York: Columbia University Press, 1987), p. 106.

29. For example, Grand Mufti Hasan Khalid, considered a Nasserist before the war, could be found supporting the American-backed government of Amine Gemayel in 1983, only to express support for an Islamic state after West Beirut fell out of government control in early 1984. See "Beirut Christians Fearful of Shift to Moslem Rule," *Washington Post*, March 12, 1984.

30. *Al-Diyar* (Beirut), August 31, 1989.

31. "Fighting at Nahr al-Bared Splits Tripoli into Two Camps," *The Daily Star*, July 3, 2007.

32. Kurt Mendenhall, "Syria's Ongoing Lebanese Adventure," *Washington Report on Middle East Affairs*, August 1988, p. 9.

33. Key Sunni figures believed to have been assassinated on orders from Syria include Shaykh Subhi Salih, deputy chairman of the Supreme Islamic Council (1986); Muhammad Shukayr, political adviser to then President Amine Gemayel (1987); Grand Mufti Hasan Khalid (1989); and MP Nazim Qadri (1989).

34. Hilal Khashan, "The Lebanese State: Lebanese Unity and the Sunni Muslim Position," *International Sociology*, Vol. 7, No. 1 (1992), p. 93.

35. A. Nizar Hamzeh and R. Hrair Dekmejian, "A Sufi Response to Political Islamism: Al-Ahbash of Lebanon," *International Journal of Middle East Studies*, Vol. 28, No. 2 (May 1996), pp. 217–229.

36. When Lebanon's Council of Maronite Bishops openly called for the withdrawal of Syrian forces in the fall of 2000, the Akkar Ulama accused it of "instigating fanaticism and strife." See "Orthodox Patriarch Defends Bkirki," *The Daily Star* (Beirut), October 4, 2000.

37. When the Council of Maronite Archbishops issued a historic statement calling for a Syrian withdrawal from Lebanon in September 2000, Qabbani issued a statement expressing "astonishment" and praising "sisterly Syria" for its "big

sacrifices to safeguard Lebanon's unity and maintain its security and stability."
Al-Safir (Beirut), September 21, 2000.
38. A. Nizar Hamzeh, "Lebanon's Islamists and Local Politics: A New Reality,"
Third World Quarterly, Vol. 21, No. 5 (2000), pp. 739–759. Hizballah's platform contained not a hint of Islamic influence.
39. "Lyrical Liberties?" *al-Ahram Weekly*, Nos. 14–20 (October 1999); "Khalife
Song Not an Insult to Islam: Fadlallah," Agence France Presse (AFP), October 4,
1999. In 1994, Dar al-Fatwa banned the compilation of articles by the recently
deceased Libyan writer (and fierce critic of Islamic orthodoxy) Sadiq al-Nay-
hum. See Dale F. Eickelman and James Piscatori, *Muslim Politics* (Princeton:
Princeton University Press, 1996), p. 156.
40. Al-Arabiya TV, April 13, 2007. Translation by British Broadcasting Corporation
(BBC) Worldwide Monitoring.
41. For more on Salafists outside of north Lebanon, see Bilal Y. Saab and Magnus
Ranstorp, "Securing Lebanon from the Threat of Salafist Jihadism," *Studies in
Conflict & Terrorism*, Vol. 30, No. 10 (2007), pp. 825–855.
42. Bernard Rougier, *Everyday Jihad: The Rise of Militant Islam among Palestinians
in Lebanon*, translated by Pascale Ghazaleh (Cambridge, MA: Harvard
University Press, 2007), pp. 49, 85.
43. "Two Moslem Fundamentalist Charity Groups Banned," AFP, January 4,
1996.
44. Human Rights Watch, "Lebanon: Torture and Unfair Trial of the Dhinniyyah
Detainees," May 7, 2003, http://web.amnesty.org/library/index/
engmde180052003.
45. *Al-Safir* (Beirut), February 8, 2003.
46. A key figure in this regard (until his assassination in 2003, apparently by Israel)
was Abd al-Sattar al-Jad (widely known as Abu Muhammad al-Masri), an
Egyptian al-Qa'ida operative who arrived at the camp in the mid-1990s.
47. For example, a foiled plot to assassinate U.S. Ambassador Vincent Battle was
allegedly financed by the Lebanese-born head of Australia's Islamic Youth
Movement, Bilal Ghazal. See "The Baggage of Bilal Khazal," *Sydney Morning
Herald* (Australia), June 4, 2004. For their alleged links to Asbat al-Ansar, see
"Clashes Leave Fatah in Poor Position," *The Daily Star*, May 22, 2003.
48. By November 2004, according to the London-based Arabic daily *al-Hayat*,
"dozens" of Lebanese Sunnis and "tens" of Palestinians from Lebanese ref-
ugee camps were fighting in Iraq. Lebanese killed in Iraq included two resi-
dents of al-Qara'un (Fadi Ghayth and Umar Darwish), two from Majdal Anjar
(Ali al-Khatib and Hasan Sawwan), and "several" from the predominantly
Sunni cities of Sidon and Tripoli. The report also mentioned the deaths of
Palestinians Muhammad Farran and the son of Ansarallah leader Jamal
Sulayman. See *al-Hayat* (London), November 8, 2004.
49. One of the earliest Lebanese arrivals, Mustapha Darwish Ramadan (aka Abu
Muhammad al-Lubnani), was said to have been the "right-hand man of Zarqawi"
until his death in a September 2004 American air strike. See *al-Rai al-Aam*
(Kuwait), September 20, 2004; "Smoke of Iraq War 'Drifting over Lebanon,'"
Washington Post, June 12, 2006.
50. The number reached 50 during the summer of 2006. See "Lebanese Salute
Their 'Martyrs' in Iraq War," *The Independent* (London), July 7, 2006.
51. Two members of the Algerian terrorist group Salafist Group for Call and
Combat (GSPC) arrested by French police in 2005 were found to have received

explosives training at a camp near Tripoli. See Emily Hunt, "Can al-Qaeda's Lebanese Expansion Be Stopped?" *PolicyWatch*, No. 1076 (Washington Institute for Near East Policy, February 6, 2006).

52. Although nominally founded by prominent preacher Muhammad Sharqiyya (aka Abu Yusuf), the main decision-makers were Abu Ramiz al-Sahmarani (aka Abu-Ramiz al-Tarabulsi), a prominent Dinniyya militant, and Imad Yasin, a former Asbat commander who had gained notoriety for instigating a shootout with Hamas in 2002.

53. The Arabic word *al-Sham* literally means "the north." In early Islamic history, it was used to refer to lands north of the Arabian Peninsula, including present-day Syria, Lebanon, and Israel. *Jund al-Sham* is sometimes translated as "soldiers of Greater Syria."

54. *Al-Nahar* (Beirut), June 26, 2004; *al-Safir* (Beirut), July 14, 2004.

55. "Uproar over Lebanon Custody Death," BBC, September 28, 2004, http://news.bbc.co.uk/2/hi/middle_east/3698028.stm.

56. The only notable exception was its 1985 kidnapping of four Soviet diplomats (one of whom was executed while in custody), which was an act of desperation intended to halt the Syrian siege of Tripoli. Current al-Tahrir leaders disavow involvement.

57. As the *New York Times* noted, "[T]he endorsement of the Shi'a Hezbollah party was critical" in Ba'abda-Alay, where the number of Shi'a voters was substantially larger than the March 14 coalition's margin of victory. See "Returning Lebanese General Stuns Anti-Syria Alliance," *New York Times*, June 14, 2005. Hizballah's endorsement was also a factor in north Lebanon, as it eroded the ability of rival Sunni politicians to mobilize the Arab nationalist current against the Hariri family.

58. In April 2006, UN Secretary General Kofi Annan warned in a report to the Security Council that the Lebanese Army has "not been authorized to prevent further movement of the ammunitions" from Syria to Hizballah bases in Lebanon. See Third Semi-Annual Report of the Secretary-General to the Security Council on the implementation of Security Council Resolution 1559 (2004), April 19, 2006, http://domino.un.org/UNISPAL.NSF/36leea1cc0 8301c485256cf600606959/abf843295c78f7f18525715e00657ba9!Open Document.

59. "Beirut Clashes Follow Geagea Amnesty," Aljazeera.net, July 20, 2005, http://english.aljazeera.net/English/archive/archive?ArchiveId=13568.

60. Hariri's newspaper, *al-Mustaqbal*, acknowledged that al-Qa'ida "has benefited from Lebanon as a transit point for individuals and logistics headed to Iraq or other Arab countries" and therefore "has not used Lebanon as an arena for confrontation." See *al-Mustaqbal* (Beirut), January 8, 2006. Translation by BBC Worldwide Monitoring; Hazim al-Amin writes in *al-Hayat*:

> Al-Qaeda benefits from Lebanon as a human and financial transit point that does not tighten its surveillance and search measures at its airports and facilities. If Lebanon is turned into a target because of a decision by al-Qaeda, it will become an area of difficulty.... There are some aspects of al-Qaeda's presence in Lebanon to which a blind eye is turned in a sense.... While most of the region's countries have doubled the financial and commercial supervision of activities linked to suspected Islamic organizations, Lebanon has not adopted any such measures. Unlike many other countries, it has not imposed special procedures for the transfer of funds through it. (See *al-Hayat* [London], August 27, 2006)

61. Graham E. Fuller, "The Hizballah-Iran Connection: Model for Sunni Resistance," *The Washington Quarterly*, Vol. 30, No. 1 (Winter 2006–2007), p. 147.
62. "The Hariri group bussed many groups in from Akkar," according to American University of Beirut professor Hilal Khashan. Quoted in "Lebanon's New War," *al-Ahram Weekly*, Nos. 24–30 (May 2007).
63. "Hezbollah, al-Qaida Mirror Islamic Split," The Associated Press, June 24, 2006.
64. *Al-Diyar* (Beirut), April 13, 2006; "Shia of Lebanon Emerge from Poverty to Face Charges of Overstepping Their Powers," *Financial Times*, May 5, 2006.
65. In fact, there has long been an undercurrent of tension between Hamas and Hizballah for this very reason. Hizballah's resumption of hostilities with Israel after the start of the 2000–2005 intifada led to a public rift between the two groups that lasted throughout much of 2001 (though this was partly due to Hizballah's attempts to recruit Palestinian terror cells directly). See "The Terror Twins," *Time*, April 30, 2001.
66. According to an Ipsos survey conducted at the end of the war, 84% of Shi'a Muslim and 46% of Sunnis believed that Hizballah "should keep its weapons," while only 21% of Druze and 23% of Christians believed it should. See *L'Orient-Le Jour* (Beirut), August 28, 2006.
67. A November 2006 survey of six Arab countries by Shibley Telhami and Zogby International found that Nasrallah was the most popular choice among respondents in Egypt, Jordan, Morocco, and the United Arab Emirates when asked to name the world leader outside their own countries they admired most (Lebanese respondents had to choose a non-Lebanese figure; he finished second among Saudi respondents). See "U.S., Israel 'Biggest Threat' to Arabs, Poll Finds," Inter Press Service, February 8, 2007; Amal Saad-Ghorayeb, "What the Moderate Arab World Is," *al-Ahram Weekly*, No. 26 (April–May 2007). Data for the poll is available at http://brookings.edu/views/speeches/telhami20070208.pdf.
68. "Hezbollah is waging a struggle against its own self-interests. Its real cause is and should remain the resistance," said al-Jama'a Deputy Secretary-General Ibrahim al-Masri after Hizballah and the FPM organized two massive demonstrations against the government in early December 2006. See "Lebanon at a Tripwire," *International Crisis Group Middle East Briefing*, No. 20 (December 21, 2006), http://www.crisisgroup.org/home/index.cfm?id=4586.
69. Michael Young, "Destruction and Deceit in North Lebanon," *The Daily Star* (Beirut), May 24, 2007.
70. *Al-Safir* (Beirut), November 28, 2006.
71. *Al-Diyar* (Beirut), February 20, 2007.
72. This was confirmed definitively by the identification of militants captured and killed in the recent violence. Of 20 Fatah al-Islam members who appeared before a military court on May 30, 2007, 19 were Lebanese. See National News Agency, May 30, 2007.
73. Of 25 militants whose bodies had been recovered by the Lebanese authorities as of May 26, 2007, 4 were identified as Saudis, according to the Saudi ambassador in Lebanon. See *al-Hayat* (London), May 27, 2007.
74. Although Lebanese troops imposed a tight blockade of the camp in March 2007, eyewitnesses in the camp said that a large shipment of weapons arrived in early May. See al-*Hayat* (London), May 27, 2007. Officials of the UN Relief and Works Agency (UNWRA) later expressed astonishment that such a large influx of men and material went undetected by either the Lebanese government's

surveillance of the camp or the mainstream Palestinian militias inside that liaison with the authorities. "Somebody hasn't been doing their job," UNWRA Commissioner-General Karen Koning Abu Zayd told the *Washington Times*. See "UN Agency Knew of Armed Foreigners in Lebanon Camp," *Washington Times*, May 24, 2007.

75. "A New Face of Jihad Vows Attacks on U.S.," *New York Times*, March 16, 2007.

76. Seymour M. Hersh, "The Redirection: Does the New Policy Benefit the Real Enemy?" *New Yorker*, March 5, 2007.

77. "There's a relationship between ourselves and Sheikh Saad [Hariri] when it's needed," Dai al-Islam al-Shahal told the *Washington Post* in June 2007. "The biggest Sunni political power is Hariri. The biggest Sunni religious power are the Salafis. So it's natural." See "Radical Group Pulls in Sunnis as Lebanon's Muslims Polarize," *Washington Post*, June 17, 2007, p. A16.

78. *Al-Hayat* (London), May 22, 2007.

9

HIZBALLAH IN LEBANON: BETWEEN TEHRAN AND BEIRUT, BETWEEN THE STRUGGLE WITH ISRAEL, AND THE STRUGGLE FOR LEBANON

Eyal Zisser

INTRODUCTION

The first anniversary of the outbreak of the Second Lebanon War fell on July 12, 2007. Many Lebanese greeted this date with a mood of sadness rather than with joyous shouts of triumph and victory celebrations. Some chose to ignore the anniversary altogether. Indeed, it would seem that most Lebanese would like to strike the war and the events of the subsequent year from the calendar. This mood is a reminder and, indeed, another clear indication of the severe blow Lebanon suffered during the war, from which it is still having trouble recovering.

Most of the country's newspapers chose to devote their anniversary-day editorials to penetrating and painful self-examinations regarding the war and its results. Reading these pieces one discovers writers who felt obligated to continue claiming that it was Israel who was defeated in the war, but even they found it difficult to ignore the ruinous results for Lebanon. Prominent among them was Talal Salman, editor-in-chief of *al-Safir* newspaper, who has been known for his close relations with Syria and for his opposition to Fuad Siniora's government and the coalition backing it—which was led by Sa'ad al-Din al-Hariri and Walid Jumblatt. Salman, who made his support for Hizballah manifest during the war in summer 2006, now, in his anniversary editorial, lamented Lebanon's gloomy situation. In his words: "A year has passed and Lebanon is still not what it was prior to the war, for it lacks the atmosphere of unity and solidarity. They are lacking in the country today more than ever before."[1]

Gloom and depression, as well as soul-searching, were also apparent in things said or written by high-ranking members of Hizballah on the occasion of the war's anniversary. To be sure, these spokesmen still tried hard to convince their supporters that Hizballah had won the war. However, it would seem that it became more and more difficult, and perhaps even impossible, as time passed, to convince the people of this victory that never was.[2] After all, it was Hizballah leader Hasan Nasrallah himself who showed regret when he admitted that if he had assumed that there was even a 1 percent chance that Israel would respond to the kidnapping of its soldiers in the way it did, then he certainly would not have given orders to carry out this deed.[3]

There was good reason for the gloom in Lebanon with which even the supporters and leaders of Hizballah greeted the anniversary of the war. A look at the Lebanese scene a year after the war reveals a shattered state on the verge of a civil war that threatens to tear it apart, or at the very least turn it back 20 years to the terrible civil war period of 1975–1990. The year after the 2006 war was a bad one even for Hizballah. True, the organization survived the Israeli attack and even managed to chalk up a number of successes during the fighting. The most important success, of course, was in preventing Israel from achieving the goals it declared when it embarked upon the war. Israel's failure, however, was clearly the result of a number of factors quite apart from Hizballah's military prowess. These mostly revolved around the failings of many of Israel's senior political and military leaders in the summer of 2006, their professional and personal deficiencies, their lack of qualifications and abilities, and, in general, their unfitness for the posts they held. Since the war, Hizballah has managed to restore a large portion of its military infrastructure, especially its stockpile of missiles and rockets. However, taking everything into consideration, it must be concluded that the fighting in 2006 brought the organization's era of glory and successes to an end. Prior to the war Hizballah had racked up a long list of achievements and victories, even if most of them were merely image- and media successes. The war opened a new chapter. Hizballah had worked very hard for many years to build up its standing. The war with Israel largely damaged that. During and after the fighting the organization found itself in a tough uphill struggle to preserve and restore its status—in the Shi'a community, in Lebanon, and in the whole Arab world.

Moreover, the war and the chain of events following it—in particular, the political crisis into which the Lebanese state was thrown in early 2007, revolving around the questions of the composition of the government and the election of a president—emphasized once again the dilemma that had been confronting Hizballah since the early 1980s, when the organization first emerged as a central actor on the political stage in Lebanon. Hizballah's dilemma has to do with its identity, which contains a tension built into its very origins and being. How is this tension—between the organization's Lebanese-Shi'a identity on the one hand and its Islamic-revolutionary identity, its commitments to Iran, and its conception of the holy jihad on the other—to be resolved? It seems, indeed, that since the war Hizballah has been finding it harder and harder to maintain the balance between Beirut and Tehran that it had tried so carefully to preserve ever since its founding. The balance now seems to be turning in favor of the Islamic-revolutionary identity, which also means turning in favor of Tehran. There is no doubt that the war and its aftermath revealed as never before, and against the desire and interests of Hizballah, the fact that the organization is the handiwork of Tehran, if not simply its instrument. Hizballah has also been exposed as an organization dedicated to and active in achieving radical and far-reaching aims. Its aim in the short term is to gain dominance over Lebanon and in the long term to turn that country into a Shi'a-dominated state ruled by Islamic law and closely linked to Iran.

THE HIZBALLAH ORGANIZATION: SOME HISTORICAL BACKGROUND

Hizballah made a stormy entrance into the center of the Lebanese political arena toward the end of 1983, when Hizballah activists delivered a series of painful blows to the Israeli, American, and French military headquarters in Lebanon. The Hizballah attacks left hundreds dead and wounded and eventually led to the withdrawal of the American and French forces, and following them, the Israeli forces, from Lebanon. Hizballah thus broke into the center of the Lebanese arena as a radical and militant organization carrying on a violent struggle against the West, and Israel in particular. It was no less determined against its political opponents domestically. The approach taken by Hizballah was influenced by two major events in the recent history of the Middle East that exerted a formative influence on the organization. The first was the Islamic Revolution in Iran, which began in December 1979 and served as a source of inspiration and model for imitation for Hizballah. The second event was the Israeli invasion of Lebanon in June 1982, which brought to a peak Israel's lengthy intervention in the affairs of that state. Israel now became an easy target against which much of the enthusiasm and radicalism characteristic of the Lebanese Shi'a, and especially the Hizballah organization, in those years could be channeled. However, these two events stood in the shadow of a third one, the civil war raging in Lebanon at the time, during which the Shi'a became central actors on the Lebanese political stage.[4]

THE SHI'A IN LEBANON: FROM THE PERIPHERY TO THE CENTER

Even before Israel's 1982 invasion of Lebanon and the Islamic Revolution in Iran, the Lebanese Shi'a began transforming themselves from a weak and passive community on the fringes of the political order into a radical and combative public struggling for a leading position in the state. This transformation began in the early 1970s as a result of several demographic, social, and economic developments that affected the Lebanese Shi'a during the second half of the twentieth century. First of all, they became the largest community in the country. They grew from 18 percent of the total population in the 1920s, when the state was founded, to 35 percent, or perhaps even 40–45 percent, of the population toward the end of the century. The rapid growth of the Shi'a population led many to migrate from the rural regions of the Lebanese Biqa and south Lebanon, where most had lived until the end of the 1950s, to the slums on the outskirts of the country's larger cities. The Shi'a migrants were condemned to a life of poverty and misery while the institutions of the state proved to be helpless or completely incapable of giving any assistance. The migration to the cities also weakened their traditional sense of belonging and social identity. Perhaps most importantly, the power of the prominent feudal notable families who had led the community until then was diminished.

The crisis situation that developed from the early 1970s onward became the breeding ground for a process of religious radicalization. In these circumstances, Musa al-Sadr, a religious figure of Iranian origin, appeared and gained a position of great influence and power in the Shi'a community. In the mid-1970s, following the outbreak of the Lebanese civil war, al-Sadr founded the Amal movement. However, in 1978 he suddenly disappeared without a trace during a visit to Libya.[5]

Several years later, following the Islamic Revolution in Iran in 1979 and the Israeli invasion of Lebanon in 1982, Hizballah forced its way into the center of the Lebanese arena, having previously gained a central position within the Shi'a community. From the beginning it represented itself as having a religious, radical, and revolutionary worldview. Naturally, it also presented itself as an alternative to Amal, which was portrayed, correctly, as more moderate and secular in character. In order to understand Hizballah's origins properly, one must remember that the major force pushing for its establishment was the Islamic regime in Iran, as it worked to unite the Shi'a factions and forces operating in Lebanon, some of which were groups that had previously left Amal. Iran wanted everyone to work together under the Hizballah framework. Iranian leader Ayatollah Khomeini himself gave Hizballah its name, which means "Party of God."[6]

HIZBALLAH: FROM THE CIVIL WAR TO THE TA'IF AGREEMENT (OCTOBER 1989)

Within several years of its founding, Hizballah began to make its move to gain a leading role in Lebanese social and political life. The organization's political platform, published in February 1985, outlined its mission and goals. The document concentrated on what it described as the uncompromising struggle with Israel until the destruction of that entity. The platform also focused on the struggle to establish an Islamic republic in Lebanon, using Iran as a model, as a stage on the way to establishing one united Islamic state covering the whole Islamic world. Joining actions to its words, Hizballah intensified its struggle with Israel in south Lebanon. At the same time, it engaged in a vigorous struggle, sometimes even involving bloody confrontations, with its main Shi'a competitor in the Lebanese arena, Amal, and no less importantly, with various Palestinian organizations working in the Palestinian refugee camps, mainly in south Lebanon and Beirut.

By the end of the 1980s Hizballah had become the leading force in the Shi'a community, and it seemed to have it within its power to take over

Lebanon—or at least those parts of the country inhabited by Shi'a—and to establish an Islamic order there on the Iranian model. However, just at the moment when Hizballah had reached its peak, it got into trouble, and for the first time had to confront a real challenge to its advance, and perhaps even to its very existence. In October 1989 the Ta'if Agreement was signed in Ta'if, Saudi Arabia. These accords ended the civil war that had made Hizballah's successes possible. A process of rehabilitation of the institutions of the Lebanese state began. This led to the disarming of most of the militias that had been active in the country. The Ta'if Agreement also laid the foundations for the establishment of a new Maronite-Sunni order, with the backing and support of Syria. These developments left the Shi'a community far behind, even though it had become the largest, and perhaps the strongest, community in the country. Then, in October 1991, two years after the signing of the Ta'if Agreement, the Middle East peace process began in Madrid. This development threatened to halt Hizballah's struggle with Israel and thus cut off one of the main sources of the organization's legitimacy and power.[7]

Faced with this threat Hizballah proved to be very pragmatic, taking whatever steps necessary in order to survive. The organization looked as if it was ready to abandon its devotion to its ideological positions, or at least to postpone their realization to the distant future. At first it did not hide its opposition to the Ta'if Agreement, but in the end it resigned itself to the reestablishment of the Lebanese state, the "Lebanon of Ta'if," and began to act in ways that would enable it to integrate into the state's institutions. Little by little Hizballah turned from being an armed militia into a social and political movement. In doing this it broadened greatly the scope of its activities among the Shi'a population all over the country. From the mid-1980s the organization began—with generous Iranian help, estimated at tens, and perhaps even hundreds, of millions of dollars yearly—to establish a network of social and welfare services that would draw the support of the Shi'a community and provide it with an alternative to the services provided by the Lebanese state, or, to be more precise, to the benefits and aid the state should have provided for this population and did not. The Hizballah network of services expanded greatly over the years as Shi'a support became firmer and firmer. To be sure many Hizballah supporters today view the organization as simply a convenient framework for political, social, and economic activities, without necessarily feeling any commitment to its ideology. However, the leadership, and certainly the hard core, remain as committed to the Hizballah worldview as in the past, and they are the ones who have power and control over the organization and its members.[8]

THE STRUGGLE WITH ISRAEL IN SOUTH LEBANON: THE WAY TO VICTORY

The struggle against Israel, or, more precisely, against the Israeli presence in the south Lebanon "security zone," continued to be an important focus of

Hizballah activity—if not the only one—until May 2000. However, in the shadow of this struggle the government of Israel, led by Ehud Barak, decided to retreat from Lebanon unilaterally. During the night of May 24, 2000, the Israel Defense Forces (IDF) carried out this decision and withdrew entirely from the "security zone" in a unilateral step taken outside the framework of any agreement or arrangement. In the eyes of many Lebanese, and Arabs and Muslims in general, the IDF's unilateral retreat from south Lebanon turned Hizballah into the leading force in the Arab struggle against Israel. The organization was now viewed as a rising power with a great future before it, both inside and outside Lebanon. People thought it was destined to play a significant regional role, especially in light of the lack of leadership and the political and ideological vacuum that characterized inter-Arab relations in those years. Some observers in Israel even expressed concern that Nasrallah was aspiring to become an all-Arab leader and model worthy of admiration and emulation, like Gamal Abdel Nasser had been.

It is not surprising that Hizballah Secretary General Sayyid Hasan Nasrallah hastened to represent this as an achievement of his organization and as an historical turning point in the Israel-Arab conflict, for, as he stated, Hizballah had managed to accomplish what no other Arab state or army had accomplished until then—the removal of Israel from territory it held, without any conditions or quid pro quo whatsoever. Even more, the Arab side did not have to commit itself to any arrangement or even to a future peace agreement with Israel. Nasrallah went on to boast that Hizballah had the key, or the formula, that would make it possible for the Arabs to prevail over Israel from now on. This formula was based upon finding out what Israel's Achilles' heel was at the present moment—namely, the fatigue and exhaustion of Israeli society and its sensitivity to preserving the lives of its soldiers. In a victory speech Nasrallah delivered on May 26, 2000, in the town of Bint Jubayl, from which the IDF had withdrawn only days before—a speech that came to be known as the "spider web" speech—Nasrallah continued to boast that

> several hundred Hizballah fighters forced the strongest state in the Middle East to raise the flag of defeat.... The age when the Zionists frightened the Lebanese and the Arabs has ended. The Zionist entity lives in fear after the defeat the occupation army suffered at the hands of the fighters of the Islamic resistance in Lebanon. This fear reigns not only in occupied northern Palestine, but also in the heart of Tel Aviv and in the depths of occupied Palestine.... Israel, which possesses nuclear weapons and the most powerful air force in the region, this Israel is weaker than a spider web.[9]

Hizballah's seeming victory over Israel in south Lebanon in May 2000, however, in fact served to intensify the existential dilemma into which the organization had been thrown following the October 1989 Ta'if Agreement that ended the Lebanese civil war. From Ta'if on, the organization's identity, goals, and course were all thrown into question. Should it continue with its close ties and commitments to Iran and the devotion to radical Islam and jihad that went with this? Or should it adopt more consistently the identity it had begun to assume since the end of the civil war, the Lebanese-Shi'a identity, with a certain Islamic coloration? Adoption of the jihadist and Iranian-oriented identity meant, of course, continuation of the struggle with Israel as well as continuation of the struggle to take over Lebanon. The struggle over Lebanon would be a political struggle, but violence would be employed whenever deemed necessary. The aim would be to change the character of the country and turn it into an Islamic state. Adoption of the more moderate Lebanese-Shi'a identity meant continuation of the trend toward "Lebanonization" that had already begun and turning the Hizballah organization into a broad-based, deeply rooted social and political move-ment acting within the Lebanese system according to the prevailing rules of the game in that country.

Hizballah resolved this dilemma in practice by adopting a policy that allowed it to have it both ways. That is, it stuck to its Islamic, revolutionary, and even jihadist, identity, mainly by continuing the struggle with Israel, even if in a low key, and it took on Lebanese trappings by acting as a political organization for all intents and purposes. This was done while cleverly trying to conceal the organization's loyalty to Iran as much as possible and the long-term goal that went with this, namely turning Lebanon into an Islamic republic ruled by Shi'a Islamic law. After all, Hizballah could take its time, or, more precisely, it seemed as if the organization's leaders, taking into con-sideration the demographic processes occurring in Lebanon, assumed that time was on their side. They were therefore prepared to wait patiently for the moment of truth and meanwhile act moderately and patiently, as called for by the Lebanese trappings they had assumed and also by the constraints they faced both within and outside the country.[10]

Nevertheless, Hizballah renewed its attacks on Israeli targets in October 2000, mainly, but not exclusively, in the Shab'a Farms area at the foot of Mount Hermon. The organization also built up an impressive military force, with Iranian and Syrian assistance, which included an arsenal of about 12,000 advanced missiles with a range covering all of northern Israel up to the city of Hadera. Finally, it began to encourage and, even more, assist and guide terrorist activities by Palestinian terrorist organizations against Israel. However, in practice, in comparison to the period that preceded the Israeli retreat from south Lebanon in May 2000, the scope of Hizballah's anti-Israel activities was greatly reduced (4,963 military attacks against Israeli positions and patrols during the years 1996–2000 versus only 22 during the 2000–2006 period). At the same time it should be noted that one localized act, the one carried out on July 12, 2006, was enough to inflame the situa-tion enormously and engulf all of Lebanon and large portions of northern Israel in a real war.[11]

In any case, from the mid-1980s Hizballah was wise enough to build itself up into an organization standing on two legs. One leg was its powerful armed militia that focused its efforts on the struggle with Israel. The other leg was the organization's political and social activities, which were aimed at

improving the lot of the Lebanese Shi'a population and eventually even challenging the existing order in the country in the name of the Shi'a community. Most students of the movement naturally focused on its military
dimension and tended to underestimate the importance of the social, economic, and political aspect. However, as the years passed, two things became
clear: that the latter activities were no less central in the eyes of the organization than the former, and, even more importantly, they had far-reaching
implications for the organization's future. Indeed, during the 1990s
Hizballah became the leading power among the Lebanese Shi'a, thanks to
the social, economic, and political infrastructure it had developed. It grew
much stronger and became much more popular than the other organization
competing for leadership of the Shi'a community, the Amal movement. A
vivid expression of this superiority can be seen in the election results of the
Lebanese parliament and the local municipalities since the end of the 1990s.
Hizballah gained clear victories over its opponents in these elections. In
light of this, since 2000 many in Lebanon and abroad have begun to suspect
that Hizballah leader Hasan Nasrallah has set himself the ambitious goal of
taking power in Lebanon by democratic means, exploiting the fact that his
Shi'a supporters constitute the largest community in the country (between
35 and 45 percent of the total population). Indeed, following the American
invasion of Iraq and the establishment of a new regime there, Nasrallah
began calling for the implementation in Lebanon of a democratic system
such as the one Americans had brought to Iraq. The implications of this were
that the Shi'a should be granted the representation due to them by virtue of
their numbers, and, eventually, they should become the majority in the state
institutions.[12]

HIZBALLAH IN THE SHADOW OF
THE CEDAR REVOLUTION (SPRING 2005)

In 2005, Hizballah's drive to take over Lebanon by democratic means, or at
least to gain a leading position in the state, was suddenly disrupted. During
the first months of that year a storm that threatened to drown Hizballah's
achievements altogether engulfed Lebanon. This turmoil came to be known
as the Cedar Revolution. The first event that must be mentioned in this context took place in September 2004, when the UN Security Council adopted
Resolution 1559 with the aim of preventing the extension of Lebanese
President Emile Lahoud's term of office for an additional three years. The
resolution called for the withdrawal of Syrian forces from Lebanon and the
disarming of Hizballah. Strong discontent in Lebanon began to emerge in
September 2004 when the parliament, ignoring the United Nations, facing a
long period of pressure from Syria, and contrary to the provisions of the
Lebanese Constitution, voted to extend Lahoud's term of office. Then, in
February 2005, former Lebanese President Rafiq al-Hariri was assassinated,
and the turbulence, demonstrations, and popular civic action increased
greatly. The turmoil reached a climax at the end of March 2005 when, thanks

to the application of international pressure, Syrian forces were compelled to leave Lebanon. Elections were held in May–June 2005, and Syria's opponents were victorious. This revolution threatened to push Hizballah to the margins of the national consensus, and, what is more, it threatened to destroy one of the organization's main sources of power—its armed military wing, which was being called upon to disarm. When the Cedar Revolution broke out in February 2005 in Beirut, Hizballah quickly sided with the Syrians in an effort to prevent their expulsion from the country. On March 8, 2005, shortly before the Syrian withdrawal later that month, Hizballah held a mass demonstration. Nearly a million of its Shi'a supporters participated in this event, which was intended to show support for the Syrians but even more to demonstrate Hizballah's power and deter the organization's opponents—both at home and abroad. However, as soon as the last Syrian soldier left Lebanese soil, all the various factors wielding power in Lebanon—the Maronites, Sunnis, and Druze together—hastened to demand publicly that Hizballah disarm, as required by UN Security Council Resolution 1559.[13]

As it turned out, the Syrians' withdrawal from Lebanon ultimately brought with it benefits for Hizballah. The organization's military ties with Syria continued and even grew stronger, but at the same time it acquired more room for political maneuver now that the Syrian forces were gone. Syria's policy in Lebanon had always been based upon the principle of "divide and rule." Thus, Damascus had worked to strengthen Hizballah militarily vis-à-vis Israel, but also to weaken it politically inside the country, or at least to keep it on a small scale and subdued. Meanwhile, Syrian President Bashar al-Asad, who at the beginning of his reign seemed to have fallen under the spell of Hasan Nasrallah, had begun to free himself from this spell and show greater independence vis-à-vis Hizballah. For this reason too the Syrians' departure from Lebanon must have eased the organization's situation.

As noted earlier, elections for the Lebanese parliament were held in May–June 2005. The victors, by a large margin, were the members of the Cedar Revolution coalition (Sunni leader Sa'ad al-Din al-Hariri, Druze leader Walid Jumblatt, and their Christian partners). However, it turned out that Hizballah had also strengthened its position among the Shi'a population. The organization's election campaign had focused on the dangers of foreign intervention in the internal affairs of Lebanon and on the principle that Hizballah should be allowed to retain its weapons of "resistance," contrary to UN Security Council Resolution 1559. Therefore, when the organization's success in the elections became evident, its leaders quickly began representing them as a "referendum" whose results justified Hizballah retaining its arms. The organization also agreed, contrary to its policy in the past, to join the new government formed in July 2005, and one of its members, Muhammad Fanish, was even appointed minister of energy and water. It appears that Hizballah hoped that by joining the government and carrying on a dialogue with the various power brokers in the Lebanese political system it could prevent the creation of a national consensus that would compel it to disarm and cease its struggle against Israel.[14]

THE GAMBLE THAT FAILED:
HIZBALLAH GOES TO WAR AGAINST ISRAEL

On the morning of July 12, 2006, Hizballah fighters attacked an IDF patrol moving along the Israeli-Lebanese border fence. Two of the Israeli soldiers were kidnapped and eight were killed. Hizballah Secretary General Hasan Nasrallah later admitted that he had thought at the time that the Israeli response would be in a minor key, localized and limited, like Israeli reactions in the past to similar Hizballah provocations. After all, there was nothing new in the present attack; the organization had frequently carried out similar ambushes from the time it renewed its anti-Israel activities in October 2000. The Israeli response this time, however, was forceful and even unprecedented. The government of Israel decided to undertake an all-out war against Hizballah.[15]

The war lasted 33 days. During that time, 153 Israeli civilians and soldiers were killed by the missiles and Katyusha rockets fired by Hizballah on northern Israel up to Haifa and in the ground fighting in south Lebanon. The war also brought ruin and destruction on the Lebanese side of the border, all the way from the Shi'a towns and villages in the border area up to the Shi'a suburbs of south Beirut. Civilian deaths in Lebanon numbered 1,287 during the fighting, together with several hundred Hizballah fighters. Nearly a million Lebanese—973,334, according to the official figures published by the Lebanese government—became refugees; including most of the residents of south Lebanon, most of whom are Shi'a. When the smoke of battle cleared, this multitude of people found that their lives had been spared but their homes had turned into mounds of rubble.[16]

As soon as the war ended, Hizballah Secretary General Hasan Nasrallah declared that his organization had clinched the victory, even a "divine" victory.[17] After all, Hizballah had survived the Israeli assault, and it even had quite a few successes in the fighting to its credit. However, when one reckons the gains and losses, one cannot ignore the severe blows the organization had sustained during the fighting. Proof of this is Nasrallah's admission that if he had assumed that there was even a 1 percent chance that Israel would respond to the kidnapping of its soldiers in the way it did, then he certainly would not have given orders to kidnap the Israeli soldiers.[18]

In Israel as well as in the West Nasrallah was largely perceived through a narrow prism as the leader of a terrorist militia with several thousand fighters and over 12,000 rockets. Those who look at Nasrallah through that narrow prism would have probably concluded that since Nasrallah continued firing rockets into Israel until the last day of the fighting he could be seen as the victor in the confrontation. However, Nasrallah was not only the leader of an armed militia. He himself did not see his organization as such, and in fact, since being appointed leader of the organization in 1992 he has dedicated his efforts toward turning his organization into something else entirely. As of July 11, 2006, Nasrallah was the leader of a political and social movement, probably the largest in Lebanon, with deep roots in the Lebanese Shi'a community. Hizballah had 14 representatives in parliament, over 4,000 representatives in local municipal councils in the country's Shi'a villages and towns, an education system with dozens of schools with around 100,000 students, a health system with dozens of hospitals and clinics caring for half a million people a year, a banking system, marketing chains, and even pension funds and insurance companies. Nasrallah devoted much of his energies in the last decade to building up his movement, or empire as it were. He viewed the creation of such an empire as his life's work—which would take him far, possibly even to a contest over the control of Lebanon.[19]

Israel damaged Nasrallah's efforts badly, and only those who had witnessed the destruction and ruin in Lebanon could comprehend just how severely the war affected the Shi'a in general and Hizballah and its leader in particular. One out of every two Shi'a living in Lebanon became a refugee during the war, and most of the Shi'a community—peasants, merchants, industrialists—returned to their homes, stores, and factories in villages and towns in southern Lebanon or in the Shi'a quarters of south Beirut to find they had lost their homes and their possessions. Indeed, Hizballah suffered an estimated damage to its institutions and enterprises of almost $3–4 billion, while the damage caused to Lebanon during the war was $20 billion.[20]

In essence, these Shi'a had no choice but to gather around Hasan Nasrallah's flag. There was no one else in Lebanon who did care about them, not the United Nations or the international community, and not even the Lebanese government whose leaders focused on the interests of the Sunni, Maronite, and Druze communities, which barely suffered in the war. This was after all the nature and character of the Lebanese system in which each community took care of itself. As such, members of the Shi'a community continued to support Nasrallah. However, the damage inflicted on the Shi'a clearly reduced Nasrallah's room for maneuver as evidenced by his admission at the end of the war, which undoubtedly was aimed at his supporters, that he did not anticipate correctly Israel's response to the kidnapping.

There is no doubt that Hasan Nasrallah enjoyed broad support in the Arab world during the war and for a short time afterward. However, his achievements were largely in the realm of image and of a temporary and fleeting character. As the days and months passed, it became clearer and clearer that Hizballah had sustained a severe blow, and, even more significantly, it became more and more evident that irreparable damage had been done to the victorious and confident image of the organization and its leader. In the wake of the war the organization found it difficult to bounce back and represent itself as "the defender of Lebanon," as it had done in the past; that is, as the party that by its very existence would ensure the integrity and security of the Lebanese state. Nor could Hizballah now represent itself as an authentic Lebanese resistance movement or as perhaps the representative of the whole Arab world, the organization that held the magic key to fighting Israel effectively.

Thus, in the wake of the war several circumstances very uncomplimentary to Hizballah became evident. First, Hizballah had presented itself as the "defender of Lebanon" but proved to be its ruination since it brought so much destruction down upon the heads of its people. Second, Hizballah's deterrent charm was now dissipated, for it had become clear that the organization could no longer carry on its military actions against Israel along the Israeli-Lebanese border and simultaneously deter Israel from striking inside Lebanon and disrupting the lives of its people in Beirut and the other parts of the country. Third, Hizballah was now perceived more and more as a Shi'a organization serving the interests of Iran, as well as being an organization sinking deeper and deeper into the quicksand of Lebanese politics.[21]

Indeed, the Sunni-Shi'a tension, on occasion reaching confrontational proportions, has become a key to understanding developments in the Middle East in recent years. It would seem that Hizballah fell victim to this tension without being able, as in the past, to obscure its ties, affinity, and even dependence and commitment to Iran. A characteristic example of this was the anger manifested by Sunnis all over the Arab world following the execution of Saddam Hussein in Iraq in January 2007. This anger was directed not only against the United States and the Shi'a government ruling in Baghdad but also against Iran and Hizballah, who made no secret of their support for the elimination of Saddam.[22] In spring 2006, before the outbreak of the Second Lebanon War, a cell made up of young Sunnis, members of the al-Qa'ida organization, was discovered in Lebanon as planning, according to Lebanese sources, to assassinate Hasan Nasrallah.[23]

Also in this context, on April 15, 2007, Deputy Secretary General of Hizballah Na'im Qasim gave an interview to the Iranian television channel al-Alam and acknowledged that Iran served as a religious authority for Hizballah. Qasim explained that

> Military attacks require the approval of Islamic law in principle. And indeed, in everything having to do with what is permitted and forbidden in the framework of jihad, we ask and consult and receive general answers. We thus act according to the religious views that obligate us in everything having to do with our regular activities and in everything having to do with jihad activity, and what obligates us, of course, is the judgment in religious law of the religious leader (*al-Walih al-Faqih*, that is, the Guardian Jurist) [meaning, in practice, Ayatollah Ali Khamene'i, the spiritual leader of Iran and of Hizballah]. Even our shelling of Israel directed against civilians, in response to the fact that they shelled civilians on our side and in order to exert pressure on them, even a thing like this requires the approval of religious law, and Hizballah does indeed receive the approval of a religious law jurist for it.[24]

It is possible that Qasim's words here were a kind of slip of the tongue intended to please Iran, since the interview was given to an Iranian TV station. Nevertheless, they still serve as another indication of the difficulty Hizballah was having after the 2006 war in maintaining the ambiguity about its identity that it had worked so hard to keep until then, the vagueness about whether it was a Shi'a Lebanese party or an organization primarily committed to Iran.

Be that as it may, since the end of the 2006 war, Hizballah leader Hasan Nasrallah has devoted himself to rehabilitating and rebuilding his power while at the same time being careful—most ironically, as never before—to keep the peace along the border with Israel. After all, he does not want to provoke any incident that could lead to a repeat of the summer 2006 confrontation.

HASAN NASRALLAH TAKES ON THE GOVERNMENT OF FUAD SINIORA, NOVEMBER 2006

On November 9, 2006, the Amal and Hizballah ministers in Fuad Siniora's government turned in their resignations. They did so in protest against the Cedar Revolution coalition's refusal to meet the Shi'a movements' demand that a "national unity government" be established in which Shi'a representation would be increased and in which representation would be granted to General Michel Aoun, who at the beginning of 2006 had become a faithful ally of Hizballah. On the face of it, this appeared to be an innocuous, and perhaps even legitimate, demand, whose aim was to advance the dialogue and mutual understanding between the religious communities and various factors holding power in Lebanon. However, it was clear to everyone that if this demand were met, and Nasrallah's representatives and allies were granted a third of the government ministries, they would then constitute a "blocking third," with the power, according to Lebanese usage, to prevent the adoption of any resolution they opposed. Nasrallah and Hizballah would thus acquire a veto power over every decision the Lebanese government might wish to take in the future.[25]

The timing of the crisis engineered by Hizballah and its partners was not accidental. It came just as the Lebanese government was about to adopt a resolution asking the United Nations to establish an international tribunal to judge those accused of assassinating former Lebanese Prime Minister Rafiq al-Hariri. The murderers had not yet been identified, but someone in the top echelons of Hizballah, and evidently in Damascus as well, had reason to fear the establishment of such a tribunal. It might demand the extradition and trial of certain senior figures in the Syrian regime, persons close to Syrian President Bashar al-Asad, who had already in the past been mentioned as implicated in the murder of Rafiq al-Hariri.

However, despite the resignation of the Shi'a ministers, or perhaps just because of it, on November 13, 2006, the government in Beirut hastened to adopt the resolution calling for the establishment of an international tribunal. In addition, Prime Minister Fuad Siniora, supported by his partners in the leadership of the Cedar Revolution coalition, rejected Hizballah's demand to alter the composition of the government.[26] The coalition members made no secret of their view that making such an alteration was tantamount to handing over control of Lebanon to Hasan Nasrallah, a move they were not prepared to make.

In response, Hasan Nasrallah announced that the "opposition"—meaning Hizballah and its partners—Amal, the followers of Michel Aoun, and other figures wielding power in the Maronite and Sunni camps opposed to the Cedar Revolution government—intended to bring its supporters out on the streets in an open-ended protest demonstration until the government fell. Nasrallah and other opposition spokesmen argued that the resignation of the Shi'a ministers removed the Siniora government's basis of legitimacy, since it no longer represented the Lebanese consensus—even if it still enjoyed a formal majority in parliament. When speaking to his supporters, Nasrallah did not even shrink from calling upon them not to be afraid of a new civil war, since, he explained, "only the weak side is afraid of such a possibility, and we are not weak."[27]

The opposition's protest demonstration was supposed to begin on November 23, 2006, the day after Lebanese Independence Day. However, on the eve of the holiday, November 21, Lebanese Minister of Industry Pierre Gemayel (leader of the Phalangist Party, one of the leading members of the Cedar Revolution coalition, and son of Amine Gemayel), was shot to death in an ambush.[28] The storm of feelings aroused by the murder moved the Hizballah people to postpone giving the signal to begin the protest activity they had planned, although they did not cancel it altogether. Therefore, about a week later, on Friday, December 1, 2006, masses of demonstrators filled the streets of Beirut. The vast majority of them were Shi'a, answering the call of their leader, Hasan Nasrallah, to go out and demonstrate until the government fell.[29]

Nevertheless, Nasrallah was not interested in forcing a final showdown or in causing a bloody civil war. On the contrary, the Hizballah leader sought a period of quiet and stability that would enable him to restore the strength of his organization after the blows it had suffered at the hands of Israel in the summer of 2006. His way was to advance slowly, gradually, patiently, and, insofar as possible, peacefully, to his goal. He thus sought to subdue Fuad Siniora and his partners and to compel them to accept at least some of his demands. Nasrallah evidently believed that even a minor achievement would turn him into the kingmaker of Lebanese politics and into the person at whose word everything would be done in the country. Even more, perhaps the whole course of events in the country could be channeled in the direction Hizballah and its leader wanted. In Lebanon and abroad there were those who had hoped that the 2006 war would create a dynamic leading to the disarming of Hizballah, and perhaps even to the weakening of its political power. In opposition to this, Nasrallah's moves were intended to create a contrary dynamic that would strengthen his position and turn him and his organization into the key factor ensuring and preserving the stability of the country. This would be accomplished by taking one small step after another toward the seizure of power, the long-term strategic goal toward which Hizballah and its leader had been aspiring for some time.

However, Fuad Siniora and the forces backing him in the Cedar Revolution (or the March 14) coalition showed themselves to be hard nuts to crack and held firm. In response, on January 23, 2007, the opposition decided to intensify its protest activity with the aim of paralyzing the state. The main streets and roads all over Lebanon were blocked, but for one day only. Still, in the violent confrontations that broke out that day and in the following days, eight demonstrators were killed. In the wake of these violent events, the Lebanese Army, for the first time since the end of the civil war, imposed a nighttime curfew on the streets of Beirut.[30]

Throughout the whole of the following year Lebanon found itself in the throes of an ongoing political crisis that paralyzed the entire political system. President Emile Lahoud announced that he did not recognize the legitimacy of the government, nor, of course, the legitimacy of its decisions. However, he refrained from firing its members even though he had the legal authority to do so. It should be remembered that Lahoud himself was perceived by the forces whose interests the government of Fuad Siniora represented as holding the office of president illegitimately because of the manner in which his term of office had been extended in September 2004, namely thanks to Syrian pressure. Lahoud received support for his position on the legitimacy of the government from the Shi'a (Amal) speaker of the Lebanese parliament, Nabih Barri. The speaker, for example, refused to convene the parliament in an effort to prevent the majority belonging to the March 14 camp from adopting a resolution calling on the United Nations to establish an international tribunal to judge those accused of assassinating former Lebanese Prime Minister Rafiq al-Hariri. Such a resolution was needed in order to ratify the decision taken by the Lebanese government in this matter. All this was absolutely necessary in order to enable the UN secretary general to set in motion the procedures for establishing the international tribunal. However, the United States and France together with their allies in Lebanon soon found a way to circumvent the obstacles in the way of establishing the international tribunal. On May 30, 2007, the UN Security Council adopted Resolution 1757. It provided for the establishment of an international tribunal under Chapter 7 of the UN Charter, which provides for the use of armed force if needed in order to implement the decisions of the Security Council. Indeed, it seems that the international tribunal train has pulled out of the station, with everything this implies, especially for the Syrian regime, which is perceived as the main suspect in the Hariri assassination. In a report published in July 2007, the Belgian investigator Serge Brammertz added fuel to the fire when he declared that he had information that would enable him to point out possible suspects in the murder, and that he would give this information to the international tribunal once it was established.[31]

Meanwhile, in Lebanon the trauma of the lengthy civil war that had ended with the 1989 Ta'if Agreement continued to play a big role in people's consciousness. It moved both Hasan Nasrallah and his opponents to act with restraint so as not to be perceived as responsible for the decline of the state into a new civil war, which would surely lead to a loss of support from their followers. Thus, the rival sides tried to find a formula for a compromise that would enable them to get off their high horses, at least until the next unavoidable crisis. The formula they came up with aimed at the following: first, ensuring the election of a new president acceptable to all sides; second, establishing a new government in which the Shi'a and Hizballah would also be represented; and third, making possible the beginning of preparations for new parliamentary elections scheduled for the spring of 2009. However, Lebanon being Lebanon, reason did not always determine the course of events.

This was given vivid demonstration on June 13, 2007, when another anti-Syrian Lebanese politician was murdered. This time the victim was MP Walid Idu, a Sunni ally of Sa'ad al-Din al-Hariri from Beirut who was known for his opposition to Syria. Later, on September 19, 2007, Phalange MP Antoine Ghanim, also an opponent of Syria and a member of Sa'ad al-Din al-Hariri and Walid Jumblatt's coalition, was murdered. Earlier, in June 2007, another Lebanese politician had, evidently under Syrian pressure, announced his resignation from the coalition. This was Mustafa Alawi, an Alawite MP from Tripoli. Thus, the majority enjoyed by the March 14 camp in the Lebanese parliament dwindled, but the members of the camp did not lose their determination to continue fighting against Syria and Hizballah.[32]

Throughout this long period of crisis Hizballah insisted that any solution to the question of the presidency must also include an improvement in the representation of the Shi'a community in the Lebanese political system. In a speech that Nasrallah delivered on October 5, 2007, in honor of Jerusalem Day, he explained to his adversaries that "[y]ou must change the Constitution, once and for all, and grant the people the right to elect and to express, once and for all, and in fact, for the first time in our history, its free and independent will." As an alternative, Nasrallah presented an original idea: "If this is not possible, then, come, let us agree to have three or five neutral, scientific, and trustworthy public opinion research organizations come and conduct surveys, so that we can know what the people desire and honor their will."[33]

President Emile Lahoud's term of office ended on November 24, 2007, and he left the presidential palace in Ba'abda. Up until that moment, and indeed, for long weeks afterward, the Lebanese politicians found it impossible to come to an agreement on Lahoud's successor. Matters were complicated even more by the speaker of the parliament, Nabih Barri. Exploiting his authority, he prevented the parliament from convening to elect a president. It should be noted that in any case, the opposition, led by Hizballah, could have boycotted any session of the parliament, thus denying the quorum needed according to accepted Lebanese practice in order for the parliament's decisions to have any validity or legitimacy.

For a time it seemed as if the rivals had reached a compromise over the new president—General Michel Suleiman—and the manner of his election. Suleiman, indeed, was not the candidate of Syria or Hizballah, but it seems that they both preferred him over their ally, Michel Aoun, who was considered to be unpredictable and megalomaniacal. Meanwhile, the contacts that had to be made in order to facilitate the election of the Lebanese president proved once again that Syria and Hizballah were essential players, without whom no political arrangement could be made in Lebanon. Whoever might seek to exclude these two would find themselves compelled to negotiate with them and obtain their agreement to any presidential election process. However, Sulayman's election was prevented by the unresolved conflict over the composition of the new government that would be formed after the election of the president.[34] Furthermore, on December 12, 2007, Brigadier General François al-Hajj, director of Operations of the Lebanese Army, was murdered. Al-Hajj had been mentioned as a candidate to replace Michel Suleiman as commander of the army. This murder was perceived as having the aim of thwarting the implementation of the compromise agreement, which was intended to bring about political calm in the country.[35]

During the first months of 2008 all efforts to resolve the crisis in Lebanon and to bring about the election of a new president failed. In the meantime, the tension between the rivals increased till a break became unavoidable. Toward the beginning of May 2008 this tension increased further. At the beginning of May a strike was declared by the unions close to Hizballah. The strike, which was to start on May 7, was declared in protest against the rising cost of living in the country. Earlier, the Lebanese government and its supporters stepped up their criticism of Hizballah. This criticism focused on the communication network that the organization established for itself in Lebanon, as well as on survey cameras that Hizballah placed in the Beirut International Airport, thereby enabling it to follow all arrivals in the country. On May 6, 2008, the government adopted a resolution to dismiss Colonel Wafiq Shuqayr, the airport's chief security officer—known for his close relations with Hizballah—and to close down Hizballah's independent communications network.[36]

Hizballah considered this decision of the Siniora government as a challenge, or, as Hasan Nasrallah put it at a press conference held in his Beirut hideout on May 7, 2008, as a declaration of war against the movement.[37] Hizballah thus decided to make a move to break the stalemate in Lebanon and to try and enforce on its enemies a solution to the crisis that would strengthen its own standing.

On May 8, 2008, Hizballah activists took over the Sunni suburbs of West Beirut. Alongside the occupation of West Beirut, Hizballah men took over the West Beirut offices of the al-Mustaqbal party, led by Sa'ad al-Din al-Hariri, and shut down transmission of its TV station, al-Mustaqbal, and its radio station, al-Sharq (Orient), in addition to setting fire to the building housing the party's newspaper, *al-Mustaqbal*—which belongs to the media empire run by the Hariri family. In addition, Hizballah surrounded the residencies of Sa'ad al-din al-Hariri and Walid Jumblatt, the leader of the Druze community, although they did not try to get into these houses.[38]

This was an impressive demonstration of the military might of Hizballah, although there was nothing surprising in this demonstration. After all, every Lebanese acknowledges the military superiority of Hizballah over all its rivals, including the Lebanese Army. It seems that Hizballah's move was calculated and cautious. Hizballah activists did not appear in uniforms and as organized forces and avoided attacking government buildings or clashing with the Lebanese Army. This was a clear message that they are not interested for the time being in bringing about a total destruction of the Lebanese political order. Indeed, in a matter of two days Hizballah activists evacuated their positions and left the streets of West Beirut, enabling the Lebanese Army to deploy its forces there. Hizballah thus sent a clear message: At will it can occupy West Beirut; at will it can evacuate it.

Yet Hizballah's impressive victory over its rivals was soon exposed as a Pyrrhic victory. The challenge facing Hizballah is not and never has been the occupation of West Beirut. Its challenge is to win the hearts of the Lebanese people, especially those who are not part of the Shi'a community. Those Lebanese who regarded Hizballah with mistrust and resentment, in the wake of the May events, now regard them with hatred. Furthermore, it is one thing to occupy West Beirut, another to govern it as an occupation army exposed to criticism and mainly resistance—the same kind of resistance Hizballah itself posed to the Israeli army in southern Lebanon. This was well perceived by Fuad Siniora, who once again discovered that in his weakness there is much strength, and that this weakness won him the support and empathy of many in Lebanon and in the Arab world at large.

Furthermore, in Lebanon there are many areas where there is no Shi'a presence. These include Tripoli in the north; some parts of the Lebanese Biqa, where local Sunni residents blocked roads to Damascus, preventing Hizballah supporters from passing; and Mount Lebanon, populated by Druze loyal to Walid Jumblatt. Efforts of Hizballah activists to enter the Druze area cost them heavy casualties.[39]

The round of violence of early May 2008, which cost the lives of over 100 Lebanese, shows that no one in Lebanon has an interest in a renewed civil war in which all would lose and no one would win. It was only a few days before an Arab reconciliatory effort began, which led to an all Lebanese summit in Doha, Qatar. On May 23, 2008, the summit produced the Doha agreement, which enabled the election of Michel Suleiman as Lebanese president two days later. Other parts of the agreement dealt with the establishment of a unity government in which the opposition headed by Hizballah would have one-third of the seats and thus the power to veto all government decisions. It also included understandings regarding the election law for the forthcoming 2009 parliamentary elections.[40] The total break has thus been delayed for the next time.

Lebanon has crossed the struggle over the identity of the president and is facing now the struggle over the composition of the government. However, it is also to face the yet-to-come struggle over the elections to the parliament, scheduled for June 2009. Altogether these flash points should be viewed as a preface to the much more significant struggle over the composite question of who is to rule Lebanon, what Lebanon's identity should be, and what course it should follow. In practice, this struggle is being carried on seriously even today, even if no one has declared it openly, and even if it is being conducted on a low flame, and, for the most part, in the political corridors of Beirut.

SUMMARY

The farther away the Second Lebanon War, the more clearly the severity of the blow suffered by the Lebanese body politic and the Lebanese people is perceived. With the war's end the country was thrown into a long drawn-out political crisis that threatened to rekindle the fires of civil war. This time such a war would be between the members of the Shi'a community, led by Hizballah on the one side, and the members of Lebanon's other communities on the other, led by the Sunnis and Druze, with the support of important elements in the Maronite community. It was not the Second Lebanon War that engendered this crisis, which is actually rooted in deep, long-term processes that Lebanon has been experiencing for many years already. However, the war definitely intensified the existing tensions, unraveled unifying stitches, and exposed wounds that could be healed only with great difficulty. In this sense the war served as combustible material thrown on the explosive "struggle for Lebanon," which now stands on the verge of becoming inflamed once again. In this struggle for the soul of the country and rule over it, Hizballah is a key player.

The war and the events following it in Lebanon revealed a large portion of Hizballah's hidden face, which it had tried to keep camouflaged up until then. In particular, the contrasts and contradictions between the organization's Lebanese identity and its loyalty to that country, on the one hand, and its Islamic-revolutionary identity with its commitments to Iran, on the other, were exposed. Hizballah had tried to bridge or obscure these troublesome conflicting elements over the years. Yet in the moment of truth it became clear that it was not prepared to renounce its partially hidden agenda—that is, its loyalty to Iran and the ideas of radical Islam and jihad. Therefore, it dragged Lebanon into a bloody battle with Israel, whose price was paid, first and foremost, by the Shi'a of Lebanon but also by many other Lebanese from other ethnic communities.

There is no doubt that Hizballah survived the 2006 war only by the skin of its teeth. Along with heavy material damage it suffered the loss of much of its prestige and the fracture of its image. Nevertheless, the organization managed to survive the war and began acting energetically to repair the damage that had been done and to prepare itself for the new battles that it would surely have to confront vis-à-vis Israel and above all vis-à-vis its opponents inside of Lebanon itself.

Precisely because the Shi'a will become the largest community in Lebanon within a few years, the power struggle between Hizballah and the Amal movement for control of this sector is of the utmost importance. Surveys conducted in Lebanon shortly after the end of the war indicate extensive support of up to 65–70 percent among Shi'a for Hizballah under Nasrallah's leadership. However, these surveys also show that the hard core of the organization's supporters comprises no more than 25–30 percent of the community.[41] This means that most of the members of the Shi'a community are not necessarily in Nasrallah's pocket, and they might well transfer their allegiance from Hizballah to Amal if the latter offers them the same hope for the future that Hizballah currently embodies. The Amal movement is a secular movement that believes in the integration of the Shi'a in Lebanese life, while Hizballah represents a radical outlook imported to Lebanon from Iran. Though the economic aid that Iran provided Hizballah allowed the organization to become a leading force within the Lebanese Shi'a community, this does not mean that an internal Shi'a conflict between Amal and Hizballah for the soul of the Shi'a community has been averted.

Against this background, the attention of many in Lebanon was drawn to the battles that broke out at the end of May 2007 between Fath al-Islam, a radical Islamic organization, and the Lebanese Army. Fath al-Islam is perceived as being connected with al-Qa'ida, but there are those in Lebanon who claim that it is an organization established and supported by Syria, since its leader, Shakir al-Abbasi, was imprisoned in Syria for several years. In any case, the armed combat began with a local incident and ended with fighting that went on for many months. In the course of the fighting Lebanese Army units assaulted the Nahr al-Barid Palestinian refugee camp, not far from Tripoli, where the Fath al-Islam fighters had found refuge. For years the Palestinian refugee camps were considered extra-territorial. Now, for the first time, the taboo on Lebanese military forces entering them was violated. Tens of thousands of camp residents fled from their homes, not from fear of the IDF this time but from blows delivered by the Lebanese Army. Many observers noted the role the army played in the battles and also the role it was playing in south Lebanon—where it had been deployed after the 2006 war—viewing these developments as expressions of the fact that the army had become an effective force that could give the Lebanese state strength in its difficult hour. Many also pointed to the fact that a very large percentage of the over 200 Lebanese Army soldiers killed in the fighting with Fath al-Islam were Shi'a and viewed this as indicating an additional option open to the members of their community: They could devote themselves to the Lebanese state and its institutions. Many Shi'a may prefer this over the Hizballah option.[42]

Given all this, the big questions are: How will Lebanon—the state, its society, and the various communities living there—treat the Shi'a community? Will it act to preserve this community and integrate it more justly and fully into the Lebanese system? The answer to these questions will determine which direction the Shi'a will choose, whether they will continue to favor coexistence with the other Lebanese communities or turn to a power struggle, and perhaps even to violence, with the aim of achieving a decisive and ruling position in the state.

These considerations lead to other questions. Is the Shi'a community really capable of taking over a leading position in the Lebanese state? Will the Hizballah organization be the agency that will lead the Shi'a to victory? True, Hizballah suffered a severe blow from the 2006 war. However, it would seem that the organization, inspired and helped by Iran, its ally and patron, is more committed than ever to continue the long and unremitting struggle it began when it was first established in the early 1980s, with the ultimate aim of taking power in Lebanon. The possibility that Hizballah might succeed in its mission has become more realistic, thanks to the demographic processes taking place in Lebanon. At the same time, however—undoubtedly to Hizballah's regret—its pursuit of power has become more exposed to public awareness and more blatant than previously because of mistakes made by the organization and its leader, Hasan Nasrallah.

Hizballah's enemies are well aware of all this and have been carrying on a vigorous campaign against the organization since the 2006 war. They focus on the claim that Hizballah's Lebanese identity and its devotion to Lebanon have always been only lip service and that the organization's real loyalty has always been, above all else, to its Islamic-revolutionary identity, and, in particular, to Iran. All things considered, it can be concluded that the coming years hold much greater opportunities but also much greater dangers for Hizballah than ever before.

NOTES

1. *Al-Safir* (Beirut), July 12, 2007.
2. *Al-Intiqad*, July 12, 2007; see also al-Manar TV, July 12, 13, 2007.
3. See Nasrallah's interview on NTV Channel, August 27, 2006. See also *al-Hayat* (London), August 28, 2006.
4. For more, see Ahmad Nizar Hamzeh, *In the Path of Hizballah* (Syracuse: Syracuse University Press, 2004); Judith Palmer Harik, *Hizballah, the Changing Face of Terrorism* (London: I. B. Tauris, 2004); Hala Jaber, *Hizballah, Born with a Vengeance* (New York: Columbia University Press, 1997); and Amal Saad-Ghorayeb, *Hizbullah, Politics Religion* (London: Pluto Press, 2002).
5. For more on the Shi'a community in Lebanon see Tamara Chalabi, *The Shi`is of Jabal `Amil and the New Lebanon, Community and Nation-State, 1918–1943* (New York: Palgrave Macmillan, 2006); Rodger Shanahan, *The Shi`a of Lebanon, Clans, Parties and Clerics* (London: I. B. Tauris, 2005); Na`im Qasim, *Hizballah, al-Minhaj, al-Tajruba, al-Mustaqbal* [Hizballah: The Path, the Experience, the Future] (Beirut: Dar al-Hadi, 2002).
6. H. E. Chehabi (ed.), Distant *Relations, Iran and Lebanon in the 500 Years* (London: I. B. Tauris, 2006); Martin Kramer, "Redeeming Jerusalem: The Pan Islamic Premix of Hizballah," in David Menashri (ed.), *The Iranian Revolution and the Muslim World* (Boulder, CO: Westview, 1990), pp. 30–105; Shimon Shapira, *Hizballah between Iran and Lebanon* (Hebrew) (Tel Aviv: Hakibbutz Hameuchad, 2000).
7. William W. Harris, *Faces of Lebanon: Sects, Wars and Global Extensions* (Princeton, NJ: Marcus Weiner Publishers, 1997).
8. Eyal Zisser, "Hizballah at the Crossroads," in Bruce Maddy-Weitzman and Efraim Inbar (eds.), *Religious Radicalism in the Greater Middle East* (London: Frank Cass, 1997), pp. 90–110; Bahman Baktiari and Augustus Richard Norton, "Lebanon End-Game," *Middle East Insight* (March/April 2000), pp. 6–9; Hamzeh, *In the Path of Hizballa*, pp. 44–79.
9. Al-Manar TV, June 6, 2000.
10. Eyal Zisser, "Hizballah at a Crossroads"; Eyal Zisser, "The Return of the Hizballah," *Middle East Quarterly*, Vol. 9, No. 4 (Fall 2002), pp. 3–12.

11. Hamzeh, *In the Path of Hizballa*, pp. 80–141; Daniel Sobelman, *New Rules of the Game, Israel and Hizballah after the Withdrawal from Lebanon* (Tel Aviv: The Jaffee Center for Strategic Studies, 2003); Eyal Zisser, "Hizballah and Israel: Strategic Threat on the Northern Border," *Israel Affairs*, Vol. 12, No. 1 (January 2006), pp. 86–106.

12. Yoram Schweitzer, "Divine Victory and Earthly Failures: Was the War Really a Victory for Hizbollah?" in Shlomo Brom and Meir Eliran (eds.), *The Second Lebanon War: Strategic Perspectives* (Tel Aviv: Institute for National Security Studies, 2007), pp. 123–134; Eyal Zisser, "The Battle for Lebanon: Lebanon and Syria in the Wake of the War," in Shlomo Brom and Meir Eliran (eds.), *The Second Lebanon War: Strategic Perspectives*, pp. 135–150.

13. Eyal Zisser, "Lebanon: The Cedar Revolution—Between Continuity and Change," *Orient*, Vol. 47, No. 4 (2006), pp. 460–484.

14. Ibid., pp. 479–482.

15. *Ha'aretz* (Tel Aviv), July 13, 2006; *Yedi'ot Aharonot* (Tel Aviv), July 14, 2006.

16. Reuters, September 12, 2006; *al-Hayat*, September 13, 2006; The Economist Intelligence Unit, "Country Report—Lebanon," No. 4 (2006).

17. Al-Manar TV, September 22, 2006.

18. Nasrallah's interview with NTV Channel, August 27, 2006; *al-Hayat*, August 28, 2006.

19. Hamzeh, *In the Path of Hizballa*, pp. 44–79.

20. Schweitzer, "Divine Victory and Earthly Failures."

21. See, e.g., *al-Nahar* (Beirut), September 15–23, 2006; al-Jazeera TV, September 26, 2006.

22. *Al-Mustaqbal* (Beirut), January 3, 6, 2007.

23. *Al-Hayat*, April 14, 15, 2006.

24. Al-Alam TV, April 15, 2007; *al-Hayat*, April 16, 2007.

25. Lebanese News Agency, February 5, 6, 2006; November 9, 2006.

26. Reuters, November 13, 2006.

27. Al-Manar TV, November 15, 20, 2006.

28. Reuters, November 21, 2006.

29. Lebanese News Agency, December 1, 2006.

30. Reuters, January 24, 26, 2007; *al-Safir* (Beirut), January 24, 2007.

31. Reuters, May 30, 2007.

32. *Al-Nahar*, June 14, 16, 2007; September 20, 2007.

33. Al-Manar TV, October 5, 2007.

34. *Al-Mustaqbal* (Beirut), November 24, 27, 2007; *al-Safir* (Beirut), November 27, 2007.

35. Reuters, December 12, 13, 2007.

36. Lebanese News Agency, May 6, 7, 2008.

37. Al-Manar TV, May 7, 2008.

38. Al-Jazeera TV Channel, May 8, 9, 2008.

39. See the website of Walid Jumblatt's Progressive Socialist Party, http://www.psp.org.lb (accessed May 9, 2008). See also *al-Nahar*, May 17, 2008.

40. *Al-Nahar*, May 23, 25, 27, 2008.

41. *Al-Nahar*, August 7, 11, 2006.

42. Lebanese News Agency, June 1, 2007; August 17, 2007; September 3, 2007.

10

THE LEBANESE SHI'A AS
A POLITICAL COMMUNITY

Omri Nir

An overall view of Lebanese Shi'a politics reveals three key issues. One is the change in the political status of the Shi'a from a secondary- to a major player in the Lebanese political arena. Second is the shift of political power within the Shi'a community from feudal families to leftist activists and later to religious politicians. Third is the political dilemma between three choices of identities—Lebanonism, Arabism, and Shiism. This chapter deals with each of these issues and examines the linkage between the three.

FROM A SECONDARY TO A KEY PLAYER
IN LEBANESE POLITICS

When examining the Lebanese Shi'a as political community one must consider some long-run processes that have taken place in Lebanon and in the Shi'a community in the course of the past 30–40 years. It is also proper to look at the current political and social status of the Lebanese Shi'a as still being in a process of change. This change has shifted the role of Lebanese Shi'a from a supporting player to a major one in Lebanese politics and society.

Up until the 1980s, Lebanese politics was led by non-Shi'a. The Druze and Maronites led the way during the emirate period of Mount Lebanon (al-Imara), between the fifteenth and nineteenth centuries, and during the period of the Ottoman autonomy district in Mount Lebanon (*al-Mutassari-fiyya*) from the second half of the nineteen century until World War I.

After the creation of the modern Lebanese entity in 1920, with new boundaries that included some Sunni- and Shi'a-populated areas in addition to Mount Lebanon, the political game was conducted by Maronites and Sunnis. These two communities continued to be dominant during the French mandate of Lebanon (1920–1946) and in independent Lebanon until the early 1980s. From the mid-1980s and, more intensely, with the stabilizing of the political map at the end of the civil war in 1990, a substantial change took place in the main roles when Shi'a and Sunnis became the new main actors.

The change in the Lebanese political map was mostly a result of the inter-communal military balance at the end of the civil war. The fact that the Shi'a emerged from the war as the militarily strongest religious community and the largest in number was only partly reflected in the new postwar political formula of the Ta'if Accord and electoral laws. This left the door open for political instability. According to the new formula the Shi'a hold 27 out of 128 seats in the parliament, about 21 percent, while in fact they comprise more than 30 percent of the Lebanese population and the largest commu-nity. The Maronites, in comparison, have 34 seats (26.5 percent), and the Sunnis 27.[1] The formula also enlarged the power of the speaker, who is always Shi'a.

In the government, the division of power is equally divided between the three major communities—the Shi'a, the Sunnis, and the Maronites. The political crisis of 2006–2008 proved that one factor for political stability is whether demography is being reflected in the distribution of political posts and powers.

The current Shi'a-Sunni struggle in Lebanon shows that political hege-mony is always the subject for conflict between the largest communities. This was the case in the three previous major conflicts in Lebanon—in 1840–1860, in 1958, and in 1975–1990. However, demography is not the only cause for strong fears among non-Shi'a communities. During the vio-lent events of May 2008, when Hizballah seized Sunni West Beirut and fighting broke out, other communities expressed strong fears of Shi'a strength—but these were rooted in previous events, including a takeover of West Beirut by the Shi'a in February 1984. In the "February Uprising" of 1984 (*Intifadat Shbat*), Amal, the dominant Shi'a militia of the time, together with the Druze militia, took control over West Beirut after Shi'a soldiers deserted the Shi'a 6th brigade of the Lebanese Army.[2] For the first time in Lebanese history the commercial and political centers of the state were under Shi'a military control.

From that point on, the Shi'a were perceived by most other Lebanese as an intimidating factor for future Lebanon. The 1984 "February Uprising" took some sleepy genies out of the bottle. As a result, an anti-Shi'a camp, com-prising most of the other Lebanese communities, was formed. In some aspects, the May 2008 takeover of Beirut was a remake of the events of 1984. In 2008 the Shi'a, this time under the leadership of Hizballah with active participation by Amal, forcibly took control of Beirut and some other areas in three days, levying a heavy price of 65 casualties and about 200 wounded.[3]

In both events, 1984 and 2008, the non-Shi'a of Lebanon shared the same fears of seeing the Shi'a emerge as the dominant political power and set the cultural and religious agenda. The principal fear is derived from the demographic situation in Lebanon, which has not only social but direct political significance given the communal proportionate division of power.

The Shi'a community is presumably the largest religious community in Lebanon although there is no official up-to-date data because no official census has been held in the country since 1932. In the last census, held still

under the French mandate, the Shi'a comprised 19.81 percent, ranked third
after the Maronites (29.11 percent) and the Sunnis (22.63 percent).[4] Even if
these results are accepted—which may be wrong given both French interests
and the objective problems of holding an accurate census—there are still
three significant factors that make the Shi'a community the largest today.[5]

One is the birthrate among the Shi'a population, which is the highest in
all Lebanese religious communities.[6] Second is the emigration of non-Shi'a
Lebanese, mainly Maronites. Lebanon faced waves of emigrations following
violent crises in the past (1860, 1958, 1975–1990), and according to some
reports, emigration of Christians out of Lebanon following the July 2006
war between Hizballah and Israel is estimated at 100,000.[7]

The third relevant impact of demography is internal migration in Lebanon.
The southern suburbs of Beirut (al-Dahiya al-Janubiyya, or, Sharit al-Ba'as)
became the largest Shi'a-populated area in the country. This is highly important because Beirut is the country's political arena and economic artery. In
the past, the Shi'a feudal leadership (al-zu'ama) was able to manipulate the
masses in the peripheries of southern Lebanon and the Biqa Valley.

Since the 1950s, and increasingly during the civil war of 1975–1990, this
manipulation became impossible as many Shi'a moved following the important role of the Shi'a militias in the capital city. These militias of Amal and
Hizballah took control over the political power in the Shi'a community during the war and in the postwar era, partly because of their ability to mobilize
the Shi'a masses for political purposes. This ability was well demonstrated
when the two Shi'a movements organized mass demonstrations during the
political crisis of 2006–2008, sometimes in the hundreds of thousands.[8]

Another fear shared by non-Shi'a communities is derived from strong
Shi'a communal organization and military strength. The military force of
Hizballah, known as the Islamic Resistance (al-Muqawama al-Islamiyya), is
well trained, equipped with the best technologies, and experienced from
fighting with Israel. It is the only Lebanese militia that remained following
the Ta'if Accord of 1989, excepting small Palestinian militias in the refugee
camps. After opposing the Ta'if Agreement initially, Hizballah accepted it
eventually—presumably following a pre-understanding with Syria, the
determining player in Lebanon at the time, on keeping its arms. This served
the Syrian interests both for regional and Lebanese struggles. Hizballah
then committed itself never to use their weapons against the Lebanese. The
military occupation of western Beirut and other areas in May 2008 was a
flagrant breach of this commitment, and Hizballah will probably face more
internal hostility in future discussions on the issue of disarmament.

The organizational abilities of the Shi'a are well demonstrated through
various events. Enormous efficiency was demonstrated in a series of election
campaigns, when the Shi'a utilized a highly organized transportation system
and headquarters. Another example of a successful Shi'a technique is the
mass demonstrations during the political crisis of 2006–2008, including the
establishment of the "city of tents" in downtown Beirut, which blocked central Beirut for 18 months. They also effectively organized reconstruction of

thousands of houses and apartments, though fewer and slower than promised, after the July 2006 war against Israel.[9]
    Another cause of concern for the non-Shi'a communities is the Shi'a link-
age to Islamism. The Shi'a community is the main paradigm of the revival of
Islam in Lebanon. Following the failure of pan-Arabism and Arab socialism
in the Middle East an accelerated process of Islamization began in the mid-
1970s. As a result, political Islam emerged in Iran, Sudan, Afghanistan,
Algeria, Egypt, and the Palestinian Authority. In Lebanon, this process
occurred mainly within the Shi'a community. This trend has also existed
among Sunnis since 2005 but in much lower numbers.[10] One of the political
expressions of Islamism in Lebanon is a growing support for Hizballah.
Islam has become attractive as a political and social framework, and Shi'a
have started to participate in growing numbers in Islamist activities—trying
to promote an Islamist agenda by supporting Hizballah.
    Hizballah itself has an ambivalent attitude toward Lebanon itself, which
influences the Shi'a as a whole. It sees the state's institutions as legitimate as
long as they serve the organization's own goals. However, when this is not
so, Hizballah views the Lebanese institutions as illegitimate. This is one of
the essential differences between Hizballah and Amal, which sees itself as a
national Lebanese movement whose vision for the future of Lebanon is
within the existing national institutions. The more the Shi'a accept the
Islamist worldview the less they respect the Lebanese national institutions.
    The fact that the Shi'a community enjoys consistent support from foreign
countries, namely Iran and Syria, is another source of fear in Lebanon. Up
until the early 1980s the Shi'a lacked foreign support, while some other
communities enjoyed the support of Western and Arab countries.[11] Today
the commitment of Western countries to the Christians and Sunnis in
Lebanon is weaker than the Iranian and Syrian commitment to the Shi'a.
Iran provides the Shi'a with economic support, arms, political backing, religious leadership, and communal activities. Iranian support is based on a
religious worldview and regional interests. Syrian support, which is based on
political, economic, and strategic interests in Lebanon, has roots going back
to the early 1970s. Since then, the Shi'a have been the most solid ally of Syria
in the country.

SHIFT OF POLITICAL POWER WITHIN
THE SHI'A COMMUNITY

In general, since the formation of the Lebanese state in 1920, political power
in the Lebanese Shi'a community has shifted between four elements. In the
first phase, which lasted until the late 1960s, political power was all in the
hands of the *zu'ama*. The prominent *zu'ama* families were al-Asad, Hamada,
al-Khalil, Usayran, and Haydar. Later on, until the early 1980s, the religious
scholar Musa al-Sadr, with the help of former leftist activists, became at least
as important as the *zu'ama*. For a decade and a half, ending in the mid-
1990s, a group of former leftist activists took the political wheel before a new

model of religious politicians took control of Shi'a politics. The shift of political power is related to social, political, and military changes that have taken place since the mid-twentieth century. Some of these processes still influence Shi'a domestic politics.

Foremost is the urbanization factor, which started among the Shi'a in the 1950s and has not stopped since. Part of the impetus for that trend was related to economic changes in the 1950s, particularly the oil industry boom, which dramatically altered the city of Beirut. It was also affected by the bad conditions of agriculture due to changes in market demand. The result was a massive exodus of Shi'a from rural areas in order to find alternative subsistence in the big cities. Between the early 1950s and the mid-1970s, almost 40 percent of the rural Shi'a population moved to the cities. As a result, 63 percent of the Shi'a became urban; 45 percent of them lived in greater Beirut.[12]

Part of the process can be seen as a direct result of "Shihabism," the policy adopted by presidents Fuad Shihab and Charles Hilu between 1958 and 1970 in which the government made earnest efforts to bridge the economic and social gaps in Lebanese society. For the first time, the Lebanese central government attempted to enforce its authority over all aspects of life and over all districts of the country. The government intended to implement programs for improvement in underprivileged areas, with special emphasis on the Shi'a in Jabil Amil. That policy risked the status of the Shi'a *zu'ama*, causing them to oppose Shihab and Hilu. In return, the two acted to promote Musa al-Sadr as a political alternative to the *zu'ama* and helped him to establish and head the Supreme Shi'a Islamic Council (1969) as the official representative body of the Shi'a. With the title of the official leader of the Shi'a community, Sadr later established the Movement of the Deprived (al-Mahrumin) and Amal. These bodies contributed greatly to the change of the political framework of the Shi'a and their political perception.[13]

As an outcome of urbanization, tens of thousands of Shi'a settled down in the southern suburbs of Beirut, free of the political influence of the *zu'ama*. Instead, they were exposed to leftist ideologies that offered them class worldviews with revolutionary passion. At the same time, Musa al-Sadr offered them a social and political struggle based on traditional Shi'a roots. In fact, Sadr and the leftist movements struggled over Shi'a public support within the traditional strongholds of the *zu'ama* too. This nibbled the popularity and political status of the *zu'ama* and strengthened the new political alternatives.

Urbanization created a political problem, since the electoral law allocated the Shi'a parliamentary seats to the traditional Shi'a-populated areas, Jabil Amil and the Biqa Valley, while the Shi'a of Beirut's suburbs were underrepresented. Urbanization is one of the reasons why the Shi'a *zu'ama* rapidly declined in the 1970s as compared to the *zu'ama* in other Lebanese religious communities. During the next decade Amal was the popular choice among most of the Shi'a in the city suburbs, and since the early 1990s the Dahiya became one of Hizballah's strongholds—with a closed compound area out of the government's authority.

The process of urbanization contributed to another social transformation, the creation of a new Shi'a middle class. Members of this class have graduated from high schools and universities in Beirut and have become doctors and lawyers. Others are the descendants of Shi'a merchants who emigrated from Lebanon to western Africa in the 1930s due to economic difficulties and returned to Lebanon in the 1990s. The new Shi'a petit bourgeois class, which pushed for political change in the early 1970s, became the ideological and economic core of Amal's supporters. In the mid-1990s some of them became supporters of Hizballah, including rich Shi'a business men in Lebanon and abroad.

In spite of the growing importance of the southern suburbs of Beirut as the largest Shi'a-populated area in the country, Jabil Amil remained the political stronghold as a result of the geographical division of the communal system.[14] According to the electoral laws following the Ta'if Agreement 14 Shi'a are elected from Jabil Amil and 8 in the Biqa Valley, while only 2 are from Beirut. In fact, the Dahiya is not considered part of Beirut, not municipally nor in the Lebanese poll book, and not cognitively. In the late 1980s, for instance, Hizballah took control over the Dahiya after pushing Amal out militarily and socially, but it began to lead Shi'a politics only after establishing itself in Jabil Amil. As many Shi'a from the Dahiya were still registered as residents of Jabil Amil and voted in their hometowns in the 1992 parliamentary elections, Hizballah was able to take advantage and gain great success. Hizballah made a distinction between Dahiya and Beirut—after almost a month of Israeli shelling of the Dahiya in July 2006, Hassan Nasrallah, Hizballah's secretary general threatened to bomb the Israeli city of Tel Aviv if Israel bombed Beirut.[15]

The 1975–1990 civil war was another essential factor in the shift of political power. In its first stages, the war gathered most Shi'a around the only Shi'a militia of the time, Amal. That gave the leaders of Amal political advantage, as during the war political influence depended on military force. In addition, Amal was the closest ally of Syria during the war, and Syria eventually took control over Lebanon in the late 1980s. As a result, Amal's leader, Nabih Barri, became an important politician whose attendance has been essential in any political deal.[16] One of the main reasons why Amal lost popularity to Hizballah in the 1990s is that Amal gave up its weapons in 1991 according to the Ta'if Accord while Hizballah kept its arms after giving a clear commitment to use them only against non-Lebanese enemies. Using arms for political purposes in May 2008 and the fact that Hizballah strengthened its leadership within the Shi'a community as a result of that violent act proves the importance of military strength in Shi'a politics.

Another factor that influenced the shift of political power was the rise of an activist political stream among the Lebanese Shi'a. This had roots in the Shi'a activism of Najaf, Iraq, during the late 1950s and the 1960s. Modern Shi'a political activism cultivated by the Iraqi Grand Ayatollahs Muhsin al-Hakim and Muhammad Baqir al-Sadr was a change from the Shi'a tradition of submissiveness. The main innovation was the idea that the Shi'a should take an active role in shaping their own destiny. Saturated with the activist political perception, bigwigs such as Musa al-Sadr, Muhammad Husayn Fadlallah, and Muhammad Mahdi Shams al-Din settled in Lebanon in the 1950s and 1960s.

Dozens of other Lebanese scholars educated in Najaf had to leave Iraq when the Iraqi Ba'th party came to power in 1968 and started to harass Shi'a scholars. In Lebanon some of them established Shi'a colleges based on the Najafi model (*Huzat Ilmiya*). Musa al-Sadr was the first to take the Lebanese Shi'a out of their political indifference during the 1960s and early 1970s and in fact created political activism in order to gain political and social improvements for the Shi'a. This was at the expense of the traditional *zu'ama*.

Yet Sadr's secular associates, who took the political wheel after his disappearance in 1978 and led the Shi'a militia in the civil war after 1980, could not limit the Shi'a activism to the national political or social arena. Shi'a activism in Lebanon got out of the control of Sadr's successors, and the activist stream advanced to link the uncompromising military stand in the war with the Shi'a religious roots of activism. The opportune moment was the February 1979 Iranian Islamist Revolution. From that point on Shi'a activism was mainly connected with religious motivation, although politically it was only the death in 1989 of the highest spiritual authority and the revolution's leader, Ayatollah Ruhollah Khomeini, that triggered Hizballah to become a dominant political power. It enabled the movement to replace Islamic activism with national activism in order to attract secular supporters.

The domination of Hizballah in Shi'a politics since the late 1990s is very much linked with the emergence of Iran as a regional superpower in the context of Iranian efforts to gain hegemony in the Middle East. With Iranian money and military support Hizballah enjoys a clear superiority against any rivals within the Shi'a community. Amal, the only possible alternative, tried to gain popularity through Lebanese government money, which was much less than the Iranian support. However, the intra-Shi'a political implication is even more meaningful since the dilemma of loyalty between Lebanon and the Shi'a state, Iran, has been sharpened. Hizballah is aware of the dilemma and is trying to satisfy both Lebanese supporters and Iran. This is the main reason for the process of "Lebanonization," which will be discussed later.

Feelings of deprivation were the main reason for the wide rift opened between the *zu'ama* and the ordinary Shi'a people in the 1930s and for the accumulated anger against the *zu'ama*. This reaction pushed many Shi'a later to join leftist movements with revolutionary social ideologies. Deprivation remained on the Shi'a agenda after the decline of the *zu'ama* and became the key factor of al-Mahrumin and Amal. The idea that the Shi'a were suffering from injustice is rooted deep in the Shi'a religious tradition; this had an important part in shaping the unique Shi'a-Lebanese identity of these movements in the 1970s and enabled Amal domination of political power in the 1970s and 1980s.

The shift of political power to the group headed by Sadr, integrating leftist activists and religious scholars, seems a paradox because of the essential difference between the secular worldview and the religious outlook. Nevertheless, that integration was probably necessary for ending the political control of the *zu'ama*. The common ground was a social struggle that was first in the list of priorities of both the religious scholars and the leftist activists. In the 1990s the communal activity in the deprived Shi'a areas was among the key factors for the growth of Hizballah.

Some regional and domestic events since 2000 also strengthened the political status of Hizballah within the Shi'a community. The Israeli withdrawal from Lebanon after 18 years of occupation in May 2000 was taken as a great military victory for Hizballah. The popularity of the movement and its leaders reached new heights, not only among the Shi'a population but also on the Lebanese street and in Arab countries.

The July 2006 war against Israel and the following Lebanese political crisis of 2006–2008 also strengthened the political status of Hizballah in the short term. The claim of military success in the battlefield in the first case let Hizballah present itself as the defender of Lebanon and seemed a contrast to the defeats of all Arab armies against Israel in previous wars. In addition, Hizballah swiftly succeeded in taking control of the restoration of damaged buildings and provided aid in the Shi'a areas with Iranian and foreign Shi'a money.

A day after the ceasefire, using its own effective staff of Jihad al-Bina'a (Hizballah's holy department of building), it started promising solutions for the newly homeless. Each family that lost its home was to receive $12,000 for renting a temporary alternative residence, until Hizballah rebuilt a permanent one.[17] This was filmed and used by the media, mainly al-Manar TV, to prove Hizballah's devotion to the Shi'a population. Jihad al-Bina'a broadened its projects and became an employer of many workers and engineers, Shi'a and non-Shi'a. Hizballah provided salaries for 35,000 Shi'a families and was the second-largest employer in Lebanon after the government.[18]

Politically, Hizballah showed excellent organizing capabilities during the war and at any rate, no alternative leadership appeared in the Shi'a community. The Amal movement became a kind of "branch" of Hizballah, and Amal's leader, Nabih Barri, functioned as a middleman between Hizballah and the "outside" world.[19]

After the war, Hizballah has had to face some difficulties. As time passed the credibility of the movement was undermined because it could not keep its promise to reconstruct quickly.[20] With United Nations Interim Force in Lebanon (UNIFIL) and the Lebanese Army also in the south the war seemed less successful, and Hizballah seemed more restricted in that area. Nevertheless, in the eyes of most Lebanese Shi'a—though not non-Shi'a Lebanese—the balance of achievements after 2006 is bigger than the failures.

FINDING A POLITICAL PATH:
BETWEEN LEBANONISM, ARABISM, AND SHIISM

The third element of Shi'a politics in Lebanon is the leadership's need to maneuver between three political options: Lebanonism, Arabism, and Shiism.

The Shi'a in Lebanon have been linked to all three political identities, with different emphases in different time periods. For example, while some Shi'a politicians opposed the French presence at the time of the mandate others supported it. While some advocated the formation of a separate Lebanese state others supported the annexation of Lebanese land to Syria. Some supported the pan-Arab Egyptian leader Gamal Abdel Nasser in the late 1950s while others opposed his ideology. Some backed the centralist policy of President Shihab in the early 1960s while others were clearly anti-Shihab. Some welcomed the Palestinian presence in Lebanon and others rejected it. Some were pro-Syrian in the 1980s, others pro-Iranian. Some held a secular way of life while others were more religiously oriented. Some adopted an activist approach and others a passive one. Personal struggles between politicians and internal feuds also played a role in these disagreements.

In spite of the inconsistency it is possible to find typical characteristics in each political period. The Shi'a *zu'ama* held a dual stand during their dominant years, until the 1960s. On the one hand they always supported a radical Arab policy, which sometimes seemed anti-Lebanese, in order to maintain public support. On the other hand, they acted to preserve the Lebanese system that served their personal, political, and demographic interests. At the time of the French mandate most of the Shi'a *zu'ama* opposed the Lebanese state and acted to promote an annexation of Shi'a-populated areas to Syria. Only in the mid-1930s did the leading Shi'a *zu'ama* join the political game. They continued to support the Arab stand during the 1958 political crisis on the question of Arabism versus Westernization and drove the Shi'a to play a significant role against the pro-Western forces.[21]

The political positions of Musa al-Sadr, the next prominent political leader, were unique in the Lebanese political arena. Sadr combined Lebanese national political targets with a Shi'a-Islamic tradition. As a religious scholar he urged for a national solution that would ameliorate the deprived Shi'a lives. At Shi'a mass gatherings he emphasized the linkage between the modern social and political struggle of the Shi'a in Lebanon during the early 1970s and the historic struggle of the Shi'a in the early days of Islam. Sadr also adopted some Arab political views, such as supporting the Syrian presence in Lebanon and supporting the Palestinian struggle in Lebanon. By adopting these policies, Sadr hoped to attract Shi'a activists from leftist movements, who held a social agenda, and to give them "esprit de corps" as Shi'a. In many aspects he personally was the combining force among all the opponents of the *zu'ama*, including religious scholars, leftist activists, rural and urban Shi'a, farmers, and liberal professionals. Therefore, he held a unique combination of Lebanese, Islamic, and Arabic political positions. His disappearance in August 1978 dismantled that coalition into separate groups.

Politically, Sadr's successors were young activists whose political background was rooted in leftist movements before they joined Sadr's Amal movement. Under Nabih Barri, Amal adopted a Lebanese political identity with some Arabism and drew away from Shi'a Islamism. One of the reasons for the political weakness of Amal in the struggle against Hizballah today is the absence of a Lebanese spiritual figure identified with the movement while Hizballah has close relations with Muhammad Husayn Fadlallah. Amal's good relations with the head of the Supreme Shi'a Islamic Council in Lebanon, Abd al-Amir Qabalan, are not enough. Although maximum efforts are made by Amal to link with Shi'a Islamism in the public consciousness, it is still recognized by most Shi'a as a secular movement.[22]

The religious politicians of Hizballah who have led Shi'a politics since the late 1990s started with a clear Shi'a-Islamic political agenda in the mid-1980s and gradually adopted a national Lebanese policy. Hizballah published its political platform in an open letter in February 1985. The platform displayed a clear religious Islamic vision, with a clear, decisive negation of Lebanon as a multi-confessional state. In October 2005 Hizballah joined the Lebanese government under the same political multi-confessional system, with a Maronite Christian still the head of the state. It was made possible due to a process in which Hizballah blurred its Islamic revolutionary dogmas and gradually adopted a Lebanese identity. This process is often called "Lebanonization."

It began with some structural changes and later with some policy modifications right after the death of its Iranian supreme leader, Ayatollah Ruhallah Khomeini in June 1989. From a structural standpoint, the movement had for the first time a Lebanese leader (secretary general) and not an Iranian one, although the spiritual leadership remained in the hands of Iranian Ali Khamene'i. The slogan "The Islamic Revolution in Lebanon" (*al-thawra al-Islamiyya fi Lubnan*) was removed from the movement's banner in order to emphasize that Hizballah is a Lebanese movement, acting within the Lebanese reality. At that stage, during the last days of the civil war when Lebanon started to implement the Ta'if Accord as a new formula for the Lebanese politics, Hizballah was struggling to gain status and influence. Hizballah opposed the agreement at first due to articles that confirmed the multi-confessional system with Christian privileges and the demand for disarmament of all militias.[23] The second important opponent to the Ta'if Accord was Maronite General Michael Aoun, who became Hizballah's ally in the Lebanese political crisis that started in November 2006.[24] Only after it became clear that the agreement would be implemented did Hizballah accept it, very likely with a promise from Syria that it would be able to keep its arms.

The next stage of "Lebanonization" was Hizballah's decision to participate in the first postwar elections during the summer of 1992, after obtaining permission from its top spiritual authority—the Iranian leader Ali Khamene'i.[25] The Hizballah's great success in these elections reflected the wish of many Shi'a for political change.[26] Over the course of time Hizballah participated in all-Lebanese national forums for reconciliation between religious groups and adversaries after the civil war. Moreover, the extensive public service system of the movement opened its gates to non-Shi'a as well, although for payment.[27]

In the mid-1990s leaders in Hizballah clearly blurred most of the Islamic revolutionary dogmas in speeches and declarations and correspondingly emphasized Lebanese nationalism. Lebanonism became a central argument in Hizballah's political platforms in further parliamentary and municipal election campaigns. The most important struggle of the movement in the 1990s, the one against the Israeli army in the "security belt" in the south, was also presented as a Lebanese struggle, not an Islamic one. The Israeli withdrawal in May 2000 was presented as a religious and political triumph but mostly as a great victory for Lebanon.[28] Lebanese flags and Hizballah's yellow ones were waved side-by-side.

Hizballah also showed loyalty to the state by handing over collaborators with Israel to the Lebanese special court martial in Beirut after the Israeli withdrawal rather than punishing them himself on behalf of the "resistance." The abduction of Israeli soldiers in October 2000 as well as in July 2006 were also presented to the Lebanese public as part of the national Lebanese struggle and as an Arab one in order to assure the release of Lebanese and Palestinian prisoners, not specifically Shi'a ones.[29] The next step was the joining of Hizballah to the government for the first time, after the 2005 parliamentary elections.

The "Lebanonization" process enabled Hizballah to break some barriers among secular Shi'a with a national- or Arab-national outlook and to become a legitimate political framework for the Shi'a community. In the Lebanese arena, the process enabled Hizballah to establish relationships with non-Shi'a groups and to become a strong player in the parliamentary game. However, the July 2006 war against Israel and the following political crisis put a question mark on this process, its depth, and its real aim.

While the war strengthened the status of Hizballah as the dominant leadership of the Shi'a and a leading power in Lebanese politics on the one hand, it revealed fundamental controversies that have been blurred during the years of the "Lebanonization" process on the other. Some of the moves taken by Hizballah during and after the war stand in contrast to the process. The fact that Hizballah justifies its actions with contradictory arguments shows it knows the value of the political line of "Lebanonization" and does not want to abandon it openly.

For instance, the abduction of the Israeli soldiers was not coordinated with any governmental factor in Lebanon in spite of the direct military and political implications it has had on the Lebanese state. To finesse this problem, Hizballah says that since the one goal of the operation was to release the Lebanese Druze Samir Quntar, it is not a Shi'a agenda but a Lebanese national issue.

Another example is the way Hizballah conducted the war with no consideration of the national implications, leaving Lebanon in ruins. Once again Hizballah justifies itself by claiming to defend Lebanon from a planned Israeli invasion and proved itself the only Lebanese military body capable of doing so. This argument also justifies the decisive stand against disarmament, an issue that was on the Lebanese political agenda before July 2006 and has remained there since. Nasrallah also tried to show Lebanese patriotism when he threatened to bomb Tel Aviv if Beirut was bombarded.[30] Accusations of Iranian involvement in the war and the blocking of the government from helping Shi'a were all rejected by Hizballah.

Whether these protestations of Lebanese patriotism were sincere or not—much if not most of the other communities reject them—they are vital if Hizballah is going to operate in Lebanese politics. To the extent, of course, that it violates Lebanese interests or is perceived as doing so by the other communities, Hizballah's power is challenged and limited.

The postwar situation raised further allegations against Hizballah on promoting Iranian and Syrian interests in Lebanon at the expense of Lebanese interests, as well as of course Shi'a interests instead of national ones. The political crisis that started in November 2006 with the resignation of the five Shi'a ministers called into question the nature of "Lebanonization" in Hizballah even more than the war did. For 18 months during the crisis, the Shi'a, under the hegemony of Hizballah, blocked national Lebanese institutions such as the government, the parliament, and the presidency. Hizballah undermined the Lebanese government although it was an elected government that represented the Lebanese electoral majority. The Shi'a political bloc used the authority of the speaker, Nabih Barri of Amal, to prevent the legislators from assembling, thus stopping the government from providing financial aid to war-damaged areas and leaving Hizballah to be the sole benefactor.

Hizballah also tried to build civilian systems parallel to those of the state, thereby acting as a state within a state. After the government tried to dismantle Hizballah's private, parallel communication system in May 2008, violence broke out. At this point, Hizballah and its allies used their weapons against the Lebanese people, contradicting their clear promise in the early 1990s. Following negotiations in Doha, Qatar, which fulfilled almost all the political demands of the Shi'a, Hizballah tried to blur the events of May by describing them as civil disobedience.[31]

When viewing the issue of the Shi'a political dilemma between Lebanonism, Arabism, and Shiism, a dynamic development can be seen. The line starts with Arabism as their first political preference between the 1920s and the 1960s, then turning to Shi'a-Islamism in the late 1980s. In between, the line crosses a unique Lebanese-Shi'a political identity, which integrates religious elements on the one hand and Lebanese national elements on the other. In the early 1990s the tendency of the imaginary line was changed once again toward the direction of Lebanese political identity, thereby blurring Islamism but still maintaining the Shi'a communal interest foremost. After the 2008 violent collisions the so-called Lebanese political identity was changed a little, and became a better representative of Shi'a political views. The Doha Agreement, the basic principles of the 2008 unity government and in the national dialogue talks, shows that anti-Shi'a political coalition accepted some of the Shi'a previous stands as the new golden path of Lebanon's politics.

CONCLUSION

The Shi'a community became a crucial factor in Lebanese politics in the post–civil war era. Political developments that occurred in the last 40 years within the Shi'a community and within Lebanese politics in general lead to the conclusion that Lebanon may well be in the middle of a slow Shi'a political and social revolution. The May 2008 takeover of Beirut by arms, which led to Shi'a political victory in a long crisis, was only another step toward the fulfillment of that revolution. Naturally, however, the Shi'a is facing difficulties in their relations with other religious communities who feel threatened by these developments. These communities, which still form the majority of the country's population, still hold their own territories, identity, and resources. Thus, the story is by no means over nor is a particular future inevitable.

The upgrade in the status of the Shi'a in the Lebanese political system in the 1980s and afterward could not have happened without the shift of political power within the community to Amal and later to Hizballah. The latter could not have become a leading political power if it had not adopted a Lebanese political identity in the early 1990s and blurred its Islamic ideology—a process known as Hizballah's "Lebanonization."

Shi'a politics in the postwar era provide two political alternatives for the Shi'a. One, represented by Amal, accepts the Lebanese state as the homeland for the Lebanese Shi'a. Its vision for the Lebanese state is based on its strong linkage to Arab nationalism and a weak linkage to Islamism. The second, represented by Hizballah, sees the Lebanese state as an instrument to fulfill a wider Islamist ideology, with some linkage to the Lebanese state and Arabism. Therefore, Hizballah accepts the Lebanese state only as long as it serves its own interests, but if the state disturbs those interests the state becomes illegitimate. That might be the proper context for explaining Hizballah's policy and statements during the political crisis of 2006–2008 and particularly the events of May 2008.

One interesting point is that political power shifted from Amal to Hizballah although it was Hizballah that adopted, at least outwardly, most of Amal's political platform while Amal did not change. History also shows that the Lebanese reality and public opinion prevent the total fulfillment of Islamist ideology.

The importance of the Shi'a clerics in politics provides another key interpretation of Shi'a politics. These figures have been continuously involved. All the substantial alterations in Shi'a politics were an outcome of activities led by religious scholars. They were the first to accept and internalize the idea of a separate Lebanese state in the 1920s and later they waved the banner of Shi'a uniqueness in Lebanon. They emphasized Shi'a-Islamism in the Supreme Shi'a Islamic Council and in Hizballah, which was a turning point in Shi'a identity. One can say that the Shi'a political leadership in the 1980s, which was dominated by politicians with leftist backgrounds, took advantage of the Shi'a-Islamist wave, while in the 1990s the religious politicians of Hizballah took advantage of the political and military position of the community—a position that was taken by the secular leadership of the 1980s.

An overall view of Shi'a politics in Lebanon leads to the conclusion that the Lebanese Shi'a did not fully adopt any political ideology. Most of them seek the best political platform in order to achieve social and political improvement. This argument is supported by the historical fact that the critical masses of Shi'a political activists were members of communist movements in the mid-1970s, of Amal in the early 1980s, and of Hizballah in the early 1990s. In 15 years they shifted their political support from a secular-leftist movement to an extremist Islamist movement.

Within this context the popularity of Hizballah should be understood as the current best platform for the Shi'a but not necessarily the future one. Two reservations should be made regarding this point. One is that Lebanon and the Shi'a are both infected by the rise of Islamism in the region, which causes more and more Shi'a to adopt a religious-Islamist worldview. Without the emergence of a political alternative or a drastic decline in Hizballah's situation there is a chance that Hizballah will not be looked at only as a means for a socioeconomic improvement but as reflecting a massive process of Islamization. The second reservation is related to the demographic process in Lebanon. The more the Shi'a get closer to being a majority the closer they will get to achieving their political and social revolution and might turn Lebanon into a much more religious Islamic state than it is today. Yet if Hizballah's ambitions or power grow, in a typically Lebanese way, the more the opposition from other communities would also intensify. This might push Lebanon into the next violent round, a negotiating process through which a political compromise could be reached in which the Shi'a would improve their position. What seems most likely, however, is that the Shi'a factor in Lebanese politics will become more important and powerful, though whether that happens and in what direction it leads Lebanon is largely dependent on Hizballah's actions. For this reason, particularly after the Shi'a takeover of West Beirut in May 2008, the anti-Shi'a political camp is partly adapting itself with Hizballah, knowing that Lebanon needs to compromise on a new common denominator that is closer to the Shi'a political line. Therefore the new middle way, until the next crisis, reflects not only Hizballah's "Lebanonization" but also Lebanon's "Hizballization."

NOTES

1. The Ta'if Accord set the number of seats in the Lebanese parliament at 108 in article 6, section II, "On Political Reforms." It was changed to 128 in the electoral law of June 1992. For more on the number of seats, see (in Arabic) Farid al-Khazan and Bul Salam, *al-Intikhabat al-Niyabiyya al-Ulaa fi Lubnan ma Ba'ad al-Harb—al-Arqam, wal-Waqa'i' wal-Dalalat* (Beirut: al-Markaz al-Islami lil-Dirasat, 1993), p. 53.
2. The "February Uprising" of 1984 was a follow-up to the "Black Saturday" heavy fighting on February 4. See *al-Nahar*, February 5, 1984. According to Nabih Barri, the leader of Amal, 14,400 Shi'a and Druze soldiers deserted the Lebanese Army. See *The Voice of the Mountain*, February 7, 1984, in: FBIS-DR, February 8, 1984, p. G7.

3. The press reported on 65–84 dead and around 200 wounded. See *al-Nahar*, May 14, 2008; and Nadim Ladki, "Lebanese Army Says Will Intervene from Tuesday," Reuters, May 12, 2008, http://www.reuters.com/article/newsOne/idUSL1250503820080512.
4. Meir Zamir, *The Formation of Modern Lebanon* (Ithaca and London: Cornell University Press, 1988), p. 98.
5. Several statistics were published in recent years. Youssef Douwayhi, based on official birth records (*sijilat al-nufus*) since 1905, published a demographic survey in *al-Nahar*, November 13, 2006, that the Shi'a are 29.05% of the population, the Sunnis are 29.06%, and Maronites are 19.47%. The study included all the Lebanese born, including those who immigrated from Lebanon; the list of registered voters published prior to the 2005 elections indicated 26.5% Sunni, 26.2% Shi'a, and 22.1% Maronite, but the registrations only include adults older than 21. See *al-Safir*, February 11, 2005, and *al-Nahar*, February 11, 2005. Majed Halawi, *A Lebanon Defined: Musa Al-Sadr and the Shi'a Community* (Boulder: Westview Press, 1992), p. 50, estimated the number of Shi'a at 1,325,499 out of a population of 4,044,784 in 1988 (32%).
6. In 1971, Shi'a showed the highest fertility rate of 3.8, followed by Sunnis (2.8) and Maronite and non-Maronite Catholics (2). See Joseph Chamie, *Religion and Fertility* (New York: Cambridge University Press, 1981), p. 85; Muhammad Faour, in "Religion, Demography and Politics in Lebanon," *Middle Eastern Studies*, Vol. 43, No. 6 (2007), p. 914, suggests that Sunni and Shi'a fertility rates are now roughly equal, based on data published by the Lebanese government in 1996. For a discussion on fertility see Mark Farha, "Demography and Democracy in Lebanon," *Mideast Monitor*, Vol. 3, No. 1 (January–March 2008), http://www.mideastmonitor.org/issues/0801/0801_2.htm#_ftnref22.
7. The Maronite patriarch Nasrallah Sfeir estimated the number of Maronites who left Lebanon after the July 2006 war in the hundred thousands. He was quoted on the U.S. Copts Association Internet site. See "The Christian Exodus from the Arab World, http://www.copts.com/english1/index.php/2007/01/10/a-christian-exodus-from-the-arab-world/ (accessed January 10, 2007); see also: Rana Fil, "Lebanon's Exodus," *Newsweek Web*, http://www.newsweek.com/id/76551 (accessed December 11, 2007).
8. *Al-Nahar*, November 20, 2006, quoted Hassan Nasrallah's speech of one day earlier in which he called Hizballah's supporters "psychologically" ready to take to the streets in mass demonstrations to support the Islamic group's demand for a national unity government. In the coming months mass demonstrations took place in central Beirut.
9. On the effective tending by Hizballah, see Jackson Allers, "MIDEAST: Hezbollah Ahead of Govt Again," http://ipsnews.net/news.asp?idnews=34687 (accessed September 12, 2006).
10. On Sunni Islamist activity after 2005, see Gary C. Gambill, "Salafi-Jihadism in Lebanon," *Mideast Monitor*, Vol. 3, No. 1 (January–March 2008), http://www.mideastmonitor.org/issues/0801/0801_1.htm.
11. The Maronites were supported by France and the West; the Sunnis and Palestinians in Lebanon were supported by most of the Arab states; the Druzes were historically supported by Britain and later by Libya; and the Orthodox by Russia and later the USSR.
12. Salim Nasr, "Roots of the Shii Movement," *MERIP Reports*, Vol. 15, No. 5 (June 1985), p. 11.

13. On the struggle between Sadr and the prominent *za'im*, Speaker Kamil al-As'ad, see Thorn Sicking and Shereen Khairallah, "The Shi'a Awakening in Lebanon," *CEMAM Reports*, No. 2 (1974), pp. 97–130.

14. Only 16,480 Shi'a voters were registered in Beirut in 2007, compared to 343,330 in the southern electoral districts of Marj Ayun, Nabatiyya, Bint Jbayl, Sa'ida, and Sur, and to 163,720 in the Biqa Valley's districts of Ba'albek and Hermel. See Mark Farha, "Demography and Democracy in Lebanon," *Mideast Monitor*, Vol. 3, No. 1 (January–March 2008), http://www.mideastmonitor.org/issues/0801/0801_2.htm.

15. Nassrallah said in a television address on August 3, 2006, after 23 days of massive Israeli strikes on Dahiya al-Janubiyya: "If you hit Beirut, the Islamic resistance will hit Tel Aviv and is able to do that with God's help." It means he does not see the Dahiya as part of Beirut. The speech is quoted in *al-Nahar*, August 4, 2006.

16. He participated in the Lebanese conventions of Geneva (1983) and Lausanne (1984); he was also a major factor in the tripartite agreement (1985) under Syrian patronage and in all the Lebanese reconciliation talks in the 1990s. Since 1984 Barri served as a minister in most Lebanese governments, and since 1992 he has been the speaker of the parliament.

17. *Al-Aharam Weekly*, No. 810 (August 31–September 6, 2006); The U.S. Department of the Treasury declared Jihad al-Binaa as a terrorist organization in February 2007. See the official statement at http://www.ustreas.gov/press/releases/hp271.htm (accessed February 20, 2007); and in the *Federal Register*, Vol. 72, No. 37, http://edocket.access.gpo.gov/2007/pdf/E7-3193.pdf (accessed February 26, 2007).

18. Nicholas Blanford, "In Lebanon, Hizbullah's Rise Provokes Shiite Dissent," *Christian Science Monitor*, December 15, 2006, http://www.csmonitor.com/2006/1215/p01s02-wome.html.

19. The war raised anti-Hizballah voices among the Shi'a community, but none of them has the potential to emerge as a political or public alternative to Hizballah in the short term. The loudest criticism comes from Shi'a Mufti Muhammad Hajj Hasan, who established "the Liberal Shi'a Stream" (al-Tayyar al-Shi'i al-Hurr); other critics are Shaykh Ali al-Amin of Tyre and Jabil Amil and, a Shi'a professor at the Lebanese University, Mona Fayyad.

20. The official assessment by the Lebanese government counted after the war more than 10,000 homes entirely destroyed, 1,255 partially destroyed, and 73,000 damaged. See http://www.rebuildlebanon.gov.lb/english/f/NewsArticle.asp?CNewsID=501 (accessed October 24, 2006).

21. Omri Nir, "The Shi'ites during the 1958 Lebanese Crisis," *Middle Eastern Studies*, Vol. 40, No. 6 (November 2004), p. 127.

22. See the emphasis on religious issues on Amal's official Internet site, and particularly the importance of the Iraqi scholar, Ali al-Sistani, http://www.amal-movement.com/.

23. The relevant articles in the Ta'if Agreement are: 2.a.6—"On the Equal Division between Christians and Muslims"; 3.b.b.—"On Freedom of Belief and Education for all Religions"; and in the second part of the accord, article 1—"On Disarmament of all Militias." For the full text of the accord in English, see http://www.al-bab.com/arab/docs/lebanon/taif.htm.

24. Hizballah and Aoun entered into political alliance in February 2006 on personal and anti-American motivations. Aoun later explained to his supporters

who rejected the alliance that the agreement assures the Lebanese national institution as well as the rules of the political game in the future, when the Shi'a might be a majority in Lebanon. For the full text of the Aoun-Hizballah agreement in English see http://yalibnan.com/site/archives/2006/02/full_english_te.php.

25. *Al-Diyar*, June 17, 1992, mentioned a fatwa addressed by Khamene'i, but other sources described it only as permission.

26. Hizballah gained eight seats and became the largest political party in parliament. See Khazan and Salam, *al-Intikhabat al-Niyabiyya al-Ulaa fi Lubnan ma Ba'ad al-Harb*, Table 32, p. 84.

27. Nizar Hamzeh, "Lebanon's Hizballah: From Islamic Revolution to Parliamentary Accommodation," *Third World Quarterly*, Vol. 14, No. 2 (1993), p. 328; and Helena Cobban, "Hizbullah's New Face," *Boston Review* (April–May 2005), http://www.bostonreview.net/BR30.2/cobban.html.

28. For example, see Nasrallah's speech: "... the resistance won its victory on May 25, 2000...these Lebanese people made the miracle of the victory that stunned the world and humiliated the Zionists" in *al-Nahar*, July 15, 2006. On the eighth anniversary of the Israeli withdrawal Nasrallah said: "... brilliant victory for Lebanon, Arabs, and the nation ..." in *al-Akhbar*, May 28, 2008.

29. After the Israeli withdrawal from Lebanon in May 2000 Nassrallah personally promised to release Samir Quntar by capturing Israeli soldiers. Quntar is a Lebanese Druze, not a Shi'a, who is imprisoned in Israel for killing civilians in a terrorist attack in 1979. The October 2000 abduction ended with the exchange of prisoners in January 2004, in which Nasrallah gained the release of 435 Arab prisoners (400 of whom are Palestinians and some Lebanese), as well as 59 bodies of Lebanese. See *Haaretz*, January 25, 2004.

30. See note 15 earlier.

31. Nasrallah was quoted in a press conference on May 8, 2008: "Our response was not a military revolution. Yes, we hit the streets, protested, cut off roads and blocked the airport. This is civil disobedience as it occurs in any country. We did not occupy Beirut, as some people are chanting, nor do we want to attack anyone." See http://yalibnan.com/site/archives/2008/05/nasrallah_vows.php.

11

ISRAEL AND LEBANON: PROBLEMATIC PROXIMITY

Jonathan Spyer

Throughout the relatively short history of their existence as modern states, Israel's and Lebanon's mutual border has proven to be largely disadvantageous to both countries. The picture is not entirely negative. In the British Mandate period, as the Jewish community of Mandate Palestine grew and developed, brisk trade and commercial relations existed between Jewish and Arab communities in the northern Galilee, and between the Christian and Shi'a Muslims of southern Lebanon.[1] Similar relations—though in a far more problematic context—reemerged to some degree in the period of Israeli occupation of part of southern Lebanon from 1985 to 2000, as large numbers of residents of the Israeli "security zone" found work across the border in Israel. However, for the most part, the proximity of Israel and Lebanon has been unfortunate for both countries.

For Lebanon, Israel's establishment was the primary cause for the eventual arrival of the Palestinian national movement to within its borders in 1970. This, in turn, was a key factor in precipitating the country's ruinous civil war, the Israel-PLO war on Lebanese soil in 1982, the partial collapse of Lebanese sovereignty after the Syrian entry in 1990, and the partial Israeli occupation of southern Lebanon until 2000. This calamitous series of events has continued until the present day, with the emergence of a powerful pro-Iranian militia among the country's ascendant Shi'a population, and this organization's subsequent use of the territory under its control to launch a ruinous war against Israel in 2006. Syrian attempts to regain influence and control in Lebanon after Damascus's involuntary withdrawal from Lebanon in 2005 have further contributed to destabilization.

From Israel's point of view, it has been the Lebanese state's weakness that has made it a thorn. The inability of Beirut to control its borders and the subsequent eruption of Palestinian nationalism into Lebanon has made the country uniquely problematic from the point of view of Israeli defense planners and strategists. With Egypt, Syria, and Jordan, Israel was able to engage in straightforward relations of either cold or hot war or peace. If the former prevailed, Israel could build deterrence, knowing full well who was ultimately the "address" and therefore responsible for anything emerging from the relevant country's borders. In Lebanon, since the early 1970s, no such assumptions have been possible. With central authority largely a fiction for long periods, Israel has had to contend with guerrilla and paramilitary organizations—Palestinian and Shi'a—partially answerable to outside interests, over whom the Lebanese state can exert little, if any, control. The result has been to make Lebanon into a location for proxy, asymmetrical wars against Israel.

This essay traces the history of Israeli-Lebanese relations. This chapter looks back to the origins of the border between the two countries, noting its very recent vintage and the starkly different state of affairs that pertained in the area that is now northern Israel and southern Lebanon during the Ottoman period.

It then goes on to outline the key episodes in the Israeli involvement in Lebanon. It notes the process whereby the Palestinian national movement became a player in internal Lebanese affairs and the effect this had on both Lebanon's internal situation and eventually on the Israel-Lebanon context. This chapter also looks into the Litani operation of 1978, the first large-scale incursion of Israeli forces into Lebanon and will provide a brief overview of the 1982 war, subsequent Israeli involvement in southern Lebanon from 1982 to 2000, and the 2006 war. It concludes with some observations regarding the key elements and likely future direction of relations between Israel and Lebanon.

ORIGINS

During the period of the Ottoman Empire, the border between Lebanon and Israel as currently constituted did not exist, nor did the Ottomans maintain administrative units called "Lebanon," "Palestine," or "Israel." In this period, travel and trade between the areas that are today divided between Lebanon and Israel was common.

Both these areas, rather, were shared out between several subdistricts. The arrival of the British and French to the region saw the creation of the modern border between then British Mandate Palestine and Lebanon. The border drawn up in 1923 remains the accepted international border today between Israel and Lebanon.[2]

During the period of the European mandatory powers, the border was relatively open and travel between Palestine and Lebanon was common. The rural areas of southern Lebanon, however, became a natural base for Arab irregular forces when widespread violence against both the British authorities and the Jews began in 1936. The fact that this area of Lebanon was a sleepy and neglected rural backwater exacerbated this process.[3]

Beirut proved to be the cradle of two contradictory political trends. On the one hand, the Lebanese capital was a center for Arab nationalist clubs and secret societies, and hence a hub for early support for the Arab cause in Palestine This tendency was exacerbated by the arrival of a number of Palestinian Arabs fleeing the disorder in Palestine after 1936.[4] On the other hand, there was a tendency in Zionist thought from the earliest days to see the Christians of Lebanon, and in particular the Maronites, as natural potential allies of their cause. This notion derived from the Maronites' pro-Western inclination and from their historical self-image as refugees from encroaching Islam.[5] Yet while there was a general feeling among the Zionists that the Lebanese Maronites were natural allies, there was also a countervailing sense that they were too small and weak a community for this fellow-feeling to have much consequence.

Lebanese troops played a small part in the war of 1948 and were pushed back by the forces of the nascent Israeli army (IDF) into Lebanon during the final, victorious phase of the war in late October 1948. The 1923 border was reestablished after the 1949 armistice. The border was sealed against infiltration and remained quiet throughout the 1950s.

The Israeli interest in the Maronites, however, did not disappear in the intervening years. Rather, a particular strand in Israeli policy thinking continued to believe in the possibility and promise of an Israeli-Maronite alliance that could lead to peace between Israel and Lebanon. In 1955, against a background of strife in Lebanon, the idea resurfaced. Moshe Sharett, then Israel's foreign minister, described how he fought "tooth and nail" against a scheme conceived of by then Prime Minister David Ben-Gurion and IDF Chief of Staff Moshe Dayan in which Israel would buy off a Maronite officer—"even a major will do"—those who conceived the scheme considered. The officer would then request Israeli intervention in Lebanon, and would come to power as an Israeli client. The scheme was still-born. Sharett's view of the Maronites would be considered prescient by many given subsequent events. He referred to them as a "broken reed."[6]

This idea never reached the operational stage (despite the far stronger position of Ben-Gurion and Dayan in the hierarchy compared with Sharett). The Israeli-Lebanese border was well guarded and quiet throughout the 1960s. Lebanon played no part in the Six Day War of 1967. An incident in 1968, however, was a harbinger of what was to come: On December 28, 1968, in retaliation to a Palestinian attack on an El Al plane at the Athens airport, which resulted in the death of an Israeli civilian, Israeli special forces carried out a raid on Beirut International Airport, in which more than a dozen airplanes were destroyed on the ground. The planes all belonged to Lebanese airlines—Middle East Airlines, Trans-Mediterranean Airways, and Lebanese International Airways. The two members of the Popular Front for the Liberation of Palestine (PFLP) who had carried out this attack had traveled to Athens from Beirut.

The 1967–1970 period was in many ways the high point in the popularity of Palestinian organizations committed to armed struggle, and Beirut had become a center of ferment and focus for these groups. In November 1969, in Cairo, PLO leader Yasir Arafat and Lebanese Army Chief of Staff Emile al-Bustani signed an agreement affording official Lebanese recognition to the "Palestinian revolution." The agreement gave the Palestinians permission to conduct the "armed struggle" from Lebanese soil, on condition that this did not undermine "Lebanon's sovereignty and welfare."[7] In retrospect, both Lebanon's welfare and its sovereignty would suffer grievous damage as a result of this decision.

THE CATALYST: THE PALESTINIAN
NATIONAL MOVEMENT IN LEBANON

The series of events that would lead to Israel's involvement in Lebanon began with the defeat of the PLO in Jordan at the hands of King Hussein's forces in 1970. A large Palestinian population of refugees and their descendants had been resident in Lebanon since 1948. Palestinian political and paramilitary activity preceded the watershed of 1970, beginning in the mid-1960s, and attempts had been made by the government of Lebanon to regulate it. However, the arrival of the leadership of Fatah to Beirut, accompanied by 3,000 Palestinian fighters, transformed the situation. Henceforth, Beirut became the international center of focus for the PLO and the place of residence of its senior leadership.

As a result, Lebanon became one of the theatres in which the conflict between Israelis and Palestinians would be played out. In 1970, Palestinian terrorists attacked an Israeli school bus en route from Moshav Avivim. Twelve schoolchildren were killed. Four years later, 21 schoolchildren were murdered in Ma'alot by terrorists of the PLO-affiliated Democratic Front for the Liberation of Palestine. In another attack, 18 Israelis were killed in Kiryat Shmona.[8] In April 1973, in an operation code-named Spring of Youth, Israeli special forces struck back at Beirut. The operation targeted three prominent leaders of Fatah—Muhammad Yusef al-Najjar, Kamal Adwan, and Kamal Nasir. All three were killed in the attack, and Israeli forces also bombed a building used by the PFLP.[9]

Civil order broke down in Lebanon in 1975, in a civil war in which the Palestinians played a central role. This period also saw the launching by Palestinian armed organizations based in southern Lebanon of attacks on Israeli targets across the border. These attacks were carried out both by Fatah gunmen and by members of the PFLP. A massacre of 37 Israelis by a Fatah armed group that crossed into Israel for the purpose set the stage for the first large-scale IDF entry into Lebanon.[10] The so-called Litani Operation of 1978 was launched on March 14 and saw IDF forces advancing across southern Lebanon to the Litani River, occupying this area for a week-long period. The operation involved 25,000 troops. It was intended to dislodge the PLO from the border area, destroy the PLO bases in southern Lebanon from where the attacks on northern Israel were emanating, and to extend the area of territory under the control of Major Sa'ad Haddad's militia. Haddad, a Greek Catholic professional military officer, had formed an anti-PLO, pro-Israeli militia in the south that would become the South Lebanese Army (SLA).[11]

In the course of the operation, the PLO was pushed back north of the Litani River, and a number of refugees headed for the north. Israeli forces withdrew after the passing of UN Security Council Resolution 425. The resolution called for immediate withdrawal of Israeli forces from southern Lebanon and established a UN military presence in southern Lebanon.[12] IDF forces departed southern Lebanon in the following weeks, handing over positions to the SLA of Major Haddad.

The entry of United Nations Interim Force in Lebanon (UNIFIL) did not usher in a period of quiet. Rather the UN forces became themselves a factor in a tense triangle, which saw them clashing with both PLO forces and Haddad's SLA.

THE ISRAELI-MARONITE ALLIANCE

Contacts between Israel and prominent Lebanese Maronite politicians had been developing since the mid-1970s against the background of the breakdown of civil order in Lebanon and the central role of the PLO in the Muslim/ leftist coalition against which the Maronites were fighting. Over time, Bashir Gemayel, scion of a leading Maronite family and most prominent among anti-Syrian Maronite leaders at the time, became the main Maronite contact for the Israelis. Other Maronite leaders were taking an opposite stance, in the wake of Syrian intervention in the civil war in support of the Maronites in September 1976. However, Bashir remained aloof from the Syrian-Maronite alliance and is considered to be centrally responsible for maintaining the Maronite link to the Israelis. In the period of calm following the Syrian intervention in 1976 Bashir worked to develop the link, which was maintained on the Israeli side by officials of the Mosad Intelligence Agency.

Throughout, Bashir's purpose was to encourage Israel to intervene against the Syrian garrison forces in Lebanon. He benefited from the Likud victory in May 1977 elections in Israel. The new Israeli government increased the level of contacts, and soon hundreds of Phalange militiamen were going to Israel for training. In December 1980, Prime Minister Menachem Begin gave a pledge to Gemayel guaranteeing the safety of the Christians of Lebanon. With tension between the Phalange and the Syrians in the area of Zahla growing, and with the Syrians preparing to install a puppet government in Beirut that would exclude Gemayel, Bashir sought to bring the situation to a head and to ensure active Israeli support for his cause. Bashir provoked a clash with the Syrians in Zahla and requested that Israel launch an air strike in support. Israel obliged, downing two Syrian helicopters. Syria in response brought Sam-6 missiles into the Zahla area, portending a serious escalation. The tension was defused with subsequent U.S. mediation, though the missiles were not removed. Yet the incident showed the extent to which Israel's alliance with the Maronites had developed—to a point that it now promised to embroil Israel deeper into the internal Lebanese situation than at any previous time.[13]

THE WAR OF 1982

The PLO had been in the process of establishing itself as a semi-conventional force in southern Lebanon. By the end of the 1970s, a virtual state-within-a-state existed in the area. Since its expulsion from Jordan in 1970, Lebanon remained the last territorial foothold available to the PLO. In the south, its officials ruled with a harsh hand. The movement concentrated 6,000 of its total of 15,000 fighters in southern Lebanon. They were backed up by a force of 60 World War II vintage T-34 tanks. With Israeli efforts at sealing the border against infiltration improving, the prospect of developing an artillery presence in southern Lebanon seemed to the PLO leadership to represent the best way of projecting a credible threat to Israel. The urgency of this process was enhanced by a growing sense that the Begin government, reelected on a narrower right-wing base in 1981, was planning to launch an operation to drive the PLO from southern Lebanon and hopefully destroy it once and for all.

The situation began to deteriorate toward war in the summer of 1981. Israel undertook the bombing of PLO concentrations in southern Lebanon beginning on May 28, 1981. The operations continued for a week. The PLO, fearing a large-scale Israeli response, offered only a minor response. After a six-week respite, the bombing began again on July 10, 1981. The PLO now responded with Katyusha rockets and barrages from its field artillery. The exchanges of fire continued for two weeks. U.S. envoy Philip Habib then brokered a ceasefire agreed upon on July 24.[14]

The ceasefire failed to deal with the PLO's arming and buildup of artillery in the south. In this way, it did not address the central Israeli concern and thus failed to halt the process of deterioration. From the Israeli point of view what was taking place in southern Lebanon was an attempt by an organization committed to Israel's destruction to organize a conventional military force that would then be used to make war on Israel at a time of the organization's choosing. The government was thus deeply concerned by the long-term implications of the PLO's control of southern Lebanon—particularly for the security of the 68 Jewish communities in the Galilee.

From the PLO's point of view, the organization was far from reaching a stage where it could pose a serious strategic threat to Israel. However, its immediate hope was to keep and build its south Lebanon enclave. The PLO therefore henceforth adopted a strategy of adherence to the ceasefire coupled with a determined drive to increase PLO forces in the area, with a particular emphasis on increasing long-range artillery capability. Thus, in the period between the July 1981 ceasefire and the Israeli invasion a year later, the PLO artillery presence in southern Lebanon more than tripled—going from 80 cannons and rocket launchers to 250 by June 1982.[15]

The spark that eventually precipitated war was the attempt to assassinate the Israeli ambassador to Britain, Shlomo Argov, on June 5, 1982, by the Abu Nidal group. Israel bombed PLO targets in southern Lebanon in retaliation. The PLO responded, and on June 6, Israeli forces invaded. The immediate goal was to push the PLO back 40 kilometers—thus putting the Galilee out of the range of the group's Katyusha rockets. From the outset, however, there were more ambitious goals to the Israeli invasion. Israel also hoped to strike a blow at Syrian influence in Lebanon and, if possible, to see

Israel's ally—Phalange leader Bashir Gemayel—elected as Lebanon's president. Should this be achieved, the way would be clear for Israel to conclude its second peace treaty with an Arab state. An additional goal of the invasion, as conceived by Defense Minister Ariel Sharon, was to bring about the eclipse and destruction of the PLO in Lebanon.

Of these goals, only the first and the last were achieved—and the last in a manner less complete than Israel had hoped. Israeli forces continued toward Beirut, destroying Syrian antiaircraft batteries on the way and laying siege on Beirut. Fighting between Israeli and Syrian forces began from June 7. On that day, the IDF destroyed two Syrian radar stations—one deep in Syrian-controlled territory north of the Beirut-Damascus highway. This was an early indication that Israel's war aims went beyond merely pushing the PLO back 40 kilometers. By June 13, Israeli forces had reached Beirut and began laying siege on PLO-controlled West Beirut. With this early, high tempo phase of the war concluded, the Israeli intention was now to bring about the removal of the PLO from Lebanon. West Beirut was subjected to Israeli air- and artillery attack.

On August 12, Yasir Arafat agreed to the departure of PLO forces from West Beirut. Through U.S. mediation, it was agreed that the PLO leadership would be relocated to Tunisia, with seven Arab states agreeing to accept a portion of the PLO's fighters.[16] The evacuation of the PLO began on August 21.

The departure of the PLO from Lebanon represented a significant achievement for Israel. With this achieved, however, Israel's more ambitious plans began rapidly to fall apart. Relations with the Phalange had become strained in the course of the initial invasion and the siege of Beirut. At the root of this was Bashir Gemayel's refusal to order his men to take part in ground operations against the PLO in West Beirut in line with Israeli expectations. On August 23, Bashir was elected president of Lebanon. On September 15, the new president was murdered in a bomb attack while addressing a group of women activists of the Phalange party in the Christian neighborhood of Ashrafiyya in East Beirut. In the days following his election, Bashir had already begun to show signs of moving away from his link with Israel, but his death in effect destroyed the Maronite alliance with Israel—which had always been far more fragile than leading Israeli policy-makers of the time had chosen to believe.

The death of Bashir placed the entire Israeli project in Lebanon in jeopardy, at a moment when it had seemed to be reaching fruition.[17] In response, Israeli forces moved to take control of West Beirut, with the intention of finishing the PLO as a military threat. In light of heavy losses while fighting in Palestinian refugee camps along the coast it was decided that Phalangist forces would be responsible for entering the large Sabra and Shatila refugee camps. The result was that Phalangist militiamen, enraged at the assassination of their leader, moved on the camps. The Christian militiamen were concerned to avenge not only the murder of Bashir but also previous massacres carried out against Christians by PLO forces, such as the massacre at Damur in February 1976.

A massacre of civilians by the Phalange subsequently took place in the refugee camps of Sabra and Shatila, which were in an area under the overall control of the IDF, on September 16–17. An Israeli commission of enquiry into the massacres found that Defense Minister Ariel Sharon bore "personal responsibility" for the massacre because of his having failed to take the "danger" that the Phalangists might commit a massacre into account when he permitted them to enter the camps.[18] Estimates of the number of victims of the massacre vary.

Israel's involvement in Lebanon had by now become a matter of deep political controversy in Israel. The Sabra and Shatila massacre galvanized Israeli opposition to the war amid claims that Defense Minister Sharon had misled the cabinet regarding the original extent of Israel's war aims. The Kahan Commission report was published on February 9, 1983, with Israeli forces still in control of southern Lebanon up to Beirut. Against the background of the report, Ariel Sharon resigned as defense minister, staying on in the cabinet as minister without portfolio. Then, in September 1983, Menachem Begin resigned as prime minister, disappearing from Israeli public life. While the precise reasons for Begin's resignation have never emerged, it is generally assumed that the pressure brought on by the events in Lebanon, and particularly by the ongoing loss of life among Israeli troops, were primary factors in bringing about his resignation.[19] Begin was replaced by former Foreign Minister Yitzhak Shamir.

The 1982 Lebanon War was very much the brainchild of Menachem Begin and Ariel Sharon, and in due course it ended the political career of the first and appeared for a time to have done the same for the second. Ultimately, Israel achieved its limited military aim of removing the PLO from Lebanon, and this undoubtedly represented a significant gain for the Jewish state. Yet this was achieved purely by Israeli arms and without connection to the Israeli-Maronite alliance that formed the political backdrop to the invasion. This alliance proved to be built on sand. Before his assassination, it was clear that Bashir Gemayel was attempting to move away from the link to Israel.[20] The Israeli link to the Maronites produced a single diplomatic achievement—a peace treaty signed between Israel and Lebanon in March 1983. This treaty recognized the 1923 border as the legitimate border between the two states. The treaty was not to the liking of the Syrians, who were far more effective power-brokers in Lebanon than the Israelis. The treaty was duly unilaterally abrogated by the Lebanese side in March 1984.[21]

Israel's alliance with the Maronites derived from a faulty analysis of the real balance of forces in Lebanon and some extremely adept lobbying on the part of the Lebanese Phalangists. Israel overestimated the strength of their Maronite allies, their sincerity, and their ability to impose their wishes on the rest of Lebanon. In the case of Prime Minister Begin, there was a genuine concern at the possible genocide of Lebanese Christians that, as a Holocaust survivor, he wished to help prevent. In the case of Defense Minister Sharon, the concern was to deliver a mortal blow to the PLO, and at the same time bring about peace between Israel and a Maronite-dominated

Lebanon. This ambition proved beyond reach. Nevertheless, the end of the PLO's role in Lebanon may have played a role in precipitating the more moderate turn taken by the Palestinian national movement at the end of the 1980s—since it definitively rendered unrealistic Palestinian ambitions to develop a conventional military force with which to challenge Israel.

1983–1985: ISRAEL MAKES NEW ENEMIES IN LEBANON

With its main Maronite ally dead, Israel attempted to work with Bashar's brother Amin and to move forward toward a peace agreement under U.S. mediation. Amin proved not strong enough to play the role envisioned for him according to this idea. Instead, amid the kaleidoscope of shifting alignments, Israel became increasingly concerned with protecting the lives of its own soldiers amid angry calls for the withdrawal of IDF forces. In August 1983, the slow process of withdrawal began, with Israel removing its forces unilaterally from the area of the Shuf mountains where it had been seeking to mediate between the Phalange and Druze forces loyal to Walid Jumblatt. Jumblatt at the time was allied to Syria, and his forces were the clearest threat to Amin Gemayel's attempt to consolidate control over the country. The United States, attempting to mediate between Gemayel and Israel, asked Israel to delay the move but this proved impossible. IDF forces withdrew to new lines along the Awali River. Predictably, Jumblatt's forces rapidly overran the area following the Israeli withdrawal, resulting in large-scale atrocities against Christian civilians.

An anti-Gemayel, anti-Israel, anti-U.S., and pro-Syrian alignment was now emerging as the key political force in the country. Among the various elements involved in this alignment, little noticed at first, were pro-Iranian Shi'a militants who had organized under the auspices of the Iranian Revolutionary Guards in the Biqa. Israel's withdrawal to the Awali river line removed the IDF from the cauldron of Beirut. But it left Israel entrenched as an occupying force in the Shi'a south of Lebanon.

The result was that in the next period, Israel found itself the unexpected target of Shi'a attacks.[22] On its entry into Lebanon, the IDF had found itself welcomed by the inhabitants of the Shi'a villages of the south. Traditionally a largely politically quietist people, the Shi'a had found themselves subject to a brutal and arbitrary rule by the PLO that had led them to see the IDF as liberators in the summer of 1982. This feeling rapidly changed, however, as Lebanon's Shi'a found themselves subject to a heavy-handed Israeli occupation. A number of inflammatory incidents deriving from Israel's ignorance of the sensibilities of Shi'a Muslims contributed to the deterioration of the situation. The Shi'a violence against the Israeli forces was carried out by two organizations—the Amal militia, which had constituted the main political force among the Lebanese Shi'a since its establishment in the 1970s, and the smaller, pro-Iranian Hizballah that would eventually eclipse Amal. The IDF remained deployed along these lines for the next two years, in the course of which the Iranian-sponsored Hizballah grew in popularity as a force combining opposition to Israeli occupation with a wider Shi'a Islamist ideology implacably opposed to Israel's existence and to the West.[23]

American forces, harried by attacks from pro-Syrian and pro-Iranian terror groups, departed from Lebanon in late 1983. Israel's peace treaty with Lebanon, as mentioned earlier, was abrogated the following year, and with this the Israeli attempt to intervene in Lebanese politics effectively came to an end. Syrian interference had proven the more ruthless force, and it was this, coupled with Israel's own faulty understanding of the nature and dynamics of Lebanese politics, that doomed Israel's ambitions.

In the meantime, Israeli forces remained deployed along the Awali river line, under increasing attack from Hizballah and Amal. In June 1985, the IDF again redeployed further south—leaving all of Lebanon save a 12-mile-wide "security zone" close to the Israeli border, which was maintained in cooperation with the SLA, the militia founded by Sa'ad Haddad and later led by Antoine Lahad. The security zone was intended to prevent attacks on Israeli communities on Israel's northern border. It largely succeeded in this while exacting a steady toll on the lives of the IDF soldiers stationed in it from the attacks of Hizballah.

THE SECURITY ZONE 1985–2000

Hizballah, which emerged as the key Shi'a force opposed to Israel in the 1990s, was simultaneously an authentic grassroots' representative of the Lebanese Shi'a and a pro-Iranian ideological Islamist movement committed to the destruction of Israel. The movement developed from its beginnings as a body known mainly for the practice of kidnapping foreigners and suicide bombings into a formidable guerrilla force in the 1990s. Hizballah maintained constant pressure on the IDF in the buffer zone, engaging in attacks on convoys, placing roadside bombs, occasional rocket attacks, and attacks on IDF outposts. Over time, the organization began to employ sophisticated weaponry, including Sagger antitank missiles.

The ending of the Lebanese civil war as a result of the signing of the Ta'if Agreement in 1989 and Syrian intervention in 1990 did not have a major effect on the situation on Israel's northern border. Ta'if permitted Hizballah to keep its weaponry, unlike other militias, because it was classified as a "resistance" group rather than a militia.[24] Syria gave it free rein to continue attacks on Israeli forces. In 1993, and again in 1996, the IDF undertook major operations beyond the security zone and deeper into southern Lebanon. Both operations—Accountability in 1993 and Grapes of Wrath in 1996—were undertaken in response to Hizballah shelling civilian communities in northern Israel. Both operations demonstrated the difficulties of locating and destroying Katyusha rocket launchers.

Israel was unwilling, however, to widen the scope of operations against Hizballah in a way that might have brought it into potential conflict with the Syrians. The result was that the situation reached an effective stalemate, with

Israel losing an average of two or three soldiers per month to Hizballah attacks. The security zone succeeded in keeping northern Israel safe from terrorist infiltration. During the period of its existence only two successful armed infiltrations of the border took place, and in both cases the gunmen were killed before carrying out their attacks.[25]

However, the maintenance of the zone also exacted a cost from IDF personnel. Israeli public discontent with the seemingly endless conflict in southern Lebanon began to increase after a helicopter accident claimed the lives of 73 soldiers in the security zone in 1997. An incident on September 5, 1997, in which 12 members of the IDF's naval commando unit were killed, further helped to erode the Israeli public's willingness to see the IDF stay in southern Lebanon.[26] A protest movement founded by Orna Shimoni, whose son was killed in southern Lebanon, demanded immediate unilateral withdrawal of the IDF from the security zone. Ehud Barak was elected prime minister in 1999 with a clear promise to withdraw Israeli forces to the international border.

Israel's unilateral withdrawal from the security zone began on May 22, 2000. It was carried out without prior consultation with Israel's SLA allies. This was because of Israeli concerns that the SLA, whose rank and file was largely Shi'a and recruited thus because of economic incentives, was infiltrated by Hizballah and therefore any information given to them would reach Hizballah. The withdrawal was completed by May 24. In its final phase, it turned into an undignified rush for the border as the SLA collapsed. A considerable amount of military equipment, including armored vehicles, was left behind and fell into Hizballah hands. Some of this equipment may still be seen in southern Lebanon, where Hizballah has converted it into monuments for its victory. At the entrance to Bint Jbayl, for example, an ancient SLA tank may be seen, with a cardboard statue of Ayatollah Khomeini triumphantly standing on it.[27] This image, perhaps more than any other, captures the essence of the last phase of Israel's involvement in southern Lebanon.

In June 2000, the United Nations confirmed that Israel's withdrawal had brought the country back to the international border and that Israel was therefore now in accordance with UN Resolution 425. Thus ended the 18-year period of Israeli military involvement on Lebanese soil. Subsequent events did not develop as Israel had hoped, however, and did not allow the Israelis to draw a line under the painful, generation-long experience with Lebanon.

The Lebanese Army failed to deploy in the south of the country, which remained under the control of Hizballah. Hizballah, meanwhile, did not transform itself into a purely political domestic force following the Israeli departure. Rather, the movement claimed that the Israeli withdrawal was not complete because, it claimed, the Shab'a Farms, a 22-square-kilometer area on the border between Lebanon and the Golan Heights, also constituted part of Lebanon. This claim did not stand up to international scrutiny.

A 2005 report by the UN secretary general stated that: "The continually asserted position of the Government of Lebanon that the Blue Line is not valid in the Shab'a Farms area is not compatible with Security Council resolutions. The Council has recognized the Blue Line as valid for purposes of confirming Israel's withdrawal pursuant to resolution 425 (1978)."[28]

The UN Security Council subsequently passed Resolution 1310, which confirmed that Israel had fulfilled its obligation to leave Lebanese territory.

Nevertheless, the Shab'a Farms claim was used as a casus belli by Hizballah, which vowed to continue attacks on Israel unless the area was ceded. The result of Hizballah's determination to continue its fight against Israel—and the failure of the Beirut government or the Syrian power-brokers in Lebanon to interfere with this—was continued tension in the north.

Ironically, the result of Israel's military intervention in 1982, and its subsequent long military occupation of southern Lebanon, was to remove the Palestinians permanently from the Lebanese political map and as a military threat to Israel—while making a new and more potent enemy in the Iranian-backed Hizballah, which pursued similar tactic of rocket fire and guerrilla attacks from the same south Lebanese area that Israeli strategists had once called Fatahland.

The period of 2000–2006 was characterized by flare-ups between Israel and Hizballah, deriving from Hizballah attempts to kidnap IDF troops. The reason for the kidnappings was ostensibly to obtain the release of Lebanese and Palestinian prisoners held by Israel. The broader purpose was also to maintain a front of military pressure on Israel, in the service of Hizballah's patrons in Tehran and latterly Damascus. In October 2000 Hizballah forces attacked an IDF patrol in the Shab'a Farms area, kidnapping three soldiers. Israel's response was restrained, particularly in comparison with the declarations of Israeli politicians during the period of the withdrawal as to what Hizballah could expect if it refused to transform itself into a purely political Lebanese force.

In addition to its periodic attacks, Hizballah also engaged during the 2000–2006 period in massive investment in its military infrastructure in southern Lebanon. The organization built an extensive system of tunnels across the area, which would enable its fighters to move unhindered in the event of conflict with Israel. The organization also, with Iranian assistance, constructed a series of observation outposts along the closed border—which they effectively administered—in order to observe the Israeli side.[29] Hizballah General Secretary Hasan Nasrallah spoke openly of the movement's intention of kidnapping more Israeli soldiers. An attempt at a kidnapping on November 21, 2005 failed when Israeli paratroopers near the village of Rajar on the border noted a Hizballah team entering Israel and drove them back.[30]

SECOND LEBANON WAR, JULY–AUGUST 2006

The Second Lebanon War began on July 12, 2006, with the shelling by Hizballah of the Israeli border villages of Zarit and Shlomi. The shelling was intended to act as a diversion for the commencement of a cross-border raid. The objective of the raid was the abduction of IDF soldiers for use as bargaining chips to secure the release of Lebanese citizens convicted of terrorist acts and incarcerated in Israel. A contingent of Hizballah fighters attacked two armored Humvees manned by IDF reservists from a combat engineering unit. Three IDF soldiers were killed, two more injured, and two abducted by the Hizballah men and taken back across the border to Lebanon. Five additional soldiers were killed, and a Merkava tank destroyed as the IDF attempted to rescue the soldiers.[31]

The Hizballah attack was met by a determined Israeli response, which began with Israeli airstrikes on Lebanese targets, including Hizballah's south Beirut headquarters and the Rafiq Hariri International airport. The Israeli response was more far-reaching than Hizballah had expected. It represented an Israeli attempt to end the long stalemate between Israel and Hizballah once and for all and to strike a decisive blow against the Iran-supported organization.

Hizballah leaders were undoubtedly surprised by the extent and ferocity of the Israeli response. However, once its dimensions became clear, the movement was able to mobilize according to prior existing plans to await the Israeli ground assault. In the following days, the movement reinforced the border villages, moving in elements of its regular force. At an early stage, however, the Israeli political leadership chose to rule out a major ground assault to the Litani River. Instead, an intensive air campaign commenced. Israel enjoyed some early successes in destroying Hizballah's long-range missile capability. Israeli defense sources claim to have destroyed around 80 percent of this capability.[32] Yet Israel found no effective answer to the launching of shorter-range missiles from the area under Hizballah control.

Hizballah would fire almost 4,000 rockets in the course of the fighting, with over 200 rockets a day fired in the final days of the war.[33] Hizballah was not able to adjust or coordinate its rocket fire in a sophisticated fashion, and hence the rockets were employed in essence as a terror weapon—designed to produce panic and disorientation among Israel's civilian population in the north.

Limited ground operations began on July 17. These consisted for the most part of what were essentially large-scale raids by Israeli forces into areas adjoining the border. Together with the air campaign and the war on the ground close to the border, the Israeli navy imposed a blockade on the Lebanese coast, which Hizballah proved unable to dislodge—despite its early success in hitting an Israeli ship, the Hanit, with a C-802 missile, badly damaging it.[34]

These, then, were the contours of the war for the greater part of its duration: limited ground operations by the IDF in an area adjoining the border, air operations up to Beirut, as well as a naval blockade; and on Hizballah's side, defense of areas under ground attack and a successful effort to maintain a constant barrage of short-range rockets on northern Israel.

This situation changed somewhat in the final days of the war, as the IDF began larger-scale and more ambitious ground operations. This phase saw the IDF push for the Litani River, achieving some tactical objectives, though with considerable loss of life.[35] The targeting of IDF armored forces in the Wadi Saluqi area, with resultant heavy IDF losses, received much publicity.[36] A ceasefire came into effect at 8:00 a.m. on August 14, 2006, following the passing of UN Resolution 1701. The end of the fighting found some IDF forces deployed at the Litani River but with Israel far from control of the entire area between the river and the Israeli-Lebanese border. Symbolic of this was Hizballah's continued ability to fire short-range missiles into Israel, which the group demonstrated by continuing the barrage until the very minute that the ceasefire went into effect.[37]

The conduct of the Second Lebanon War, and in particular the perceived failure of Israel to achieve its stated objectives, such as the freeing of the two kidnapped soldiers and the disarming of Hizballah, led to a mood of deep disquiet in Israel in the months that followed the war.

The aims of the war from Israel's point of view had been defined in the cabinet on July 19, 2006. They included the following:

- Freeing the kidnapped soldiers and bringing them back to Israel, with no conditions.
- The cessation of the firing of missiles and rockets against the citizens of Israel and against Israeli targets.
- Complete implementation of Resolution 1559, including the disarming of all the militias as well as the imposition of its sovereignty by the Lebanese government throughout its territory, and also the deployment of the Lebanese Army along the border with Israel.[38]

Following the ceasefire, it was clear that of these objectives only the second half of the third had been achieved. This led to the widespread and clearly justified sense later summed up in the final report of the Winograd Committee of the war as a "great and grave missed opportunity."[39]

Many international observers felt that the mood of pessimism that very noticeably descended on Israel in the weeks following the war was exaggerated.[40] Resolution 1701, which ended the fighting, changed the situation in southern Lebanon to Israel's advantage, in that it ended the de facto Hizballah domination of the southern border area that had pertained since the unilateral Israeli withdrawal in May 2000. According to the resolution, control of the south and of the border would be taken over by a beefed up UNIFIL force and by the Lebanese Army's deployment in the south for the first time since 2000.[41]

The loss of the control of the border and of freedom of operation south of the Litani was a significant setback for Hizballah. Clearly, however, much would depend on the extent to which the international community would prove determined in ensuring the implementation of the resolution. It was also evident that these achievements notwithstanding, Israel had failed to achieve the greater number of its goals as the Israeli government itself had defined them, and the performance of the army—in particular the ground forces—was cause for deep concern and disquiet regardless of the clear damage inflicted on Hizballah in the course of the war and by its outcome. Hizballah, for its part, declared that the war represented a "divine victory" for the movement.[42] The movement initially claimed to have suffered minimal losses. As the underdog, it was able to point to the generally acknowledged impressive performance of its fighters in the defense of southern Lebanese towns and the failure of Israel to destroy the organization's infrastructure of command or to kill any of the senior leaders of the movement. A statement made by Hizballah leader Hasan Nasrallah in an interview with a Lebanese TV channel shortly after the war, however, indicated a more complex response to the war within Hizballah. Nasrallah said that had the movement known of the likely IDF response to the kidnapping operation, it would have never carried out the kidnappings. This statement became the subject of much interpretation and speculation.[43]

SINCE THE WAR

Since 2006 Lebanon has been wracked by renewed internal political instability, deriving from an attempt by Hizballah to capitalize politically on its performance in the war and to achieve veto power in the Lebanese governing coalition. The long period of political standoff between pro-Iranian Hizballah and the pro-Western March 14 coalition has brought the country to the brink of renewed civil war.

The changes wrought by Resolution 1701 began to be implemented in the period following the war. The open, armed Hizballah presence in southern Lebanon disappeared. UNIFIL was increased from 2,000 to 13,000 troops. Lebanese military forces deployed in the south, taking control of the border.[44]

However, there is deep concern in Israel at the manner in which 1701 has been implemented. UN forces have not deployed in the eastern part of the country, adjoining the border with Syria. The result has been an unhindered rearming of Hizballah starting almost immediately after the ceasefire in 2006. By summer 2008, Hizballah was reckoned by Israeli military officials to have entirely replaced losses in ordnance experienced in the 2006 war and in fact to have increased the number of missiles under its control when compared to the pre-July 2006 period.[45]

Many observers consider that a renewal of hostilities between Hizballah and Israel is a matter of time. Lebanon has become—not for the first time—one of the key locations in which the central power struggle of the Middle East is being played out. That struggle now is between pro-U.S. states and an alliance grouped around Iran. In Lebanon Hizballah represents the pro-Iranian side, with the largely Sunni, Saudi-supported March 14 movement representing the pro-U.S. forces. As of now Hizballah has succeeded in preserving the absolute autonomy of its military infrastructure, enabling it to renew conflict with Israel at a time of its choosing (even if the presence of UNIFIL continues to restrict its ability to operate openly south of the Litani River). The ongoing regional tension and the enmity between Iran and Israel suggest that the long and ruinous history of war between Israel and various armed factions committed to its demise on Lebanese soil is probably not yet over.[46]

Conclusion

Israel's involvement with Lebanon has been related from the outset to the weakness of Lebanese central state authority, and for a while also to the Israeli sense that the Christians of Lebanon represented a natural ally for Israel. The latter idea is now defunct in Israeli thinking, following the experience of 1982–1984. The consensus to be found among Israeli officials dealing with Lebanon is that Moshe Sharett's statement of 1955 that the Christians were a "broken reed" is now confirmed.[47] As a consequence of this, Israel currently has no dealings with any of the major political actors within Lebanon.

However, while large-scale Israeli adventures to make alliance with political forces within Lebanon are part of the past, the weakness of the Lebanese state and central authority remain very much part of the present. One of the results of this weakness, which is itself a product of the country's divided sectarian makeup, is its vulnerability to outside penetration, and therefore its oft-repeated, luckless fate as the launching ground for attacks by various forces (the PLO, Syria, now Iran and Hizballah) against Israel, its southern neighbor—with whom the majority of Lebanese have no particular dispute or quarrel. This fact remains the core reality behind Israel's relations with Lebanon. It is—unfortunately for both countries—unlikely that the final word in this story has been written.

Israel itself must take some of the responsibility for the direction of events. Specifically, Israeli policy-making was gripped by a kind of inertia in the period following the departure of the PLO from Beirut. This was partially the result of the alliance with the Maronites and the faith that Israeli policy-makers had placed in it. Yet in staying entrenched across southern Lebanon, long after the relationship with the Maronites had gone sour, Israel incurred the enmity of southern Lebanese Shi'a and allowed the Iranian-supported Hizballah to capitalize on this enmity for its own much larger hostility toward Israel. Many leading Israeli policy-makers agree in retrospect that Israel should have withdrawn to the international border by 1984.[48]

The bitter opposition of Hizballah to Israel and the movement's deep entrenchment among the Shi'a of Lebanon served to confound expectations that Israel's May 2000 withdrawal would mark the end of major conflict in that area. These are now part of the reality of the region and are considered by many observers to be likely at some point in the future to lead to further open conflict.

Notes

1. Laura Zittrain Eisenberg, "Do Good Fences Make Good Neighbors?: Israel and Lebanon after the Withdrawal," *Middle East Review of International Affairs (MERIA) Journal*, Vol. 4, No. 3 (2000), p. 18.

2. "Country Profile: Lebanon," UK Foreign and Commonwealth Office, http://www.fco.gov.uk.
3. See Frederic C. Hof, *Galilee Divided: The Israel-Lebanon Frontier 1916–1984* (Boulder, CO: Westview, 1985).
4. Zittrain Eisenberg, "Do Good Fences Make Good Neighbors?" p. 19. See also Fouad Ajami, *The Dream Palace of the Arabs* (New York: Pantheon, 1998), pp. 26–110 for an examination of the interaction between Lebanon and Arab nationalism.
5. Reuven Ehrlich, *The Lebanon Tangle: The Policy of the Zionist Movement and the State of Israel towards Lebanon, 1918–1958* (Tel Aviv: Maarachot, 2000). Also Laura Zittrain Eisenberg, *My Enemy's Enemy: Lebanon in the Early Zionist Imagination, 1900–1948* (Detroit: Wayne State University Press, 1994).
6. Zeev Schiff and Ehud Ya'ari, *Israel's Lebanon War* (London: Counterpoint, 1984), p. 14.
7. Helena Cobban, *The Palestinian Liberation Organisation: People, Power and Politics* (Cambridge: Cambridge University Press, 1984), p. 47.
8. Gal Luft, "Israel's Security Zone in Lebanon—a Tragedy?" *Middle East Quarterly*, Vol. 8, No. 3 (September 2000), pp. 13–20.
9. See Ahron Bregman, *Israel's Wars: A History since 1947* (London: Routledge, 2002) for a more in-depth account of this operation.
10. *Zeev Maoz and Ben D. Mor, Bound by Struggle: The Strategic Evolution of Enduring International Rivalries* (Ann Arbor: University of Michigan Press, 2002), p. 192.
11. Schiff and Ya'ari, *Israel's Lebanon War*, pp. 24–25.
12. Resolution 425, complete text, Mideast Web, http://www.mideastweb.org.
13. Schiff and Ya'ari, *Israel's Lebanon War*, pp. 29–30.
14. Ibid., p. 37.
15. Ibid., p. 84.
16. Ibid., p. 227.
17. Thomas Friedman, *From Beirut to Jerusalem* (London: Collins, 1990), p. 157.
18. Report of the Commission of Inquiry into the events at the refugee camps in Beirut, February 8, 1983, Israel Ministry of Foreign Affairs, http://www.mfa.gov.il.
19. James D. Atwater, "Begin Drops a Bombshell," *Time*, September 5, 1983, http://www.time.com.
20. Schiff and Ya'ari, *Israel's Lebanon War*, p. 233.
21. "Decades of Conflict in Lebanon, Israel," CNN, July 14, 2006.
22. Friedman, *From Beirut to* Jerusalem, p. 179.
23. See Amal Saad-Ghorayeb, *Hizbullah: Politics and Religion* (London: Pluto Press, 2002).
24. Magnus Ranstorp, *Hizb'allah in Lebanon: The Politics of the Western Hostage Crisis* (New York: St. Martin's Press, 1997).
25. Luft, "Israel's Security Zone in Lebanon," pp. 13–20.
26. Ibid.
27. As witnessed by the author, January 1, 2008.
28. "Introduction of Hizbollah in Lebanon," al-Jazeera, July 13, 2006. http://www.chinadaily.com.cn.
29. Shimon Shapira, "Countdown to Conflict: Hizballah's Military Build-Up and the Need for Effective Disarmament," *Jerusalem Issue Brief*, Vol. 6, No. 8, Jerusalem Center for Public Affairs, August 2006, http://www.jcpa.org/brief.
30. "IDF Responds to Hizbullah attack on Northern Border," Ministry of Foreign Affairs, November 21, 2005, http://www.mfa.gov.il.

31. Greg Myre and Steven Erlanger, "Clashes Spread to Lebanon as Hezbollah Raids Israel," *New York Times*, July 12, 2006, reprinted in *International Herald Tribune*, September 12, 2006.

32. Steven Erlanger, "Israel Committed to Block Arms and Kill Nasrallah," *New York Times*, August 20, 2006. See also Noam Ophir, "Look Not to the Skies: The IAF vs. Surface to Surface Rocket Launchers," *Strategic Assessment*, Vol. 9, No. 3 (November 2006), pp. 18–23.

33. Yaakov Katz, "Katyusha Defence at Least 4 Years Away," *Jerusalem Post*, October 11, 2006.

34. Barak Ravid, "Israel to UN: Hezbollah Has Tripled Its Land-to-Sea Missile Arsenal," *Haaretz*, October 31, 2006.

35. Adrian Blomfield, "Israel Humbled by Arms from Iran," *Daily Telegraph*, August 16, 2006.

36. Yaakov Katz, "Wadi Saluki Battle: Microcosm of War's Mistakes," *Jerusalem Post*, August 29, 2006. See also Nava Tsuriel and Eitan Glickman, "The Canyon of Death," *Yediot Ahronot*, August 18, 2006.

37. As witnessed by the author, August 14, 2006.

38. Final Report of the Winograd Committee, January 30, 2008, p. 219.

39. Ibid., p. 41.

40. See, e.g., John Keegan, "Why Israel Will Go to War Again—Soon," *Daily Telegraph*, November 3, 2006. The author, a distinguished British military historian, attributes postwar assessments that considered the war a Hizballah victory to be largely a reflection of bias against Israel in the international media.

41. See full text of Resolution 1701, http://www.un.org.

42. "Hezbollah Leader Claims 'Divine Victory,'" Associated Press, September 21, 2006.

43. Herb Keinon, "Nasrallah: I Would Not Have Kidnapped Troops Had I Known the Outcome," *Jerusalem Post*, August 28, 2006.

44. Unifil Website, http://www.un.org.

45. "UN Report: Israel Says Hizballah's Arsenal Includes 30,000 Rockets," *International Herald Tribune*, March 4, 2008, http://www.iht.com/articles.

46. See Jonathan Spyer, "Lebanon, 2006: Unfinished War," *Middle East Review of International Affairs (MERIA) Journal*, Vol. 12, No. 1 (March 2008), http://www.meriajournal.com.

47. Schiff and Ya'ari, *Israel's Lebanon War*, p. 14.

48. Nahum Barnea, "Uri Lubrani Leaves Lebanon," *Yediot Ahronot*, June 23, 2000. Cited in Eisenberg, "Do Good Fences Make Good Neighbors?"

12

AMERICA AND THE LEBANON ISSUE

David Schenker

The U.S. can protect us from another superpower but not from a regional power like Israel or Syria. The U.S. is not ready to escalate the battle to the degree Syria is.[1]
    —Former Lebanese Ambassador to Washington Abdullah Bouhabib

A small and weak state with few natural resources and no oil, Lebanon has not traditionally been considered a U.S. national security policy priority in the Middle East. In fact, with the notable exception of crises involving two military interventions, in recent decades Lebanon has been somewhat of a backwater of U.S. policy.

Since the 1950s, the United States has sporadically demonstrated intense interest in developments in Lebanon. Twice—in the 1950s and 1980s—Washington deployed troops to Lebanon to protect what were defined as U.S. national interests. And more recently, in 2007, the U.S. government deemed the stability of Lebanese government to be so important that levels of U.S. Foreign Military Financing (FMF) were increased more than seven-fold, making Lebanon the second largest per capita recipient of U.S. military assistance worldwide.[2]

Despite these significant commitments, however, historically U.S. involvement in Lebanon has been reluctant. Given that country's presumed negligible strategic value, Washington has largely preferred where possible to steer clear of the Byzantine world of Lebanese politics. More often than not, Washington's policy toward Beirut has been reactive, driven by crises rather than by a proactive effort to enhance the bilateral relationship or by abiding strategic necessity.

Perhaps more detrimental to both Lebanese and U.S. interests, for much of the past 20 years Washington has largely viewed relations with Beirut through the prism of Damascus, and specifically through the lens of Israeli-Syrian peacemaking. In this context, Lebanon—with Washington's bless-ing—was essentially diplomatically reduced to the status of Syrian appendage. Without regard to Lebanon's sovereignty or national interests, the United States ceded Lebanese decision-making to Damascus in hopes of forging an Israeli-Syrian deal.

When the United States has been interested in Lebanon, it has largely been at times when Beirut was threatened by outside states and non-state actors seeking to permanently alter the orientation of the state. Lebanon has been a perennial battleground for regional and ideological influence. In part, external meddling has been so prevalent because Lebanon comprises alternately competing and conciliatory religious and ethnic communities. With no demographically, politically, or militarily dominant community, these communities have traditionally sought out alliances with states and non-state actors for protection, inviting intervention and, not infrequently, foreign occupation.

Not surprisingly, this complex dynamic of internal Lebanese politics and outside intervention has proven a challenging environment for Washington to understand, much less navigate. Consequently, although the United States has had exorbitant influence in the Middle East in the past 50 years, the U.S. impact on Lebanon has been limited.

The absence of a focused, consistent, and ongoing U.S. role in Lebanon constitutes an opportunity missed. For Lebanon, while small, is an intellectual center of the Middle East and has a significant impact in shaping regional trends. This influence, as well as Lebanon's central geographic position, accentuates the strategic import of Beirut to Washington.

What follows is a discussion of U.S. policy toward Lebanon, with a focus on Washington's policy in the aftermath of the 2005 Cedar Revolution. To explain Washington's current disposition toward Beirut, however, it is first necessary to discuss U.S. military interventions in Lebanon in 1958 and 1982. These two developments—with profoundly differing consequences—inform the context of U.S. policy vis-à-vis Lebanon today.

1958 MILITARY INTERVENTION

"United States forces are being sent to Lebanon," said President Dwight Eisenhower in July 1958, "to protect American lives and by their presence to assist the Government of Lebanon in the preservation of Lebanon's territorial integrity and independence, which have been deemed vital to United States national interests and world peace."[3]

U.S. policy toward Lebanon in the 1950s was shaped largely by regional trends that threatened and sometimes removed pro-West regimes in the Middle East. The most significant of these was the 1952 coup in Egypt that toppled the pro-Western regime of King Faruq, bringing to power the Free Officers—a group of Arab nationalist military men sympathetic to the Soviet Union. Gamal Abdel Nasser, who eventually emerged as the charismatic leader of this group, posed a real concern for Washington.

A few years later, after a series of coups and a tilt toward increased Communist influence within the Syrian military, Damascus officially joined this anti-West camp: In 1956, Syria signed a pact with the Soviet Union. In 1955, in an attempt to stave off rising Arab nationalist and pro-Soviet sentiment in the region the United States brokered the Baghdad Pact, a pro-West military alliance between Turkey, Iran, and Iraq.

Meanwhile in Beirut, in 1952, Western-oriented Chamile Chamoun was elected president. Chamoun sought closer ties with the United States, even as Arab nationalist currents were sweeping Beirut and the region. By the mid-1950s, according to the U.S. Department of State, Beirut had become a "center for the propagation and dissemination of communist propaganda in the Middle East."[4] Even so, following Egypt's 1956 nationalization of the Suez Canal and the subsequent tripartite attack (by Israel, Britain, and France) to reverse Nasser's move, Lebanon was one of few Arab states not to cut ties with Britain and France. Increasingly, however, Chamoun and Lebanon's pro-West government were under siege by the largely Sunni pro-Nasser Arab Nationalists.

In 1957, largely in response to the perceived spread of Communism in the region, President Eisenhower issued the Eisenhower Doctrine, a policy statement in which the former general declared the "preservation of the independence and integrity of the nations of the Middle East" as "vital to the national interest." In this context, Eisenhower requested, and subsequently received, congressional authorization for the United States to deploy its troops to any Middle East state in need of such assistance.[5] Perhaps not surprisingly, in 1957 Lebanon under Chamoun was the only Arab country to accept the Eisenhower Doctrine. Later that year—as Chamoun's position in Lebanon deteriorated—the United States and Britain began to develop contingency plans for military intervention in Lebanon.[6]

The establishment in 1958 of the United Arab Republic (UAR)—a political, economic, and military union between Egypt and Syria—generated concern in Washington and among U.S. allies in the region. At the same time, Chamoun's efforts to solidify his rule—by engineering a constitutional change allowing him to serve a second term—were generating more resentment at home. By May 1958, there was an armed insurrection in Beirut, led by Lebanese Sunni Muslims who viewed the Christian president's policies as a violation of the 1943 National Pact.

According to Chamoun, the revolt—which would eventually claim some 2,000 lives—was backed by Syria and Egypt. U.S. policy-makers agreed. As President Eisenhower later wrote, increased border crossings from Syria into Lebanon indicated to the United States that Nasser would eventually move to bring Lebanon "under his influence."[7] Based on this assessment, the United States decided to intervene on behalf of the legitimate Lebanese government—but, prior to any deployment, Washington first needed to receive "an appropriate request from Lebanon's duly constituted government."[8]

The request from Chamoun came a few months later, when on July 14, 1958, a coup in Iraq replaced the Western-backed Hashemites with the revolutionary regime of Abd al-Karim Qasim. In the aftermath of the coup, Chamoun requested U.S. military intervention within 48 hours.[9] U.S. Marines landed in Lebanon on July 15 and over the next three weeks, the contingent reached some 14,000 Marines.

U.S. troops were deployed in Beirut and at the airport in support of the Lebanese government. As a condition of the U.S. deployment, Chamoun

agreed to step down (and not serve an unprecedented second term), and the
United States brokered a deal whereby Lebanese Armed Forces (LAF) Chief
of Staff General Shihab was elected president. The rebels, in turn, were
granted amnesty. With the conflict defused, U.S. troops returned home in
October 1958.

EISENHOWER, THE UNITED NATIONS, AND RATIONALE

Although in retrospect the deployment seemed a rational decision, at the time
it was a risky endeavor.[10] At the most basic level, the concern was that the
deployment might somehow provoke the Soviets. The Eisenhower
administration was not entirely sure how the LAF would respond to the
Marine landing either. Although the LAF had remained largely "neutral"
throughout the previous months of civil unrest, Chamoun's request for U.S.
assistance was not supported by the Sunnis; so at the time, the Lebanese military's reaction to the impending U.S. military presence was an unknown.

The Eisenhower administration made three public statements on July 15,
1958, the day of the Marine landing in Beirut. These statements emphasized
that the government of Lebanon had requested U.S. forces and that these
forces were necessary to "protect American lives," and "assist the government of Lebanon to preserve its territorial integrity and political
independence."[11] In his broadcast to the American people that day,
Eisenhower also recalled the "indifference" of the League of Nations—the
predecessor to the United Nations—to aggression that "made World War II
inevitable."

Notably, the administration's three major statements—to the American
people, to Congress, and the president's statement regarding the Lebanese
government's appeal—all mentioned the United Nation's insufficient role in
Lebanon. In June 1958, as violence increased in Lebanon, the United
Nations had dispatched observers to Lebanon "insuring that further outside
[Syrian] assistance to the insurrection would cease."[12] The administration
considered this effort to stem the flow of weapons from Syria to be "helpful"
but not enough.

Indeed, Eisenhower told Congress that "given developments in Iraq, the
measures thus far taken by the United Nations Security Council are not sufficient to preserve the independence and integrity of Lebanon."[13] "More will
be required" Eisenhower noted, "than the team of United Nations observers
now in Lebanon."[14] U.S. forces would be withdrawn, he said, only after the
United Nations had taken "effective steps" to safeguard Lebanese
independence.

Eisenhower explicitly linked the deployment to support for justice and
international law. "Indirect aggression and violence are being promoted in
the Near East in clear violation of the provisions of the UN Charter," he
said. If the United States failed to support the principles of the UN Charter,
"the result would be to open the flood gates to direct and indirect aggression throughout the world."[15]

The deployment and the articulated principled stand had the added benefit of demonstrating U.S. seriousness of purpose. Years later, with the benefit of perspective, Eisenhower wrote of the Lebanon experience: "The Communists had come to be aware of our attitude and there was reason to think that they respected it."[16]

U.S. INVOLVEMENT IN LEBANON IN THE 1980S

A second event that shapes U.S. policy-making toward Lebanon today is Washington's bitter experience associated with the U.S. contingent's deployment to Lebanon in 1982–1983 as part of the Multi National Force (MNF). Contrary to the 1958 deployment, a well-defined mission with realistic and achievable goals, the 1982–1983 deployment of American forces in Lebanon was ill-defined, and its security was largely dependent on the perceived neutrality of the United States.

Fearing the possibility of becoming enmeshed, Washington had largely stayed clear of the Lebanese civil war, which began in 1976. Still, the United States was not viewed as neutral—and subsequently, U.S. personnel in Lebanon came under fire. In 1976, U.S. Ambassador Francois Melloy and the embassy's economic counselor were kidnapped and killed.

Although Washington initially hesitated, eventually the United States supported entry of a Syrian "peacekeeping" intervention force into Lebanon.[17] With the Syrians in Lebanon, U.S. involvement early in the war was focused on preventing war between the Syrians and Israelis, who viewed the Syrian deployment in Lebanon a threat. To accomplish this goal, Washington helped broker the "red lines"—an understanding between the Israelis and Syrians that essentially divided Lebanon into spheres of influence, and limited the size of Syrian troop deployments and weapons systems.[18]

This equation changed when the Israelis invaded Lebanon in March 1982. Of course, the Israelis had entered Lebanon before, most notably during Operation Litani in 1978, when some 25,000 troops crossed the border. That incursion had prompted the UN Security Council to pass Resolution 425, demanding an Israeli withdrawal from Lebanon and establishing the UN Interim Force in Lebanon (UNIFIL). However, the 1982 invasion was different, both in scope and in breadth: 70,000 Israeli troops entered Lebanon in an operation that reached Beirut in pursuit of PLO forces.

Following the Israeli invasion, the United States reengaged diplomatically in Lebanon. That summer, U.S. Ambassador Phillip Habib mediated the evacuation of PLO forces from Beirut, overseen by contingents of U.S., French, and Italian troops. The PLO departed from Lebanon by September 1, and the 800 U.S. Marines were redeployed on September 10. Israeli forces remained in Lebanon.

In the aftermath of the Lebanese Forces massacre of hundreds of Palestinian civilians at the Sabra and Shatila refugee camps on September 16, 1982—in an area under Israeli security responsibility—the Lebanese government requested deployment of an international force in Lebanon, and the

Reagan administration responded. On September 20, in conjunction with the French and Spanish, Washington announced the establishment of a Multi National Force (MNF), and on September 29, the initial group of what would eventually be 1,800 U.S. Marines were deployed to Beirut. At the time, the deployment order indicated only a 60-day mission,[19] with rules of engagement that stated that U.S. forces were not to engage in combat, they were to exercise restraint to avoid conflict escalation and becoming involved in factional violence, and to maintain neutrality.[20]

Essentially the Marine's mission entailed constituting a U.S. "presence" on Lebanese soil. The mandate of the MNF was to provide an "interposition force" and assist the government and the LAF in Beirut and its environs. This entailed providing training to the LAF and, later, providing ammunition that was employed against Syrian surrogates, amongst others. The Marines would leave, according to then Assistant Secretary of State for Near East and South Asia Nicholas Veliotes, "just as soon as the evacuation of Syrian, Israeli, and Palestinian forces is complete and the Lebanese Army is able to do its job countrywide."[21]

Interestingly, even as the United States was deploying troops to Beirut, by October 1982 Israeli and Lebanese officials were engaged in a bilateral discussion of a withdrawal and a potential peace agreement, and apparently making progress toward a deal. According to Lebanese diplomatic sources, however, Washington opposed a Lebanese-Israeli deal, fearing an Arab economic boycott of Beirut.[22] As one U.S. official explained it, "[A] full peace treaty was too ambitious." In the end, the Lebanese opted for U.S. mediation, which focused on an Israeli withdrawal taking for granted that Syria would eventually pull out.

To this day, the Reagan administration's role in scuttling a bilateral deal is astounding. As one former high-ranking U.S. official said, in retrospect the administration's major mistake was "to pull the Lebanese out of the Israeli embrace and dump them on the Syrian's mercy."[23]

On the political front, Washington continued to press forward with its own negotiated settlement in Lebanon—in particular Syrian and Israeli withdrawals—via its envoys Phillip Habib and Morris Draper, but these efforts remained largely unsuccessful in spite of the personal diplomacy of then Secretary of State George Shultz.

At the same time, the U.S. Marines in Lebanon, who had been quietly supporting the government of Lebanon and the LAF, were losing the image of neutrality. In mid-March 1983, a grenade was thrown at a U.S. MNF patrol, wounding five Marines.[24] Then, in April—almost eight months after the deployment of the Marines—the U.S. Embassy in Beirut was bombed, killing 60 people, including 17 Americans.

By May, however, the diplomatic effort seemed to bear fruit: On May 17, 1983, Israel and Lebanon signed a peace agreement that stipulated withdrawals of both Israeli and Syrian forces. Washington was optimistic, but in short order the agreement disintegrated. The primary problem appears to have been Syria. Washington assumed that Lebanese and Israeli consent to the May 17 pact was enough, but at the end of the day, the United States could not convince the Syrians to withdraw. According to one U.S. diplomat:

We should have been better prepared to deliver and deal with the Syrians. We didn't do a good enough job, either diplomatically or militarily.... We did not give enough attention when the groundwork was being laid for the agreement to parallel talks with Syria to see if they'd cooperate. Everyone agrees that Syria was important and we should do something, and no one did anything.[25]

The Lebanese had a similar interpretation of developments. As then Lebanese Ambassador to Washington Abdullah Bouhabib saw it:

We thought it [the May 17 Agreement] was done because a superpower had committed itself to the goal—our objective of liberating a small democracy from foreign forces. We didn't see the limitations of the superpower....The United States can protect us from another superpower but not from a regional power like Israel or Syria. The United States is not ready to escalate the battle to the degree Syria is.[26]

In the months following the attack on the U.S. Embassy, the Marines stationed at Beirut International Airport were increasingly targeted by mortars, artillery, and sniper fire—and in August 1983, for the first time, the Marines responded. That September, U.S. naval gunfire was employed in direct support of the Marines. By the end of September 1983, the environment was "hostile."[27]

A month later, on October 23, 1983, the Marine Barracks at Beirut International Airport was destroyed by a car bomb, killing 241 Marines. In a separate attack on the same day, 56 French paratroopers were killed in a separate attack. Iranian-affiliated Islamic Jihad claimed responsibility for the Marine Barracks attack, but a U.S. court later determined—during a civil claim brought by families and victims in September 2003—that the Shi'a terrorist organization Hizballah was responsible for the attack.[28]

On October 24, President Reagan indicated that despite the attack, U.S. forces would remain in place. "We have vital interests in Lebanon," he said. Then, in early December 1983, U.S. forces began to clash with the Syrians; Damascus fired on U.S. F-14 reconnaissance aircraft over Lebanon and later downed two U.S. aircraft, killing one airman and taking another prisoner. The United States responded to these Syrian provocations by firing the 16-inch guns of the battleship *New Jersey* at Syrian positions in Lebanon.

The situation was deteriorating on the ground, but Reagan was rhetorically, at least, still committed to the force deployment in Lebanon. "As long as there is a chance for peace," he told the *Wall Street Journal* on February 3, 1984, "the mission remains the same. If we get out, that means the end of Lebanon." It would have a "pretty disastrous result" for Washington, as well, Reagan said. Three days later, however, on February 7, 1984, Reagan announced the phased withdrawal of 1,400 Marines. By the end of February, U.S. forces had quit Lebanon.

Several explanations are typically offered for the precipitous collapse of U.S. policy in Lebanon in the aftermath of the Marine barracks bombing. Most focus on the lack of a clear mission in the first place along with changing conditions on the ground. In 1984, then Secretary of Defense James Schlessinger told the Senate how U.S. forces ended up in the crosshairs. In short, he said, this development occurred as the "transformation of the Marine role from that of peacekeeping mission, however amorphous, [became] that of a participant in a complex struggle."[29]

Serious deficiencies in U.S. policy also played a role in the collapse, in particular the lack of a clearly articulated U.S. mission in Lebanon. This lack of clarity reflected the deep divisions in the Reagan administration at the time regarding the use of force. Then Secretary of State George Shultz was an advocate for robust use of the U.S. military assets to promote U.S. foreign policy interests; Secretary of Defense Casper Weinberger took a more cautious approach and was said to have argued against a more robust policy vis-à-vis Lebanon and Syria.[30] The result was a policy that neither stabilized Lebanon nor protected U.S. interests and personnel.

THE DARK YEARS: THE 1990S

Lebanon's civil war officially ended in November 1989 with the signing of the Ta'if Agreement. In addition to revising the 1943 National Pact to some extent, particularly regarding the details of the power-sharing arrangement, Ta'if established the terms for a Syrian withdrawal from Lebanon.

According to Lebanese sources, Washington played an important, behind-the-scenes role in the negotiation of Ta'if, working closely with Rafiq Hariri. While the agreement resulted in an official end to the hostilities, Syria did not leave Lebanon. Indeed, some two years later, ostensibly with U.S. blessing, the Syrian presence in Lebanon was seemingly made permanent.

When Iraq's Saddam Hussein invaded Kuwait in August 1990, Washington embarked on building an international coalition to participate in the military operation to liberate the small Gulf emirate. Secretary of State James Baker enlisted 34 states to participate in the operation, including Syria, a state with which U.S. ties at the time were tenuous at best. The announced quid pro quo for Syrian participation was a postwar good faith effort on Washington's part to broker a Syria-Israel peace deal. In Lebanon, however, it was—and continues to be—widely held that an unannounced component of this deal was that in exchange for Syrian participation in the coalition, Washington would tolerate the ongoing Syrian occupation of Lebanon.

While there is no record of any such deal—and U.S. diplomats involved in the discussions continue to deny this collusion[31]—there is little doubt in Lebanon that this is what occurred. Clearly, based on what subsequently occurred, this is what Damascus inferred. In the aftermath of the Gulf War,

Syria remained in Lebanon and consolidated control over its weaker neighbor. Washington and Beirut sporadically engaged diplomatically during the 1990s—Secretaries of State Baker and Warren Christopher visited Beirut in the early 1990s—but the priorities for the United States in the bilateral relationship had shifted. The principal U.S. interest in Lebanon had become the Israeli-Syrian peace process, and as such, Lebanese matters started to fall within the purview of U.S.-Syrian relations and, to a lesser extent, U.S.-Israeli ties.

The April 1996 Israel-Hizballah understanding—in which the parties agreed to avoid future targeting of civilians—is a good example of how the United States consulted with Syria on Lebanese issues in the 1990s. On April 11, 1996, Israel initiated a military operation in Lebanon with the stated purpose of stopping Hizballah rocket fire into northern Israel. Operation Grapes of Wrath, as it was known, lasted nearly two weeks and resulted in hundreds of dead Lebanese civilians and dozens of Israeli and Lebanese injured. A ceasefire between Hizballah and Israel was brokered by Secretary of State Warren Christopher, in consultation with Syrian and Lebanese officials.[32] The understanding consisted of an agreement to no longer target civilians on both sides of the border.

While many argue that the agreement proved durable—it lasted until the summer 2006 war—the agreement also contained a number of problematic aspects, foremost of which was that it raised the stature of Hizballah to that of a state, further legitimating the Shi'a militia. Interestingly, even though Syria was the occupying force in Lebanon at the time and was a principal party consulted in the agreement, no positive constraining role for Damascus was envisioned vis-à-vis Hizballah. Not surprisingly, given Syrian input, the understanding solidified Hizballah's position outside the control of the Lebanese state. In so doing, ultimately, this agreement sowed the seeds for the 2006 war.

LEBANON AND THE BUSH ADMINISTRATION

In the aftermath of the al-Qa'ida attack on the United States on September 11, 2001, Washington moved quickly to change its disposition toward the Middle East. The Bush administration started to pursue a policy of democracy promotion in the region with an eye toward undermining Islamist ideology. It also redefined how it would deal with state sponsors of terrorism, especially those states developing weapons of mass destruction. In this context, during his January 29, 2002 State of the Union Address, President Bush described Iran, Iraq, and North Korea as an "axis of evil" with which to contend. "The United States of America will not permit the world's most dangerous regimes to threaten us with the world's most destructive weapons," he said.

The administration's paradigm change put Syria—which had occupied Lebanon for nearly 30 years—in a different light. Syria, of course, continued its support for several terrorist groups and was developing WMD, which were the two criteria that defined membership in the "axis." At the same time, though, Syria was providing Washington with some useful assistance in the campaign against al-Qa'ida, which effectively purchased Damascus a pass on accountability for its other nefarious activities.

However, Syrian behavior in the lead-up to the U.S. invasion of Iraq changed the dynamic. Before the war, in 2002, the administration had publicly requested that Congress not pass the Syria Accountability and Lebanese Sovereignty Restoration Act (SAA)—a set of sanctions to be leveled against Damascus in response to Syria's support for terrorism and occupation of Lebanon.[33]

In the months leading up to the war, despite complaints from Washington, Syria provided Iraq with military materiel. As a matter of policy, the Syrian government also facilitated the movement of insurgents into Iraq before and during the war, a practice that resulted in Syria becoming the leading transit point for foreign fighters entering post-Saddam Iraq. This unhelpful Syrian policy resulted in a reevaluation of administration disposition toward Damascus.

After months of egregious Syrian provision of support to the insurgency, President Bush finally relented in his opposition to the SAA, and on December 12, 2003, he signed the Syria Accountability and Lebanese Sovereignty Restoration Act into law, which included among other things, the demand that Syria withdraw from Lebanon. In May 2004, the administration began implementing economic sanctions against Syria.

Despite passage of the SAA, Damascus continued to press its interests in Lebanon. Top on the list was ensuring the extension of the term for the Syrian-appointed president of Lebanon, Emile Lahoud. Damascus was making great efforts—via a campaign of intimidation against Lebanese lawmakers—to extend the term of Lahud, which was slated to end in October 2004.[34]

In an unprecedented development, the Bush administration also weighed in against Syria's attempts to dictate the president of Lebanon. In June 2004, for example, he stated that "the people of Lebanon should be free to determine their own future, without foreign interference or domination."[35] At the same time, Washington was taking steps to rally the international community to clip Syria's wings in Lebanon.

Foremost among these U.S. diplomatic endeavors was UN Security Council Resolution 1559, which was passed on September 2, 2004. The U.S. UN delegation was a driving force behind this resolution, which called for the withdrawal of "foreign" (i.e., Syrian) forces from Lebanon, the "disbanding and disarmament" of militias (i.e., Hizballah), and which declared support for "free and fair electoral process in Lebanon's upcoming presidential elections...without foreign interference or influence."[36]

Even the threat of 1559 could not deter the Syrians from pressing forward on installing Lahoud for another term. Indeed, just days before the resolution passed, Syria engineered a change in the Lebanese Constitution, effectively ensconcing Lahoud for three more years. Damascus's intransigence on the Lahoud issue increased support in the Security Council for the resolution, helping the United States and its European allies to pass this controversial measure.

By 2004, Washington had started to view Syria as a real problem. At the same time, the administration saw the occupation of Lebanon—which strengthened Syria and Hizballah, and was viewed negatively by the vast majority of Lebanese—as a target of opportunity for democracy promotion and leverage on Damascus. When former Lebanese Premier Rafiq Hariri was assassinated in February 2005, the United States held Syria responsible, withdrew its ambassador from Damascus, and started to back the pro-freedom, anti-Syria movement in Lebanon.

In the weeks after the Hariri killing, the Bush administration amplified its demand for the end of the Syrian occupation. U.S. calls echoed those of the opposition within the Lebanese government, including, most prominently, those articulated by the Maronite Christian gathering known as the Qornet Shehwan. One typical statement read: "The road to salvation and independence is represented by a full withdrawal of the Syrian army and intelligence from Lebanon."[37]

At the same time, the Lebanese opposition orchestrated a series of large protests in downtown Beirut in Martyr's Square, not far from the Grand Serail, raising the pressure on the pro-Syrian Lebanese government. U.S. statements became even more ubiquitous following the resignation of the pro-Syrian prime minister and his government on February 28, 2005.

Soon after, Washington made dozens of statements against the Syrian presence and in support of the opposition. On March 1, Secretary of State Condoleezza Rice and French Foreign Minister Michel Barnier issued a joint statement saying: "We fully support the Lebanese people in their pursuit of an independent, democratic and sovereign Lebanon, free of outside interference and intimidation."[38] A day later President Bush affirmed her remarks, saying: "I applauded the press conference...where both of them stood up and said loud and clear to Syria, you get your troops and your secret services out of Lebanon so that good democracy has a chance to flourish.... The world is speaking with one voice when it comes to making sure that democracy has a chance to flourish in Lebanon."[39]

The same day Bush was making his remarks, Under Secretary of State for Democracy, Human Rights, and Labor Paula Dobriansky praised the political upheaval and mass demonstrations in Beirut, comparing them to similar democratic movements around the world: "There was a rose revolution in Georgia, an orange revolution in Ukraine and, most recently, a purple revolution in Iraq. In Lebanon, we see growing momentum for a cedar revolution that is unifying the citizens of that nation to the cause of true democracy and freedom from foreign influence."[40]

Meanwhile, the State Department continued to hammer Damascus for its noncompliance with UN Security Council Resolution 1559. As State Department Deputy Spokesman Adam Ereli said on March 2, 2005: "The simple way to put this is we're not hearing what 1559 calls for, which is full and immediate withdrawal of all foreign forces from Lebanon."[41]

The support from Washington emboldened an already energized opposition, which orchestrated a huge popular rally in Beirut on March 14—the one-month anniversary of Hariri's assassination. An estimated 1.5 million Lebanese—nearly a third of the population—attended the demonstration, and a month later, under increasing pressure, Syria withdrew its troops and its visible intelligence presence from Lebanon.

Two months later, in May and June 2005, Lebanon went to the polls for parliamentary elections and voted the anti-Syrian "March 14" coalition into government, with a slim majority of 72 of 128 seats. With a new Lebanese government in place led by Prime Minister Fuad Siniora—who had previously served as finance minister in Rafiq Hariri's government—Washington moved to upgrade the bilateral relationship with Beirut. From 2005 to 2008 the United States provided unprecedented levels of financial and diplomatic support to Lebanon.

DIPLOMATIC SUPPORT AT THE UNITED NATIONS

Even though France was excellent at taking credit for being Lebanon's great friend, in my experience it was usually the United States that pushed the envelope furthest on behalf of Lebanese democracy.

—John Bolton[42]

Perhaps the most important—although least visible—element of U.S. assistance for the pro-West Lebanese government was Washington's diplomatic support to Beirut within the United Nations. Before the Cedar Revolution, the Bush administration played a key role in the passage of UN Security Council Resolution 1559. After the 2005 elections that brought March 14 coalition to power, U.S. efforts to support the Lebanese government in the world body picked up steam.

From 2005 through early 2008—at a time when the administration was broadly seen as not engaging in effective diplomacy—U.S. diplomats at the United Nations built a strong coalition within the Security Council to press an agenda aimed at protecting the March 14–led government vis-à-vis Syria, Iran, Hizballah, and its Lebanese allies. During this period 15 of 243 Security Council resolutions dealt directly with Lebanon, which was a relatively high number given the size and influence of this small state. In fact, the time focused on Lebanon within the United Nations was significantly higher during this period, seemingly placing Beirut at the epicenter of UN deliberations.

While some of these resolutions dealt with the extension of the UNIFIL mandate and were not particularly controversial, many others were tendentious and required adept and focused U.S. diplomacy with states not traditionally considered Washington's allies in the United Nations. The effectiveness of U.S. action in the Council, in particular from 2005 to 2007, was largely attributable to the improbable convergence of France and John Bolton.

Known for his direct style, Bolton shocked many critics by proving an adept diplomat and coalition-builder during his two-year tenure as U.S. ambassador to the United Nations. The ambassador was personally committed to the administration's "Freedom Agenda" as it pertained to Lebanon and considered Syria to be a negative factor, an assessment solidified during his previous tenure from 2001 to 2005 as undersecretary of state for arms control in the State Department.

Bolton's accomplishments were made possible, in part, by the changes in French policy that accompanied the Hariri assassination in February 2005. In the aftermath of the former premier's murder, Paris became an unlikely U.S. ally in support of March 14 (and the effort to pressure Damascus) within the Security Council and, as a result, Washington was able to engineer several critical resolutions and insert strong language—critical of Syrian behavior—in other more innocuous resolutions.

Key Lebanon-related Security Council resolutions passed from 2005 to 2007 include UN Security Council Resolution 1595 (April 2005), which established an international independent investigation commission into the Hariri murder to "help identify its perpetrators, sponsors, organizers, and accomplices"; UN Security Council Resolution 1664 (March 2006), which acknowledged the establishment by the government of Lebanon of the legal basis and framework for an international tribunal to prosecute Hariri's murderers; UN Security Council Resolution 1686 (June 2006), which extended UN technical assistance to Beirut regarding other terrorist attack investigations since October 2004; and UN Security Council Resolution 1701 (August 2006)—the terms of a ceasefire between Israel and Hizballah—which among other things called for deployment of LAF forces in South Lebanon, the augmentation of UNIFIL forces, and the disarmament of militias (i.e., Hizballah).

The resolutions' passage was by no means assured. The U.S. UN delegation had to do some diplomatic heavy lifting to get these sharply worded resolutions passed. Bolton served as a critical engine for retaining the focus on Lebanon and the Hariri assassination and keeping the pressure on Syria.[43] Not only did this involve a lot of effort and discussions with the Russians about language, it also required quite a bit of cajoling of the French delegation to the United Nations—which was concerned about the impact of these tough resolutions on Syrian behavior.[44]

However, the crowning achievement of U.S. diplomacy within the United Nations that benefited Lebanon was the passage in May 2007 of UN Security Council Resolution 1757, which established a special tribunal to prosecute Hariri's killers. Passing this resolution was no mean feat: It was plausible that at least one state sympathetic to Syria would veto the action to protect the Asad regime from prosecution. Even so, U.S. diplomats helped pave the way for a final vote that included ten for the tribunal and five abstentions. Not a single country voted against the tribunal.

Washington's diplomatic support for the democratically elected March 14–led government extended well beyond its work at the United Nations.

From 2005 to 2008, the White House issued dozens of statements about Lebanon, condemning assassinations of Cedar Revolution leaders, and demanding Syrian compliance with UN Security Council Resolutions. Still other statements from senior administration officials focused on the demand that Damascus recognize and respect Lebanese sovereignty.

In one case, the White House even issued a statement apparently based on an intelligence intercept regarding a Syrian plot to undermine the Lebanese government and stymie the tribunal. "We are...increasingly concerned by mounting evidence that the Syrian and Iranian governments, Hizballah, and their Lebanese allies are preparing plans to topple Lebanon's democratically-elected government," the White House statement read, continuing, "one goal of the Syrian plan is to prevent the current Lebanese government from approving the statute for an international tribunal...any such effort to side-line the tribunal will fail."[45]

BUSH ADMINISTRATION'S FINANCIAL SUPPORT TO LEBANON

By and large, the decades of Syrian occupation were lean years for U.S. foreign assistance to Beirut. In 1983, U.S. grants to Lebanon were significant, reaching nearly $154 million, including $52 million in economic aid and $100 million in military assistance. In the years that followed, however, U.S. largess toward Lebanon diminished considerably, to less than $20 million total per year. Between 1985 and 2005, aside from about $500,000 per year in International Military Education and Training (IMET), this assistance included no funding for LAF military materiel.

All this changed with the arrival of the Bush administration and the attacks of September 11, 2001. In 2002, Washington raised Lebanon's Economic Support Funds (ESF) baseline by nearly $20 million per year, to approximately $36 million annually. Then, after the Cedar Revolution, in 2006—with the Syrian military out of Lebanon—the administration started to dramatically increase Foreign Military Financing (FMF).[46]

The United States did enter into a multiyear commitment to provide economic assistance to Lebanon in December 1996—during the Clinton administration. Earlier that year in April, Israel had launched Operation Grapes of Wrath, a military action aimed at curtailing Hizballah Katushya rocket bombardments of northern Israel. In addition to the loss of life, Lebanon suffered an estimated $500 million in damage, including most prominently the destruction of much of the state's electrical grid. Later that year, Washington organized the Friends of Lebanon conference, during which it committed—and later delivered—$60 million in aid over five years, from FY97 to FY01.

Relative to Lebanese requirements, however, this U.S. assistance was largely symbolic. After all, as a consequence of years of civil war, occupation, and rebuilding, Lebanon had by 2005 acquired some $40 billion in debt. By 2003, the servicing on this debt alone had become a crushing $3 billion a year, equivalent to nearly 40 percent of Lebanon's national budget.

In the initial years of the Bush administration, although Washington upped the level of ESF, it did not participate in either the Paris I (February 2001) or Paris II (November 2002) donor conferences organized by the French to help alleviate economic pressures on Beirut. After the Cedar Revolution, however, the administration invested itself more fully in the success of the Lebanese government, and when the Paris III conference convened in January 2007—to fund the reconstruction of Lebanon following the summer 2006 Israel-Hizballah war—the United States attended and was a key player, pledging $890 million of the $7.6 billion in total commitments.[47]

In 2008 the administration requested $53.2 million in ESF for Lebanon, a baseline that absent a change in the composition of the Lebanese government (such as a full Hizballah takeover) will likely persevere.

U.S. MILITARY ASSISTANCE TO THE LAF

Increases in U.S. economic support to Beirut after the Cedar Revolution were significant. Yet Washington's new outlook on the post-Syrian domination Lebanese government was perhaps best represented by the robust level of military assistance that started flowing to the LAF. The aid started slowly. In 2006—after 10 years of no funding—the United States provided the LAF with $1 million in FMF. Then, in 2007, the baseline U.S. funding was set at nearly $5 million but was augmented by a significant supplemental and other discretionary funding totaling nearly $300 million. Between 2006 and 2008, Washington provided some $410 million in security assistance to the LAF.[48]

The Pentagon has been extremely creative and effective in channeling funds and materiel to its Lebanese counterparts. In 2006, for example, the Department of Defense worked to ensure that Lebanon was eligible for a new funding mechanism called "1206 funding." Subsequently, the Pentagon provided $10 million to the LAF to improve capacity, in particular via the purchase of spare parts for vehicles, APCs, and helicopters.[49]

U.S. military assistance proved decisive in the May 2007 conflict between the LAF and the al-Qa'ida-affiliate Fath al-Islam. After members of Fath al-Islam executed two dozen LAF soldiers, the LAF initiated a military campaign against the terrorist group. In the initial days of the campaign, however, the LAF reportedly exhausted up to 40 percent of its ammunition stocks. To enable the LAF to fight on, the Pentagon expedited the shipment of over 40 C-130 transport planes brimming with military materiel to Beirut within a week of the outbreak of fighting.

The airlift was no mean feat. It required a lot of creative thinking—the United States used an Acquisition and Cross Servicing Agreement (ACSA) mechanism to dispatch the weapons and ammunition quickly—and a real effort to cut through standard timelines and procedures. Military materiel provided by the United States in this airlift included over 10 million rounds of all types of ammunition.

Through 2008 the United States had delivered a broad range of equipment to the LAF, including nearly 300 humvees and 200 cargo transport
trucks, with a commitment to provide an additional 300 humvees, coastal
patrol boats, and refurbishment of helicopters. According to the State
Department, DoD has provided the LAF with "[t]he same front-line weapons
that the U.S. military troops are currently using, including assault rifles,
automatic grenade launchers, advanced sniper weapons systems, anti-tank
weapons, and the most modern urban warfare bunker weapons."[50]

U.S. Security assistance to Lebanon also included the purchase of equipment for the Internal Security Forces (ISF). Through the summer of 2008,
the procurement included nearly 100 police cruisers, 60 Ford Explorers, and
14 APCs. The U.S. government likewise agreed to assist the ISF with capac-
ity-building and technical assistance as part of its assistance package to
reconstruct the Nahr al-Barid refugee camp.

Washington's support for the LAF, which was focused on building the
capacity of this key national institution, was the lynchpin of U.S. support
aimed at strengthening the central government of Lebanon led by the
March 14 coalition. In addition to provision of equipment, the effort included a longstanding allocation of IMET—approximately $700,000 per
year—which in 2006 paid for more than 130 Lebanese servicemen to receive
training in the United States. So important was this aspect of training that
the administration requested an increase to $1.5 million for 2008.

While it seemed an uncontroversial endeavor, however, the Hizballah-led
opposition and its Christian allies—principally the Free Patriotic Movement
led by General Michel Aoun—have by and large viewed this support with
suspicion.

In fact, the increased U.S. involvement with the LAF generated a lot of
criticism and conspiracy theories among the opposition. Several visits in particular by senior U.S. military and Department of Defense officials to Beirut,
including CENTCOM Commander Admiral Fallon and J5 Director Major
General Robert Allardice, fueled the concerns. Undersecretary of Defense
for Policy Eric Edelman's—the third highest-ranking official in the
Pentagon—visits to Lebanon in 2007–2008 were also the focus of intense
scrutiny from Hizballah and its allies.

During many of these visits, Defense Department officials signed funding
commitments with the LAF, while other missions carried military materiel.
The then assistant secretary of defense for international security affairs traveled to Beirut in November 2006 and signed a deal with Lebanese Defense
Minister Elias Murr to provide the LAF with $10.6 million. When
Undersecretary Edelman traveled to Beirut in May 2007, he brought with
him body armor and helmets.[51] During Fallon's trip in August 2007, he
announced delivery of 130 humvees.[52]

Nevertheless, the opposition used these visits as an opportunity to try and
discredit Washington and the March 14–led government. The story of what
occurred following one of Ambassador Edelman's trips to Beirut is instructive. While in Beirut in October 2007, during an interview with LBC

television Edelman said that the United States would like to see a "strategic partnership" with the LAF to undermine Hizballah's excuse to bear arms.[53] Days later, the Lebanese opposition daily *al-Safir* reported that Washington was planning to build an airbase in northern Lebanon. The story was subsequently picked up by Hizballah's television station, al-Manar and Iranian Press TV.[54] The implication was that the United States needed this base to attack Syria—and Hizballah. Days of denials by the United States and Lebanese governments followed.

Of course, this rumor planted by the opposition was totally fabricated, but it served to raise concerns about U.S. intentions in Lebanon. Washington's goal via supporting the LAF was decidedly more benign than Hizballah had suggested. As Assistant Secretary of Defense Peter Rodman said in 2006, U.S. aid was designed to "assist Lebanon in building its capacity to protect its borders and establish sovereignty over all its territory."[55] Clearly, however, even this modest goal proved threatening to Hizballah.

FURTHER U.S. ACTIVITIES IN SUPPORT OF THE GOVERNMENT OF LEBANON

In addition to the significant provision of financial, military, and diplomatic support, from 2005 to 2008 Washington pursued a number of other initiatives in an effort to try and strengthen the central government of Lebanon vis-à-vis Hizballah and the opposition. Although it is counterintuitive, the administration's position during the 2006 summer war between Israel and Hizballah was one such example. Instead of pushing for an immediate ceasefire to end the hostilities, in the belief that Israel was poised to deal a severe blow to the organization, Washington remained silent. The hope in Washington, of course, was that a Hizballah military setback would redound to increased Lebanese government sovereignty.

Not only did the six-week war not result in a meaningful blow to Hizballah, the Shi'a militia emerged from the conflict with a burnished reputation in the region. The organization and its leader were lionized in the Arab world for seemingly dealing Israel its first ever military defeat. As a result, Israeli deterrent capabilities were dramatically compromised. In the process, the reputation of the Lebanese government emerged tarnished, as it had initially severely criticized Hizballah for provoking the war in the first instance.

A more subtle tact taken by Washington in support of Beirut involved the use of targeted financial measures to undermine opposition fundraising efforts abroad and achievements in Lebanon. In addition to several executive orders focused specifically on Syria—which were clearly intended to pressure Syria with regard to Lebanon—in 2007, the administration issued two financial measures focused on strengthening the March 14–led government.

On August 2, 2007, President Bush issued an executive order (EO) "Blocking Property of Persons Undermining the Sovereignty of Lebanon or Its Democratic Processes and Institutions," an edict targeting the assets of those who contribute to the "breakdown of the rule of law in" or support "the reassertion of Syrian control" over Lebanon.[56] This EO was broadly interpreted to be targeting FPM leader Michel Aoun, who was until then believed to have an impressive U.S.-based fundraising network.[57] In Washington, Aoun—who was politically allied with Hizballah—was viewed as a significant obstacle to the election of a new president in Lebanon. According to senior U.S. officials, shortly after the executive order was issued, Aoun's North American fundraising dried up.

Then, in February 2007, the U.S. Department of Treasury designated the Hizballah subsidiary Jihad al-Bina'a or "Construction Jihad" a terrorist entity. The organization had been established with Iranian support in the early 1990s, but it flourished in the immediate aftermath of the summer 2006 war, when it was called upon to reconstruct decimated Shi'a areas of Lebanon. Jihad al-Bina'a's postwar construction work garnered a lot of popularity for Hizballah at the expense of the state.

By designating Jihad al-Bina'a terrorist, Washington effectively limited the organizations' access to international financial institutions. Perhaps more importantly, the move supported the central government's own effort to prevent Hizballah from translating the reconstruction into political capital. The government eventually lost this battle, but for months the government, with U.S. backing, succeeded in preventing Hizballah from becoming the exclusive agent of Lebanese Shi'a by refusing to issue individual government compensation for war-related losses directly to Hizballah, to Jihad al-Bina'a, or to the Jihad subsidiary Wa'd (Promise).

Washington also tried to enhance the credibility and international legitimacy of the democratically elected government vis-à-vis Hizballah through continual senior-level meetings with senior administration officials, whether in Washington or in Beirut. These included several White House meetings—including with Prime Minister Fuad Siniora and March 14 leaders and parliamentarians Walid Jumblatt, Sa'ad Hariri, and Nayla Muawwad—between 2006 and 2008. Secretary of State Condoleezza Rice also paid a few visits to Beirut in 2007 and 2008, where she met with government officials.

Other U.S. efforts to support the March 14–led government were decidedly less effective. In February 2008, Washington deployed the guided missile destroyer USS *Cole* to Lebanon's shores. The move appeared to be intended as a warning to Hizballah that it should not retaliate against Israel for assassinating Hizballah's Chief Operations Officer Imad Mughniyya. (Mughniyya had been killed by a car bomb in Damascus earlier that month; no one has yet claimed responsibility for the action.) The *Cole* deployment was widely viewed with derision in Lebanon, based on the understanding that regardless of how Hizballah responded the ship's arsenal would not be deployed against the group. While it was intended to demonstrate U.S. resolve in support for the government of Lebanon, in fact, it was viewed as a sign of U.S. weakness.

Another ill-advised U.S. initiative that was supposed to provide some benefit to the Lebanese government—but which had the exact opposite effect—was the Annapolis (Palestinian) peace conference, convened on November 27, 2008. Annapolis was intended to jumpstart the moribund Israeli-Palestinian negotiations, presumably having a positive effect on developments in the neighboring states. For the Lebanese government, however, the timing of the conference and Washington's atavistic commitment to Syrian participation proved highly damaging.

The conference took place in the midst of the Lebanese presidential elections, a process obstructed by the Hizballah-led opposition. Preoccupied with Annapolis the administration did not focus on the election period but instead subcontracted the diplomacy to the French, who failed to broker an agreement between the government and the opposition. In the process, the French discredited March 14 coalition candidates and undermined the authority of Maronite Patriarch Boutros Sfeir by compelling him to publicly weigh in on acceptable candidates—who were subsequently rejected by Syria.

Before Annapolis, March 14 had repeatedly stated that the only two acceptable candidates for the position were Boutros Harb and Nassib Lahud, two March 14 stalwarts, and Washington had publicly supported this position. However, in the weeks leading up to the conference, the Lebanese government grew increasingly concerned with the prospect that Washington was preparing to rehabilitate Damascus—to end support for the international Hariri tribunal in favor of pursuing peace negotiations between Syria and Israel.

The concern was justified. After all, since the 1990s the Lebanese have understood that Syrian participation in the first Gulf War (to oust Saddam from Kuwait) was the result of a deal with Washington granting Syria hegemony over Lebanon. While there is little evidence to suggest that such a deal ever was made, the perception persists and informs Lebanese politics. After the conference, these views were reinforced by the State Department spokesman's comments that Syria's participation in Annapolis had been "constructive."

A day after the conference ended the Lebanese government's resolve to continue supporting its candidates for president collapsed. The demoralized majority capitulated under pressure and accepted the Hizballah and Syrian-supported candidate for president, Lebanese Armed Forces (LAF) Chief of Staff Michel Suleiman, who had been anointed Chief of Staff by Damascus in 1998. Damascus and Hizballah subsequently pocketed the government concession and pressed for more compromises from the majority. Eventually, in a great defeat for March 14, Suleiman was elected president in the summer of 2008.

Annapolis was not the only administration misstep regarding the Lebanese presidential elections. U.S. policy regarding the elections was problematic from the very beginning. In Lebanon, where the (Maronite Christian) president is elected by parliament, a debate emerged between the government and the opposition regarding whether a two-thirds' quorum was required to proceed with a vote if a president had not been elected 10 days before the end of the previous president's term. March 14 argued that the quorum was not required; the opposition said it was. The interpretation was crucial because at the time, the majority held just 68 of 127 seats.

March 14 threatened to move ahead with a strict majority vote to elect the president—a move that likely would have triggered Hizballah-led violence in Lebanon—and was looking for tangible support from Washington to proceed. The administration demurred. Worse, Washington told March 14 that it would support the move "if the Patriarch did," placing this key political decision in the hands of Lebanon's Maronite Christian leader. Washington had punted on the decision, as it was clear that the Patriarch—who was trying to avoid further divisions within his confession—had already announced that he did not concur with the 50 percent plus one formula.

CONCLUSION

The 2005 Cedar Revolution and the subsequent election of the March 14–led government presented Washington with both opportunities and challenges. From the beginning, it was clear that Syria, Iran, and these states' Lebanese allies led by Hizballah would look to undermine the government at every turn. The administration viewed the struggle in Beirut as a micro-cosm of the larger battle of ideas in the region—a conflict between moderate pro-West states (a group that included Jordan, Egypt, and Saudi Arabia) and militant anti-West states led by Syria and Iran. Committed as a matter of policy to the Freedom Agenda, the Bush administration was compelled to protect its embattled ally in Beirut.

Yet Washington's policy options were limited. The situation on the ground in Lebanon was not dissimilar to 1958 and 1983: A moderate government in Beirut had requested U.S. assistance to help it withstand its opponents who were receiving strong backing from external powers. For Washington, leaving March 14 to the mercy of Hizballah, Syria, and Iran was not an option. At the same time, however, the experience of 1983 had left the United States with a bitter aftertaste, with an understanding of its limitations in playing Lebanese politics. Even if the United States had not had over 100,000 troops on the ground in Iraq, deployment of American soldiers in Lebanon again was out of the question. In Washington, this was an issue on which there was overwhelming bipartisan consensus.

Thus the administration was compelled to find effective tools to strengthen the weak government without using U.S. force. What it chose to do was to try and bolster the March 14 coalition through provision of robust financial support to Lebanese institutions. This meant providing economic grants to Lebanon, particularly in the aftermath of the summer 2006 war, and more prominently, by establishing a close working relationship with the LAF.

Of course, Washington was under no illusions as to the potential short-term effectiveness of the LAF as a protector of national institutions. Clearly, no one in the U.S. government believed that the LAF could be called upon to "disarm" Hizballah. Although nationally respected, it was well understood that the organization was largely representative of

Lebanon's demographics and as such subject to the same political problems facing the country writ large. Washington knew that the LAF was unlikely to be deployed in politically controversial matters, lest it fragment along religious lines. Nevertheless, the primary avenue employed by the administration to insulate the central government from threats and ensure its survival was the LAF.

Given the prevailing assessment of the Lebanese Army's disposition, it was unclear exactly what Washington expected of the organization. When Hizballah established its tent city in 2006, effectively closing down Beirut and surrounding the Grand Serail, the LAF took no actions; when Hizballah militarily attacked Beirut in 2008, the LAF was missing in action. Whatever faith the administration had in the LAF was either misplaced or premature. Building the kind of capacity and loyalty to the state that trumps sectarian identity is, at best, going to be a long-term project.

The other avenue pursued by the administration to secure its allies in Beirut was to pressure Syria: by working to keep the Hariri tribunal and violations of UN Security Council resolutions center stage at the international body; by senior administration officials making pronouncements at home and abroad; and via the implementation of a broad range of unilateral sanctions against Damascus. While administration statements proved irritants to Damascus, the sanctions were a bust. Sanctions imposed under the Syria Accountability and Lebanese Sovereignty Restoration Act of 2004 were grossly ineffective: Trade between Washington and Damascus tripled over a three-year period.

U.S. efforts to keep Lebanon in the limelight within the international framework between 2005 and 2008 were more successful. Notably, Washington was able to build and maintain—at least through the summer of 2008—a broad coalition to isolate Syria in anticipation of the international Hariri tribunal and in support of Lebanon. However, the longer the tribunal takes, the shakier the coalition becomes. By July 2008 France, which had proven the strongest of U.S. partners on the Lebanon-Syria front, seemed to be poised to welcome Damascus back into the international fold, thereby threatening the unified front.

Washington's support for the international tribunal is a key element of U.S. support for Beirut. Should the court implicate senior Asad regime officials, the hope among March 14 is that it will weaken the regime and chasten its behavior regarding Lebanon. This may be true, but it will accrue little benefit if March 14 is no longer in power and if there is a shift in Washington's disposition vis-à-vis Beirut.

As for the status of the government of Lebanon itself, the administration backed the March 14 coalition-led government when it came to power in 2005, even though the government essentially was a national unity government with Hizballah. In 2006, Hizballah bolted from the government in a cabinet dispute surrounding the international tribunal. Yet as of July 2008— in the aftermath of Hizballah's May 2008 takeover of Beirut and the negotiated agreement a month later in Doha—the Shi'a militia and its allies are once again in the government. Furthermore, the policy statement guiding this national unity government includes a recognition of Hizballah's right "to resist" (i.e., conduct military operations against Israel), outside of government control.[58]

For now, despite the reintegration of Hizballah into the Lebanese government and the problematic ministerial statement, Washington will continue to back the government majority. However, it is unclear that Washington would continue to do so if the March 14 coalition does not again win a majority in the elections scheduled in spring 2009. U.S. support for Lebanon, including financial and materiel support to the LAF, is to a large extent based on the pro-West orientation of the government. Should this calculus change—and if Hizballah and its allies control the government—in the view of Washington, Lebanon would start to bear a striking similarity to Gaza ca. 2008, under Hamas. In short, many in the United States would likely start to view Lebanon as a terrorist-controlled state.

Since the late 1950s, U.S.-Lebanese relations have vacillated between intense bilateral involvement and detachment. Given what is currently at stake in Lebanon—the survival of the only pro-West democratically elected government in the Arab world—continued U.S. interest and robust bilateral ties are all but assured for the immediate future. The defeat of March 14 would be a real setback for both Washington and Beirut. Based on the historical pattern, it would also signal an end to the renaissance of the U.S.-Lebanese relationship that started in 2005.

NOTES

1. Former Lebanese ambassador to Washington, Abdullah Bouhabib, quoted in Lally Weymouth, "Mideast: How the United State Skewed the Outcome in Lebanon," *Los Angeles Times*, March 11, 1994.
2. Alfred B. Prados, "CRS Report for Congress: Lebanon," *Congressional Research Service*, October 10, 2007.
3. Dwight D. Eisenhower, "Special Message to the Congress on the Sending of U.S. Forces to Lebanon," July 15, 1958 at www.presidency.ucsb.edu/ws/index. php?pid=11132.
4. "World Strength of the Communist Party Organization," Annual Report 10, Department of State Bureau of Intelligence & Research. (Washington, DC: DOS, 1958). Quoted in Erika Alin, "U.S. Policy and Military Intervention in the 1958 Lebanon Crisis," in David W. Lesch (ed.), *The Middle East and the U.S.: A Historical and Political Reassessment*, 3rd edition (Boulder, CO: Westview, 2003), p. 152.
5. The Eisenhower Doctrine was approved by a joint resolution of Congress of March 9, 1957.
6. Barry M. Blechman and Steven S. Kaplan, "Force without War: U.S. Armed Forces as a Political Instrument," Brookings Institution, Washington, DC, 1978.
7. Dwight D. Eisenhower, *Waging Peace* (New York: Doubleday and Company, 1965), p. 265. Eisenhower wrote: "The Lebanon-Syrian border was open to a steady influx of Syrians who meant no good to Chamoun's government," p. 267.

8. Ibid., p. 267.
9. Ibid., p. 270.
10. Eisenhower told Congress that the deployment may have "serious consequences."
11. "Broadcast to the American People Following the Landing of the U.S. Marines at Beirut, July 15, 1958," Dwight D. Eisenhower Memorial Commission, http://www.eisenhowermemorial.org/speeches/19580715%20Broadcast%20to%20the%20American%20People%20Following%20the%20Landing%20of%20United%20States%20Marines%20at%20Beirut.htm.
12. "Special Message to the Congress on the Sending of U.S. Forces to Lebanon," http://www.presidency.ucsb.edu/ws/index.php?pid=11132.
13. Ibid.
14. "Statement by the President on the Lebanese Government's Appeal for United States Forces," http://www.presidency.ucsb.edu/ws/index.php?pid=11131&st=&st1.
15. "Broadcast to the American People Following the Landing of the U.S. Marines at Beirut, July 15, 1958."
16. Eisenhower, *Waging Peace*, p. 291.
17. David Binder, "Envoy Says U.S. Erred in Beirut Policy," *New York Times*, May 27, 1976.
18. Yair Evron, *War and Intervention in Lebanon* (Baltimore: Johns Hopkins University Press, 1987), p. 200.
19. Ralph A. Hallenbeck, *Military Force as an Instrument of U.S. Foreign Policy* (New York: Prager, 1991), p. 34.
20. DoD Commission Report, pp. 35–37, www.ibiblio.org/hyperwar/AMH/XX/MidEast/Lebanon-1982-1984/DOD-Report/Beirut-1.html.
21. Nicholas Veliotes testimony before Congress, March 9, 1983, cited in John Kelly, "Lebanon: 1982–1984," in Jeremy R. Azrael and Emil A. Payin (eds.), *U.S. and Russian Policymaking with Respect to the Use of Force* (Santa Monica: RAND Corporation, 1996).
22. Lally Weymouth, "Who Lost Lebanon? Why U.S. Policy Failed," *Los Angeles Times*, March 11, 1984. Some sources say that then U.S. Middle East negotiator Phillip Habib "went ballistic" when he found out about the pending agreement and demanded that Lebanese President Amin Gemayel not sign it.
23. Ibid.
24. Report of the DoD Commission on Beirut International Airport Terrorist Act, October 23, 1983, p. 38.
25. Weymouth, "Who Lost Lebanon? Why U.S. Policy Failed."
26. Ibid.
27. Report of the DoD Commission on Beirut International Airport Terrorist Act, p. 39.
28. The families were awarded $123 million in damages by the U.S. court.
29. James Schlesinger testimony before the Senate Committee on Foreign Relations, 1984.
30. For a more comprehensive discussion of this dynamic, see David C. Martin and John Walcott, *Best Laid Plans: The Inside Story of America's War against Terrorism* (New York: Simon And Schuster, 1988). Of note, then Special Envoy to the Middle East for President Reagan Donald Rumsfeld sided with Shultz.
31. Interview with Ambassador Dennis Ross, former Special Envoy, U.S. Department of State, December 19, 2007.

32. "Israel-Lebanon Ceasefire Understanding," *USIP Website*, April 26, 2006, http://www.usip.org/library/pa/israel_lebanon/il_ceasefire_1996.html.

33. Clauses in the bill were later added condemning Syrian behavior vis-à-vis undermining stability in Iraq.

34. Detlev Mehlis, *Report on the International Independent Investigation Commission Established Pursuant to Security Council Resolution 1595* (Beirut, Lebanon: United Nations, October 19, 2005), pp. 15–19, www2.un.int/Countries/Lebanon/12100145848403.pdf. According to the interviews in the report, shortly before the assassination, Asad reportedly told Hariri that "Lahoud should be viewed as his personal representative" in Lebanon and that "opposing him is tantamount to opposing Assad himself." Asad then warned that he "would rather break Lebanon over the heads of" Hariri and influential Druze political leader Walid Jumblatt "than see his word in Lebanon broken" to Lahud.

35. http://www.whitehouse.gov/news/releases/2004/06/20040605-6.html, June 5, 2004.

36. http://daccessdds.un.org/doc/UNDOC/GEN/N04/498/92/PDF/N0449892.pdf?OpenElement.

37. Sam F. Ghattas, "Opposition Wants Syria Out of Lebanon," *Associated Press*, March 2, 2005.

38. Carolyn Wheeler, "Syrian Isolation Grows as France and U.S. Demand Lebanon Pullout," *The Guardian*, March 2, 2005, http://www.guardian.co.uk/world/2005/mar/02/syria.lebanon?commentpage=1.

39. Remarks by President George Bush, Anne Arundel Community College, Arnold, Maryland, *Federal News Service*, March 2, 2005.

40. Roy Eccleston, "U.S. Praise as Cedar Revolution Takes Root," *The Australian*, March 2, 2005.

41. State Department Regular Briefing, Adam Ereli, Deputy Department Spokesman, State Department Briefing Room, Washington, DC, March 2, 2005.

42. John Bolton, *Surrender Is Not an Option* (New York: Simon and Schuster, 2007), p. 385.

43. Ibid., pp. 271–412. Bolton provides some detail on the passage of UN Security Council Resolution 1636, for e.g., which called on UN member states to freeze assets of suspects in the Hariri murder.

44. Ibid., p. 385.

45. "White House Calls for Support for Sovereign Lebanon," Office of the Press Secretary, November 1, 2006, http://www.whitehouse.gov/news/releases/2006/11/20061101-1.html.

46. Alfred B. Prados, "CRS Report to Congress: Lebanon," *Congressional Research Service*, November 23, 2007, p. 36.

47. "International Conference for Support to Lebanon-Paris III: Second Progress Report," Government of Lebanon, Ministry of Finance, July 2, 2007; $120 million of the U.S. package included a public-private partnership project between OPIC and Citigroup to provide financing through Lebanese banks to provide loans to Lebanese citizens and businesses.

48. "U.S. Army Major General Robert R. Allardice Visits Lebanon," Embassy of the United States, Beirut, Lebanon, Press Release, July 15, 2008, http://lebanon.usembassy.gov/latest_embassy_news/press-releases08/prodc071508.html.

49. Donna Miles, "Lebanon to Be among First Beneficiaries of New DoD Funding Authority," *Military Connection*, August 4, 2006, http://www.militaryconnection.com/news/august-2006/funding-authority.html.

50. "The U.S. Provides More Support to the Lebanese Armed Forces," Embassy of the United States, Beirut, Lebanon, Press Release, May 30, 2008, http://lebanon.usembassy.gov/latest_embassy_news/press-releases08/pr053008.html.

51. "Undersecretary of Defense for Policy Eric Edelman Visits Lebanon," USEMB Beirut Press Statement, May 31, 2008, http://lebanon.usembassy.gov/latest_embassy_news/press-releases08/pr053109.html.

52. "Lebanon's Army Receives 130 Armored Humvees from U.S.," *Ya Libnan*, August 30, 2007, http://yalibnan.com/site/archives/2007/08/lebanons_army_r_2.php.

53. "U.S. to Build 'Strategic Partnership' with Lebanese Army, Says Pentagon Official," Associated Press, October 18, 2007, http://www.iht.com/bin/printfriendly.php?id=7953956.

54. "Lebanon U.S. Base to Counter Qaeda, Hezbollah or Russia?" *Al Manar*, October 18, 2007, http://www.almanar.com.lb/NewsSite/NewsDetails.aspx?id=27111&language=en. See also "U.S. to Build Military Base in Lebanon," *Press TV*, October 17, 2007, http://www.presstv.ir/detail.aspx?id=27498&sectionid=351020203. The story that appeared in the Lebanese press was a recycling of yet another conspiracy.

55. "U.S. Grants Lebanon $10.5 Million in Military Aid," Reuters, November 9, 2006, http://www.alertnet.org/thenews/newsdesk/L09141085.htm.

56. "Executive Order: Blocking Property of Persons Undermining the Sovereignty of Lebanon or Its Democratic Processes and Institutions," The White House, Office of the Press Secretary, August 2, 2007, http://www.whitehouse.gov/news/releases/2007/08/print/20070802-1.html.

57. In the early 1990s, Aoun had been the leading Lebanese opposition to Syrian occupation. Following his return to Lebanon in 2006 from decades in exile, however, Aoun allied himself politically with Hizballah. Aoun not only became a vocal proponent of "the resistance," he actively cooperated with Hizballah to prevent the election of a Lebanese president.

58. Bayan Wizari," Government of Lebanon, Ministerial Statement, August 5, 2008, http://www.nowlebanon.com/Arabic/NewsArticleDetails.aspx?ID=53639&MID=114&PID=46.

INDEX